Citrix® XenApp® 6.5 Expert Cookbook

Over 125 recipes that enable you to configure, administer, and troubleshoot a XenApp® infrastructure for effective application virtualization

Esther Barthel MSc

BIRMINGHAM - MUMBAI

Citrix® XenApp® 6.5 Expert Cookbook

First published: January 2014

Production Reference: 1210114

Published by Packt Publishing Ltd.
Livery Place
35 Livery Street
Birmingham B3 2PB, UK.

ISBN 978-1-84968-522-1

www.packtpub.com

Cover Image by Aniket Sawant (aniket_sawant_photography@hotmail.com)

Credits

Author
Esther Barthel MSc

Reviewers
Dragos Madarasan
Shankha Mukherjee
Peter Nap
Sebastien Sollazzo

Acquisition Editor
Kevin Colaco

Lead Technical Editor
Anila Vincent

Technical Editors
Shashank Desai
Krishnaveni Haridas
Jinesh Kampani
Arwa Manasawala
Veena Pagare
Shruti Rawool
Aman Preet Singh

Copy Editors
Deepa Nambiar
Karuna Narayanan
Kirti Pai
Lavina Pereira
Laxmi Subramanian

Project Coordinator
Kranti Berde

Proofreaders
Ting Baker
Lindsey Thomas

Indexer
Mariammal Chettiar

Production Coordinator
Aditi Gajjar Patel

Cover Work
Aditi Gajjar Patel

Notice

The statements made and opinions expressed herein belong exclusively to the author and reviewers of this publication, and are not shared by or represent the viewpoint of Citrix Systems®, Inc. This publication does not constitute an endorsement of any product, service, or point of view. Citrix® makes no representations, warranties or assurances of any kind, express or implied, as to the completeness, accuracy, reliability, suitability, availability, or currency of the content contained in this publication or any material related to this publication. Any reliance you place on such content is strictly at your own risk. In no event shall Citrix®, its agents, officers, employees, licensees, or affiliates be liable for any damages whatsoever (including, without limitation, damages for loss of profits, business information, or loss of information) arising out of the information or statements contained in the publication, even if Citrix® has been advised of the possibility of such loss or damages.

Citrix®, Citrix Systems®, XenApp®, XenDesktop®,and CloudPortal™ are trademarks of Citrix Systems®, Inc. and/or one or more of its subsidiaries, and may be registered in the United States Patent and Trademark Office and in other countries.

About the Author

Esther Barthel MSc has been working in different roles and functions as an IT consultant since she finished her Masters degree in Computer Science in 1997. She has worked as a web developer, database administrator, and server administrator until she discovered how **Server-Based Computing** (**SBC**) combined servers, desktops, and user experience in one solution. She has been specializing in virtualization solutions such as SBC, VDI, application, and server virtualization for over seven years now and currently works as a senior consultant at PepperByte, where she designs and implements Citrix® solutions for both small-business and large-enterprise infrastructures scaling from 100 to 15,000 users.

Ever since she hosted introduction days for technical female student candidates, Esther has been sharing her passion and knowledge for IT. What started out as small internal meetings to report on the latest technologies is growing from technical blog posts into international presentations at Citrix® User Groups and events like E2EVC. There's no surprise that she has now taken up the challenge to write her first technical book, *Citrix® XenApp 6.5 Expert Cookbook*, for a well-known publisher, *Packt Publishing*, offering a selection of recipes (how-to's) that allow experienced Citrix® XenApp® administrators to automate, monitor, troubleshoot, and manage advanced XenApp® infrastructures.

Esther is a **Citrix Certified Professional - Apps and Desktops** (**CCP-AD**), **Citrix Certified Integration Architect** (**CCIA**), and **RES Software Certified Professional** (**RCP**).

You can follow her on social media on her blog (http://www.virtues.it), on Twitter at @virtuEs_IT, or contact her directly through e-mail, techwriting@cognitionit.com.

Acknowledgments

I would like to thank Jozé Danen for all her love, patience, and understanding for the months it took to write this book. But even more so, I would like to thank her for her support and endless understanding while I struggled to balance work and life and spent many passionate hours delivering the best user experience, presenting enthusiastically, and sharing my knowledge with the community. Thank you, my love, for always being there to cheer me on!

A big thanks to my parents and sister as well who encouraged me to go for that Master of Science degree and have fun in my job. Mom, Dad, and sis, thank you so much for telling me over and over again how proud you are even though you might not always understand my technical rants.

I would also like to thank Sjaak Laan, the author of the book *IT Infrastructure Architecture, Lulu.com*, for being a great role model even though he might not be aware of it at all. And last but not least, Daniel Nikolic, CEO at PepperByte and Denamik, for sharing my vision and supporting my ambitions.

Special thanks to Carl Webster, Andrew Morgan, Helge Klein, Dane Young, Yoni Avital, Michel Stevelmans, Jason Poyner, and all other contributors to the Citrix® community for helping me show the power of community sharing and introducing their powerful tools and scripts!

About the Reviewers

Dragos Madarasan is a support engineer for one of the fastest growing companies in Eastern Europe. After working as a freelance IT consultant and working for a Fortune 500 company, he now enjoys tackling complex scenarios and using his knowledge to bridge the space between IT and business needs.

Dragos publishes interesting cases on his personal blog, and whenever time permits, he enjoys taking part in the ITSpark community as a technical writer and speaker.

Shankha Mukherjee has over six years of experience in the IT Industry. He is currently working as a Windows L2 engineer at Accenture Services Pvt. Ltd., supporting client infrastructure for Windows, Citrix, and VMware.

He has a BTech degree in Information Technology. Previously, he has worked as a reviewer for the book, *Getting Started with Citrix XenApp 6.5, Packt Publishing*.

> I would like to thank Packt Publishing for giving me this opportunity again and would definitely look forward to more such opportunities.

Peter Nap is an experienced Microsoft and Citrix® specialist with 14 years of experience mostly in server-based computing environments. His main areas of expertise are XenApp®, XenDesktop®, Microsoft Windows Server deployments and virtualization of applications, servers, and operating systems.

In his free time, he maintains his own website (`http://napplications.nl`) with free tools for ICT professionals because programming in C# is his passion. Currently, he is working for CGI as an infrastructure architect.

Peter Nap also reviewed the following titles for Packt Publishing:

- *Getting Started with XenApp 6.5*
- *XenDesktop 5.6 Cookbook*
- *XenDesktop 5 Starter*

Sebastien Sollazzo was born near Paris in France, and since 2005, he has been living in Quebec City, Quebec province, Canada. He has begun working with Citrix® products with Citrix® Metaframe 1.8 on Microsoft Windows NT4. Following every new iteration of Citrix® product, he has taken every opportunity to enhance his knowledge about each aspect of virtualization. He knows Citrix® products (XenApp®, XenDesktop®, Provisioning, NetScaler, and Branch Repeater), Microsoft (every Windows version, Active Directory, GPO, User Profile, and Printers), VMware (every vSphere version), Antivirus (Trend Micro, Kaspersky, and Symantec) very well and has a good knowledge of every technology involved in virtualization, such as Firewall (Checkpoint), IIS Server, DataBase (SQL, Oracle), and Scripting.

In 2009, Sebastien Sollazzo created his own company, Virtuel TI Inc, based in Quebec City, with a colleague, Michel Lajoie, to provide professional services for virtualization product to customers. Being an expert in all virtualization aspects, Virtuel TI consists of many specialized people in many technologies, which mainly include Citrix® and VMware , as well as strong expertise on Microsoft and Trend Micro technologies.

> I would like to thank my wife for giving me enough time to achieve all professional challenges such as my company and this book. Being a passionate man is not easy every day when 15 minutes of work gets extended to 1 or 2 hours. She always helps me surpass myself and takes care of the family, helping me find the right balance between work and family/leisure time.

www.PacktPub.com

Support files, eBooks, discount offers and more

You might want to visit www.PacktPub.com for support files and downloads related to your book.

Did you know that Packt offers eBook versions of every book published, with PDF and ePub files available? You can upgrade to the eBook version at www.PacktPub.com and as a print book customer, you are entitled to a discount on the eBook copy. Get in touch with us at service@packtpub.com for more details.

At www.PacktPub.com, you can also read a collection of free technical articles, sign up for a range of free newsletters and receive exclusive discounts and offers on Packt books and eBooks.

http://PacktLib.PacktPub.com

Do you need instant solutions to your IT questions? PacktLib is Packt's online digital book library. Here, you can access, read and search across Packt's entire library of books.

Why Subscribe?

- ▶ Fully searchable across every book published by Packt
- ▶ Copy and paste, print and bookmark content
- ▶ On demand and accessible via web browser

Free Access for Packt account holders

If you have an account with Packt at www.PacktPub.com, you can use this to access PacktLib today and view nine entirely free books. Simply use your login credentials for immediate access.

Instant Updates on New Packt Books

Get notified! Find out when new books are published by following @PacktEnterprise on Twitter, or the *Packt Enterprise* Facebook page.

Table of Contents

Preface

Classified as a server-based computing solution, Citrix® XenApp® offers companies a solution for Windows applications to be virtualized, centralized, and managed in the datacenter and delivered to end users from a single application portal (or store) at any time, any place, and any device. Making use of Microsoft's Remote Desktop Services, Citrix® XenApp® hosts multiple user sessions on a single Windows Server while supporting enhanced user experience through the Citrix® HDX technology that delivers bandwidth-efficient, high-quality multimedia. Combined with Citrix® Web Interface or StoreFront, users are provided with a single portal or store that unlocks the published applications and desktops. With the NetScaler Gateway, secure remote access is also supported.

By combining products such as Citrix® XenApp®, Citrix® License Server, Citrix® Web Interface or StoreFront, NetScaler Gateway, and Microsoft's Remote Desktop Services, you can implement a full XenApp® infrastructure to deliver Windows applications and desktops to end users.

Citrix® XenApp® 6.5 Expert Cookbook will not only focus on Citrix® XenApp® as a product but will take all components of the XenApp® infrastructure into account and offer practical guidelines to install, configure, maintain, and script all parts of that infrastructure.

What this book covers

Chapter 1, *Remote Desktop Services*, covers the foundation of each Citrix® XenApp® infrastructure by offering practical how-to's for installing, configuring, and troubleshooting Microsoft's Remote Desktop Services, both Session Host and License Server.

Chapter 2, *Citrix® License Server*, provides practical guidelines for installing, configuring, and troubleshooting the Citrix® License Server.

Chapter 3, *Citrix® Web Interface*, offers different recipes for installing, configuring, and troubleshooting the Citrix® Web Interface.

Chapter 4, *Citrix® StoreFront*, zooms into the successor of the Citrix® Web Interface with practical guidelines for installing, configuring, and troubleshooting Citrix® StoreFront.

Chapter 5, The NetScaler Gateway, enables the implementation of remote access to Citrix® XenApp® published desktops and applications with guidelines for configuring, managing, and troubleshooting the NetScaler Gateway.

Chapter 6, XenApp® Management, focuses on Citrix® XenApp® management activities by offering practical how-to's for configuring load evaluators, worker groups, printing, and the HDX Mediastream Flash Redirection.

Chapter 7, XenApp® Maintenance and Monitoring, zooms in on the available tools to support administrators with Citrix® XenApp® maintenance and monitoring tasks.

Chapter 8, XenApp® Policies, provides practical guidelines for XenApp® policy configurations for printing, shadowing, assigning load evaluators, redirecting client drivers, and enhancing user experience.

Chapter 9, XenApp® Troubleshooting, offers practical how-to's for troubleshooting XenApp servers and user sessions.

Chapter 10, PowerShell and Command-line Tooling, focuses on command-line tools and PowerShell scripts to automate maintenance and monitor tasks in a XenApp® infrastructure.

Chapter 11, XenApp® Infrastructure Best Practices, covers the best practices provided by Citrix® for different aspects in a XenApp® infrastructure, such as virtualization, computer and user settings, policies, profiles, antivirus, and high availability.

Chapter 12, Citrix® Community, introduces you to the Citrix® community and many tools and scripts that are developed by its members. Based on their own practical experiences, each tool or script will compliment the Citrix® XenApp® infrastructure and its administrative activities.

What you need for this book

This book covers more than just Citrix® XenApp® 6.5 as it will focus on all the required infrastructure components to deliver published desktops and applications to end users.

To test each and every step, script, command line, and management tool discussed in this book, a small lab environment was used with the following virtual machines:

- **CBDC01.cblab.local**: This is a Windows Server 2008 R2 domain controller with additional software installed to support the XenApp® data store (SQL Server 2008 R2 database), RD license server and Citrix® License Server (Version 11.9) roles.

- **CBXA01.cblab.local**: This is a Windows Server 2008 R2 XenApp® 6.5 controller host with additional software installed for the Citrix® Web Interface (Version 5.4).

- **CBXA02.cblab.local**: This is a Windows Server 2008 R2 XenApp® 6.5 session host with additional software installed for Citrix® StoreFront (Version 2.1).

▶ **CBCNG01**: This is a virtual NetScaler Gateway appliance (Version 10.1 build 118.7.nc) hosting the virtual servers that support remote access for the Web Interface and StoreFront.

▶ **Win701**: This is a standalone virtual desktop with Windows 7 Professional (64-bit) to represent a remote user. Additional software is installed for the Citrix® Receiver (Version 4.0) and online plug-in (Version 14.0)

▶ **Win702.cblab.local**: This is a domain-joined virtual desktop with Windows 7 Professional (64-bit). It represents an internal office user. Additional software is installed for the Citrix® Receiver (Version 4.1) and Online Plug-in (Version 14.1).

The following is a graphical representation of the XenApp® infrastructure created in the lab environment:

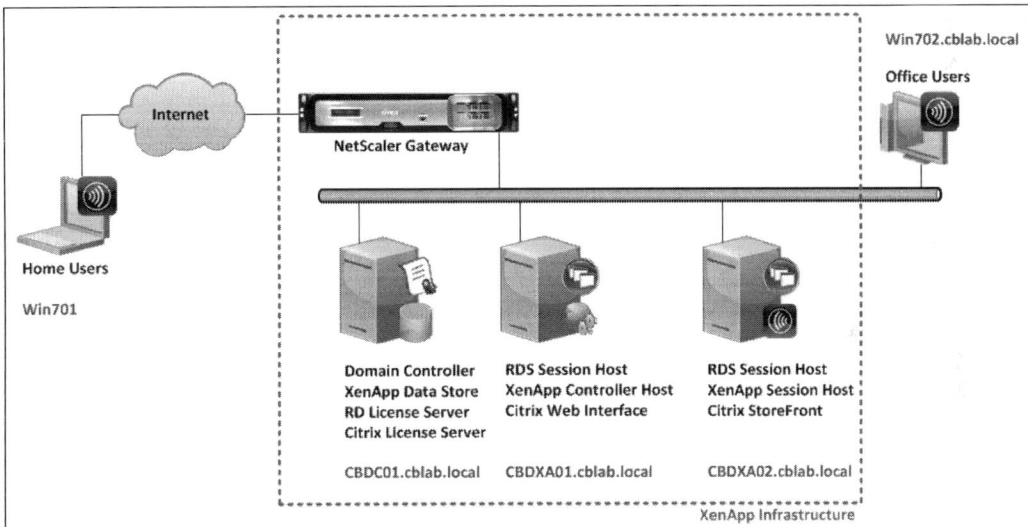

The following software were used to build the Citrix® XenApp® infrastructure:

▶ Windows Server 2008 R2

▶ Citrix® XenApp® 6.5

▶ Citrix® Web Interface 5.4

▶ Citrix® StoreFront 2.1

▶ Citrix® Receiver 4.0

Who this book is for

This book is for Citrix® XenApp® experts who want to get hands-on knowledge of the guidelines for the advanced features and configurations not only of Citrix® XenApp® but also of all the components of a XenApp® infrastructure.

Citrix® XenApp® administrators who have read *Getting Started with Citrix XenApp 6.5*, by *Guillermo Musumeci, Packt Publishing,* and are looking for instructions to go beyond the management consoles will also like this book. Each chapter offers recipes that focus on additional management, installation, and configuration scripts based upon command-line tools and PowerShell.

Conventions

In this book, you will find a number of styles of text that distinguish between different kinds of information. Here are some examples of these styles, and an explanation of their meaning.

Code words in text, database table names, folder names, filenames, file extensions, pathnames, dummy URLs, user input, and Twitter handles are shown as follows: "To use the RDS provider you simply need to change your location to the RDS drive by using the `Set-Location` cmdlet"

A block of code is set as follows:

```
netstat -a > tcpconn.txt
```

Any command-line input or output is written as follows:

```
servermanagercmd.exe –install RDS-Licensing -logPath C:\logs\log.txt
-restart
```

New terms and **important words** are shown in bold. Words that you see on the screen, in menus or dialog boxes for example, appear in the text like this: "clicking the **Next** button moves you to the next screen".

Warnings or important notes appear in a box like this.

Tips and tricks appear like this.

Reader feedback

Feedback from our readers is always welcome. Let us know what you think about this book—what you liked or may have disliked. Reader feedback is important for us to develop titles that you really get the most out of.

To send us general feedback, simply send an e-mail to `feedback@packtpub.com`, and mention the book title via the subject of your message.

If there is a topic that you have expertise in and you are interested in either writing or contributing to a book, see our author guide on `www.packtpub.com/authors`.

Customer support

Now that you are the proud owner of a Packt book, we have a number of things to help you to get the most from your purchase.

Downloading the color images of this book

We also provide you a PDF file that has color images of the screenshots/diagrams used in this book. The color images will help you better understand the changes in the output. You can download this file from `https://www.packtpub.com/sites/default/files/downloads/5221EN_ColoredImages.pdf`.

Errata

Although we have taken every care to ensure the accuracy of our content, mistakes do happen. If you find a mistake in one of our books—maybe a mistake in the text or the code—we would be grateful if you would report this to us. By doing so, you can save other readers from frustration and help us improve subsequent versions of this book. If you find any errata, please report them by visiting `http://www.packtpub.com/submit-errata`, selecting your book, clicking on the **errata submission form** link, and entering the details of your errata. Once your errata are verified, your submission will be accepted and the errata will be uploaded on our website, or added to any list of existing errata, under the Errata section of that title. Any existing errata can be viewed by selecting your title from `http://www.packtpub.com/support`.

Piracy

Piracy of copyright material on the Internet is an ongoing problem across all media. At Packt, we take the protection of our copyright and licenses very seriously. If you come across any illegal copies of our works, in any form, on the Internet, please provide us with the location address or website name immediately so that we can pursue a remedy.

Please contact us at `copyright@packtpub.com` with a link to the suspected pirated material.

We appreciate your help in protecting our authors, and our ability to bring you valuable content.

Questions

You can contact us at `questions@packtpub.com` if you are having a problem with any aspect of the book, and we will do our best to address it.

1
Remote Desktop Services

In this chapter, we will cover the following topics:

- ▶ Scripting a command-line installation of the RD License Server
- ▶ Configuring the RD License Server
- ▶ Scripting a command-line installation of the RD Session Host
- ▶ Configuring the RD Session Host
- ▶ Configuring RDS settings with Microsoft Group Policies
- ▶ Revoking RDS Device CALs with RD License Manager
- ▶ Creating RDS Per User CALs reports
- ▶ Using the Licensing Diagnosis snap-in for RD Session Hosts
- ▶ Troubleshooting RD License Server discovery
- ▶ Troubleshooting RD License Issuance
- ▶ Rebuilding the RD License Database
- ▶ Recovering your RDS CALs to a new RD License Server

Introduction

A **Citrix XenApp** (**CXA**) infrastructure consists of many components to ensure that its users can start a published desktop or an application. One of the core components in the infrastructure is the **Remote Desktop Services** (**RDS**) role that can be installed on a Windows Server, allowing multiple and simultaneous desktop sessions to run on one Windows Server. This chapter offers a number of tips and tricks to manage, monitor, and troubleshoot the RDS Windows server role within the XenApp infrastructure.

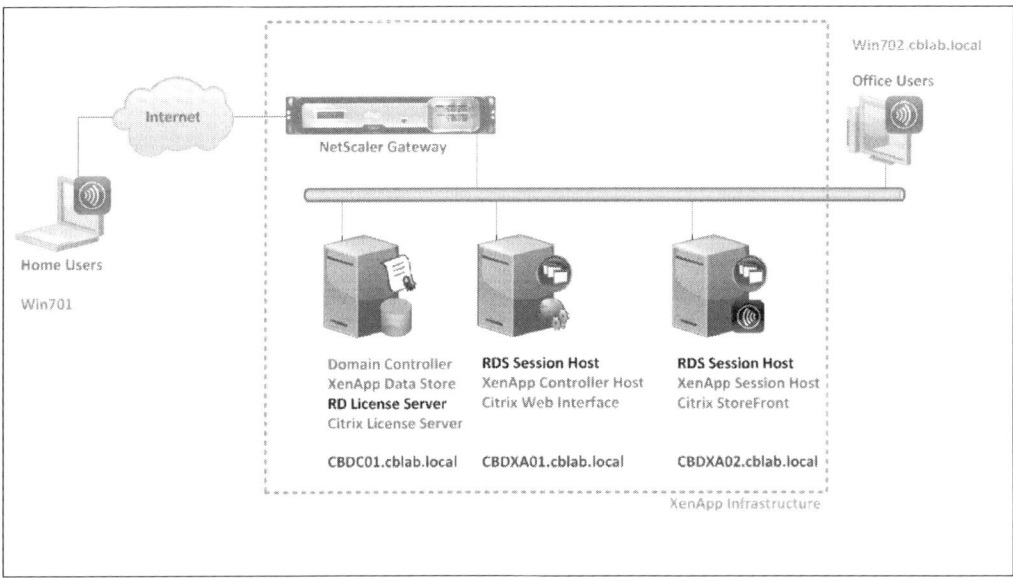

The Citrix® XenApp infrastructure relies on two important Remote Desktop role services—the **Remote Desktop** (**RD**) **License Server**, which manages the RDS **Client Access Licenses** (**CALs**) that are required to start a Remote Desktop session on a Windows Server and the **Remote Desktop** (**RD**) **Session Host** that actually runs the user sessions on the Windows Server.

Scripting a command-line installation of the RD License Server

This recipe will show you how to build an unattended installation for the RD License Server by using command-line instructions. In this way, you can create an unattended installation sequence for your XenApp infrastructure deployment.

Getting ready

To install the RD Licensing Role Service you need to install and set up a new Windows Server 2008 R2 server or add the Windows Role Service to an existing server.

To build an unattended installation for the RD License Server, you can use the `servermanagercmd.exe` command to add the Windows Role Service to the server.

How to do it...

To add the RD License Server service to a Windows server, follow this step:

1. Run the following command line on a Windows Server 2008 R2 server:

```
servermanagercmd.exe -install RDS-Licensing -logPath C:\logs\log.
txt -restart
```

How it works...

When you run the `servermanagercmd.exe` command, the following message is shown:

```
Servermanagercmd is deprecated and not guaranteed to be supported in
future releases of Windows. We recommend that you use the Windows
PowerShell cmdlets that are available for Server Manager.
```

Even though it might no longer be supported in future releases, it still works with Windows Server 2008 R2 to create an unattended installation to add Windows features, roles, or services to Windows Server 2008 R2. You can run the `servermanagercmd.exe` command with various parameters.

To check the installed roles and features on a Windows Server 2008 R2 server, you can use the following command line:

```
servermanagercmd -query [<query.xml>] [-logPath <log.txt>]
```

Windows Server 2008 R2 uses the following parameters:

► `-query`: This specifies an optional XML file used to save the results of the query
► `-logPath`: This specifies an optional log file other than the `%windir%\temp\servermanager.log` path used by default

When you want to change the installed roles and features on a Windows Server 2008 R2 server, you can add the following parameters to the `servermanagercmd` command:

```
servermanagercmd [-install|-remove] <Id> [-allSubFeatures]
[-resultPath <result.xml>] [-restart] [-whatIf] [-logPath <log.txt>]
```

This command uses the following parameters:

▶ `-install`: This installs the specified role, role service, or feature on the Windows Server

▶ `-remove`: This removes the specified role, role service, or feature from the Windows Server

▶ `-resultPath`: This specifies the XML file that saves the results of the command

▶ `-logPath`: This specifies an optional log file other than the `%windir%\temp\servermanager.log` file used by default

There's more...

You can read more about `servermanagercmd.exe` on Microsoft TechNet: `http://technet.microsoft.com/en-us/library/ee344834(v=ws.10).aspx`.

If you are not comfortable using a deprecated command or if you want to use a method that will be supported in future Windows server releases, you can also use Windows PowerShell to install the required Windows Server 2008 R2 roles and features. Windows PowerShell 2.0 is installed by default on the server. The following PowerShell commands will install the RD Licensing Role Service on the server:

```
Import-Module ServerManager
Add-WindowsFeature –Name RDS-Licensing –LogPath <log.txt> -Restart
```

You can read more about the Add-WindowsFeature PowerShell cmdlet on Microsoft TechNet: `http://technet.microsoft.com/en-us/library/ee662309.aspx`.

See also

▶ The *Configuring the RD License Server* recipe

Configuring the RD License Server

This recipe will show you how to configure the RD License Server by using Windows PowerShell scripts to create an unattended installation for the configuration of your XenApp infrastructure.

Getting ready

In order to configure the RD Licensing Role Service, you need to have the RD License Server installed. You can use the unattended installation directions in the previous recipe for installing the RD License Server.

To run the provided PowerShell commands, the default execution mode for PowerShell scripting needs to be changed so that the commands can be run on the server. You can change the PowerShell execution mode from `Restricted` to `RemoteSigned` with the following PowerShell command:

```
Set-ExecutionPolicy RemoteSigned -Force
```

How to do it...

To configure the RD License Server through command-line tools and/or scripts and build an unattended configuration script, follow these steps:

1. Run the following Windows PowerShell script to configure the RD License Server:

```
# Import the RDS PowerShell module
Import-Module RemoteDesktopServices
# Navigate to the RDS Provider for Windows PowerShell
Set-Location RDS:
# Navigate to the RD License Server configuration
cd   RDS:\LicenseServer\Configuration
# Config required info fields for the activation process
Set-Item -Path .\FirstName -Value Test
Set-Item -Path .\LastName -Value User
Set-Item -Path .\Company -Value CBlab
Set-Item -Path .\CountryRegion -Value "Netherlands, The"
# Optional info can be configured with the following lines
Set-Item -Path .\eMail -Value   <Email>
Set-Item -Path .\OrgUnit -Value <OU>
Set-Item -Path .\Address -Value <Address>
Set-Item -Path .\City -Value <City>
Set-Item -Path .\State -Value <State>
Set-Item -Path .\PostalCode -Value <PostalCode>
# Navigate to the RD License Server configuration
cd   RDS:\LicenseServer
# Activate the RD License Server
Set-Item -Path .\ActivationStatus -Value 1 -ConnectionMethod AUTO
-Reason 5
```

You can use the Get-Help command to get more information on the available options per item, which is as follows:

```
Get-Help Set-Item -Path RDS:\LicenseServer\
ActivationStatus -Detailed
```

2. Add the purchased RDS CALs by using the provided wizard.

Using a PowerShell script to automatically add the purchased RDS CALs requires detailed knowledge of the license agreement arrangements with Microsoft and Windows PowerShell only currently supports adding RDS CALs through the automatic connection method. To keep away from adding fraud sensitive information such as your Microsoft agreement number or purchased License keys to commonly available scripts, I recommend adding the RDS CAL packs manually to the configured RD License Server rather than automating these steps in your PowerShell scripts.

How it works...

When you import the Remote Desktop Services module in Windows PowerShell, the Remote Desktop Services (RDS) provider is also included. This provider enables you to configure RDS settings through Windows PowerShell by allowing you to change the RD License Server and RD Session Host server settings with default PowerShell cmdlets, such as Get-Item, Set-Item, New-Item, and Get-ChildItem.

To use the RDS provider, you simply need to change your location to the RDS drive by using the following Set-Location cmdlet:

```
Set-Location RDS:
```

To view the current configuration of the RD License Server, use the following Get-ChildItem cmdlet:

```
Get-ChildItem .\LicenseServer\Configuration
```

With the Set-Item cmdlet, you can change a setting by specifying the location of the configuration item and the new value that has to be set, as shown in the following command line:

```
Set-Item -Path RDS:\LicenseServer\Configuration\<ConfigItem> -Value
<ConfigItemValue>
```

The `Set-Item` cmdlet uses the following parameters:

- ▶ `-Path`: This path specifies the configuration item whose settings need to be changed
- ▶ `-Value`: This specifies the new value for the specified configuration item

Activating your RD License Server is also done with the following `Set-Item` cmdlet:

```
Set-Item –Path RDS:\LicenseServer\ActivationStatus -Value <Status>
-ConnectionMethod <ConnectionMethod> -Reason <Reason>
```

The `Set-Item` cmdlet uses the following parameters:

- ▶ `-Path`: This path specifies the configuration item whose settings need to be changed.
- ▶ `-Value`: This specifies the new value for the specified configuration item. Valid entries for `ActivationStatus` are 1 (Activate) or 0 (Deactivate).
- ▶ `-ConnectionMethod`: This specifies the connection method used for the activation process. Currently only AUTO is supported for PowerShell cmdlets.
- ▶ `-Reason`: This specifies the reason for the activation. Valid entries are 0 (server redeployed), 4 (server upgraded), and 5 (first-time activation).

As mentioned in the *How to do it...* section, you can use the `Set-Item` cmdlet to install the purchased RDS CAL packs. The required parameters for the cmdlet depend upon the used license type and agreement with Microsoft. When you are uncertain about the parameters you will need to provide, use the following `Get-Help` cmdlet to find the required parameters and corresponding values:

```
Get-Help New-Item -Path RDS:\LicenseServer\LicenseKeyPacks -Detailed
```

The next two examples show you how the required parameters change depending on your license type.

An example of the required parameters for an open license:

```
New-Item -Path RDS:\LicenseServer\LicenseKeyPacks -ConnectionMethod
AUTO -LicenseType OPEN -LicenseNumber 0000000 –AuthorizationNumber
'XXXXXXXXXXXXXXX' -ProductVersion 1 -ProductType 1 -LicenseCount 1
```

An example of the required parameters for a retail license:

```
New-Item -Path RDS:\LicenseServer\LicenseKeyPacks -ConnectionMethod AUTO
-LicenseType RETAIL -LicCode 'XXXXX-XXXXX-XXXXX-XXXXX-XXXXX'
```

If you receive a permission denied error when running the PowerShell command, check out the Microsoft Knowledge Base article available at `http://support.microsoft.com/kb/2648662/en-us`.

Adding RDS CALs normally has to be performed only once during the initial configuration of the RD License Server as scripting this part of the configuration is subjected to the license type used. The manual installation of the CALs takes far less time than developing and testing the required PowerShell commands.

 To avoid addition of fraud sensitive information such as your Microsoft Agreement number or purchased License keys to commonly available scripts, I recommend adding the RDS CAL packs manually to the configured RD License Server and to avoid automating these steps in your PowerShell scripts.

There's more...

You can read more about the RDS provider for Windows PowerShell at Microsoft TechNet: `http://technet.microsoft.com/en-us/library/ee791871(v=WS.10).aspx`.

If you are not comfortable running the provided PowerShell script, you can always configure and activate your RD License Server manually by following the instructions from Microsoft TechNet available at `http://technet.microsoft.com/en-us/library/cc770368.aspx`, and add RDS CAL license packs manually by following the instructions from Microsoft TechNet available at `http://technet.microsoft.com/en-us/library/cc770368.aspx`.

See also

▸ The *Scripting a command-line installation of the RD License Server* recipe

Scripting a command-line installation of the RD Session Host

This recipe will show you how to build an unattended installation for the RD Session Host by using command-line instructions. In this way, you can create an unattended installation sequence for your XenApp infrastructure deployment.

Getting ready

To install the RD Session Host server Role Service, you need to install and set up a new Windows Server 2008 R2 server or add the Role Service to an existing server.

How to do it...

To add the RD Session Host server Role Service to a Windows server, follow these steps:

1. Run the following command-line on a Windows Server 2008 R2 server:

    ```
    servermanagercmd.exe -install RDS-RD-Server -logPath C:\logs\log.
    txt -restart
    ```

 A restart is required when installing the RD Session Host role to complete the installation.

How it works...

The `servermanagercmd.exe` command is explained in detail in the *Scripting a command-line installation of the RD License Server* recipe.

There's more...

As an alternative method to the deprecated `servermanagercmd.exe`, you can use Windows PowerShell to install the the Windows Role Service. You can use the following PowerShell command to add the RD Session Host Role Service:

```
Import-Module ServerManager

Add-WindowsFeature –Name RDS-RD-Server –LogPath <log.txt> -Restart
```

See also

►   The *Configuring the RD Session Host* recipe

Configuring the RD Session Host

This recipe will show you how to configure the Remote Desktop Session Host by using PowerShell scripts to create an unattended installation and configuration for your XenApp infrastructure.

Getting ready

To configure the RD Session Host, you need to have the RD Session Host role installed on a Windows server. You can use the unattended installation directions from the previous recipe for the installation of the RD Session Host.

To run the provided PowerShell commands, you will need to change the default execution mode for PowerShell to a less restrictive mode on the server.

You can change the PowerShell execution mode from `Restricted` to `RemoteSigned` by running the following PowerShell command:

```
Set-ExecutionPolicy RemoteSigned -Force
```

How to do it...

To configure the RD Session Host, perform the following step:

1. Run the following PowerShell script to configure your RD Session Host:

```
# Import the RDS PowerShell module
Import-Module RemoteDesktopServices
# Navigate to the RDS Provider for Windows PowerShell
Set-Location RDS:
# Set General settings
cd RDS:\RDSConfiguration\TempFolderSettings
Set-Item -Path .\DeleteTempFolders -Value 1
Set-Item -Path .\UseTempFolders -Value 1
cd RDS:\RDSConfiguration\SessionSettings
Set-Item -Path .\SingleSession - Value 1
Set-Item -Path RDS:\RDSConfiguration\UserLogonMode -Value 0
# Set the License Mode: Per User = 4, Per Device =2
cd RDS:\RDSConfiguration\LicensingSettings
Set-Item -Path .\LicensingType -Value 2
# Specify the RD License Server by its FQDN
New-Item -Path .\SpecifiedLicenseServers -Name CBDC01.cblab.local
```

These are the basic settings that are required by the XenApp infrastructure. All other settings are focused on the RDP-TCP protocol used by RDS and not the ICA protocol that will be used by the XenApp servers.

[   The RDP-TCP settings are not discussed in detail in this book.]

How it works...

How the Remote Desktop Services provider works is explained in the *Configuring the RD License Server* recipe.

The RD Session Host-specific information can be found by using the following PowerShell command to view the current configuration for the RD Session Host server:

```
Get-ChildItem .\RDSConfiguration
```

To set the license mode for the RD Session Host, you can use the following command:

```
Set-Item -Path RDS:\RDSConfiguration\LicensingSettings\LicensingType
-Value <LicenseMode>
```

The `Set-Item` cmdlet uses the following parameters:

▸ `-Path`: This path specifies the configuration item whose settings need to be changed.

▸ `-Value`: This specifies the new value for the specified configuration item. Valid entries for the `LicensingType` are `2` (per device) or `4` (per user).

To specify an RD License Server for the RD Session Host to use, you can use the following `New-Item` cmdlet to add the server information:

```
New-Item -Path RDS:\RDSConfiguration\LicensingSettings\
SpecifiedLicenseServers -Name <FQDNLicenseServer>
```

The `New-Item` cmdlet uses the following parameters:

▸ `-Name`: This specifies the **Fully Qualified Domain Name** (**FQDN**) of the RD License Server

There's more...

You can read more about the RDS provider for Windows PowerShell at Microsoft TechNet: `http://technet.microsoft.com/en-us/library/ee791871(v=WS.10).aspx`.

If you are not comfortable with running the provided PowerShell scripts, you can always configure your RD Session Host manually by following the instructions from Microsoft TechNet: `http://technet.microsoft.com/nl-nl/library/dd996653(v=ws.10).aspx`.

See also

▶ The *Scripting a command-line installation of the RD Session Host* recipe

▶ The *Configuring RDS settings with Microsoft Group Policies* recipe

Configuring RDS settings with Microsoft Group Policies

This recipe shows you how to use Microsoft Group Policies to ensure all XenApp servers will have the same Remote Desktop Services settings applied within your infrastructure by applying the settings to your servers from a centrally configured location with Microsoft Group Policies.

Getting ready

To use Microsoft Group Policies and configure the required settings for your XenApp servers, you need to have the Group Policy Management feature installed on Windows Server 2008 R2 and be able to start the Group Policy Management Console on at least one of your servers.

You also need to ensure that the XenApp servers (or at least the RD Session Host servers) are put in their own **Organizational Unit (OU)** within Active Directory. This ensures you can attach **Group Policy Objects (GPOs)** with the required Group Policy settings to the server OU in Active Directory.

How to do it...

To configure RDS settings with Group Policies, follow these steps:

1. Open the Group Policy Management Console by navigating to **Start | Run | gpmc.msc**.

2. Select the Active Directory OU that contains the XenApp or RD Session Host servers.

3. Click on the menu and navigate to **Action | Create a GPO in this domain | Link it here...**.

4. Enter a clear and explanatory name for your GPO, leave the Source Starter GPO set to **none**, and click on **OK**.

5. Select the newly created GPO.

6. Click on the menu and navigate to **Action | Edit...**.

7. Configure your RDS related settings and close Group Policy Management Console when you have finished.

[ The most common RDS related settings that can be configured through Group Policies are explained in the next section.]

How it works...

You can find all the RDS-related policy settings for Windows servers by navigating to **Computer Configuration | Policies | Administrative Templates | Windows Components | Remote Desktop Services | Remote Desktop Session Host** within the Group Policy Editor.

You can configure the following RDS Session Host settings:

Subfolder	Settings	Configuration
Temporary folders	Do not delete the `temp` folder upon exit	This specifies whether RDS retains a user's per-session temporary folders at logoff.
		Not configured = Temp folders are deleted unless specified otherwise.
Temporary folders	Do not use temporary folders per session	This specifies whether RDS creates session-specific temporary folders.
		Not configured = per-session temporary folders are created unless specified otherwise.
Connections	Restrict RDS users to a single RDS session	This specifies whether users are restricted to a single remote RDS session.
		Enabled = users who log on remotely will be restricted to a single session.
Connections	Allow users to connect remotely using RDS	This specifies whether remote access is allowed using RDS.
		Not configured = the RDS setting determines whether a remote connection is allowed.
Licensing	Set the Remote Desktop licensing mode	This specifies the type of RDS client access license (RDS CAL) required: Per User or Per Device.
		Enabled = Policy setting overrules installation settings.
Licensing	Use the specified RD License Servers	This specifies the order in which an RD Session Host server attempts to locate RD License Servers.
		Enabled = RD Session Host server first attempts to locate the specified license servers. If this fails, it will attempt an automatic license server discovery.

These are the basic settings that are required by the XenApp infrastructure to be set. All other policy settings are focused on the RDP-TCP protocol used by Windows Remote Desktop Services and not the ICA protocol that is used by the XenApp servers.

 The RDP-TCP settings are not discussed in detail in this book.

There's more...

You can read more on All Group Policy Settings for Remote Desktop Services in Windows Server 2008 R2 at Microsoft TechNet: `http at //technet.microsoft.com/en-us/library/ee791756(v=ws.10).aspx`.

See also

▶   The *Configuring the RD Session Host* recipe

Revoking RDS Device CALs with the RD License Manager

This recipe will show you how to manually revoke RDS Device CALs with the RD License Manager to manage the amount of available RD Licenses in your XenApp infrastructure.

Getting ready

To manage RDS Device CALs, a RD License Server needs to be installed and activated in the XenApp infrastructure. The RD License Server must also be issuing RDS Device CALs to client devices connecting to the RD Session hosts by the RDP protocol. Use the RD License Manager to check whether RDS Device CALs are issued by the RD License Server.

How to do it...

To revoke RDS Device CALs, follow these steps:

1. Open the RD License Manager by navigating to **Start | Run | licmgr**.

2. Double-click on the RD License Server in the right pane.

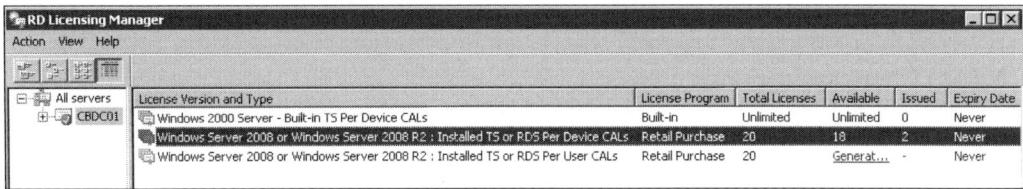

3. Double-click on **Installed TS or RDS Per Device CALs**, as shown in the previous screenshot

4. Right-click on the **Per Device CAL** that you want to revoke and select **Revoke License**.

5. Click on **Yes** to confirm the revocation of the CAL.

6. Click on **OK**.

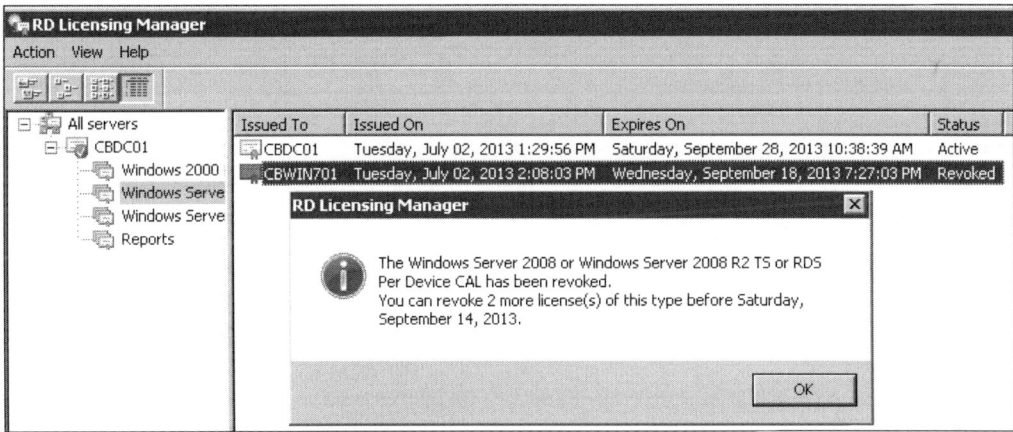

The status of the revoked Per Device CAL has now been changed to **Revoked**.

How it works...

Each RD Session Host needs to be configured with an RD License Server and the RD licensing mode to run user sessions. The configured RD licensing mode determines the type of RDS CAL that will be requested from the RD License Server. This can either be a Per User or a Per Device RDS CAL.

When a user wants to set up a Remote Desktop session on an RD Session Host, the host will check whether or not a valid RDS CAL is presented and will request an RDS CAL with the RD License Server, if one cannot be provided. The following flowchart provides a (simplified) view of the process followed by the RD Session Host to check and request an RDS Device CAL for the client device:

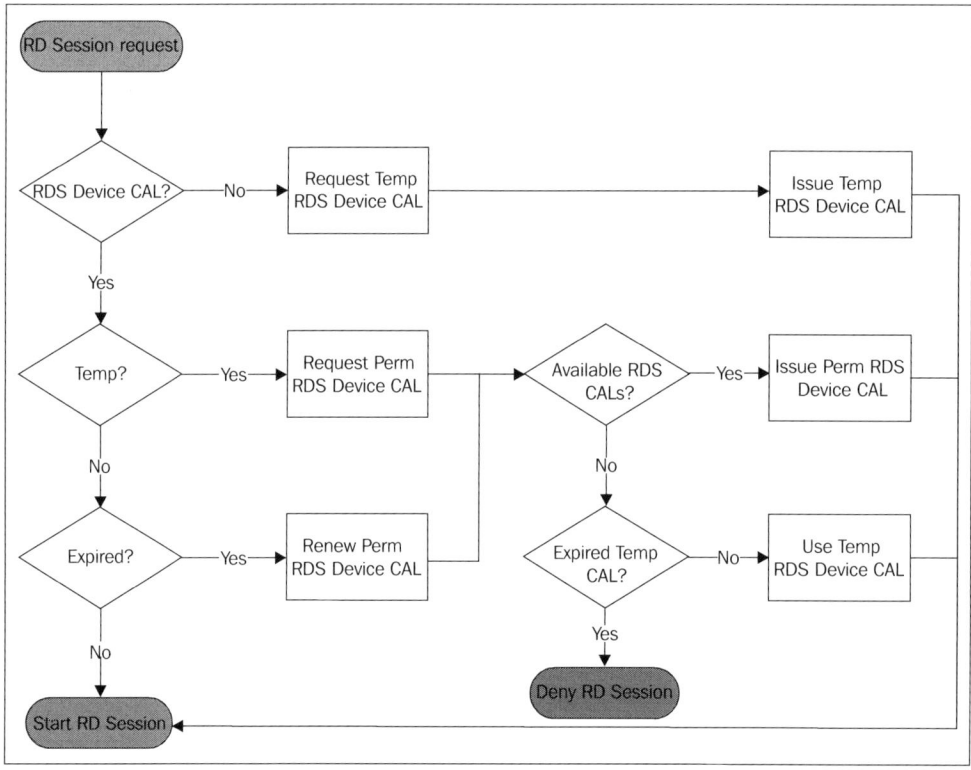

If the device cannot present an RDS Device CAL, a temporary RDS Device CAL will be issued by the RD License server. If the device presents a temporary or expired RDS Device CAL, a permanent RDS Device CAL will be issued if the RD License Server has RDS Device CALs available. If no RDS Device CALs are available, no permanent RDS Device CAL can be issued and the issued RDS Device CAL is not replaced on the client device. If a valid temporary CAL is available, a Remote Desktop session can still be started; if not, the request is denied, and the Remote Desktop session is denied.

An RD License Server can always issue temporary CALs whether it is activated or not. An unlimited supply of temporary RDS CALs is installed by default on each RD License Server. Temporary RDS CALs are valid for 90 days.

Each permanent RDS CAL issued by the RD License server is automatically configured with an expiry date. This date is a random period of 52 to 89 days from the request date. The expiry date for each RDS CAL is logged by the RD License server to ensure that when the expiry date is reached, the RDS CAL is automatically returned to the pool of available RDS Device CALs on the RD License Server. The returned RDS CAL can be issued immediately to a new device when a CAL is requested.

If by any chance you want to return a RDS Device CAL to the pool of available CALs before it is expired, you can use the RD Licensing Manager to revoke a Per Device CAL.

 Keep in mind that only RDS Per Device CALs can be revoked and not RDS Per User CALs.

The revocation of RDS Device CALs is only meant to return issued CALs for devices that are no longer in use and there is no mechanism to dynamically manage your license pool. You are only allowed to revoke up to 20 percent of the CALs within a period of two and a half months.

There's more...

You can read more about Remote Desktop licensing at Microsoft TechNet at `http://technet.microsoft.com/en-us/library/cc772298.aspx`.

You can read more about Remote Desktop licensing at Microsoft TechNet at `http://technet.microsoft.com/en-us/library/cc772298.aspx`.

To keep track of the issued RDS Device CALs and automatically generate reports, you can use the Visual Basic script that is developed and provided on Microsoft's MSDN website to generate RDS Per Device CAL reports. The following screenshot is an example of such a report:

```
Administrator: Command Prompt                                    _ □ X
Microsoft Windows [Version 6.1.7601]
Copyright (c) 2009 Microsoft Corporation.  All rights reserved.

C:\Temp\Scripts>cscript GeneratePerDeviceReport.vbs -Server localhost
Microsoft (R) Windows Script Host Version 5.8
Copyright (C) Microsoft Corporation. All rights reserved.

KeyPackID,LicenseID,IssuedToMachine,HWID,ExpiryDate
3,2,CBDC01,000234471145d9ee9c64c73e02ec3804dbff,20130928083839.000000-000
3,8,CBWIN701,00000000000000000000000000000000000000,20130918172703.000000-000

C:\Temp\Scripts>_
```

You can download the script and read more about it at Microsoft's MSDN blog at `http://blogs.msdn.com/b/rds/archive/2007/08/10/generating-per-device-license-usage-reports-for-ts-license-servers-running-windows-server-2008.aspx`.

See also

▸ The *Scripting a command-line installation of the RD License Server* recipe

▸ The *Configuring the RD License Server* recipe

▸ The *Creating RDS Per User CALs Reports* recipe

Creating RDS Per User CALs Reports

This recipe will show you how to create RDS User CAL reports from the RD Licensing Manager. Unlike RDS Device CALs, the issued RDS User CALs are not shown in the management console. A report has to be created to get an overview of the issued RDS Per User CALs.

Getting ready

In order to manage your RDS Per User CALs, you need to have an RD License Server installed and activated so that it can issue RDS User CALs. In addition to this, you also need to have RDS Per User CALs installed on your RD License server and have your RD Session Host servers configured for the Per User license mode. This will ensure that your RD Session Host will request a valid Per User RDS CAL to be presented for each user that starts a Remote Desktop session on the server.

 You can check the previous recipes in this chapter for directions on setting up and configuring your RD License Server and RD Session Hosts.

How to do it...

You can check whether your RD License server is issuing RDS Per User CALs with the RD Licensing Manager. Unlike the Per Device CALs where all issued licenses are shown in the console, a report has to be generated to get an overview of the issued RDS Per User CALs. Follow these steps to generate the report:

1. Open the RD License Manager by navigating to **Start | Run | licmgr**.

2. Double-click on **RD License Server** in the right pane.

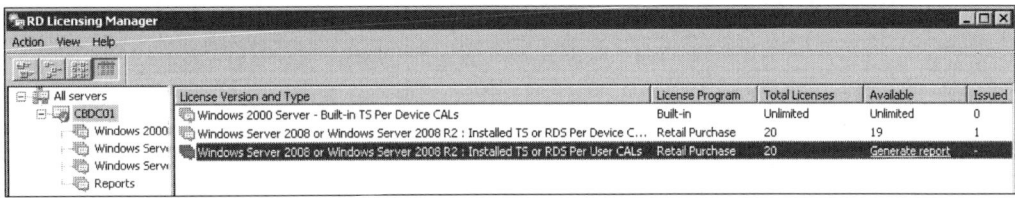

3. Check if RDS Per User CALs are installed (shown in the right pane of the previous screenshot).

4. Right-click on **Reports** in the left pane and select **Create Report | Per User CAL Usage....**

5. Select **Entire Domain** and click on **Create Report**.

6. Click on **OK**.

7. Right-click on the newly created report in the **Reports** overview and select **Save As**.

8. Save the report as a Comma Delimited (CSV) file.

You can view the report with either Notepad or Microsoft Excel as shown in the following screenshot:

```
RDSPerUserCALS20130707.csv - Notepad
File  Edit  Format  View  Help
CAL Usage Report
RD License Server:,"CBDC01"
Report Date:,"Sunday, July 07, 2013 1:02:42 PM"
Report Scope:,"Domain"

Issued to User,CAL Version,Expires On
CBLAB\cbtester01,Windows Server 2008 or Windows Server 2008 R2,Sunday, September 01, 2013 8:27:26 PM
CBLAB\cbtester02,Windows Server 2008 or Windows Server 2008 R2,Sunday, September 01, 2013 8:28:03 PM
CBLAB\cbtester03,Windows Server 2008 or Windows Server 2008 R2,Sunday, September 01, 2013 8:28:44 PM

CAL Version,CAL Type,Installed CALs,CALs in Use,CAL Availability
Windows Server 2008 or Windows Server 2008 R2,Per User,20,3,Available
```

There's more...

If you want to automate the generation of the Per User RDS CAL usage reports, you can also run the following PowerShell script:

```
# Import the RDS PowerShell module
Import-Module RemoteDesktopServices
# Navigate to the RDS Provider for Windows PowerShell
Set-Location RDS:
# Generate the Per User CAL report
```

```
cd RDS:\LicenseServer\IssuedLicenses\PerUserLicenseReports

New-Item -Path . -Name PerUser20130707 -Scope DOM

# Check report settings

Get-ChildItem -Path .\20130707_133613\Win2K8-Win2K8R2

Get-Item -Path .\20130707_133613\Win2K8-Win2K8R2\IssuedLicenses\*
```

The report name is automatically generated and based on the creation date of the report.

 It is currently not possible to specify a custom report name with the `-Name` parameter for the `New-Item` cmdlet to generate a Per User CAL usage report.

See also

▶ The *Scripting a command-line installation of the RD License Server* recipe

▶ The *Configuring the RD License Server* recipe

▶ The *Scripting a command-line installation of the RD Session Host* recipe

▶ The *Configuring the RD Session Host* recipe

▶ The *Configuring RDS settings with Microsoft Group Policies* recipe

Using the Licensing Diagnosis snap-in for RD Session Hosts

This recipe will show you how to use the Licensing Diagnosis snap-in of the RD Session Host Configuration console. This snap-in allows you to check the health of your RD Session Host configuration and the communication with the RD License server.

Getting ready

In order to use the Licensing diagnosis snap-in, you need an installed and configured RD Session Host and an installed and configured RD License server as well. In order to read information on the RD License server with the Licensing Diagnosis snap-in, you also need to run it with a user account that has administrator privileges on the RD License server.

How to do it...

To use the Licensing Diagnosis snap-in, follow these steps:

1. Open the RD Session Host Configuration console by navigating to **Start | Run | tsconfig.msc**.

2. Click on **Licensing Diagnosis** in the left pane:

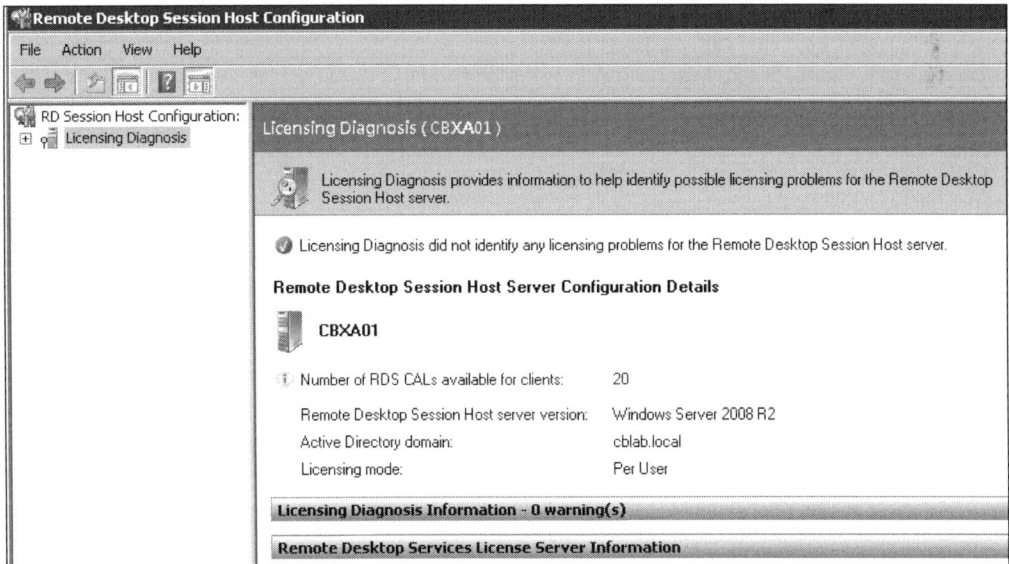

3. Select the RD License server in the **Remote Desktop Services License Server Information** pane to view more details on the RD License server:

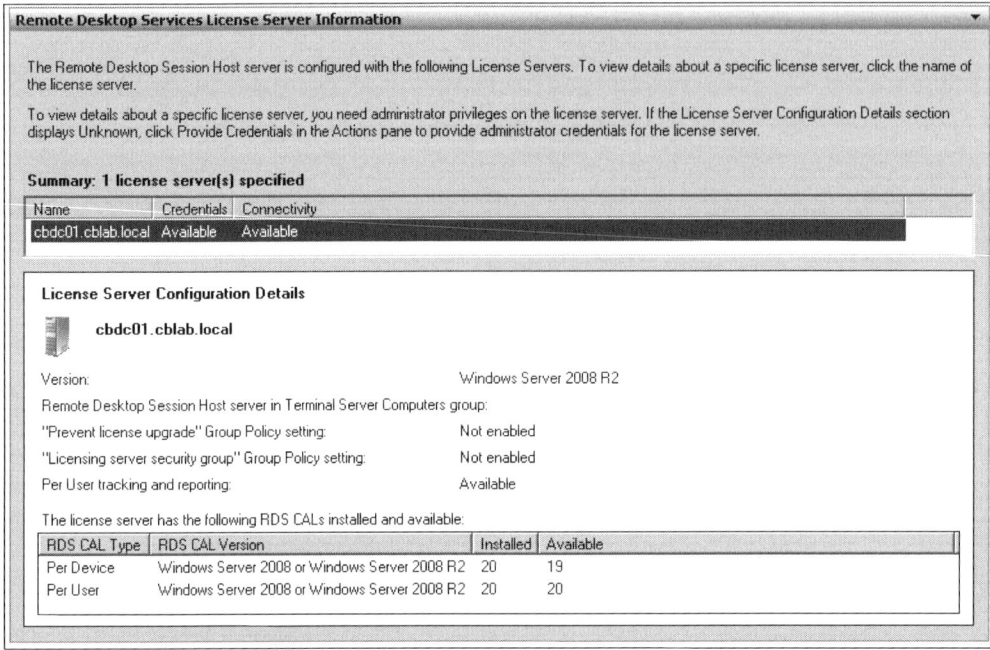

If the Licensing Diagnosis snap-in detects problems reading the RD Session Host configuration or has problems communicating with the RD Licensing Server, it will show clear warnings and/or error messages in the Licensing Diagnosis Information pane.

 The *How it works...* section of this recipe will provide more details on the different error messages that can be shown and their common fixes.

How it works...

The Licensing Diagnosis snap-in provides administrators with a quick diagnostic tool to check the configuration of the RD Session Host and the communication to and from the RD License servers. It will also provide clear error and warning messages when problems are detected.

Administrative privileges

To use the Licensing Diagnosis snap-in, it must be executed on the RD Session Host with an account that has local administrator permissions on the host. If your account does not have these permissions, a warning is shown when Licensing Diagnosis is selected in the left pane:

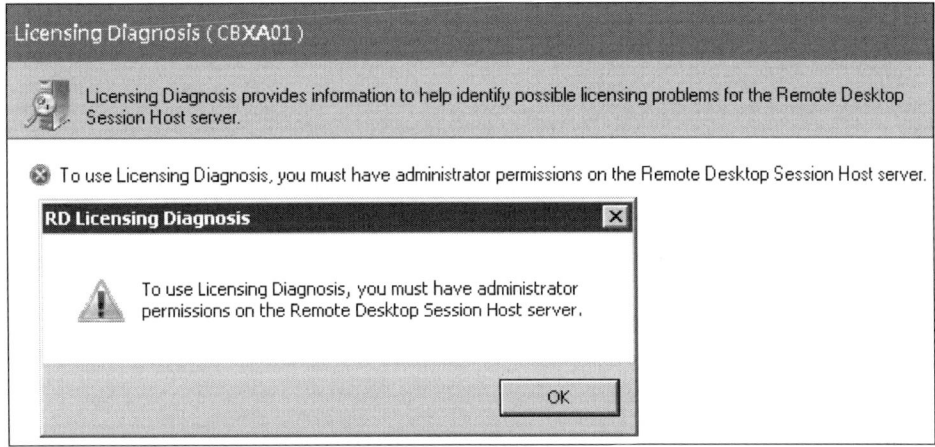

To view the RD License server information, the same account also needs administrative privileges on the RD License server. Without those privileges, the following error will be shown:

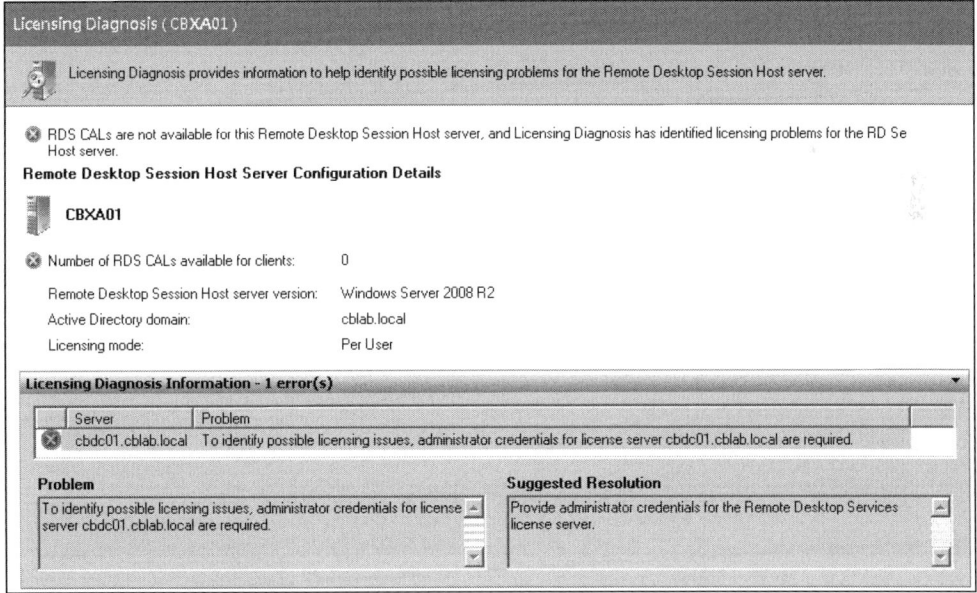

It is possible to provide separate credentials in the management console for the RD License server. By selecting the license server in the Remote Desktop Services License Server Information pane, and by selecting **Provide Credentials** from the **Action** menu, you can enter the required account information. After providing the right credentials, the RD Licensing server information is shown and no errors are reported.

RD Licensing service not started

When the RD License service is not started, the following error is shown:

```
License server <LicenseServerName> is not available. This could be caused
by network connectivity problems, the RD Licensing service is stopped
on the license server, or RD Licensing is no longer installed on the
computer...
```

Make sure the RD Licensing service is started on the RD License server. If it is not started, start the service and refresh the Licensing Diagnosis information to see if the problem is resolved.

There's more...

You can read more on Licensing Diagnosis problems at the MSDN blog at `http://blogs.` `msdn.com/b/rds/archive/2008/02/01/licensing-diagnosis-problems-and-` `resolutions.aspx`.

See also

▶ The *Configuring the RD License Server* recipe

▶ The *Configuring the RD Session Host* recipe

▶ The *Troubleshooting RD License Issuance* recipe

Troubleshooting RD License Server discovery

This recipe will show you how to troubleshoot the RD License Server discovery.

How to do it...

As of Windows Server 2008 R2, automatic discovery of the RD License Server is no longer supported. To check whether a RD License Server is configured, follow these steps:

1. Open the Windows registry by navigating to **Start | Run | regedit**.

2. Check the content of the following key:

    ```
    HKLM\SYSTEM\ControlSet001\services\TermService\Parameters\
    LicenseServers\SpecifiedLicenseServers
    ```

3. If no RD License server is specified, specify the correct server name and retest the RD License Server discovery.

4. If a RD License server is specified, test whether a connection can be made to the server with Telnet:

```
telnet <RDLicenseServer> 135
```

 If a connection can be made through telnet, a blank screen with a blinking prompt will be shown. Press *Ctrl +]* to close the connection and *Q* to exit the Telnet client.

How it works...

When installing a RD License server, a discovery scope needs to be provided for the server. Previous versions of Windows Server (2000, 2003, and 2008) Terminal Services were able to use a discovery process to automatically find the **Terminal Server** (**TS**) License server by checking the Active Directory for specified TS License servers.

This automatic discovery process is no longer supported for the RD Session Host servers running on Windows Server 2008 R2 and later. You are now required to specify a RD License server in the RD Session Host configuration or through Group Policy settings. If errors report that no RD License Server can be found by the RD Session Host, make sure a RD License server is configured through the RD Session Host Configuration console or through Microsoft Group Policy settings. You can check the following registry key for the specified License Server entries:

```
HKLM\SYSTEM\ControlSet001\services\TermService\Parameters\LicenseServers\
SpecifiedLicenseServers
```

If a RD License Server is specified, make sure the RD Licensing service is running and network connectivity is available between the RD Session Host and the RD License Server. RD Licensing uses **Remote Procedure Call** (**RPC**) over TCP port 135 and a dynamically assigned port above 1024. For communication with Microsoft Clearinghouse during activation and the RDS CAL installation process, internet communications over TCP port 443 are required as well.

You can install the Telnet client to check network connectivity on a Windows Server 2008 R2 server by running a command prompt as Administrator and using the following command line:

```
pkgmgr /iu:"TelnetClient"
```

This will run the Windows Package Manager and install the Telnet client.

 For more information on the port numbers used by Windows services, check Microsoft's Knowledge Base: http://support.microsoft.com/ kb/832017 and http://support.microsoft.com/kb/154596.

See also

▸ The *Configuring the RD License Server* recipe

▸ The *Troubleshooting RD License Issuance* recipe

Troubleshooting RD License Issuance

This recipe will show you how to troubleshoot problems concerning Remote Desktop Licenses being issued to devices or users trying to set up a RD session.

How to do it...

To troubleshoot RD License Issuance, follow these steps:

1. Open the Event Viewer by navigating to **Start | Run | eventvwr.msc**.

2. For RDS Per Device CALs, navigate to **Windows Logs | System**.

3. Search for informational events with ID 82.

4. For RDS Per User CALs, navigate to **Applications and Services Logs | Microsoft | Windows | TerminalServices-Licensing | Admin**.

5. Search for informational events with ID 4143.

6. If no entries are found, RD licenses are not issued.

 Check for known events in the table in the next section to find a solution for common RD License server problems.

How it works...

For troubleshooting purposes, a quick list of common RD Licensing error messages and their recommended solutions are provided in the following table:

ID	Error message	Solution
17	One or more RD Licensing certificates on server "%1" are corrupt. RD Licensing will only issue temporary licenses until the server is reactivated.	When a RD Licensing server is activated with the automatic connection method, Microsoft Clearinghouse sends the server a digital certificate chain that validates the ownership and identity of the server. On February 26, 2010, a certificate that was part of this digital certificate chain expired and it is flagged as a corrupt certificate by the RD License server. A hotfix is available at Microsoft's Knowledge Base: http://support.microsoft.com/kb/983385.

ID	Error message	Solution
20	The RD license server "%1" does not have a sufficient number of permanent RDS CALs for product "%3". Only "%2" permanent RDS CALs remain.	Buy additional RDS CALs of the right type (User/Device) and install them on the RD license server.
21	The RD license server "%1" does not have any remaining permanent RDS CALs of the type "%2". As a result, the RD license server cannot issue RDS CALs of the type "%2" to the RD Session Host server "%3".	Check the RD licensing mode configured on the RD Session Host server. Make sure it matches the type of RDS CALs installed on the RD license server.
22	The RD license server "%1" does not have any RDS CALs installed and registered with the Microsoft Clearinghouse for product "%2". Therefore, the RD license server cannot issue RDS CALs of the type "%2" to the RD Session Host server "%3".	Buy and install the required RDS CALs.
38	The RD license server cannot issue a RDS CAL to the client because of following error: "%1!s!"	The RD License server installation has become corrupted. Reinstall the RD License server role.
		To preserve the issued license information, back up the RD Licensing database folder (%windir%\system32\LServer) before removing the role.
4105	The RD license server cannot update the license attributes for user "%1!s!" in the AD Domain "%2!s!". Ensure that the computer account for the license server is a member of Terminal Server License Servers group in AD domain "%2!s!".	Make sure the RD License server is a member of the Terminal Server License Servers group in AD.
		For a RD license server installed on a DC, the Network Service account also needs to be a member of that group. To track or report the usage of RDS Per User CALs, a reboot is required.

Issuance of RDS Per User CALs

Issued RDS Per User CALs are logged in the Event log by Information entries with the Event ID 4143. These will appear in the **Applications and Services Logs** section under **Microsoft | Windows | TerminalServices-Licensing | Admin**.

Issuance of RDS Per Device CALs

Issued RDS Per Device CALs are logged in the Event log by Information entries with the Event ID 82 in the **Windows Logs** under **System**.

Reissue a RDS Per Device CAL

RD Licensing information concerning RDS Per Device CALs are stored on the client device in the registry:

`HKLM\SOFTWARE\Microsoft\MSLicensing.`

To remove the Per Device CAL from the client device, you can delete the hardware ID and store subkeys from the registry and reboot the client. The client device will request a new CAL at the next RD session.

 Always create a backup of the registry when editing or deleting keys and values.

When the entire MSLicensing registry key is deleted and needs to be recreated, you will have to run the Remote Desktop connection as an administrator with the corresponding privileges to have sufficient rights to create the corresponding registry keys.

 You can provide any user credentials for the RD Session as these are used to log on to the RD Session Host, not to create the registry keys.

There's more...

For a complete overview of Remote Desktop Services Events in Windows Server 2008 R2, check out Microsoft TechNet at `http://technet.microsoft.com/en-us/library/ff404148%28v=ws.10%29.aspx`.

See also

- ▸ The *Configuring the RD License Server* recipe
- ▸ The *Configuring the RD Session Host* recipe
- ▸ The *Configuring RDS settings with Microsoft Group Policies* recipe

- ▶ The *Using the Licensing Diagnosis snap-in for RD Session Hosts* recipe
- ▶ The *Troubleshooting RD License Issuance* recipe

Rebuilding the RD License Database

This recipe will show you how to rebuild the RD Licensing database to solve Remote Desktop License server issues.

Getting ready

To automatically rebuild the RD Licensing database, the computer running the RD Licensing Manager needs to have internet access (TCP port 443). The RD License server itself does not require internet access, only the computer running the management console.

Check if your RD License Server is configured for Automatic connection (recommended) through the properties of your RD License Server in the RD License Manager, before you start the rebuilding process.

How to do it...

To automatically rebuild the RD License server, follow these steps:

1. Open the RD License Manager by navigating to **Start | Run | licmgr**.
2. Right-click on **RD License Server** in the left pane and select **Manage Licenses**.
3. Click on **Next** in the **Manage licenses Wizard Welcome** screen.
4. A connection to Microsoft Clearinghouse is set up.
5. Select **Rebuild the license server database** in the action select step.
6. Provide a reason for the rebuild action and click on **Next**:

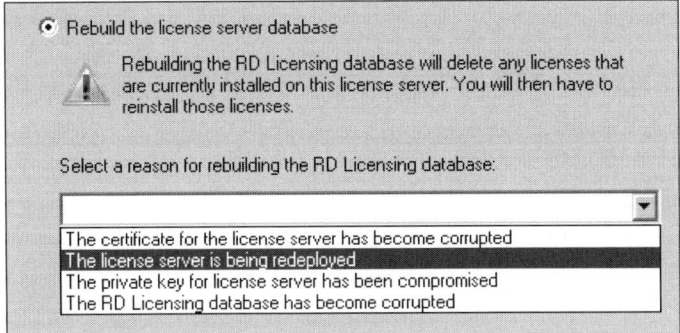

7. Read the warning message.

8. Select the **Confirm deletion of licenses currently installed on this license server** checkbox and click on **Next**.

9. The RD Licensing database has been deleted.

10. Click on **Next** to reinstall the licenses in the reinstalling licenses step.

11. Select your **License program** and click on **Next**:

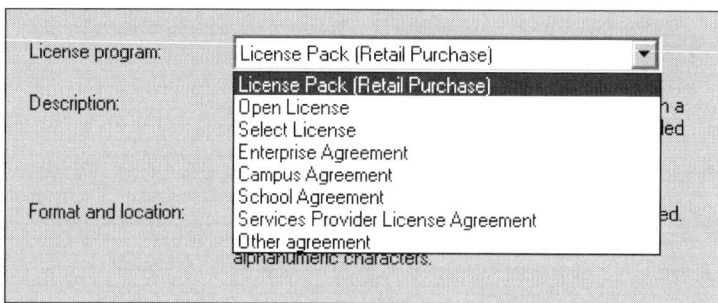

12. Fill out the required license information (**License Code**, **Agreement number**, and so on), and click on **Next**.

13. Your licenses are being reinstalled.

14. Select **Continue** if you need to install more licenses and repeat steps 11 to 13.

15. Select **Finish rebuilding the RD License database** in the reinstalling additional licenses step and click on **Next**.

16. Complete the Manage Licenses Wizard by clicking on **Finish**.

17. Select the **RD License server** in the left pane and check if the installed licenses are shown in the right pane and whether all licenses are available or not.

 New licenses might not be checked out unless your client device or user has a temporary or expired RDS CAL and a renewal request is made. When a valid CAL is presented to the RD Session Host no request will be made with the RD License Server and no CAL will be checked out.

There's more...

You can read more about rebuilding the RD Licensing Database at Microsoft TechNet: http://technet.microsoft.com/nl-nl/library/ff817600%28v=ws.10%29.aspx.

See also

▶ The *Configuring the RD License Server* recipe

▶ The *Revoking RDS Device CALs with the RD License Manager* recipe

▶ The *Creating RDS Per User CALs Reports* recipe

▶ The *Recovering your RDS CALs to a new RD License Server* recipe

Recovering your RDS CALs to a new RD License Server

This recipe will show you how to recover your RDS CALs to a new RD License server when you cannot restore your original server or when you simply need to transfer your licenses to a new RD License server.

Getting ready

In order to automatically rebuild the RD Licensing database, the computer running the RD Licensing Manager needs to have internet access (TCP port 443). The RD License server itself does not require internet access, only the computer running the management console.

Also check if your RD License Server is configured for automatic connection (recommended) through the properties of your RD License Server in the RD License Manager.

How to do it...

To automatically recover your licenses to a new RD License server, follow these steps:

1. Add the Remote Desktop Licensing server role to the new RD License server.

2. Open **RD License Manager** (by navigating to **Start | Run | licmgr** on the new RD License server).

3. Activate the new RD License Server without adding any licenses.

4. Right-click on the **RD License Server** in the left pane and select **Manage RDS CALs**.

5. Click on **Next** in the **Manage RDS CALs Wizard welcome** screen.

6. A connection to Microsoft Clearinghouse is set up.

7. Select **Migrate RDS CALs** from another license server to this license server.

8. Select a reason for migrating and then click on **Next**:

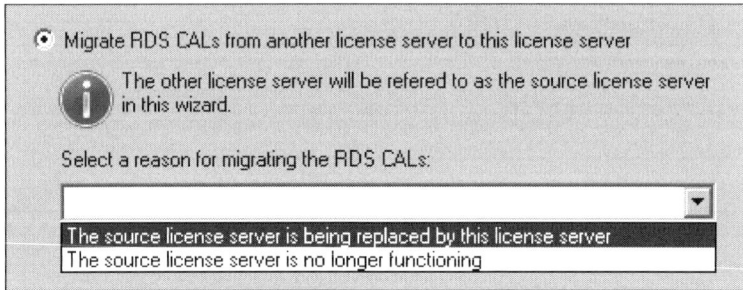

9. If you select the **The source license server is being replaced** option, provide the following information:

   ❑ The source license server name or IP address

   ❑ Whether or not it is still available

   ❑ The operating system

   ❑ The original RD License server ID

10. If you select the **The source license server is no longer functioning** option, accept the agreement not to use your source license server as RD License server and agree to manually remove the RDS CALs from your original RD License server.

11. Click on **Next**.

12. Follow steps 11 to 16 from the *How to do it...* section of the previous recipe to install the RDS CALs.

There's more...

You can read more about recovering (or migrating) RDS CALs at Microsoft TechNet at `http://technet.microsoft.com/en-us/library/dd851844.aspx`.

See also

▸ The *Scripting a command-line installation of the RD License Server* recipe

▸ The *Configuring the RD License Server* recipe

▸ The *Rebuilding the RD License Database* recipe

2
Citrix® License Server

In this chapter, we will cover the following topics:

- ► Scripting a command-line installation and configuration of the Citrix® License Server
- ► Installing the license files on your Citrix® License Server manually
- ► Configuring console user accounts for the management console
- ► Monitoring the Citrix® license usage on the Dashboard
- ► Changing port numbers on the Citrix® License Server
- ► Clustering the Citrix® License Server with Microsoft Clustering
- ► Finding your Citrix® License Server version
- ► Recovering your password when locked out of the Licensing Administration Console
- ► Using LSQuery, a License Server Data Collection Tool
- ► Resetting the license count
- ► Troubleshooting tools for the Citrix® License Server

Introduction

A XenApp infrastructure consists of many components to ensure that users can start a published desktop or application. In addition to the RDS License Server that allows the usage of Windows Remote Desktop Services, Citrix components are required to obtain their licenses from a **Citrix License Server** (**CLS**).

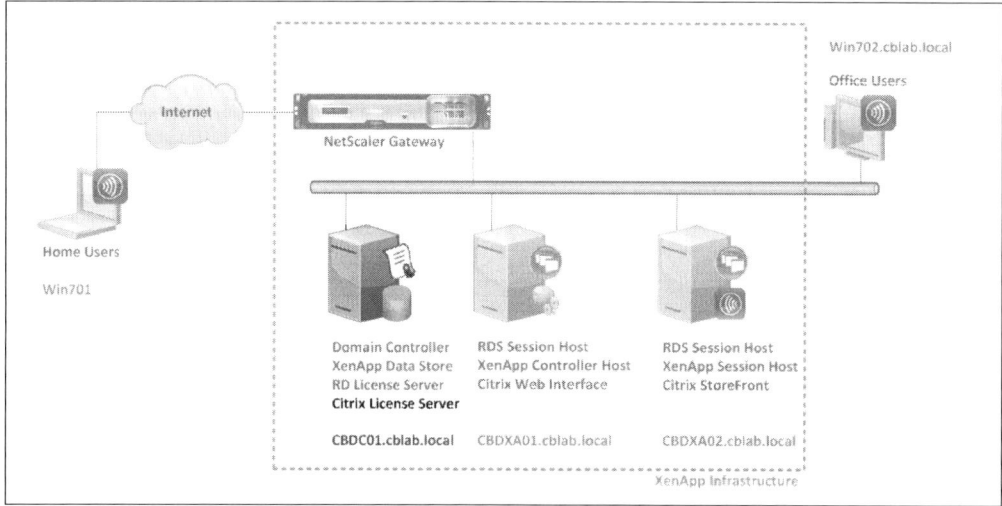

You can use multiple Citrix License Servers in your infrastructure. Due to the limited resources a Citrix License Server consumes and a grace period of 30 days (where a Citrix product can function normally without contacting a CLS), having only one Citrix License Server in your infrastructure will be sufficient for most designs.

Citrix does offer a Citrix License Server Virtual Appliance for Citrix XenServer. This appliance allows you to run a preinstalled Citrix License Server that can easily be configured when run for the first time. The virtual appliance is designed for lab environments or only to provide Citrix XenServer licenses. Using the virtual appliance in a production environment to host all Citrix components licenses is not supported.

Scripting a command-line installation and configuration of the Citrix® License Server

This recipe will show you how to build an unattended installation script for the **Citrix License Server** (**CLS**) using a command-line installation.

Getting ready

To install the Citrix License Server, you will need a Windows Server (2003, 2008, and 2008 R2 are supported) with at least Microsoft .NET Framework 3.5 installed.

How to do it...

The CLS can be installed with the XenApp installation wizard or using the provided MSI file. Follow these steps to create an unattended installation:

1. Run the following command for an unattended installation and port configuration of the CLS:

```
msiexec.exe /i ctx_licensing.msi /log clsinstall.log /qn
LICSERVERPORT=27000 VENDORDAEMONPORT=7279 MNGMTCONSOLEWEBPORT=8082
ADMINPASS=<password>
```

How it works...

To create a command-line installation for an MSI file, you can use the `msiexec.exe` executable provided on each Windows Server:

```
msiexec.exe /i /qn <misfile> /norestart /log <log.txt>
```

The command line uses the following parameters:

- ▶ `/i`: This parameter installs the provided MSI file
- ▶ `/qn`: This parameter sets the user interface level to **No UI**
- ▶ `/log`: This parameter specifies a logfile for the installation process

You can read all about the `msiexec` command-line options at Microsoft TechNet at `http://technet.microsoft.com/en-us/library/cc759262(v=ws.10).aspx`.

With each MSI file, more parameters that are specific to the MSI file can be provided. Often these parameters provide additional installation information. With the `ctx_licensing.msi` file, you can provide the following additional parameters:

- ▶ **LICSERVERPORT**: This is the port number that will be used by the Citrix License Server. The default port number is 27000.
- ▶ **VENDORDAEMONPORT**: This is the port number used by the Citrix License Server vendor daemon. The default port number is 7279.
- ▶ **MNGMTCONSOLEWEBPORT**: This is the port number used by the Citrix License Server web console. The default port number is 8082.
- ▶ **ADMINPASS**: This is the password that will be set for the admin console user.

  ▶ **CTX_CLUSTER_RESOURCE_DLL_PATH**: This is the location where the cluster resource DLL will be stored. This is used only when installed in a cluster mode.

  ▶ **REGISTER_CTX_LS_CLUSTERING**: Use "no" for cluster node 1 and "yes" for cluster node 2. This is only used when installed in a cluster mode.

There's more...

You can read more about the command-line installation of the Citrix License Server at Citrix's eDocs at `http://support.citrix.com/proddocs/topic/licensing-119/lic-install.html`.

See also

  ▶ The *Configuring console user accounts for the management console* recipe

  ▶ The *Changing port numbers on the Citrix® License Server* recipe

  ▶ The *Clustering the Citrix® License Server with Microsoft Clustering* recipe

Installing the license files on your Citrix® License Server manually

This recipe will show you how to manually install the license files on your Citrix® License Server.

Getting ready

In order to install the license files manually on your **Citrix License Server** (**CLS**), you should have the Citrix License Server installed. You should also have a Customer Account on the Citrix website and know your server's hostname.

How to do it...

To retrieve your license files from Citrix, you need to perform the following steps:

1. Go to `http://www.citrix.com`.

2. Click on the **My Account (Log In)** link in the top-right corner of the site, and enter your **Login ID** and **Password**.

3. Click on the **All Licensing Tools** link under **Licensing**.

4. Click on the **Activate and Allocate Licenses** link (or click on the **Single Allocation** if you have your license code available).

5. Follow the instructions and presented steps to allocate your license(s).

6. Enter your **Host ID** (host name) and confirm the allocation.

7. Click on **OK** to download your license file to your device.

To manually install the license files on the CLS, follow these steps:

1. Open your License Administration Console (**Start | All Programs | Citrix | Management Consoles**) or browse directly to the URL (`http://localhost:8082`).

2. Click on **Administration** in the top-right corner of the window.

3. Enter a username and password with administrative privileges.

4. Click on **Vendor Daemon Configuration** in the left pane of the window.

5. Browse to the license file and click on **Import License**.

6. Click on the **Administer** link in the left column of the Citrix Vendor Daemon.

7. Click on **Reread License Files**.

8. Check if the new licenses are shown on the **Dashboard**.

How it works...

There are different ways and steps to manually install your license files on the Citrix License Server. The different steps are discussed in detail in the following sections.

Retrieve your server's hostname

To assign your license files to your CLS, you need to provide the correct hostname of your server. The hostname provided is case sensitive. You can find the hostname of your CLS in the **Administration** part of your CLS console in the **System Information** tab, as shown in the following screenshot:

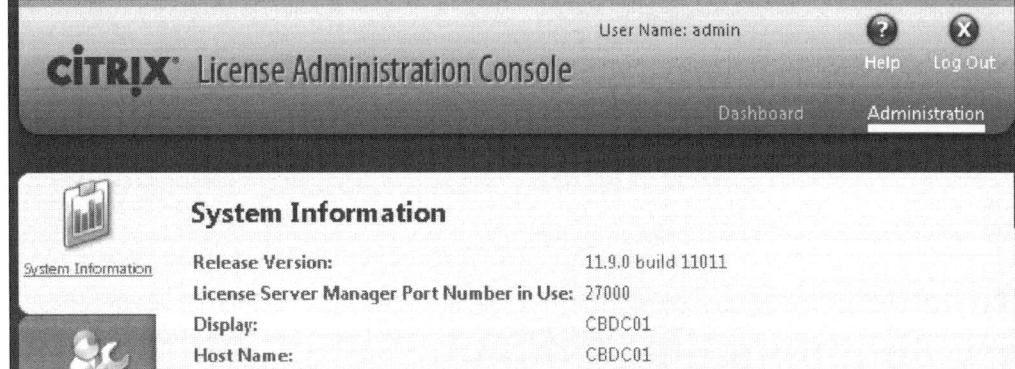

You can also find the hostname of your CLS by running the following command:

```
C:\Program Files (x86)\Citrix\Licensing\LS\lmhostid.exe -hostname
```

Manually install your license files

To manually install your license file(s) on the CLS, you can copy the downloaded file(s) to the `MyFiles` directory of your license server.

The default location of the `MyFiles` directory is as follows:

▸ For 64-bit OS: `C:\Program Files (x86)\Citrix\Licensing\MyFiles`

▸ For 32-bit OS: `C:\Program Files\Citrix\Licensing\MyFiles`

Reread your license files on the Citrix License Server

To ensure that your copied license files are reread by the CLS, you can run the following command:

```
C:\Program Files (x86)\Citrix\Licensing\LS\lmreread -c @localhost
```

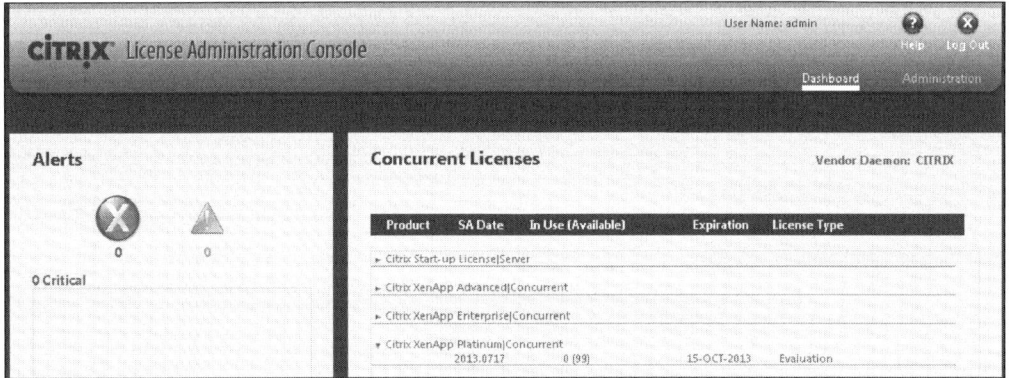

You can check the CLS console **Dashboard** to see if your licenses are correctly installed, as shown in the previous screenshot.

 For the purpose of this book, we have installed Evaluation XenApp licenses in our demo lab.

There's more...

You can read more on manually adding your license files at Citrix's eDocs at `http://support.citrix.com/proddocs/topic/licensing-119/lic-install-license-files.html`.

You can read more on the *My Account All Licensing Tool* at Citrix's Knowledge Center at `http://support.citrix.com/article/ctx131110`.

You can read more on the `lmreread` command at Citrix's eDocs at `http://support.citrix.com/proddocs/topic/licensing-119/lic-admin-cmds-reread-lic-r.html`.

See also

▸ The *Scripting a command-line installation and configuration of the Citrix® License Server* recipe

▸ The *Monitoring the Citrix® License usage on the Dashboard* recipe

Configuring console user accounts for the management console

This recipe will show you how to add additional user accounts to your **Citrix License Server** (**CLS**) management console.

How to do it...

The CLS management console manages its own user accounts and roles. To create a new user account, perform the following steps:

1. Open your License Administration Console (**Start | All Programs | Citrix | Management Consoles**) or browse directly at `http://localhost:8082`.
2. Click on the **Administration** link in the upper-right corner of the window.
3. Provide the required credentials to log in.
4. Click on the **User Configuration** tab.
5. Click on **New User**.
6. Provide the required information (**User Name**, **Password**, and **Role**) and whether the user must change the password at the next logon and click on **Save**.
7. The user account can now be used to log in for the administration part of the management console.

How it works...

The CLS License Administration Console manages user accounts by itself. These accounts are not related to the local Windows user accounts or even Active Directory user accounts.

When adding a new user account to the console, you can choose two different roles for the account. The roles and corresponding rights are as follows:

Rights for the User role:

- ▸ View Dashboard (licenses and alerts)
- ▸ Change password
- ▸ Select the console language

Rights for the Administrator role:

- ▸ Log on to administration
- ▸ View system information
- ▸ Manage users
- ▸ Configure alerts
- ▸ Configure the server
- ▸ Configure the vendor daemon
- ▸ Import license files

 If you do not configure the option **Require user to log on to view Dashboard** (**Administration | Server Configuration | User Interface**) then everyone can view the Dashboard.

The **Dashboard** page is the landing page for the Citrix License Administration Console.

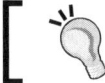 Account names are case sensitive, limited to 60 characters, and cannot contain spaces.

There's more...

You can read more on how to configure Console users at Citrix's eDocs at `http://support.citrix.com/proddocs/topic/licensing-119/lic-lmadmin-users-b.html`.

See also

▶ The *Scripting a command-line installation and configuration of the Citrix® License Server* recipe

▶ The *Monitoring the Citrix® License usage on the Dashboard* recipe

▶ The *Finding your Citrix® License Server version* recipe

▶ The *Recovering your password when locked out of the Licensing Administration Console* recipe

Monitoring the Citrix® license usage on the Dashboard

This recipe will show you how to monitor your Citrix license usage on the License Administration Console Dashboard of **Citrix License Server** (**CLS**).

How to do it...

To monitor the Citrix License usage, follow these steps:

1. Open your License Administration Console (**Start | All Programs | Citrix | Management Consoles**) or browse directly to http://localhost:8082.

2. The **Dashboard** page is the landing page of the License Administration Console.

3. Click on the arrow in front of the **Citrix Startup License|Server** to view details on the servers that requested a startup license from the CLS.

4. Click on **Hosts** to get a list of servers by hostname.

5. Click on the icon of a red circle with a white cross in the left pane of the window to view critical alerts logged by the license server.

6. Click on the icon of a yellow triangle with a white exclamation mark to view warnings logged by the license server.

How it works...

The Citrix License Administration Console Dashboard is the landing page of the web console, and shows licenses and alerts information for the Citrix products that are included in the license files:

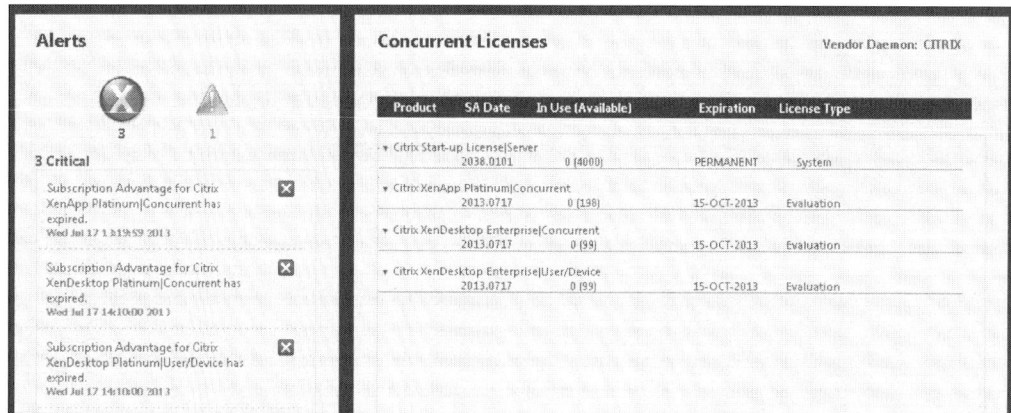

By checking the Dashboard regularly, you can keep track of the licenses in use, expiration dates for your licenses, **Subscription Advantages** (**SA**), and the hosts that claimed a startup license.

The **Hosts** link appears in the last column of the license information table if the licenses are checked. Clicking on the link will open a pop-up window with a list of hosts and the licenses used by those hosts.

In addition to the license information, you can also check the alerts to see if actions are required to keep your licenses up-to-date or whether you can run your available licenses. To view the different types of alerts, you can click on the representing icons in the **Alerts** pane. The critical alerts are shown by default.

Alerts are not cleared automatically. You can manually clear an alert by clicking on the red-squared x that is shown in the top-right corner of each alert.

There's more...

You can read more on Monitoring Licenses and Alerts at Citrix's eDocs at `http://support.citrix.com/proddocs/topic/licensing-119/lic-lmadmin-dashboard.html`.

Changing port numbers on the Citrix® License Server

This recipe will show you how to change the port numbers used by the different **Citrix License Server** (**CLS**) services, such as the licensing service, web console service, and vendor daemon service.

How to do it...

The port numbers can be changed using the License Administration Console, which can be opened by performing the following steps:

1. Open your License Administration Console (**Start | All Programs | Citrix | Management Consoles**) or browse directly to `http://localhost:8082`.
2. Click on the **Administration** link in the upper-right corner of the window.
3. Provide the required credentials to log on.
4. Check the currently assigned ports by clicking on the **System Information** tab.

The Console Web Server port can be changed by performing the following steps:

1. Click on the **Server Configuration** tab.
2. Click on **Web Server Configuration**.
3. Change **HTTP Port**.
4. Click on **Save**.
5. Restart the Citrix Licensing service (`net stop/start "Citrix Licensing"`).

 When you change the Console Web Server port number, you will have to reload the Citrix License Administration Console, and use the new port number in the URL.

The License Server Manager port can be changed by performing the following steps:

1. Click on the **Server Configuration** tab.
2. Click on **License Server Configuration**.
3. Change **License Server Manager Port**.
4. Click on **Save**.
5. Restart the Citrix Licensing service (`net stop/start "Citrix Licensing"`).

The Vendor Daemon port can be changed by performing the following steps:

1. Click on the **Vendor Daemon Configuration** tab.

2. Click on the **Administer** link in the column on the left-hand side of Citrix Vendor Daemon.

3. Change **Vendor Daemon Port**.

4. Click **Save**.

5. Restart the Citrix Licensing service (`net stop/start "Citrix Licensing"`).

 The Citrix License Server refreshes its information every 15 minutes. To force an update, you can restart the Citrix Licensing service.

How it works...

When installing and configuring your Citrix License Server, you need to provide port numbers for the different services that are used by the server. These services are as follows:

▸ Console web server (default 8082)

▸ License server manager (default 27000)

▸ Vendor daemon (default 7279)

If you want to change these ports after the installation, you will need to use the License Administration Console.

There's more...

You can read more on changing the port number at Citrix's eDocs at `http://support.citrix.com/proddocs/topic/licensing-119/lic-lmadmin-ports-change.html`.

Clustering the Citrix® License Server with Microsoft Clustering

This recipe will show you how to build a redundant licensing solution by clustering your Citrix License servers with Microsoft Clustering techniques.

Getting ready

Before installing the Citrix licenses servers, you need to have built your Microsoft cluster following Microsoft's guidelines. Keep in mind that the Failover Clustering feature is only available on the Windows Server 2008 R2 Enterprise or DataCenter editions, not on the Standard edition. To build the Failover cluster, you can follow the step-by-step instructions on the blog post at `http://www.elmajdal.net/win2k8/Installing_Failover_Clustering_With_Windows_Server_2008_R2.aspx`.

How to do it...

The following steps describe how to set up your clustered Citrix License Servers:

1. Start your installation on the active node of the cluster (ensure that node 1 is your active node and has all the shared resources).

2. Run the command prompt as administrator (right-click on the shortcut and click on **Run as Administrator**).

3. Use the following command to start the Citrix License Server installation wizard:

    ```
    msiexec.exe /i ctx_licensing.msi CTX_CLUSTER_RESOURCE_DLL_
    PATH="C:\ctxlic" REGISTER_CTX_LS_CLUSTERING="No" /log "clsinstall.
    log"
    ```

4. Accept the license agreement and click on **Next**.

5. Select the cluster-shared drive as the drive for the destination folder path on the **Change Destination Folder** page.

6. Accept the default port numbers for the Citrix License Server services on the **Configuration** page.

7. Finish the installation.

8. Use the Cluster Administrator console to activate the second node as the active cluster node.

9. Run the command prompt as administrator (right-click on the shortcut and click on **Run as Administrator on the second node**).

10. Use the following command to start the Citrix license server installation wizard:

    ```
    msiexec.exe /i ctx_licensing.msi CTX_CLUSTER_RESOURCE_DLL_
    PATH="C:\ctxlic" REGISTER_CTX_LS_CLUSTERING="Yes" /log
    "clsinstall.log"
    ```

11. Repeat step 4 to step 7.

12. Open the License Administration Console by opening the URL, `http://<clustername>:8082` and import your license file. Or copy your license file to the `MyFiles` folder on the shared cluster drive and use the following command to re-read your licenses:

```
lmreread -c @<clustername>
```

How it works...

To install the Citrix License Server on a Microsoft cluster, two additional parameters must be provided with the MSI installer to ensure that the installation wizard is cluster aware:

- `CTX_CLUSTER_RESOURCE_DLL_PATH`: This is the location (local folder on each cluster node) where the cluster resource DLL will be stored. It is used only when installed in the cluster mode.

- `REGISTER_CTX_LS_CLUSTERING`: This argument is used only when installed in the cluster mode. Use "no" for cluster node 1 and "yes" for cluster node 2.

You will need to start the installation using the following command line:

```
msiexec.exe /i <misfile> CTX_CLUSTER_RESOURCE_DLL_PATH="<localpath>"
REGISTER_CTX_LS_CLUSTERING="[Yes|No]" /log <logfile.log>
```

It uses the following parameters:

- `/i`: This parameter specifies the provided MSI file that must be installed by the `msiexec.exe` command

- `/log`: This parameter specifies a logfile for the installation process

The installation wizard will ask you to specify the destination folder. The folder must be located on the cluster-shared drive (not the quorum drive) to ensure that both cluster nodes will use the same Citrix License Server configuration and license files.

There's more...

You can read more on building Windows Server 2008 R2 Failover Clustering at Microsoft's TechNet at `http://blogs.technet.com/b/aevalshah/archive/2012/05/15/windows-server-2008-r2-failover-clustering-best-practice-guide.aspx`.

You can read more on installing the Citrix License Server on a Clustered-Enabled Server at Citrix's eDocs at `http://support.citrix.com/proddocs/topic/licensing-1110/lic-cl-install-t.html`.

You can also read more on CLS High Availability with Microsoft Failover Cluster on Windows Server 2008 R2 at the Citrix Knowledge Center article at http://support.citrix.com/article/CTX132842.

See also

▶ The *Scripting a command-line installation and configuration of the Citrix® License Server* recipe

Finding your Citrix® License Server version

This recipe will show you how to find your **Citrix License Server** (**CLS**) version number.

How to do it...

To find the correct version number of your Citrix License Server, follow these steps:

1. Open the Windows registry (**Start | Run | regedit**).
2. Check the content of the following key:

   ❑ For 32-bit OS: `HKLM\SOFTWARE\Citrix\LicenseServer\Install\Version`

   ❑ For 64-bit OS: `HKLM\SOFTWARE\Wow6432Node\Citrix\LicenseServer\Install\Version`

 With access to the Citrix License Administration Console, you can also check the version number at the **Administration | System Information** tab.

There's more...

You can read more on finding your CLS version at Citrix's eDocs at http://support.citrix.com/proddocs/topic/lic-find-by-version/lic-find-doc-by-version-c.html.

 The link also provides you with an overview of the CLS included with each Citrix product release and links to additional documentation.

See also

▶ The *Scripting a command-line installation and configuration of the Citrix® License Server* recipe

▶ The *Recovering your password when locked out of the Licensing Administration Console* recipe

Recovering your password when locked out of the Licensing Administration Console

This recipe will show you how to recover a lost password for your **Citrix License Server** (**CLS**) Administration Console user.

How to do it...

If you happen to forget the password for your Administration Console admin user (installed by default), you can use the following procedure to restore your admin password and enabling you to log into the console again:

1. Run an editor such as WordPad as administrator (right-click on the shortcut and click on **Run As Administrator**).

2. Open the file `server.xml` (located by default at `C:\Program Files (x86)\Citrix\Licensing\LS\conf\server.xml`).

3. Search for the string that starts with:

   ```
   <user firstName="System" id="admin"
   ```

4. Replace the encrypted password for this account with a new password in clear text, and change the value of the **passwordExpired** setting to **true**.

5. The original line will now look similar to the following line of code:

   ```
   <user firstName="System" id="admin" lastName="Administrator"
   password="recovered" passwordExpired="true" privileges="admin"/>
   ```

6. Save the file.

7. Restart the Citrix Licensing service (`net stop/start "Citrix Licensing"`).

8. Open the Citrix Licensing Administration Console and log into the **Administration** section with the newly set password.

9. You will now be asked to change your password.

 Once you change your password, it will be encrypted again, and stored in the `server.xml` file. The line will then look similar to the following lines of code:

```
<user firstName="System" id="admin"
lastName="Administrator" password=" (ENC-01)N2q
50bsAujjKibnV+00PPFJ2tvhf00xEN0mJL1x+W/DJ808F"
passwordExpired="false" privileges="admin"/>
```

See also

▶ The *Configuring console user accounts for the management console* recipe

Using LSQuery, a License Server Data Collection Tool

This recipe will show you how to use the LSQuery tool to collect information on your **Citrix License Server** (**CLS**) and check its health.

How to do it...

As of CLS Version 11.9 and higher, you can use a new License Server Data Collection Tool from Citrix to check the health and configuration of your Citrix License Server.

To use LSQuery, follow these steps:

1. Go to `http://support.citrix.com/article/CTX133160` and download the LSQuery tool ZIP file.

2. Unzip the file to a local folder on the license server.

3. Run `LSQuery.exe` by double-clicking on it.

4. Click on **Run** when you get the **Open File** security warning pop-up window.

5. Select **File | Collect from the menu** to start collecting the data from your CLS:

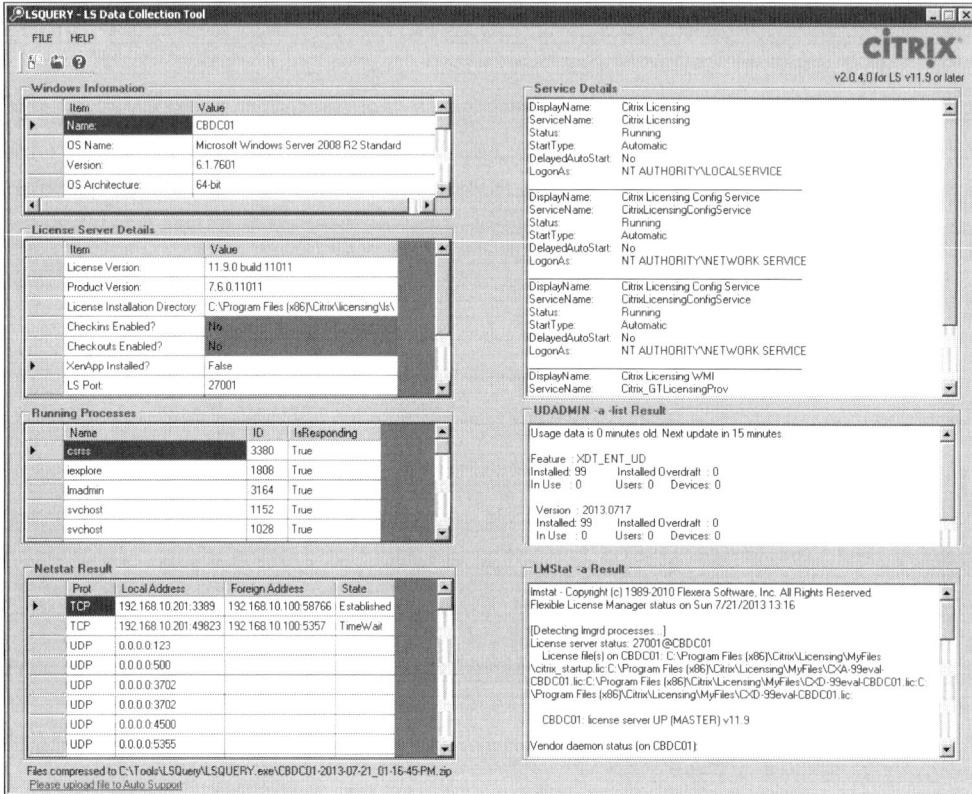

How it works...

With LSQuery, you can quickly check the configuration details of your license server, such as the version and port numbers:

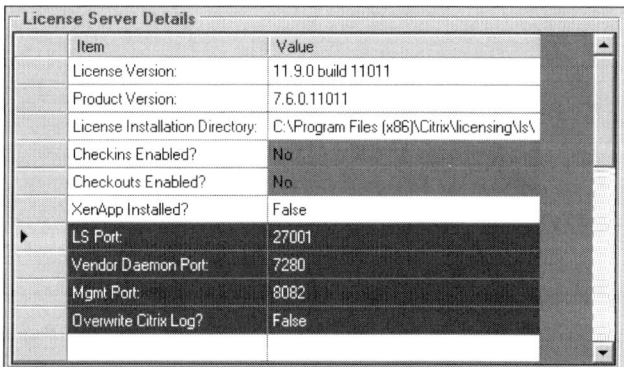

You are also able to see the direct result for the most common License Server tools such as `netstat`, `lmstat`, and `udadmin`:

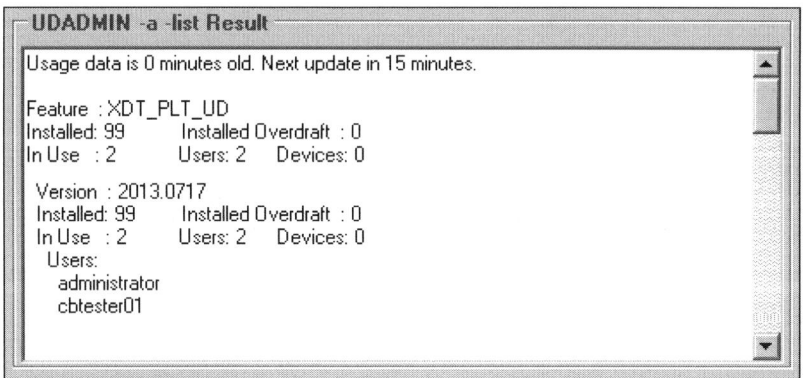

There's more...

If you want to run LSQuery without a **Graphical User Interface** (**GUI**), you can run the following command in an elevated command prompt:

```
lsquery -nogui
```

LSQuery creates a zipped output file each time it collects data. The zipped file can be named as, `<CLSservername>-<date>_<timestamp>.zip`, and can be sent to Citrix Auto Support to be analyzed by the Citrix Support Team.

If you want to read more on how to collect data for troubleshooting licensing issues, check out the Citrix Knowledge Center at `http://support.citrix.com/article/CTX127314`.

See also

- ► The *Monitoring the Citrix® License usage on the Dashboard* recipe
- ► The *Finding your Citrix® License Server version* recipe
- ► The *Resetting the License count* recipe
- ► The *Troubleshooting tools for the Citrix® License Server* recipe

Resetting the license count

This recipe will show you how to reset your license count for the Citrix XenDesktop User and/ or Device licenses that can be managed with the Citrix License Server. Citrix User/Device XenDesktop licenses can also be used for a Citrix XenApp 6.5 Farm as long as the right license type is configured with a Citrix Policy for the XenApp servers.

With the new Citrix XenDesktop Named licenses that can also be assigned to your Citrix XenApp Farm, licenses are no longer just checked out for the duration of a user session, but are permanently checked out and linked to a user or device account. With the permanently named licenses, you will need to actively manage the checked out licenses for accounts that have become obsolete within your Enterprise due to the fact that the user or device account is no longer in use.

How to do it...

To manage the named licenses, follow these steps:

1. Run the command prompt as administrator (right-click on the shortcut and select **Run as Administrator**).

2. Change to the LS subdirectory of the Citrix License Server installation folder:

   `cd C:\Program Files (x86)\Citrix\Licensing\LS`

 By default, the Citrix License Server is installed in the `C:\Program Files (x86)\Citrix\Licensing` directory on 64-bit systems and in the `C:\Program Files\Citrix\Licensing` directory on 32-bit systems.

3. To retrieve a list of named licenses that are checked out by a user or device, you can run the following command:

   `udadmin.exe -list`

 You can even use `udadmin.exe -list > C:\cmdexport.txt` to export the results of the `udadmin` command to a text file.

4. A list of the Device/User accounts, license types, and check-out dates are shown in the following screenshot:

```
C:\Program Files (x86)\Citrix\Licensing\LS>udadmin -list
Usage data is 0 minutes old. Next update in 15 minutes.

Devices:
cbwin701 XDT_PLT_UD 2013.0717
cbwin702 XDT_PLT_UD 2013.0717


C:\Program Files (x86)\Citrix\Licensing\LS>
```

5. To return a device license to the pool of available named licenses, you can run the following command:

    ```
    udadmin.exe -f XDT_PLT_UD -device cbwin702 -delete
    ```

```
Administrator: Command Prompt                                        _ □ ×
C:\Program Files (x86)\Citrix\Licensing\LS>udadmin -list
Usage data is 13 minutes old. Next update in 3 minutes.

Devices:
cbwin701 XDT_PLT_UD 2013.0717
cbwin702 XDT_PLT_UD 2013.0717

C:\Program Files (x86)\Citrix\Licensing\LS>udadmin -f XDT_PLT_UD -device cbwin70
2 -delete
Deletion successful.
C:\Program Files (x86)\Citrix\Licensing\LS>udadmin -list
Usage data is 0 minutes old. Next update in 15 minutes.

Devices:
cbwin701 XDT_PLT_UD 2013.0717

C:\Program Files (x86)\Citrix\Licensing\LS>_
```

6. To return a user license to the pool of available named licenses, you can run the following command:

    ```
    udadmin.exe -f XDT_PLT_UD -user cbtester02 -delete
    ```

How it works...

To manage named licenses, you can perform different actions depending on the license type in use. The available actions are explained in the following sections.

A Citrix License Server can manage different licenses for different Citrix products. For Citrix XenApp, you can configure the use of different license types:

▸ XenApp (Concurrent)

▸ XenDesktop (Concurrent)

▸ XenDesktop User Device

The concurrent license types will only check out a user license when the user is running a Citrix XenApp session. If the user logs off the session, the license is returned to the license pool on the Citrix License Server, and can be used by the next user that logs on.

The XenDesktop User Device license type is for named accounts (user or device) and remain checked out even when a user is not running a session. To remove licenses that are still checked out by a device or user account that is no longer in use, you can use the `adadmin.exe` tool to remove a user or device license.

To check the XenDesktop User Device licenses currently in use, you can run the following command in an administrator command prompt:

`udadmin -f <feature> -list [-a]`

This command uses the following parameters:

- ► `-f`: This parameter specifies the featured license file. Valid entries are `XDT_ENT_UD`, `XDT_PLT_UD` or `XDT_STD_UD`.

- ► `-list`: This parameter displays the users and devices with licenses.

 You can use the `-a` parameter with `udadmin.exe` to sort license usage by feature and version.

To delete a licensed user or device from a specified feature, run the following command for a device:

`udadmin -f <feature> -device <devicename> -delete`

or run the following command for a user:

`udadmin -f <feature> -user <username> -delete`

These commands use the following parameters:

- ► `-f`: This parameter specifies the featured license file. Valid entries are `XDT_ENT_UD`, `XDT_PLT_UD` or `XDT_STD_UD`.

- ► `-device`: This parameter specifies the device account.

- ► `-user`: This parameter specifies the user account.

- ► `-delete`: This parameter releases the license for one device or user.

 The license information is updated every 15 minutes on your Citrix License Server. If you want to speed up the update, you can restart the Citrix Licensing service.

Deleting a license will not disrupt any current sessions. When you accidentally delete a valid license, it will be reissued at the next connection.

There's more...

You can read more on `udadmin.exe` at Citrix's eDocs at `http://support.citrix.com/proddocs/topic/licensing-119/lic-admin-cmds-list-deletes-user-device-r.html`.

For those administrators who prefer a Graphical User Interface instead of using the command line, Bram Wolfs has developed the UDadmin GUI, a free tool providing a GUI for the `udadmin` command. You can find the tool developed by *Bram Wolfs* at `http://bramwolfs.com/2013/08/06/udadmin-gui-a-free-tool-to-manage-xendesktop-userdevice-licenses/`.

See also

▸ The *Monitoring the Citrix® License usage on the Dashboard* recipe

▸ The *Using LSQuery, a License Server Data Collection Tool* recipe

Troubleshooting tools for the Citrix® License Server

This recipe will show you how to use the most common troubleshooting tools to check the health of the **Citrix License Server** (**CLS**). These troubleshooting tools are default tools provided by the operating system or tools that are part of the Citrix License Server installation.

How to do it...

Citrix has provided several command-line tools for troubleshooting your CLS. The tools are installed by default at `C:\Program Files (x86)\Citrix\Licensing\LS`, and can be run from this location with an administrator command prompt. To troubleshoot the License Server, follow these steps:

1. Check the running licensing processes with the following command:

   `tasklist /SVC`

2. The following processes are part of the licensing process: `lmadmin.exe`, `CtxLSPortSvc.exe`, and `Citrix.LicensingConfig.Sd`.

3. Check whether the server is listening for requests on the right TCP ports with the following command:

   `netstat -a > tcpconn.txt`

4. It is recommended that you export the results of the command to a file as the list of TCP listening ports usually runs quite long. A file makes searching for specific ports much easier.

5. Check for the configured Citrix License Server port numbers in the License Administration Console.

6. The default ports are 27000 (License Server Manager), 7279 (Vendor Daemon), and 8082 (Management Console).

7. Monitor the status of your license server with the following command:

```
lmstat -c @localhost -a
```

8. Validate your licenses and test the checkout process by running the following command:

```
lmdiag -c @localhost -n
```

 Citrix provides the LSQuery tool that will run all the preceding commands and collect the information in a ZIP file. This information is ready to be sent to the Citrix Support Team if required.

How it works...

There are different command-line tools available for troubleshooting the Citrix License Server. Each command-line tool is discussed in a separate section as follows:

tasklist

A tasklist is a Windows tool that displays a list of currently running processes on the local computer or on a remote computer. To view the list of running processes, run the following command:

```
tasklist /SVC
```

Check for the processes `lmadmin.exe` (Citrix Licensing), `CtxLSPortSvc.exe`, and `Citrix.LicensingConfig.Sd` in the list:

```
Image Name                      PID Services
========================= ==== ==================================
System Idle Process           0 N/A
System                        4 N/A
lmadmin.exe                1504 Citrix Licensing
CtxLSPortSvc.exe           1532 CtxLSPortSvc
CITRIX.exe                 1692 N/A
Citrix.LicensingConfig.Sd 2212 CitrixLicensingConfigService
tasklist.exe               4016 N/A
```

netstat

Netstat is a Windows tool that displays the active TCP connections and ports on which the computer is listening. To view the active TCP connections, run the following command in a command prompt:

```
netstat -a
```

Check for the following lines to confirm that CLS is listening on all the configured ports:

```
Active Connections
    Proto   Local Address           Foreign Address         State
    TCP     0.0.0.0:7279            CBDC01:0                LISTENING
    TCP     0.0.0.0:8082            CBDC01:0                LISTENING
    TCP     0.0.0.0:27000           CBDC01:0                LISTENING
```

lmutil

Citrix offers a set of command-line licensing utilities in the `C:\Program Files (x86)\Citrix\Licensing\LS` folder. To get a list of the available licensing utilities, run the following command from that location in a command prompt:

```
lmutil.exe
```

> When combined with one of the listed commands, it will execute the preceding command.

lmstat

To monitor the status of your license server and verify the license check-out data, you can run the following command:

```
lmstat -c @localhost -a
```

> lmstat also gives an overview of the license files it uses.

lmdiag

You can use the `lmdiag` tool to test if your licenses are valid. When you run `lmdiag`, it will attempt to check out a license. To test whether a license can be checked out, run the following command:

```
lmdiag -c @localhost -n
```

> To export the results of a command-line tool to a text file, you can use the "
> > " (export to file in the overwrite mode) or ">>" (export to file in the append
> mode) switch with your command.
>
> To create a text file containing all running processes, use the following
> command:
>
> ```
> tasklist /SVC > proceslist.txt
> ```

There's more...

You can read more on tasklist and netstat at Microsoft's TechNet at `http://technet.microsoft.com/en-us/library/cc730909(v=ws.10).aspx` and `http://technet.microsoft.com/en-us/library/ff961504(v=ws.10).aspx`.

You can read more on lmstat and lmdiag at Citrix's eDocs at `http://support.citrix.com/proddocs/topic/licensing-119/lic-admin-cmds-status-r.html` and `http://support.citrix.com/proddocs/topic/licensing-119/lic-admin-cmds-diag-checkout-prob-r.html`.

You can read more on how to collect data for troubleshooting licensing issues at Citrix's Knowledge Center at `http://support.citrix.com/article/CTX127314`.

See also

▶ The *Monitoring the Citrix® License usage on the Dashboard* recipe

▶ The *Finding your Citrix® License Server version* recipe

▶ The *Using LSQuery, a License Server Data Collection Tool* recipe

3
Citrix® Web Interface

In this chapter, we will cover the following topics:

- ▶ Scripting a command-line installation of the Citrix® Web Interface
- ▶ Creating a Citrix® Web Interface XenApp® website
- ▶ Customizing the Citrix® Web Interface look
- ▶ Creating a Citrix® Web Interface XenApp® Services Site
- ▶ Configuring site settings with webinterface.conf
- ▶ Building your own language pack
- ▶ Load Balancing your Citrix® Web Interface with Microsoft NLB
- ▶ Speeding up the Web Interface first logon time
- ▶ Fixing pass-through authentication
- ▶ Troubleshooting application launch errors
- ▶ Configuring application launch settings

Introduction

A XenApp infrastructure consists of many components to ensure users can start a published desktop or application. **Citrix Web Interface** (**CWI**) offers users a portal of the published applications, desktop, and/or resources assigned to them.

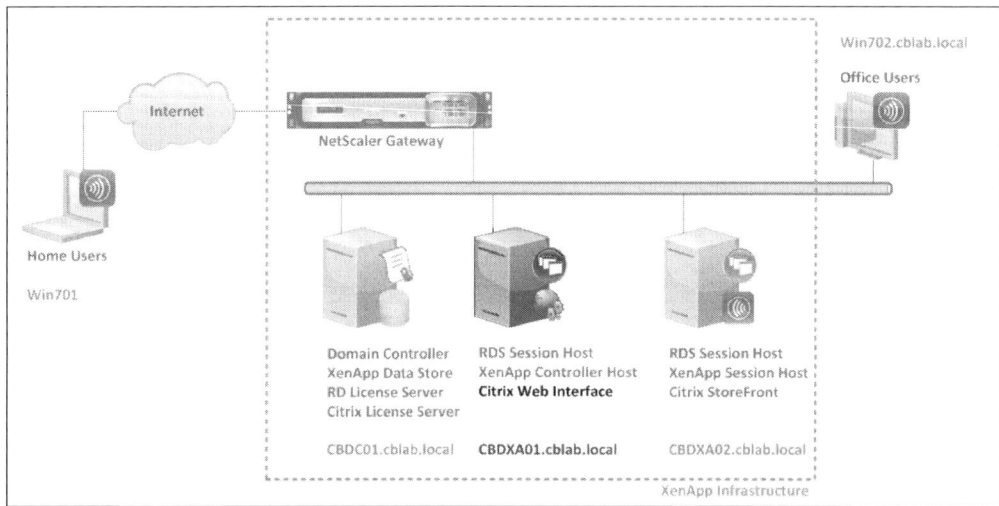

Access to the published content can be gained through a XenApp website or a XenApp Services Site created on CWI. A XenApp website offers a web portal for published applications and/or desktops, whereas a XenApp Services Site enables the Citrix Receiver to integrate the resources with the **Start** menu on a Windows device. CWI authenticates users, connects to the Citrix XenApp Farm, and enumerates the available applications and/or desktops. When a user selects an application, CWI will automatically create an ICA file to launch the application or desktop.

Scripting a command-line installation of the Citrix® Web Interface

This recipe will show you how to build an unattended installation for the CWI by using command-line instructions. This way, you can create an unattended installation sequence for your XenApp infrastructure deployment.

Getting ready

To install Citrix Web Interface 5.4.2 in your XenApp infrastructure on a Windows 2008 R2 server, you need to install the following prerequisites:

- ▶ Windows **Internet Information Services** (**IIS**) 7.5
- ▶ .NET Framework 3.5 SP1
- ▶ Visual J#.NET 2.0 SE
- ▶ ASP.NET 2.0

How to do it...

To install Citrix Web Interface, perform the following steps:

1. Run the following script to install the required Windows server roles:

```
:: Web Server (IIS) Role and required services
servermanagercmd -install Web-Server -logPath <logfile>


:: Web Server > Application Development > ASP.NET
servermanagercmd -install Web-Asp-Net -logPath <logfile>


:: Management Tools > IIS 6 Management Compatibility
:: > IIS 6 Metabase Compatibility
servermanagercmd -install Web-Metabase -logPath <logfile>


:: Enable pass-through & pass-through with smart card auth:
:: Web Server > Security > Windows Authentication
servermanagercmd -install Web-Windows-Auth -logPath <logfile>


:: Enable smart card authentication:
:: Web Server > Security > Client Certificate Mapping
Authentication
servermanagercmd -install Web-Client-Auth -logPath <logfile>
```

2. Run the following script to install the required .NET Framework 3.5 SP1:

```
servermanagercmd -install AS-NET-Framework -logPath <logfile>
```

3. Run the following script to extract files from the Visual J# 2.0 Second Edition installer package:

```
.\JSharp20_SE\vjredist64.exe /C /T:.\vjredist64
```

4. Run the following script to install Visual J# 2.0 SE:

```
.\vjredist64\install.exe /q /l ".\<logfile>"
```

5. Run the following script to install Citrix Web Interface 5.4.2. You can add the following lines to the script to install the Citrix Web Interface:

```
::wait for installer to finish by using the ping statement
ping 127.0.0.1 -n 10 > nul


:: install Citrix Web Interface 5.4.0
".\CWI54\WebInterface.exe" /q /v <logfile>


::wait for installer to finish by using the ping statement
ping 127.0.0.1 -n 5 > nul


:: install Citrix Web Interface 5.4.2 update
".\CWI542\WebInterface.exe" /q /v <logfile>


::wait for installer to finish by using the ping statement
ping 127.0.0.1 -n 5 > nul
```

Take the following note from Citrix's eDocs into account when installing the Citrix Web Interface:

 If IIS is not installed when you install .NET Framework, you must install IIS and reinstall the framework, or install IIS and run the `aspnet_regiis.exe -i` command in `C:\Windows\Microsoft.NET\Framework\<Version>` directory.

How it works...

The `servermanagercmd.exe` file is explained in detail in the *Scripting a command-line installation of the RD License Server* recipe in *Chapter 1, Remote Desktop Services*.

There's more...

As an alternative method to the deprecated `servermanagercmd.exe` file you can use Windows PowerShell to install the Windows Role Services. The following PowerShell command adds the Role and Role Services:

```
Import-Module ServerManager
Add-WindowsFeature -Name Web-Server,Web-Asp-Net,Web-Metabase,Web-
Windows-Auth,Web-Client-Auth,AS-NET-Framework -LogPath <logfile>
-Restart
```

You can read more on the `Add-WindowsFeature` PowerShell cmdlet at Microsoft TechNet found at `http://technet.microsoft.com/en-us/library/ee662309.aspx`.

You can read more on installing the Citrix Web Interface on IIS at Citrix eDocs found at `http://support.citrix.com/proddocs/topic/web-interface-impington/wi-install-web-interface-iis-task-gransden.html`.

You can download **Hotfix WI540MSI002** (Version 5.4.2.) for CWI 5.4 for Windows at Citrix Knowledge Center found at `http://support.citrix.com/article/CTX130660`.

See also

▶ The *Creating a Citrix® Web Interface XenApp® website* recipe
▶ The *Building your own language pack* recipe

Creating a Citrix® Web Interface XenApp® website

This recipe will show you how to create a XenApp® website on your CWI by using the `sitemgr.exe` command. This enables you to create an unattended XenApp website configuration for your XenApp infrastructure deployment.

Getting ready

To create a XenApp website with the `sitemgr.exe` tool, you need to have CWI installed on your server. During the installation of the Citrix Web Interface, `sitemgr.exe` is placed in the program folder for CWI.

The default location of this folder is `C:\Program Files (x86)\Citrix\Web Interface\<version>` for 64-bit Windows servers, and `C:\Program Files\Citrix\Web Interface\<version>` for 32-bit Windows servers.

How to do it...

To create a XenApp website with `sitemgr.exe`, perform the following step:

1. Run the following command:

    ```
    sitemgr -c "WIDest=1:/Citrix/XenApp,WIDefaultSite=Yes,FarmName=CBX
    AFarm,
    XMLService=CBXA01;CBXA02,XMLSPort=8080,XMLSProtocol=HTTP,
    AppAccessMethods=Remote;Streaming,AuthenticationPoint=
    WebInterface,AllowUserPasswordChange=Expired-
    only,UIBranding=Applications" -g "<logfile>"
    ```

The resulting configuration set from the preceding command is shown in the following screenshot:

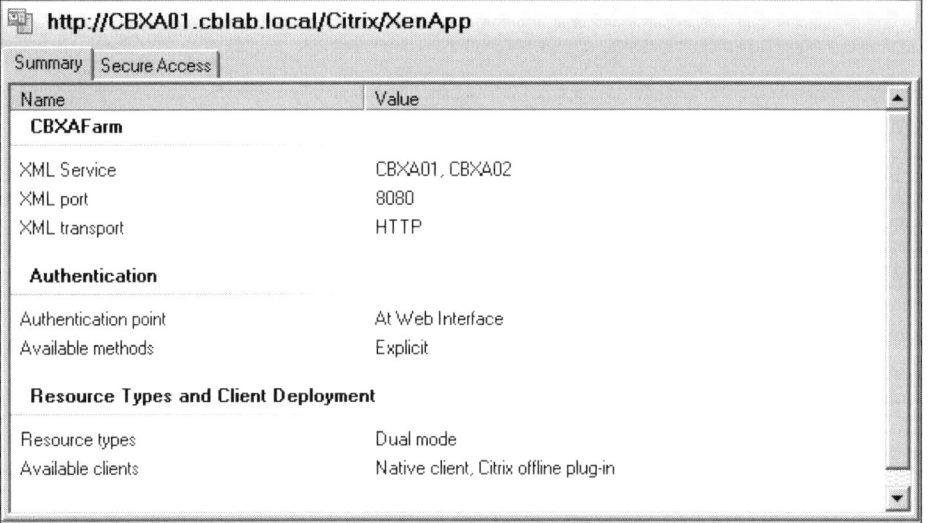

How it works...

To script the creation of a XenApp website, you can use `sitemgr.exe` provided in the CWI program folder as follows:

```
sitemgr –<action> <sitedefinition> -g <logfile>
```

The preceding command line uses the following syntax and parameters:

- ▸ `action`: This defines whether a new site is to be created (c) or an existing site is to be modified (m), or removed (r).
- ▸ `sitedefinition`: This defines a comma separated list of argument and value pairs that contain the site specifications. The options are explained in the following table.

▶ `logfile`: This defines the path and filename to log the operations performed by `sitemgr`.

The following table explains the options available for the site definition string to specify the XenApp website configuration:

Option	Explanation
`WIDest=<IISSite>:<path>`	Creates a new XenApp website at the specified path within the provided IIS site. Each IIS site is identified by a unique number. The default IIS site has the number 1.
`WICurrent=<IISSite>:<path>`	Selects an existing XenApp website for modification or removal at the specified path within the numbered IIS site.
`WIDefaultSite=Yes|No`	Specifies whether the site will be the default website for the IIS web server.
`FarmName=<FarmName>`	Specifies the name of the Citrix XenApp Farm.
`XMLService=<ServiceList>`	Lists the names of XenApp Controller Hosts running the Citrix XML service in the specified XenApp Farm. Use semicolons to separate server names.
`XMLSPort=<XMLport>`	Specifies the XML port number used by the Citrix XenApp Controller Host XML Service.
`XMLSProtocol=HTTP|HTTPS|SSL`	Specifies the protocol used by the Citrix XenApp Controller Host XML Service.
`AppAccessMethods=<MethodList>`	Lists the resource delivery methods for the site. The available methods are `Remote` and `Streaming`. Use semicolons to separate methods.
`AuthenticationPoint=` `WebInterface|AccessGateway`	Specifies the point of authentication for the XenApp website.
`AllowUserPasswordChange=` `Never|Always|Expired-only`	Specifies whether users are allowed to change their password through the Citrix Web Interface.
`UIBranding=` `Applications|Desktops`	Configures the user interface to focus on the delivery of applications (default) or desktops.

You can use `sitemgr -m` to modify an existing site or `sitemgr -r` to remove a site from the Citrix Web Interface.

There's more...

You can read all about the `sitemgr` command-line options by running the `sitemgr -h` command.

See also

▸ The *Scripting a command-line installation of the Citrix® Web Interface* recipe

▸ The *Creating a Citrix® Web Interface XenApp® website* recipe

▸ The *Creating a Citrix® Web Interface XenApp® Services Site* recipe

▸ The *Configuring site settings with webinterface.conf* recipe

Customizing the Citrix® Web Interface's look

This recipe will show you how to customize the look and feel of your Citrix Web Interface 5.4 XenApp website.

Getting ready

In order to test the configured customizations to the site, make sure you present the site in full graphics mode by selecting the following site appearance options through the Citrix Web Interface Management console for your XenApp website:

▸ **Web Site Appearance | Layout**

  ❑ Overall Layout: Full graphics

  ❑ Display Settings: all selected

  ❑ Change View Settings: all selected

  ❑ Tab Settings: Separate tabs

▸ **Web Site Appearance | Appearance**

  ❑ Logon Screen: Full

How to do it...

To change the look and feel of the XenApp website, perform the following steps:

1. Browse to the XenApp site folder on the Citrix Web Interface server (by default, the site is located at `C:\inetpub\wwwroot\Citrix\XenApp`)

2. Open the `.\media` subfolder

3. Replace the following image files to change site images without changing the code:

- ❑ `CitrixLogoHeader.png` (or `.gif`)
- ❑ `CitrixXenApp.png` (or `.gif`)
- ❑ `Devices.png` (or `.gif`)
- ❑ `CitrixWatermark.png` (or `.gif`)
- ❑ `HDX.png` (or `.gif`)
- ❑ `CitrixXenAppLoggedoff.png` (or `.gif`)
- ❑ `DevicesLoggedoff.png` (or `.gif`)
- ❑ `CitrixLogoDarkLoggedOff.png` (or `.gif`)
- ❑ `HDXLoggedOff.png` (or `.gif`)
- ❑ `IcaComboAll.ico`

 The `.png` files are used when the **Full Graphics Display** mode is configured. When the **Low Graphics Display** mode is configured, the `.gif` files are used.

4. To add a company logo to the logon page header modify `.\app_data\include\loginStyle.inc`

5. Configure whether images must be displayed or not by modifying `.\app_data\include\fullstyle.inc`

6. Change the hyperlink used in the footer by modifying `.\app_code\PagesJava\com\citrix\wi\controls\FooterControl.java`

7. Change background colors and/or images by modifying `.\app_data\include\fullstyle.inc`

8. Add a logo to the logon box by modifying `.\app_data\include\loginMainForm.inc`

How it works...

You can customize your XenApp website by changing pictures, parts, and configuration files for the different sections of your site. To make changes to the configuration, browse to your XenApp site (the default site is located at `C:\inetpub\wwwroot\Citrix\XenApp`).

We'll display the logon page in our examples as most customizable options are covered on this page as you can see in the following screenshot:

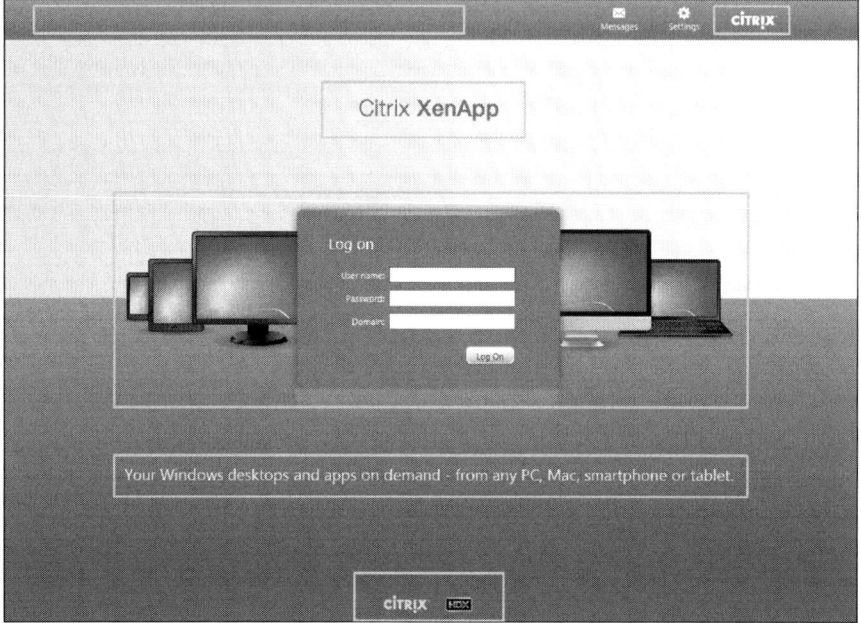

Image file locations

To change the look and feel of your XenApp website, you can replace the used images with your own versions. By using the same filenames you don't have to modify any code.

The following files are used by the XenApp website:

- The Logon page
  - **Header**: `CitrixLogoHeader.png`
  - **Body**: `CitrixXenApp.png` and `Devices.png`
  - **Footer**: `CitrixWatermark.png` and `HDX.png`
- The Applications/desktops page
- The Logout page
  - **Body**: `CitrixXenAppLoggedoff.png` and `DevicesLoggedoff.png`
  - **Footer**: `CitrixLogoDarkLoggedOff.png` and `HDXLoggedOff.png`
- Other
  - **Favicons**: `IcaComboAll.ico`

All used images are located in the .\media folder of the XenApp website. The PNG files are used for the full Graphics Display mode, and a GIF counterpart file is used for the low Graphics Display mode. When replacing the images, keep in mind that you need to replace both PNG and GIF files accordingly.

Add a company logo to the logon page header at `.\app_data\include\loginStyle.inc`

You can add a company logo to the logon page header by editing the corresponding **Cascade Style Sheet** (**CSS**) file. Apply the following modification to the file:

Original code	New code

`-->`
`</style>`
	`#headerLeft {`
	`    width: 100%;`
	`    background: url("../media/<newLogoImage>") no-`
	`repeat;`
	`    }`
	`-->`
	`</style>`

Don't display the images

For each image file used in the site you can specify whether or not the image needs to be shown by modifying the settings in the corresponding style file at `.\app_data\include\fullstyle.inc`

Remove the Citrix logo from the header by applying the following modification:

Original code	New code

`#headerLogo {`
`    padding: 11px 0 11px 18px;`
`}`
	`#headerLogo {`
	`    padding: 11px 0 11px`
	`       18px;`
	`    display: none;`
	`}`

Remove Citrix XenApp from the body by applying the following modification:

Original code	New code
| ```
#horizonTop img {
  padding-top: 75px;
}
``` | ```
#horizonTop img {
  padding-top: 75px;
  display: none;
}
``` |

Remove the device images from the body by applying the following modification:

Original code	New code
| ```
horizonPage .mainPane {
  position: relative;
  top: -120px;
  background: url(...) no-repeat
center 30px;
  color: white;
  padding: 0;
  overflow: auto;
}
``` | ```
.horizonPage .mainPane {
  position: relative;
  top: -120px;
  background: none;
  color: white;
  padding: 0;
  overflow: auto;
}
``` |

Remove the tagline from the body by applying the following modification:

Original code	New code
| ```
#horizonTagline {
  color: #F2F2F2;
  font-size: 180%;
  font-weight: normal;
  margin: 50px 0 0 0;
  padding-bottom: 10px;
  text-align: center;
}
``` | ```
#horizonTagline {
  color: #F2F2F2;
  font-size: 180%;
  font-weight: normal;
  margin: 50px 0 0 0;
  padding-bottom: 10px;
  text-align: center;
  display: none;
}
``` |

To enter a custom tagline, you need to modify the language string pages. This is discussed in a separate recipe in this chapter.

Remove the Citrix logo from the footer as follows:

Original code	New code
| ```
#footer img
{
    padding: 0 8px;
    vertical-align: middle;
}
``` | ```
#footer img
{
    padding: 0 8px;
    vertical-align: middle;
    display: none;
}
``` |

Remove the HDX logo from the footer as follows:

Original code	New code
| ```
horizonPage #hdxLogo {
    display: inline;
}
``` | ```
horizonPage #hdxLogo {
    display: none;
}
``` |

Change the hyperlink used in the footer

When you decide to change the images used for the Citrix and HDX logo in the footer of the page, keep in mind that these logos also have hyperlinks attached to them. To change the hyperlink for the images, you must modify the corresponding Java settings file: `.\app_code\ PagesJava\com\citrix\wi\controls\FooterControl.java`.

Remove the hyperlink for the used images in the footer as follows:

Original code	New code
| ```
public class FooterControl {
    private String footerText =
"";
    private static final String
        FOOTER_LINK_APPS =
        "http://www.citrix.com";
    private static final String
    FOOTER_LINK_DESKTOPS =
        "http://www.citrix.com/
xendesktop";
    private static final String
HDX_LINK =
        "http://hdx.citrix.com";
``` | ```
public class FooterControl {
    private String footerText =
"";
    private static final String
    FOOTER_LINK_APPS = "<newURL>";
    private static final String
FOOTER_LINK_DESKTOPS =
    "<newURL>";
    private static final String
HDX_LINK =
    "<newURL>";
``` |

Change background colors and/or images

Not only can you change the images on the site, but you can also adjust color schemes by changing the background colors and images for the site. To specify different color codes or images for the site, you will need to modify the settings in the corresponding style file at `.\app_data\include\fullstyle.inc`.

Change the background color/image for the top half of the logon page as follows:

Original code	New code

<pre>#horizonTop {
    width: 100%;
    height: 325px;
    background: #FDFDFD
       url("../media/
HorizonBgTop.png") no-repeat
top left;
    text-align: center;
}</pre>
	<pre>#horizonTop {
	    width: 100%;
	    height: 325px;
	    background: #FFFFFF;
	    text-align: center;
	}</pre>

Change the background color/image for the bottom half of the logon page as follows:

Original code	New code

<pre>horizonPage {
    background: #566169 url("../
media/HorizonBgBottom.png")
repeat-x left 325px;
}</pre>
	<pre>horizonPage {
	    background: #FFFFFF;
	}</pre>

Change the background color/image for the top half of the logout page as follows:

Original code	New code

<pre>loggedOut #horizonTop {
    background: #515151
url(<%=ClientInfoUtilities.
getImageName(wiContext.
getClientInfo(), "../media/
HorizonBgTopLoggedOff.png")%>)
no-repeat top left;
}</pre>
	<pre>loggedOut #horizonTop {
	    background: #000000;
	}</pre>

Change the background color/image for the bottom half of the logout page as follows:

Original code	New code
| ```
loggedOut {
  background: #383A3B
    url(<%=ClientInfoUtilities.
getImageName(wiContext.
getClientInfo(), "../media/
HorizonBgBottomLoggedOff.
png")%>) repeat-x top left;
}
``` | ```
loggedOut {
  background: #000000
    url(<%=ClientInfoUtilities.
getImageName(wiContext.
getClientInfo(), "../media/
HorizonBgBottomLoggedOff.
png")%>) repeat-x top left;
}
``` |

With some additional code modifications, you can add a logo to the logon box that is shown on the logon page of the site. To specify the image file to be used, you will need to modify the settings in the corresponding style file: `.\app_data\include\loginMainForm.inc`.

Add a logo to the logon box on the logon page as follows:

Original code	New code
| ```
%>
<table class="loginForm">
<%
if (viewControl.
getShowLoginTypeOptions()) {
%>
``` | ```
%>
<table class="loginForm">
<% // added table row and
cell %>
<tr><td rowspan="6"
valign="Top"
align="left"><img src="../
media/<yourLogoFile>"
alt=""></td></tr>
<% // end table row and cell
%>
<%
if (viewControl.
getShowLoginTypeOptions()) {
%>
``` |

With these changes, you can create your own customized XenApp website.

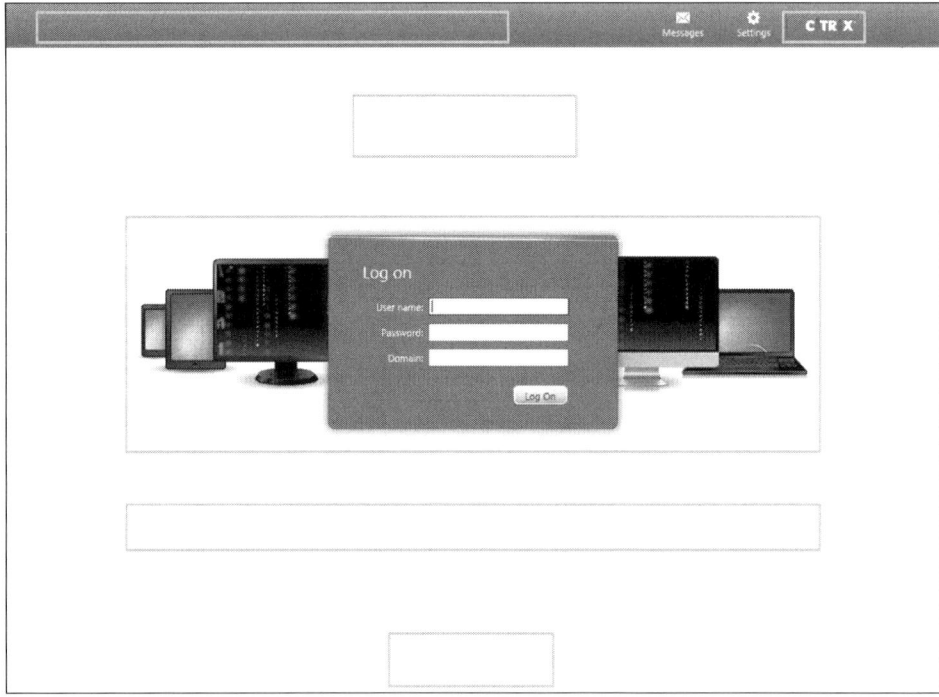

There's more...

You can read more on Citrix Web Interface modifications on Citrix's Support Forums at
`http://forums.citrix.com/thread.jspa?threadID=278818`.

Creating a Citrix® Web Interface XenApp® Services Site

This recipe will show you how to create a XenApp Services Site on your CWI by using the
`sitemgr.exe` command. This enables you to create an unattended XenApp Services Site
configuration for your XenApp infrastructure deployment.

Getting ready

To create a XenApp Services Site with the `sitemgr.exe` tool, you need to have the Citrix
Web Interface installed on your server. During the installation of the Citrix Web Interface,
`sitemgr.exe` is placed in the program folder for the Citrix Web Interface.

The default location of this folder is `C:\Program Files (x86)\Citrix\Web Interface\<version>` (64-bit), or `C:\Program Files\Citrix\Web Interface\<version>` (32-bit).

How to do it...

To create a XenApp Services Site with `sitemgr.exe`, perform the following steps:

1. Run the following command:

   ```
   sitemgr -c "PNADest=1:/Citrix/PNAgent,FarmName=CBXAFarm,XMLService
   =CBXA01;CBXA02,XMLSPort=8080,XMLSProtocol=HTTP,AppAccessMethods=Re
   mote;Streaming,AuthenticationPoint=WebInterface,AllowUserPasswordC
   hange=Expired-only" -g "createServicesSite.log"
   ```

The resulting configuration set from the preceding command is shown in the following screenshot:

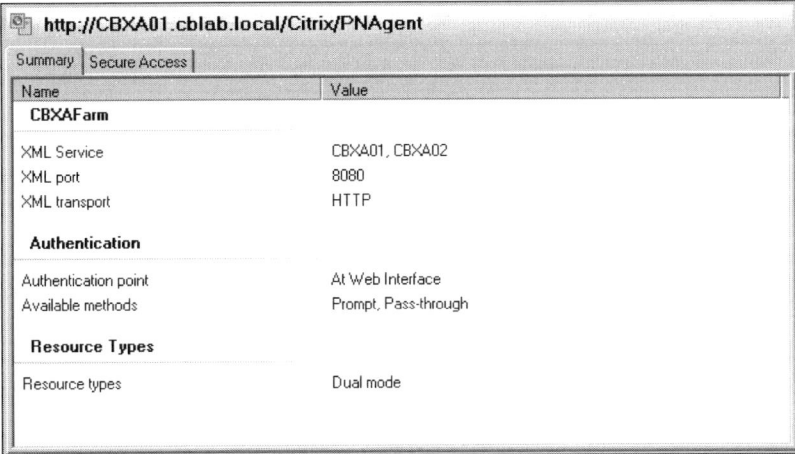

How it works...

To automate the creation of a XenApp Services Site, you can use `sitemgr.exe`. This executable is provided in the Citrix Web Interface program folder, which is located by default at `C:\Program Files (x86)\Citrix\Web Interface\<version>`. To create a XenApp Services Site, run the following command:

```
sitemgr -<action> <sitedefinition> -g <logpath>
```

The preceding command uses the following syntax and parameters:

▶ `action`: This defines whether a new site is to be created (c) or an existing site is to be modified (m), or removed (r).

▶ `sitedefinition`: This defines a comma separated list of argument and value pairs that contain the site specifications. The options are explained in the following table.

▶ `logpath`: This defines the path and filename to log the operations performed by `sitemgr`.

The following table explains the options available for the site definition string to specify the XenApp Services Site configuration:

Option	Explanation
`PNADest=<IISSite>:<path>`	Creates a new XenApp Services Site at the specified path within the provided IIS site. Each IIS site is identified by a unique number. The default IIS site has the number 1.
`PNACurrent=<IISSite>:<path>`	Selects an existing XenApp Services Site for modification or removal of the specified path within the numbered IIS site.

The `Sitemgr.exe` file and the parameters used to create a XenApp website are also explained in detail in the *How it works...* section of the *Creating a Citrix® Web Interface XenApp® website* recipe. An overview of the overall site parameters are listed there.

There's more...

You can read all about the `sitemgr` command-line options by running the `sitemgr -h` command.

You can read more on Specifying Initial Configuration Settings for a site at Citrix's eDocs found at `http://support.citrix.com/proddocs/topic/web-interface-hardwick/wi-specify-initial-config-gransden.html`.

See also

▶ The *Scripting a command-line installation of the Citrix® Web Interface* recipe

▶ The *Creating a Citrix® Web Interface XenApp® website* recipe

▶ The *Configuring site settings with webinterface.conf* recipe

Configuring site settings with webinterface.conf

This recipe will show you how to modify the `webinterface.conf` file of your XenApp Web or Services site to change the basic configuration settings for your **Web Interface** (**WI**) site.

Getting ready

To configure the XenApp website settings using the `webinterface.conf` file, the CWI software needs to be installed and the XenApp website needs to be created in advance.

 Some settings for the XenApp website can only be set with the `webinterface.conf` file, like the Multiple Launch Prevention settings explained in the *Configuring application launch settings* recipe.

How to do it...

To configure additional XenApp website settings, perform the following steps:

1. Open the `webinterface.conf` file in a text editor such as Notepad.

    The `webinterface.conf` file is an `ini` file that lists all settings in an alphabetical order.

2. To change the `farm` settings, edit the line that starts with the following:

   ```
   Farm1=CBXA01,CBXA02,Name:CBXAFarm,XMLPort:8080,Transport:HTTP,SSLR
   elayPort:443,BypassDuration:60,LoadBalance:Off,TicketTimeToLive:20
   0,RADETicketTimeToLive:200
   ```

3. To change the appearance, authentication, and client detection settings, search for the corresponding settings in the file and change its configuration.

    Many settings are explained in the *How it works...* section in more detail.

How it works...

The `webinterface.conf` file contains all the configuration settings for your XenApp website or XenApp Services site and is located (by default) in the following folder:

`C:\inetpub\wwwroot\Citrix\<site-name>\conf`

> When changing the `webinterface.conf` file settings, make sure the Citrix Web Interface Management console is not in use as it changes the file content. To activate the changes made to `webinterface.conf`, you need to restart the **Internet Information Service (IIS)** by using `iisreset` as is explained at Citrix eDocs found at `http://support.citrix.com/proddocs/topic/web-interface-impington/wi-configure-wrapper-gransden.html`.

The following are some of the basic settings that can be configured in the file:

▶ Configure the WI site Server Farms settings with the following command line:

`Farm<number>=<XMLServicesList>,Name:<FarmName>,XMLPort:<XMLPort>,Transport:<TransportType>,SSLRelayPort:<SSLRelayPort>,BypassDuration:<BypassTime>,LoadBalance:<LBswitch>,TicketTimeToLive:<TTL>,RADETicketTimeToLive:<RadeTTL>`

The preceding command line uses the following parameters:

- ❏ `number`: This is a unique number to differentiate between Farm configurations, starting with 1 to a max of 512.
- ❏ `XMLServicesList`: This is a comma-separated list of XenApp Farm servers that run the XML Service (XenApp Controller Hosts).
- ❏ `FarmName`: This is a XenApp Farm name.
- ❏ `XMLPort`: This is a port used by the XML Service.
- ❏ `TransportType`: This is a network communication protocol (either HTTP, HTTPS, or SSL) used by the XML Service.
- ❏ `SSLRelayPort`: The SSL Relay port is used by the XML Service (default: `443`). This setting is entered irrespective of whether SSL is selected as `TransportType` or not.
- ❏ `BypassTime`: This is the time (in minutes) a failed server will be bypassed for XML requests.
- ❏ `LBswitch`: This sets load balancing for the Farm servers, either as `On` or `Off`.

❑ `TTL`: This is the time (in seconds) the ICA session ticket will be valid.

❑ `RadeTTL`: This is the time (in seconds) the Streaming session ticket will be valid.

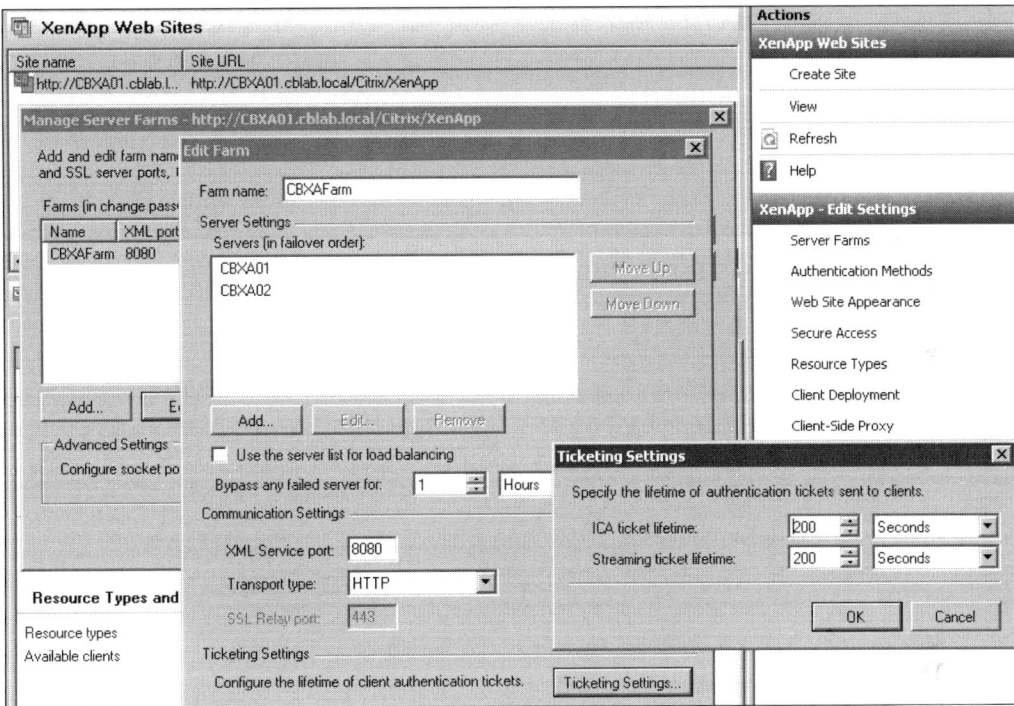

▶ Specify the return address of the XenApp server (FQDN or IP address) using the setting:

`AddressResolutionType=dns-port|ipv4-port`

You can use the `RecoveryFarm<number>` setting to specify a XenApp Farm that can be used for disaster recovery.

▶ Specify whether users are allowed to customize their ICA settings using the setting:

`AllowCustomize<Setting>=On|Off`

The preceding command uses the following syntax:

❑ `Setting`: This specifies which ICA settings (Audio, Layout, ClientPrinterMapping, Reconnect, and so on) users may or may not alter. These can be for the **General**, **User Experience**, and **Devices** settings.

▶ Preconfigure the WI site User Interface using the following settings:

```
UserInterfaceBranding=Applications|Desktops
UserInterfaceLayout=Auto|Normal|Compact
UserInterfaceMode=Simple|Advanced
CompactViewStyles==<ViewStyleList>
ViewStyles=<ViewStyleList>
```

The preceding code uses the following parameters:

▶ `ViewStyleList`: a comma-separated list specifying the available View styles a user can select to view the published applications and desktops. Avaliable styles are: Icons, Details, List, Tree and Groups.

▶ Configure the WI site authentication methods using the following settings:

```
AuthenticationPoint=WebInterface|AccessGateway
WIAuthenticationMethods=<AuthList>
DomainSelection=<DomainList>
HideDomainField=On|Off
LoginDomains=<DomainList>
RestrictDomains=On|Off
```

The preceding code uses the following syntax:

▶ `AuthList`: This is a comma-separated list that specifies the available methods that are selected for the WI site. The available methods are `Explicit` (Explicit), `Pass-through` (SingleSignOn), `Pass-through with smart card` (CertificateSingleSignOn), `smart card` (Certificate), and `Anonymous` (Anonymous).

▶ `DomainList`: This specifies the domains (NetBIOS names, comma separated) used for user authentication (LoginDomains) and are presented in the domain selection box on the logon screen.

▶ Personalize WI site messages using the following settings:

```
AppSysMessage_<LangCode>=<Message>
AppWelcome_Message_<LangCode>=<Message>
FooterText_<LangCode>=<Message>
LoginSys_Message_<LangCode>=<Message>
LoginTitle_<LangCode>=<Message>
PreLoginMessageButton_<LangCode>=<Message>
PreLoginMessageText_<LangCode>=<Message>
PreLoginMessageTitle<LangCode>=<Message>
WelcomeMessage_<LangCode>=<Message>
```

The predecing code uses the following parameters:

▶ `LangCode`: This is the language code (en, fr, nl, and so on) used to specify the language assigned to the personalized message

▶ `Message`: This is the personalized message to be shown

▶ Configure the WI site session time out using the following settings:

```
WebSessionTimeout=<Minutes>
```

▶ Configure client detection settings using the following settings:

```
ClientIca<OS>>=Filename:<FileName>,Directory:<Directory>,
Mui:[Yes|No],Version:<Version>
ClientDefaultURL=<URL>
ClientProxy=<ProxySubnet>,<ProxyType>,<ProxyAddress>
```

The preceding code uses the following parameters:

❑ `OS`: This specifies the Citrix Receiver client type. The available types are LinuxX86, Mac, SolarisSparc, SolarisX86, and Win32.

❑ `FileName`: This specifies the installation file to be sent to the client through Client Detection.

- ❑ `Directory`: This specifies the directory in which the installation file is placed. Client Detection checks for the directory in the Clients folder at `C:\ Program Files (x86)\Citrix\Web Interface\<version>`.

- ❑ `Version`: This specifies the minimum version of the Citrix Receiver that is checked by Client Detection.

- ❑ `URL`: This specifies the download link for OS types that are not enabled and specified for Client Detection.

- ❑ `ProxySubnet`: This specifies the subnet that is associated with proxy settings. To apply the settings to all Citrix clients use `*`.

- ❑ `ProxyType`: This specifies the proxy type that is used. Valid types are: `Auto`, `WpadAuto`, `Client`, `None`, `SOCKS`, and `Secure`.

- ❑ `ProxyAddress`: This specifies a proxy address and proxy port when the `SOCKS` or `Secure` type is configured. Otherwise use `-`.

There's more...

You can read more on each setting in the `webInterface.conf` file at Citrix's eDocs found at `http://support.citrix.com/proddocs/topic/web-interface-impington/wi-webinterface-conf-parameters-gransden.html`.

See also

- ▶ The *Building your own language pack* recipe
- ▶ The *Configuring application launch settings* recipe

Building your own language pack

This recipe will show you how to build your own language pack for the CWI site. By building your own language pack, you can change the default language for your **Web Interface** (**WI**) site.

How to do it...

To change the display language of the Web Interface sites, perform the following steps:

1. Create your own language pack by following the directions in the *How it works...* section or use an available language pack.

2. Open the `InstallLanguage.conf` file located by default at `C:\Program Files (x86)\Citrix\Web Interface\<version>`, and change the language code in the following line to the desired code (`nl` for instance):

   ```
   Language=en
   ```

 Each website configured in the Citrix Web Interface will use the specified language for the XenApp Web and Services sites when the corresponding language files are available.

To change the language for the Client Detection process, perform the following steps:

1. Create your own language pack by following the directions in the *How it works...* section or use an available language pack.

2. Browse to `C:\Program Files (x86)\Citrix\Web Interface\<version>\clientDetection\localizedContent`.

3. Replace the `clientwizard_strings.properties` file in this folder with your translated version.

To change the language for the first load page for a XenApp website, perform the following steps:

1. Go to `C:\inetpub\wwwroot\Citrix\<siteName>`.

2. Edit `default.html` and translate `Loading` in the following line:

   `<title>Loading</title>`

3. Edit `loading.html` and translate the following lines:

   ```
   <title>Loading</title>
   <h3>One Moment Please...</h3>
   ```

How it works...

If you want another language as your default Web Interface language or as a language your users can choose from, you can translate the English language files and build your own language pack.

 The default language for the CWI is English. These language files should not be removed or deleted to keep from breaking the WI site.

Customize the language for the Citrix Web Interface

To customize the language for the CWI, you need to create your own copies of the English language files and replace the `Locale en` with your language code in each filename. The language files are located (by default) in the following folder:

```
C:\Program Files (x86)\Citrix\Web Interface\<version>\languages
```

- `en.lang`
- `accessplatform_strings_en.properties`
- `common_strings_en.properties`
- `eventlog_strings_en.properties`
- `help_strings_en.properties`
- `lid_strings_en.properties`
- `mpssourceimpl_strings_en.properties`
- `pnagent_strings_en.properties`
- `pnagentimpl_strings_en.properties`
- `radeimpl_strings_en.properties`
- `ssl_strings_en.properties`
- `webpnimpl_strings_en.properties`
- `xmlclient_strings_en.properties`

To implement your own CWI language pack, perform the following steps:

1. Copy the preceding specified English language files to your own language files, and replace the `en` language code with your own language code.

2. Translate the content of each language file.

To set your language as the default for the CWI, open `C:\Program Files (x86)\Citrix\Web Interface\<version>\InstallLanguage.conf` and replace en in the line `Language=en` with your language code.

Customize the language for Client Detection

Client Detection language files are stored in the folder:

- `C:\Program Files (x86)\Citrix\Web Interface\<version>\clientDetection\help`
- `C:\Program Files (x86)\Citrix\Web Interface\<version>\clientDetection\localizedContent`
- `C:\Program Files (x86)\Citrix\Web Interface\<version>\clientDetection\media`

To apply your own language to Client Detection, perform the following steps:

1. Go to `C:\Program Files (x86)\Citrix\Web Interface\<version>\clientDetection\help`.

2. Create a new folder with your language code (Locale) as its name.

3. Copy the content from the `en` folder to your language folder.

4. Translate all `.txt` files in the folder

5. Replace all `.png` images from the `media` subfolder with language-specific PNG files.

6. Go to `C:\Program Files (x86)\Citrix\Web Interface\<version>\clientDetection\localizedContent`.

7. Copy the `clientwizard_strings.properties` file to the `en` folder. This ensures that the English language strings are secured for future reference.

8. Create a new folder and name it as your language code.

9. Copy the content from the `en` folder to your language folder.

10. Translate the `clientwizard_strings.properties` file.

11. Replace the `clientwizard_strings.properties` file in the root folder with your translated version.

> Unfortunately, Client Detection language settings are determined by the `clientwizard_strings.properties` file in the `localizedContent` folder, so you can only have one language active and need to replace this file with your own translated file from the subfolder to apply your own language pack.

Customize the language on the first loading page

If you want to ensure your language is used on each page of the CWI, you will need to perform the following last steps to ensure the starting page of each site is also translated correctly. As with Client Detection, only one language can be set for these pages. Perform the following steps to present the loading page in your own language:

1. Go to the webroot of your XenApp website, located by default at `C:\inetpub\wwwroot\Citrix\<siteName>`.

2. Edit `default.html` and replace the title code with your language's equivalence to load and save the changes. Search for and translate the following line:

   ```
   <title>Loading</title>
   ```

3. Edit `loading.html` and translate the following lines:

   ```
   <title>Loading</title>
   <h3>One Moment Please...</h3>
   ```

Are there language packs out there?

To aid you with the language packs, I've run a quick scan on the Internet to see if custom language packs are already available for the Citrix Web Interface. So here's what I found:

Dutch language packs

Luckily for me, *Jeroen Tielen* has already built a great Dutch language pack that comes with its own installer for Citrix Web Interface 5.4.0 and 5.4.2. You can find the installers on his site.

CWI 5.4.2: `http://www.jeroentielen.nl/citrix-web-interface-5-4-2-nederlandse-vertaling/`

CWI 5.4.0: `http://www.jeroentielen.nl/citrix-webinterface-5-4-0-nederlandse-vertaling/`

> IIS uses Microsoft .NET Framework to show Windows error messages. If these messages need to be shown in the correct language, you need to install the corresponding language pack for .Net Framework.

Norwegian language packs

I also found a Norwegian language pack containing translated `common_strings` and `accessplatform_strings` files for CWI 5.4 on the **wedelIT** site at `http://wedelit.no/index.php?option=com_jdownloads&Itemid=92&view=viewcategory&catid=2`.

There's more...

You can check which locales are recognized and supported by your Windows version at Microsoft's MSDN found at `http://msdn.microsoft.com/en-us/goglobal/bb896001`.

If you want to apply some more customizations to the Citrix Web Interface, you can check out the Citrix Web Interface SDK for version 5.4 at Citrix's Developer Network found at `http://community.citrix.com/display/xa/Web+Interface+SDK`.

See also

▸ The *Creating a Citrix® Web Interface XenApp® Services Site* recipe

Load balancing your Citrix® Web Interface with Microsoft NLB

This recipe will show you how to use Microsoft's **Network Load Balancing** (**NLB**) to build a redundant CWI infrastructure based upon Load Balancing techniques.

Getting ready

When using Load Balancing, ensure both the Citrix Web Interface servers run the same configuration for the configured WI sites by performing the following steps:

1. Create a XenApp website with the same name on the second CWI server by using the same `sitemgr` command:

   ```
   sitemgr -c "WIDest=1:/Citrix/XenApp,WIDefaultSite=Yes,FarmName=CBX
   AFarm,
   XMLService=CBXA01;CBXA02,XMLSPort=8080,XMLSProtocol=HTTP,
   AppAccessMethods=Remote;Streaming,AuthenticationPoint=WebInterface
   ,AllowUserPasswordChange=Expired
   -only,UIBranding=Applications" -g "createWebSite.log"
   ```

2. Copy `webinterface.conf` from the first node to the second node to ensure both sites are configured identically.

3. Apply the same language pack modifications to both the sites.

How to do it...

To Load Balance the Citrix Web Interfaces with Microsoft NLB, perform the following steps:

1. Install the NLB feature on a Windows Server 2008 R2 server with the following PowerShell command:

   ```
   Import-Module ServerManager

   Add-WindowsFeature -Name NLB -LogPath <log.txt> -Restart
   ```

2. Run the following script on the first node of the cluster to create and configure the first NLB Cluster node:

   ```
   # Import NLB PowerShell module

   Import-Module NetworkLoadBalancingClusters

   # Create a new Cluster

   New-NlbCluster -HostName CBXA01 -InterfaceName "LAN" -
   ClusterPrimaryIP 192.168.10.204 -SubnetMask 255.255.255.0 -
   ClusterName CBNLB01 -OperationMode multicast

   # Add a node to the Cluster

   Get-NlbCluster -HostName CBXA01 | Add-NlbClusterNode -NewNodeName
   CBXA02 -NewNodeInterface "Local Area Connection 2"

   # Remove the default port rule

   Get-NlbClusterPortRule | Remove-NlbClusterPortRule -Force

   # Add a specific port (HTTP) rule for load balancing

   Get-NlbCluster | Add-NlbClusterPortRule -StartPort 80 -EndPort
   80 -Affinity None -Mode Multiple -Protocol TCP
   ```

```
# Add a specific port rule (HTTPS) for load balancing
Get-NlbCluster | Add-NlbClusterPortRule -StartPort 443 -
EndPort 443 -Affinity None -Mode Multiple -Protocol TCP
```

3. Run the following script on the first node of the cluster to add the second server to the NLB Cluster:

```
# Add a node to the Cluster
Add-NlbClusterNode -HostName CBXA01 -InterfaceName "LAN" -
NewNodeName CBXA02 -NewNodeInterface "LAN"
```

When a NetScaler **Application Delivery Controller** (**ADC**) appliance is available, it will also support Load Balancing. You can find instructions for load balancing Citrix Web Interface on a NetScaler ADC at Citrix's eDocs found at `http://support.citrix.com/proddocs/topic/netscaler-traffic-management-10-1-map/ns-lb-setup-wrapper-con.html`.

There's more...

You can read all about How to Configure Windows NLB and Web Interface at Citrix's Knowledge Center found at `http://support.citrix.com/article/CTX108812`.

You can read all about Network Load Balancing at Microsoft's TechNet at `http://technet.microsoft.com/en-us/library/cc725691.aspx`.

The `servermanagercmd` executable is explained in detail in *Scripting a command-line installation of the RD License Server* recipe in *Chapter 1, Remote Desktop Services*.

You can find an overview of the available NLB cmdlets in Windows PowerShell at Microsoft's TechNet found at `http://technet.microsoft.com/en-us/library/ee817138.aspx`, and view common NLB scenarios at Microsoft's MSDN found at `http://blogs.msdn.com/b/clustering/archive/2009/11/24/9927791.aspx`.

Speeding up the Web Interface's first logon time

This recipe will show you how to speed up the first logon time of your Citrix Web Interface. A user may experience a very slow startup of the XenApp website when he is the first user to logon to the site after a reset of the Internet Information Services.

How to do it...

To speed up the Web Interface first logon time, perform the following steps:

1. Open the `aspnet.config` file.

2. Add the following code before the `</runtime>` tag:

   `<generatePublisherEvidence enabled="false"/>`

3. Save the file.

 You might need to open the file with a file editor run as administrator to be able to save the changes.

You can find the `aspnet.config` file in the following folder:

- ► 32-bit: `C:\Windows\Microsoft.NET\Framework\v2.0.50727`
- ► 64-bit: `C:\Windows\Microsoft.NET\Framework64\v2.0.50727`

This will disable the CRL check for only .NET Framework 2.0 and the Citrix Web Interface, and not for all machine processes. To disable the CRL check for all processes, you will need to modify the `.\CONFIG\machine.config` file.

How it works...

After restarting IIS or rebooting the Web Interface server, it takes up to one minute to get the welcome page for the first user. This is caused by a **Certificate Revocation List** (**CRL**) check from .NET Framework 2.0, which needs to access the Microsoft Certificate Revocation List servers to verify Authenticode assembly due to the fact that it is Authenticode signed by Microsoft. When the server has no Internet access, the .NET Framework will try for up to 15 seconds to access the CRL servers before a time out is reached, and the process will continue without the CRL check.

 By default the `CitrixWebInterface<version>AppPool` application pool is restarted every night at 2 a.m. by IIS. This recreates the first user's slow loading page experience every morning unless the CRL check is fixed.

You can choose to manually disable the CRL check for .NET Framework 2.0 to speed up the process and site loading on the Citrix Web Interface.

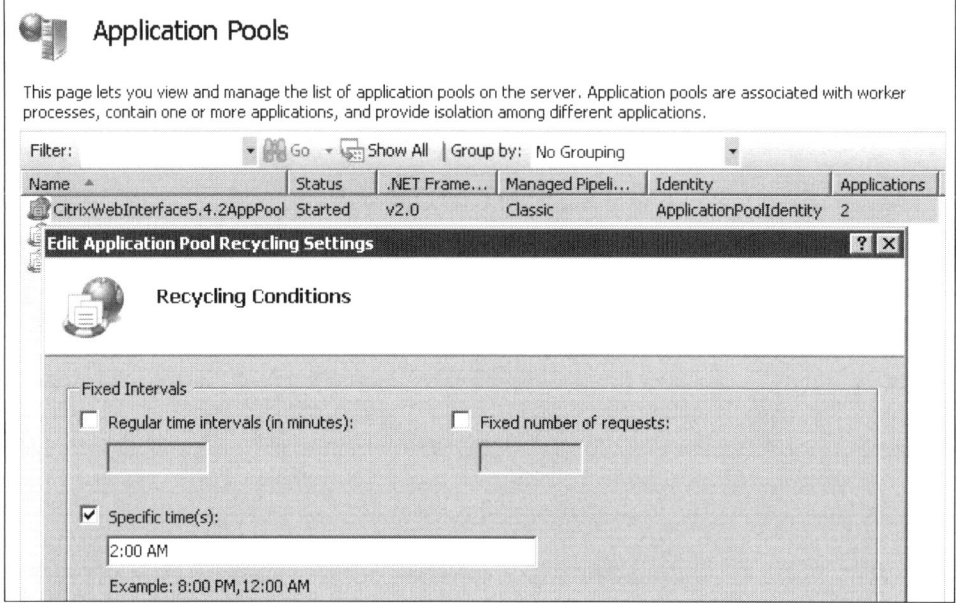

There's more...

You can read more on the .NET Framework 2.0 fix at Microsoft's Knowledge Base found at http://support.microsoft.com/kb/936707/en-us.

You can read more on speeding up the Citrix Web Interface startup at Citrix's Knowledge Center found at http://support.citrix.com/article/CTX117273.

Fixing pass-through authentication

This recipe will show you how to check your pass-through configuration for the CWI and fix any configuration errors that might have occurred.

How to do it...

There are two configurations to check for the pass-through configuration. You will need to check both the client and the server configuration to ensure the pass-through is configured the right way.

To check the IIS server settings, perform the following steps:

1. Check whether the Windows Authentication IIS Windows Role Services is installed by running the following PowerShell script:

   ```
   Import-Module ServerManager
   ```

   ```
   Get-WindowsFeature Web-Windows-Auth
   ```

   ```
   Administrator: Windows PowerShell
   PS C:\> Import-Module ServerManager
   PS C:\> Get-WindowsFeature Web-Windows-Auth

   Display Name                                          Name
   -----------                                           ----
                 [X] Windows Authentication              Web-Windows-Auth

   PS C:\> _
   ```

2. Use the following command to enable Windows Authentication:

   ```
   %windir%\system32\inetsrv\appcmd set config
   /section:windowsAuthentication /enabled:true
   /useKernelmode:true
   ```

To check the Citrix Web Interface settings, perform the following step:

1. Check if pass-through is enabled as Authentication Methods for the XenApp website by searching for the following lines in `C:\inetpub\wwwroot\Citrix\<sitename>\conf\webinterface.conf`:

   ```
   AllowCustomizeAutoLogin=On
   ```

   ```
   AutoLoginDefault=On
   ```

   ```
   EnableKerberosToMPS=On
   ```

   ```
   WIAuthenticationMethods=SingleSignOn
   ```

To check the Citrix XenApp Session Host settings, perform the following step:

1. Check if at least the latest critical updates are installed on your XenApp server by cross referencing the install hotfixes with the list of critical public updates at `http://support.citrix.com/product/xa/v6.5_2008r2/`.

[Please note that hotfix XA650W2K8R2X64001 (superseded by Hotfix Rollup Pack 2) fixes a problem with pass-through authentication on XenApp 6.5 servers.]

To check the Citrix Receiver client settings, perform the following steps:

1. Check if the Citrix Receiver for Enterprise is installed.

2. Ensure the Citrix Receiver for Enterprise is installed with the following parameters to enable pass-through authentication:

   ```
   CitrixReceiverEnterprise.exe /includeSSON ENABLE_SSON="Yes"
   ```

 You can download the Citrix Receiver Enterprise version from the Citrix Downloads site by selecting Citrix Receiver and the Legacy Client Software. Select the Receiver for Windows 3.x (Legacy PNA) version to download a Citrix Receiver Enterprise version.

3. Check if **Single Sign-On** (**SSO**) is enabled on the client by checking if the `ssonsvr. exe` process is running and by checking the following registry keys:

   ```
   HKLM\SOFTWARE\Citrix\ICA Client\SSON\Enable="true"
   ```

   ```
   HKLM\SOFTWARE\Citrix\PNAgent\EnablePassThrough=1
   ```

4. Check if the required policy settings are configured and applied to the Client Device.

5. To apply the required settings, the `icaclient.adm` file needs to be added to the policy and the following configurations needs to be set:

   ```
   Computer Configuration | Policies | Administrative Templates |
   Classic Administrative Templates | Citrix Components | Citrix
   Receiver | User authentication
   ```

   ```
   Policy setting: Local user name and password
   ```

   ```
   State: Enabled
   ```

   ```
   Enable pass-through authentication: selected
   ```

   ```
   Allow pass-through authentication for all ICA connections:
   selected
   ```

 You can find the `icaclient.adm` file at the Client Device at `C:\Program Files\Citrix\ICA Client\Configuration` (32-bit) or `C:\Program Files (x86)\Citrix\ICA Client\Configuration` (64-bit).

There's more...

Read more on installing and configuring Citrix Receiver for Pass-Through Authentication at Citrix's Knowledge Center found at `http://support.citrix.com/article/CTX133982`.

Read more on Enabling Pass-Through Authentication at Citrix's eDocs found at `http://support.citrix.com/proddocs/topic/web-interface-impington/wi-enable-pass-through-authentication-gransden.html`.

Troubleshooting application launch errors

This recipe will show you how to troubleshoot some common application launch errors that are returned by the CWI.

How to do it...

To troubleshoot application launch errors, perform the following steps:

1. Check if ActiveX Filtering is applied when Internet Explorer 9 and later versions are used on the Client Device.

 A small blue circle with a crossed line in it will be shown between the address bar and the refresh icon to indicate that ActiveX Filtering is actively applied to the site.

2. Disable ActiveX Filtering (**Tools | Active Filtering**) and refresh the web page.

3. Check if the client can resolve the XenApp server FQDN by using the following command:

   `ping <ServerFQDN>`

4. Check if firewall rules are not blocking ICA traffic by using the following command:

   `telnet <IPaddress> 1494`

5. Disable the DNS address resolution for the XenApp servers with an applied Citrix XenApp Computer policy setting if XenApp server IP-addresses need to be returned.

6. Check the current load for a XenApp server with the following command:

   `qfarm /load`

 The `qfarm` command is explained in detail in *Chapter 10, PowerShell and Command-line Tooling*.

How it works...

In addition to using the `Repair` option to troubleshoot the configured site on the CWI you might want to check some of the given solutions to known error messages.

ActiveX Filtering in Internet Explorer 9 and up

When using Internet Explorer 9, client detection might not function properly and you might be faced with the error message shown in the following screenshot, while trying to launch an application. In addition to the error message, you will also see a small blue icon next to the address bar indicating that some content is filtered.

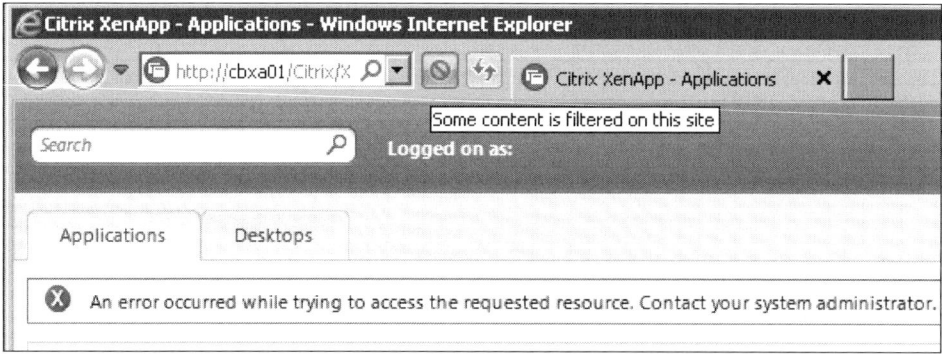

This indicates that ActiveX filtering is enabled and is preventing the user from launching the published applications.

To fix the problem, you need to disable the ActiveX filtering altogether through the menu (**Tools | Active Filtering**) or for the specific site by clicking on the blue icon and selecting **Turn off ActiveX Filtering**. The latter option will not disable ActiveX Filtering at a global level.

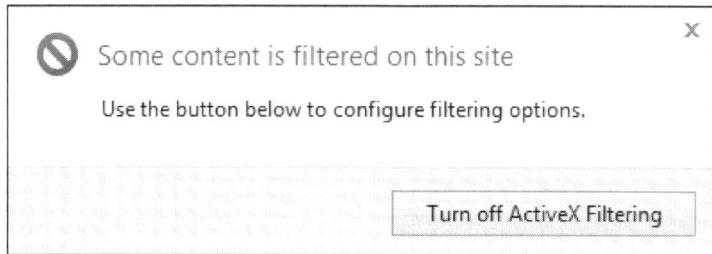

To view the sites for which ActiveX Filtering is turned off, you can check out the registry key: HKCU\Software\Microsoft\Internet Explorer\Safety\ActiveXFilterExceptions

XenApp server's name resolution

When a user launches a published application, he/she might receive the following error:

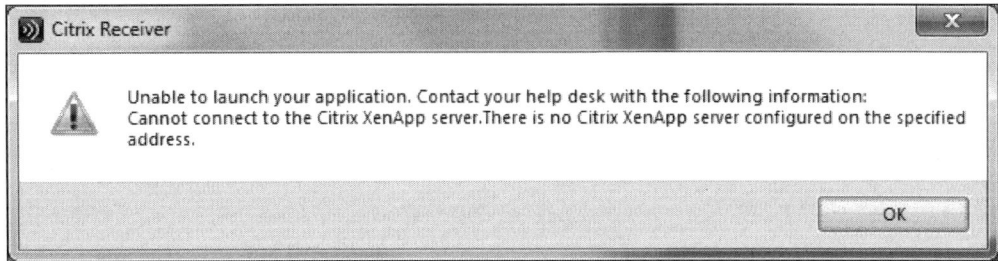

This error usually indicates a network connection error to the XenApp server. To check if the client can connect to the XenApp server, you will need to know whether the ICA file contains the IP address of the XenApp server (the DNS Address resolution is disabled through the XenApp policy), or the FQDN (the DNS Address resolution is enabled).

To view the ICA file, perform the following steps:

1. Change **File Type Association** for ICA files on the client (**Control Panel | Programs | Default Programs | Associate a file type...**). Associate .ica with Notepad instead of Citrix Connection Manager.

2. Launch a published application from the Web Interface and save the file.

 The .ica file can also be found in the temp folder of a user, which can be located by default at C:\Users\<username>\AppData\Local\Temp, when the application is still being launched. By default, the .ica file will be deleted when the application is closed.

3. Open the ICA file to view the applied settings.

4. Check the content of the ICA file and look for the following lines:

   ```
   [<ApplicationName>]
   Address=<FQDN-server>:1494
   ```

5. Check if the client can resolve the FQDN by using the following command:

   ```
   ping <FQDN-server>
   ```

6. Check if the firewall rules are correct by using the following command:

   ```
   telnet <ip-address> 1494
   ```

7. Disable the DNS address resolution in the XenApp policies if IP addresses need to be used.

Load Evaluator settings

You might have to check the Load Evaluator settings for your XenApp servers when users are receiving the following error message while launching a published application and `Event ID 31003` is logged on CWI:

All the Citrix XML Services configured for `farm <FarmName>` failed to respond to this XML Service transaction.

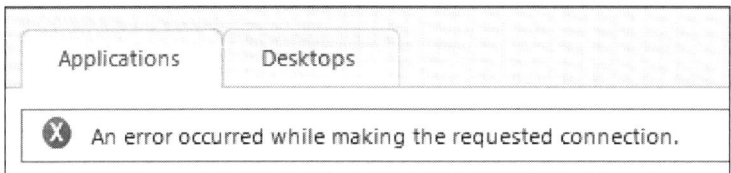

There might be a problem with the assigned Load Evaluator for the XenApp servers. Check the current load with the `QFARM` command as explained in the *Getting Farm information with QUERY/QFARM* recipe in *Chapter 10, PowerShell and Command-line Tooling*.

There's more...

You can read more on How to Obtain an ICA file through the CWI at Citrix's Knowledge Center found at `http://support.citrix.com/article/CTX111820`.

You can find an overview of the Logged Messages and Event IDs for the Citrix Web Interface 5.4 at Citrix's eDocs found at `http://support.citrix.com/proddocs/topic/web-interface-impington/wi-log-messages-event-ids-hardwick.html`.

Configuring application launch settings

This recipe will show you how to configure special application handling by configuring settings on the CWI. This enables you to automatically launch an application when a user logs in, to specify applications that need to start in a Windowed mode instead of the Seamless mode, and to prevent users from launching multiple instances of an application by clicking too enthusiastically on the icons.

How to do it...

To configure advanced application launch settings, perform the following steps:

1. To configure the automatic launch of an application, open `C:\inetpub\wwwroot\Citrix\<Site>\app_code\PagesJava\com\citrix\wi\pages\site\Applist.java`.

2. Replace `DesktopInfo` by `ApplicationInfo` in the following command:

   import com.citrix.wing.webpn.DesktopInfo;

3. Replace `DesktopInfo` by `ApplicationInfo` in the following command:

   if ((singlePublishedItem != null) && (singlePublishedItem
   instanceof DesktopInfo))

 The automatic launch of a published application only works when the user only has one published application available. When more applications are presented by the Citrix Web Interface, this setting will not work.

4. To start an application in Windowed mode while all other applications are started in the Seamless mode, add the following lines for the application to `C:\inetpub\wwwroot\Citrix\<SiteName>\conf\default.ica`:

   [<AppName>]

   TWIMode=Off

   DesiredHRES=1024

   DesiredVRES=768

5. To prevent the launch of multiple instances of the same application by a user clicking on a published application more than once, edit `C:\inetpub\wwwroot\Citrix\<SiteName>\conf\webinterface.conf` and configure the following setting:

   MultiLaunchTimeout=<NumberOfSeconds>

How it works...

Here are some quick tips to enhance your user experience through some simple Web Interface configuration tweaking.

Configure an application autolaunch

Configuring your Web Interface to automatically start a published desktop can be done through the `AutoLaunchDesktop` setting in the `webinterface.conf` file.

This simple configuration only works for published desktops and only when the user has one desktop published. If more desktops and/or published applications are available on the Web Interface or if only a published application is used, the autolaunch configuration fails.

You can create an application autolaunch configuration by modifying some of the Java code of the Web Interface at:

```
C:\inetpub\wwwroot\Citrix\<Site>\app_code\PagesJava\com\citrix\wi\
pages\site\Applist.java.
```

Change the code as shown in the following lines of code:

Original line	`import com.citrix.wing.webpn.DesktopInfo;`
New line	`import com.citrix.wing.webpn.ApplicationInfo;`

Original line	`if ((singlePublishedItem != null) &&` `(singlePublishedItem instanceof DesktopInfo))`
New line	`if ((singlePublishedItem != null) &&` `(singlePublishedItem instanceof ApplicationInfo))`

1. Restart IIS (run the `iisreset` command)

 As with the desktop autolaunch configuration, this method only works when the user has only one published application available through the Web Interface. The site also needs to be added to the **Trusted Sites** in the Internet Explorer for the autolaunch feature to work.

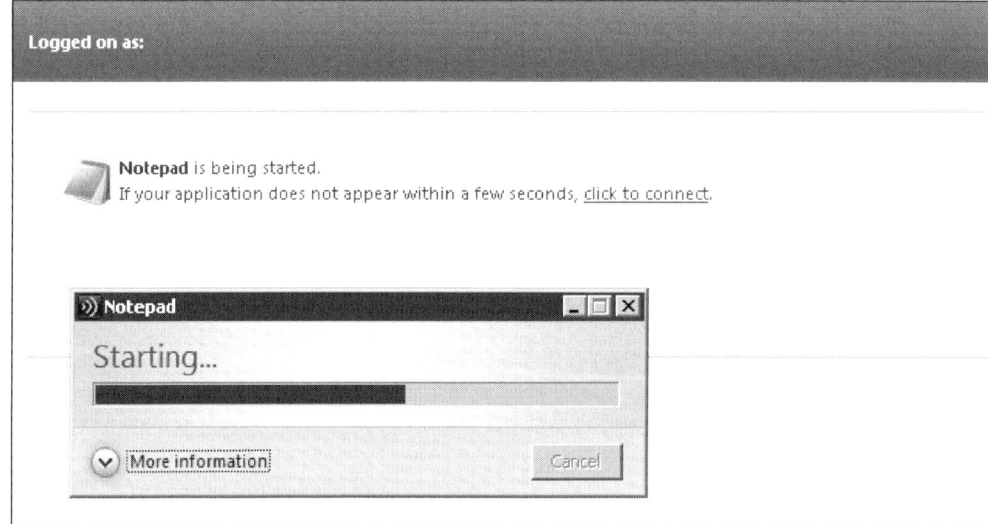

Start a specified application in Windowed mode

Some published applications do not integrate well with your local desktop and therefore running them in the Seamless mode is not the best option. To run a single application in the Windowed mode while keeping the Seamless setting for all other applications, the `default.ica` file must be edited:

`C:\inetpub\wwwroot\Citrix\<SiteName>\conf\default.ica.`

Add the following lines to the file for the required application (based upon the `ApplicationName` property of the published application):

Original code	New code

`[ApplicationServers]`
`Application=`
	`[ApplicationServers]`
	`Application=`
	
	`[<AppName>]`
	`TWIMode=Off`
	`DesiredHRES=1024`
	`DesiredVRES=768`

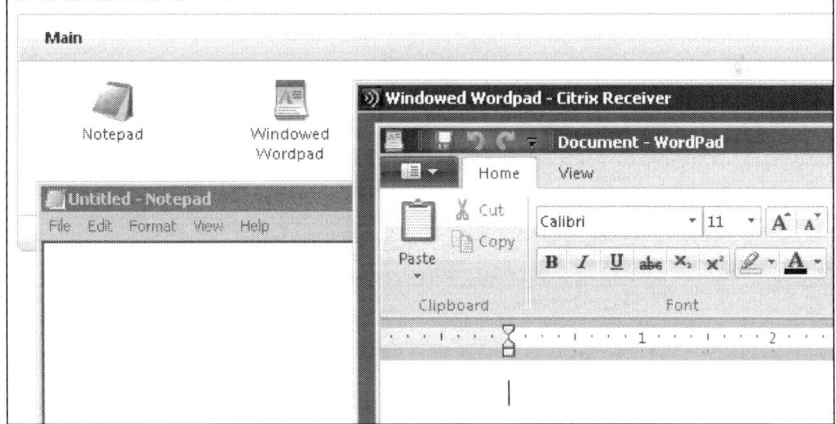

Prevent multiple launches for the same application

A published desktop or application is started with a single click on the icon at the Web Interface. Internet Explorer does not always show progress information while the Citrix Receiver is starting the desktop or application in the background. As no progress is shown, users are tempted to double-click on the icon wondering if the application or desktop has started at all. This can result in unintentionally starting multiple instances of the same desktop or application, which can be confusing for users.

To prevent multiple application or desktop launches, a time out can be configured with the following setting at `C:\inetpub\wwwroot\Citrix\<SiteName>\conf\webinterface.conf`:

`MultiLaunchTimeout=<NumberOfSeconds>`

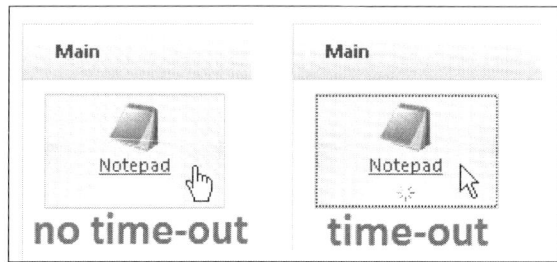

After the first click, the application is launched and you are no longer able to start a second instance within the time-out period. In addition, a very small progress indicator is added to the icon during the time-out period.

There's more...

You can read more on How to Configure AutoLaunch for a Single Published Application on WI 5.x at the Citrix Knowledge Center found at `http://support.citrix.com/article/CTX125277`.

You can read more on How to Configure WI to Launch Certain Applications in Windowed Mode at Citrix's Knowledge Center found at `http://support.citrix.com/article/CTX116357`.

You can read more on How to Configure Multiple Launch Prevention at Citrix's Knowledge Center found at `http://support.citrix.com/article/CTX124612`.

4
Citrix® StoreFront

In this chapter, we will cover the following topics:

- ▶ Scripting a command-line installation of Citrix® StoreFront
- ▶ Configuring a StoreFront Store
- ▶ Configuring StoreFront Receiver for Web
- ▶ Configuring Remote Access for a Store
- ▶ Configuring StoreFront for mobile devices
- ▶ Configuring StoreFront Receiver for Web using configuration files
- ▶ Managing application behavior by adding keywords
- ▶ Changing the Server Base URL
- ▶ Troubleshooting StoreFront Errors

Introduction

A XenApp infrastructure consists of many components to ensure that users can start a published desktop or application. Each Citrix component within the XenApp infrastructure runs as part of the entire chain to offer users published applications, desktops, and/or resources.

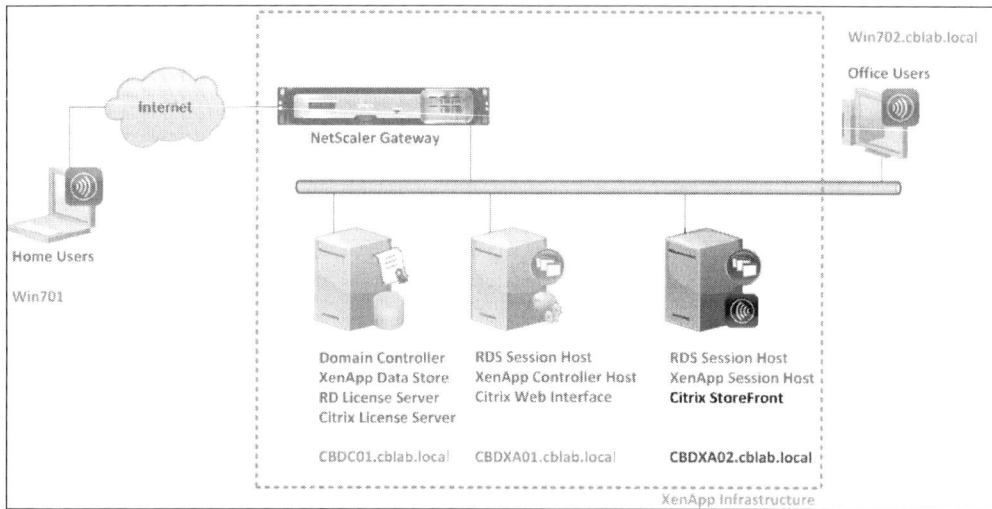

When Citrix XenDesktop 7 was announced at Citrix Synergy, Citrix also announced the End of Life for Citrix Web Interface as can be viewed on the Lifecycle Milestones for Citrix XenDesktop, as shown in the following screenshot:

Product Releases	Version	GA Date*	EOM Date*	EOL Date*
XenApp for Windows Server 2008 R2	6.5	24-Aug-11	24-Feb-16	24-Aug-16
Web Interface	5.x	2-Jun-08	17-Dec-14	14-Jun-15

* Lifecycle Phases: GA (General Availability), EOM (End of Maintenance), EOL (End of Life). For definitions of these terms, click here

In addition to the End of Life announcement, Citrix also introduced **Citrix StoreFront (CSF)** as the replacement of the **Citrix Web Interface** to better support mobile devices and integrate SaaS and web applications and even data into a single App Store.

Citrix StoreFront is one of the components of CloudGateway Enterprise and is also referred to as CloudGateway Express in the first communication by Citrix. As of June 28, 2013 CloudGateway Enterprise has been renamed to **XenMobile App Edition**.

This chapter will show you how to install, manage, monitor and troubleshoot Citrix StoreFront Version 2.0, as it is shipped with **XenDesktop 7.0**, the successor to XenApp 6.5.

Scripting a command-line installation of Citrix® StoreFront

This recipe will show you how to build an unattended installation script for CSF using a command-line installation.

Getting ready

You can install Citrix StoreFront 2.0 on Windows Server 2008 R2 SP1 Servers (Enterprise and Standard editions) and Windows Server 2012 servers (Datacenter and Standard editions).

Prior to the installation of CSF, check the presence of the following prerequisites:

- IIS

    - Common HTTP Features (Default Document, HTTP Errors, Static Content, and HTTP Redirection)

    - Health and Diagnostics (HTTP Logging)

    - Security (Request Filtering and Windows Authentication)

    - Application Development (.NET Extensibility, Application Initialization, ASP.NET, ISAPI Extensions, and ISAPI Filters)

    - Management Tools (IIS Management Console, IIS Management Scripts, and Tools)

- .NET Framework 3.5.1

 CSF can be installed as part of the XenDesktop 7 installation or a separate download pack can be downloaded from the Citrix website.

How to do it...

Follow these steps to create an unattended installation of Citrix StoreFront:

1. Run the following command to install StoreFront and the Receiver clients:

    ```
    CitrixStoreFront-x64.exe -silent -WINDOWS_CLIENT C:\Install\
    CitrixReceiver_v4_0.exe -MAC_CLIENT C:\Install\CitrixReceiver_
    v11_8.dmg
    ```

 The previously mentioned prerequisites are automatically installed when they are not present on the system.

How it works...

You can install Citrix StoreFront with the following command:

```
CitrixStoreFront-x64.exe [-silent] [-INSTALLDIR <installdir>]
```

```
[-WINDOWS_CLIENT <ReceiverForWindows>] [-MAC_CLIENT <ReceiverForMac>]
```

The preceding command uses the following syntax:

► `silent`: A silent installation of Citrix StoreFront will be performed.

► `INSTALLDIR`: This specifies the directory where StoreFront will be installed. By default this is `C:\Program Files\Citrix\Receiver StoreFront\`.

► `WINDOWS_CLIENT`: This specifies the full path of the Receiver for Windows installation file to be copied to in the StoreFront installation folder. By default this is `C:\Program Files\Citrix\Receiver StoreFront\Receiver Clients\ Windows\`.

► `MAC_CLIENT`: This specifies the full path of the Receiver for Mac installation file to be copied to in the StoreFront installation folder. By default this is `C:\Program Files\Citrix\Receiver StoreFront\Receiver Clients\Mac\`.

There's more...

You can read more on installing StoreFront at a command prompt on Citrix's eDocs at `http://support.citrix.com/proddocs/topic/dws-storefront-21/dws-install-command.html`

You can download the StoreFront installation pack and Citrix Receiver installers from the following location: `http://download.citrix.com/downloads.html`

See also

▸ *The Configuring a StoreFront Store recipe*

Configuring a StoreFront Store

This recipe will show you how to configure the basic settings of the CSF server.

Getting ready

While using Citrix StoreFront, it is recommended by Citrix to use an HTTPS connection to the Store and install the required certificate on **Internet Information Service (IIS)**.

Microsoft TechNet offers further instructions for Server Certificates in IIS 7 at `http://technet.microsoft.com/en-us/library/cc732230(v=ws.10).aspx` and for SSL binding to a site at `http://technet.microsoft.com/en-us/library/hh831632.aspx#SSLBinding`.

By default, the Citrix Receiver is configured to only connect to Citrix StoreFront through HTTPS. When HTTP is used, ensure that the Citrix Receiver configuration is changed as described in Citrix's Knowledge Center at `http://support.citrix.com/article/CTX134341`.

 The Citrix StoreFront server in the lab environment was configured to use HTTP instead of HTTPS and no additional certificates were required.

How to do it...

After the installation, you can configure the basic settings for your StoreFront server by following these manual steps:

1. Open the StoreFront Management Console by navigating to **Start | All Programs | Citrix | Citrix StoreFront**.

2. Click on **Create a new deployment** in the **Enter** pane.

3. Check the base URL specified and click on **Next**. The deployment is then created (this may take a moment).

4. Enter a Store name and click on **Next**.

5. Click on **Add** to enter the Delivery Controller configuration.

6. Enter **Display name**.

7. Select the **Delivery Controller** type.

8. Click on **Add** to enter your XenApp Controller Hosts.

9. Select the transport type and the corresponding communication port of the XML service.

10. Click on **OK**.

11. Repeat steps 5 to 10 if you want to enter more Delivery Controllers.

12. Click on **Next**.

13. Select **None** as your Remote Access and click on **Create**. The Store is now created.

14. Click on **Finish**.

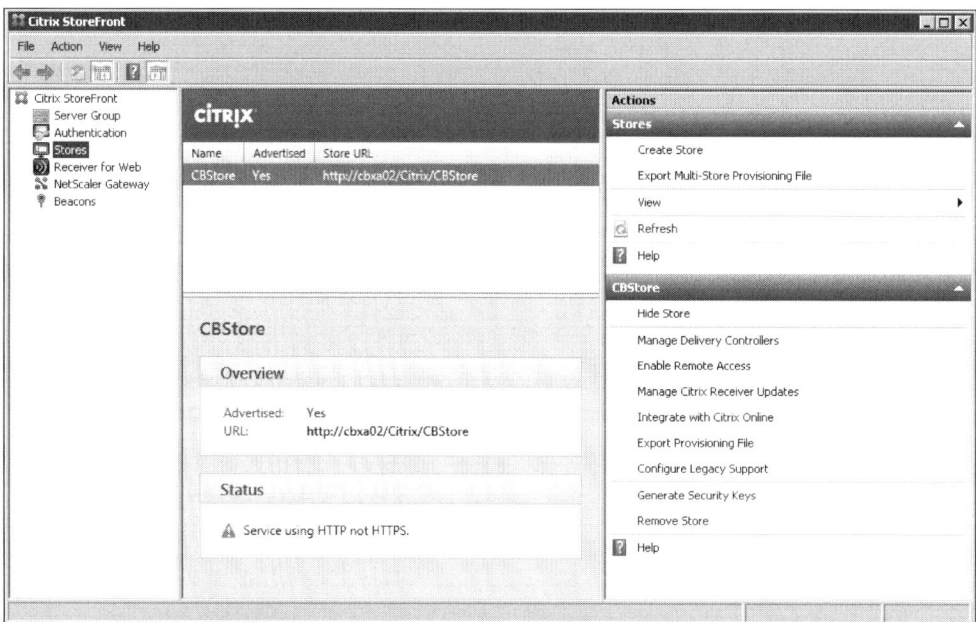

There's more...

You can read more on creating a new deployment and Citrix's eDocs at `http://support.citrix.com/proddocs/topic/dws-storefront-21/dws-deploy-multi.html`.

See also

▶ *The Configuring the StoreFront Receiver for website recipe*

▶ *The Configuring Remote Access for a Store recipe*

▶ *The Configuring StoreFront for mobile devices recipe*

Configuring StoreFront Receiver for the Web

This recipe will show you how to configure the Receiver for Web of the CSF server with the StoreFront Management Console.

How to do it...

The StoreFront Receiver for Web is automatically configured during the configuration of your CSF store. When you need to re-create the Receiver for Web or simply want to add another Receiver for Web, follow these manual steps:

1. Open the StoreFront Management Console by navigating to **Start | All Programs | Citrix | Citrix StoreFront**.

2. Select Receiver for Web from the left pane.

3. Click on **Create website** in the **Action** pane.

4. Select the Store you want to connect to with your Receiver for Web.

5. Enter the website path and click on **Create**.

6. Click on the link if you want to try out the Store.

7. Click on **Finish**.

 Some options cannot be configured through the Management Console. Check the *Configuring Receiver for Web Using configuration files* recipe for instructions on further customizing the Receiver for Web.

See also

▸ The *Configuring StoreFront Receiver for Web using configuration files recipe*

Configuring Remote Access for a Store

This recipe will show you how to configure Remote Access to your Store by using the connection between CSF and **NetScaler Gateway** (**NG**).

Getting ready

Before you can configure the NetScaler Gateway options for Citrix StoreFront, a NetScaler Gateway (virtual) appliance needs to be installed and configured in your XenApp infrastructure. Check out *Chapter 5, The NetScaler Gateway,* for instructions on configuring, administrating, and troubleshooting a Citrix NetScaler Gateway.

How to do it...

To configure Remote Access for a Store, the Authentication Service must be selected first. After setting up the Authentication Service, the Remote Access settings can be configured and activated on the Store.

 The configuration of the NetScaler Gateway will be addressed in *Chapter 5, The NetScaler Gateway.*

To set up the required authentication service for Remote Access, follow these steps:

1. Open the StoreFront Management Console by navigating to **Start | All Programs | Citrix | Citrix StoreFront**.

2. Select **Authentication** from the left pane.

3. Click on **Add/Remove Methods** in the **Action** pane.

4. Select **Pass-through from NetScaler Gateway** and click on **OK**.

5. Select the **Pass-through from NetScaler Gateway Authentication Method** in the center pane and click on **Configure Trusted Domains** in the **Action** pane.

6. Configure the following **Trusted Domain** settings:

   ❏ **Allow users to log on from**: This is for trusted domains only

   ❏ **Trusted domains**: This adds the NetBIOS name of your domain

   ❏ **Default domain**: This is to select your domain

7. Click on **OK**.

8. Click on **Configure Delegated Authentication** and ensure the option **Fully delegate credential validation to NetScaler Gateway** is not selected (unless you will be using smart cards).

 This book will not cover Smart Card Authentication and the required configuration for StoreFront.

9. Click on **OK**.

To set up the required NetScaler Gateway configuration for Remote Access, follow these steps:

1. Open the StoreFront Management Console by navigating to **Start** | **All Programs** | **Citrix** | **Citrix StoreFront**.

2. Select **NetScaler Gateway** from the left pane.

3. Click on **Add NetScaler Gateway Appliance** in the **Action** pane.

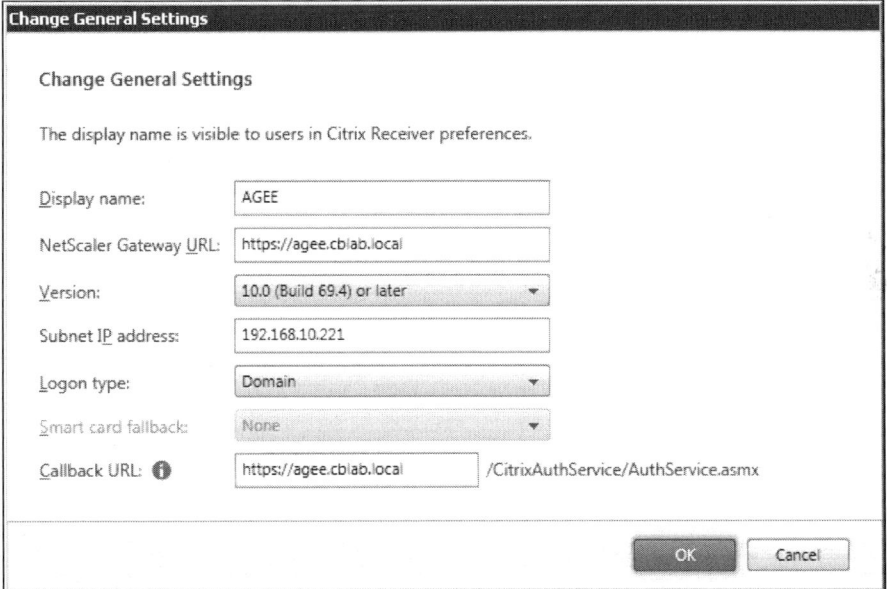

4. Configure the following general settings:

    ❏ **Display name**: This requires a descriptive display name

    ❏ **NetScaler Gateway URL**: This requires the URL of the NetScaler Gateway VIP (as used on the SSL certificate)

    ❏ **Version**: This specifies the right version of the NetScaler appliance

    ❏ **Subnet IP address**: This requires the NetScaler MIP or SNIP configured for the XenApp subnet

    ❏ **Logon type**: Select the domain

    ❏ **Callback URL**: This URL is based upon the NetScaler AGEE VIP

> The different IP address type definitions are explained in Chapter 5, *The NetScaler Gateway*.

5. Click on **Next**.

6. Click on **Add** to enter **Secure Ticket Authority (STA) URL**.

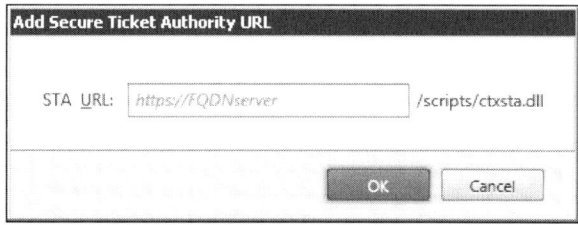

7. Enter the STA URL (syntax: `http(s)://<ControllerHostFQDN>:<XMLPort>`).

> By default, XML port 80 is used. If a different port is used, it has to be included in the STA URL by extending the FQDNserver with a colon and the XML port number.

8. Select **Enable session reliability** if you want users to be able to reconnect to the published applications and/or desktops.

9. Select **Request tickets from two STAs, where available** if you have multiple XenApp Controller Hosts in your XenApp Farm and want to offer redundancy.

10. Click on **Create**.

11. Click on **Finish**.

The final step in configuring Remote Access is to ensure it is activated for the Store. Follow these steps to activate Remote Access on the Store:

1. Open Management Console by navigating to **Start | All Programs | Citrix | Citrix StoreFront**.

2. Select **Stores** from the left pane.

3. Select **Store** in the center pane and click on **Enable Remote Access** in the **Action** pane.

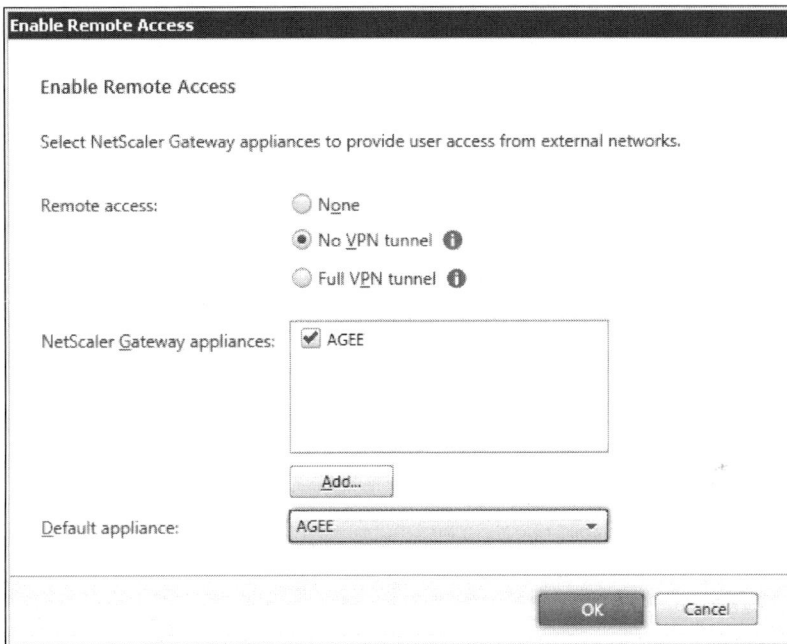

4. Configure the following settings:

   - **Remote access**: No VPN tunnel (only ICA Proxy is required)

   - **NetScaler Gateway appliances**: Select the previously configured NetScaler Gateway configuration

   - **Default appliance**: Select the previously configured NetScaler Gateway configuration

5. Click on **OK**.

6. Test your configuration by opening the external URL and logging in.

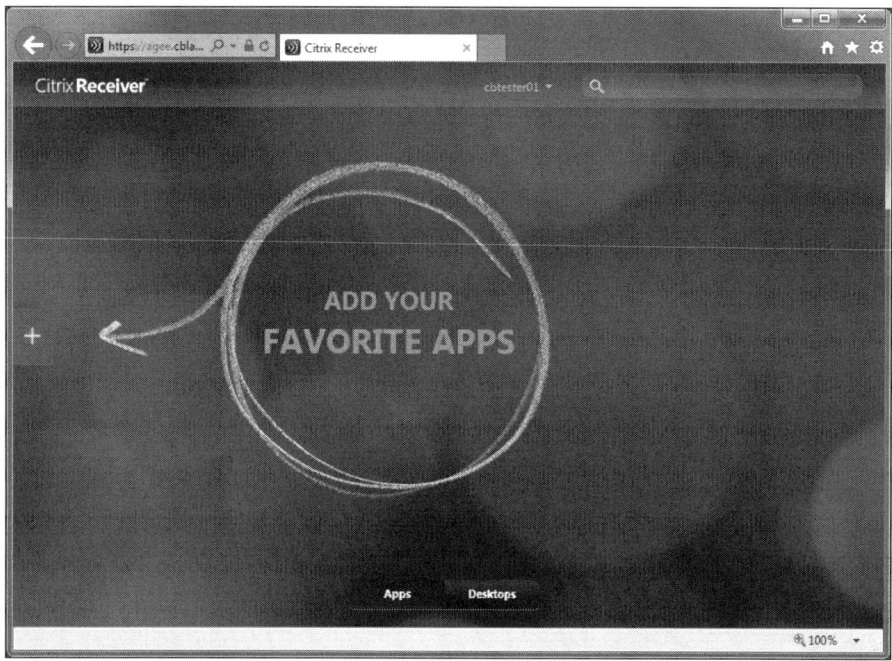

There's more...

You can read more on configuring the Authentication Service at Citrix's eDocs at `http://support.citrix.com/proddocs/topic/dws-storefront-21/dws-manage-auth-service.html`.

You can read more on configuring Remote Access at Citrix's eDocs at `http://support.citrix.com/proddocs/topic/dws-storefront-21/dws-deploy-multi-appliance.html`.

See also

  ▶ *The Configuring a StoreFront Store recipe*
  ▶ *The Configuring the StoreFront Receiver for website recipe*
  ▶ *The Configuring StoreFront for mobile devices recipe*

Configuring StoreFront for mobile devices

Mobile Device access for CSF is also known as legacy support. Legacy support describes the support for the previously available XenApp Web Services sites in **Citrix Web Interface** (**CWI**) or PNAgent support. This recipe will show you where legacy support can be configured for the Store.

How to do it...

In StoreFront 1.2, you needed to manually activate legacy support for the Store as it was not enabled by default. With CSF 2.0, it is enabled by default for each Store. To check the configuration (and URL) for legacy support, follow these steps:

1. Open the StoreFront Management Console by navigating to **Start | All Programs | Citrix | Citrix StoreFront**.

2. Select **Stores** from the left pane.

3. Click on **Configure Legacy Support** in the **Action** pane.

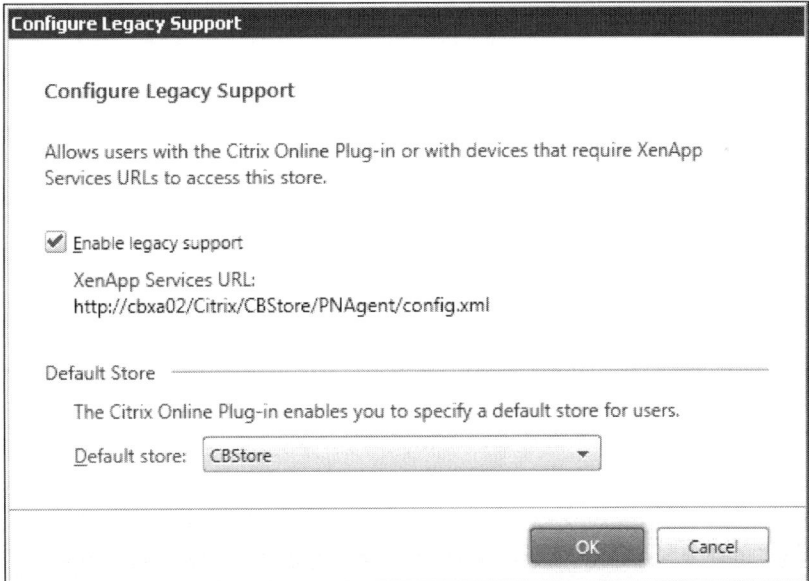

4. Ensure legacy support is enabled and copy the **XenApp Services URL** for future reference as shown in the previous screenshot.

5. To test legacy support, install the Citrix Receiver on a client device and enter the XenApp Services URL (or server name for unsecure connections) to connect to the Store. This allows Android devices to connect to StoreFront as well.

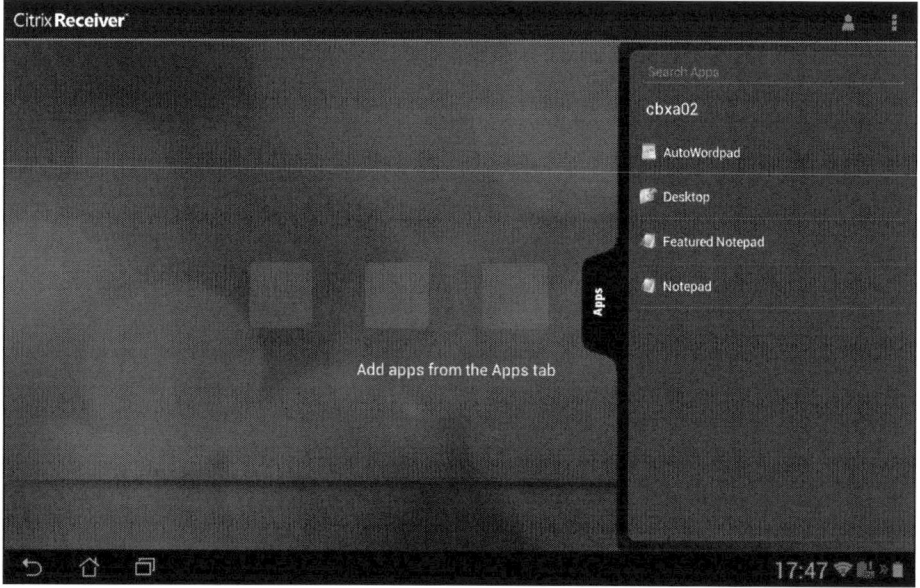

There's more...

You can read more on legacy support for StoreFront at Citrix's eDocs at `http://support.citrix.com/proddocs/topic/dws-storefront-21/dws-configure-pna-auth.html`.

See also

- ▸ *The Configuring a StoreFront Store recipe*
- ▸ *The Configuring Remote Access for a Store recipe*

Configuring StoreFront Receiver for the Web using configuration files

This recipe will show you how to configure additional Citrix StoreFront Receiver for Web settings that cannot be set through the management console by editing the appropriate configuration file. This allows further personalization of the Citrix Receiver for Web user experience.

How to do it...

To change advanced StoreFront Receiver for Web settings, follow these steps:

1. Open the configuration file at `C:\inetpub\wwwroot\Citrix\<ReceiverForWebFolder>`.

2. To personalize the Receiver for Web, find the `userinterface` element within the file and configure attribute settings for the workspace control, receiver, auto launch, and shown tabs.

3. To configure client detection settings, find the `pluginAssistant` element within the file and configure attribute settings for the different Receiver clients (Windows, MacOS, and HTML5).

4. To configure the life time of the authentication token, find the `authentication` element within the file and configure the `tokenLifetime` and `Method` attributes.

5. To configure the time out for the StoreFront Receiver for Web session, find the `sessionState` element within the file and configure the `timeout` attribute with the required minutes.

> The available settings for the mentioned elements are described in more detail in the following *How it works...* section.

How it works...

With the Citrix StoreFront Management Console, you can only configure the basic settings of the StoreFront Citrix Receiver for Web. Additional settings must be configured by editing the configuration files directly and changing the different XML elements and their values.

The Receiver for Web configuration is set with the `web.config` file located in the Receiver for Web folder. By default, this file can be found at `C:\inetpub\wwwroot\Citrix\<ReceiverForWebFolder>\web.config`.

To personalize the Citrix Web Receiver, here are some configuration options:

```
<userInterface ... autoLaunchDesktop="true">
```

The `autoLaunch` attribute of the `userInterface` element controls whether the published desktop is automatically started (`true`) or not (`false`). The auto launch only works if a user has only one published desktop available through the Citrix Receiver for Web.

```
<workspaceControl enabled="true" autoReconnectAtLogon="true"
logoffAction="disconnect" showReconnectButton="false"
showDisconnectButton="false" />
```

The `workspaceControl` element controls the connection settings of the Citrix Receiver for Web. You can specify whether the Reconnect and Disconnect options are added to the drop-down menu under the username in the top bar of the Citrix Receiver for Web. If workspace control is not enabled, the option to reconnect to previous sessions will not be available or shown in the drop-down menu, regardless of the configuration. The `logoffAction` attribute controls if a user session is logged off (terminate), disconnected (disconnect), or is kept running and active when users log off from the Citrix Receiver for Web (none).

```
<receiverConfiguration enabled="true" downloadURL="…" />
```

 To configure Follow-Me-Data and allow sessions to roam between different devices, set `autoReconnectAtLogon` to `true` and `logoffAction` to `disconnect`.

When the `receiverConfiguration` element is enabled, users are offered a provisioning file to automatically configure the Citrix Receiver with the required Store information. This way a user can directly connect to the Store without using the website. To stop the site from offering the file, you have to set `enabled` to `false`. This removes the **Activate** option from the logoff drop-down menu.

```
<uiViews showDesktopsView="true" showAppsView="true"
defaultView="desktops" />
```

The `uiViews` element controls which tabs are shown in the Citrix Receiver and which tab will be shown by default. You control the visibility of each tab to either be shown (`true`) or hidden (`false`). The default view can be set to either show the desktops tab (desktops) or the application tab (apps).

```
<pluginAssistant enabled="true" upgradeAtLogin="false">
<win32 path="clients/Windows/…" />
<macOS path="clients/Mac/…" minimumSupportedOSVersion="10.6"/>
<html5 enabled="On" platforms="…"launchURL="…" preferences=""
singleTabLaunch="false" />
```

The `pluginAssistant` element controls whether client detection is performed or not by setting the enabled attribute to `true` or `false`. The `upgradeAtLogin` attribute determines whether or not users are offered a client upgrade if an older version is detected. The location of the provided installation file is set for each operating system separately with the corresponding subelements `<win32 />`, `<macOS />`, and `<html5 />`. You can change the default behavior for HTML5 where applications and desktops are started in new browser tabs by setting `singleTabLaunch` to `true`.

You can use the `UpdateWindowsReceiverLocation.ps1` and `UpdateMacOSReceiverLocation.ps1` scripts from the `Scripts` folder in the StoreFront installation directory to place the client installation files in the right directories.

```
<authentication tokenLifeTime="08:00:00" method="Auto" />
```

The `authentication` element determines the lifetime of the token that allows users to use the XenApp published resources without having to re-authenticate.

```
<sessionState timeout="20" />
```

The `sessionState` element determines the timeout value for the user to stay logged in to the Citrix Receiver for Web.

There's more...

You can read more on the different configuration file options at Citrix's eDocs at `http://support.citrix.com/proddocs/topic/dws-storefront-21/dws-configure-wr-conf-file.html`.

If you also want to customize the appearance of the Receiver for Web, check out the Citrix blogpost at `http://blogs.citrix.com/2013/06/26/customizing-receiver-for-web-in-storefront-2-0/`.

And for those Dutch readers that are looking for a language pack, *Jeroen Tielen* has made one for StoreFront 2.0 at `http://www.jeroentielen.nl/nederlandse-vertaling-citrix-storefront-2-0/`.

See also

▶ *The Configuring the StoreFront Receiver for website recipe*

Managing application behavior by adding keywords

This recipe will show you how to manage application behavior in StoreFront by adding keywords to your published application.

How to do it...

To use keywords to manage application behavior, follow these steps:

1. Open Citrix AppCenter by navigating to **Start | Administrative Tools | Citrix | Management Consoles | Citrix AppCenter** on a XenApp Controller Host.

2. Expand **XenApp | <XAFarm> | Applications**.

3. Right-click on a published application and select **Application properties**.

4. Select **Name** in the **Properties** pane.

5. Enter KEYWORDS followed by the desired keywords in the **Application Description**.

6. Click on **OK**.

Log on to the Citrix Receiver and check to see if the applied keyword settings are shown in the Receiver (like a featured section in the application list and/or an automatically added application).

 The different keywords that can be applied are discussed in the following *How it works...* section in more detail.

How it works...

To influence the application behavior in StoreFront, you can add special keywords to the published application description field in XenApp. The special keywords that can be used are described in the following table:

Keyword	Explanation
Auto	Automatically subscribe the user to this application.
Featured	Adds a Featured Apps category to the Receiver to store these marked applications.
TreatAsApp	Special keyword for a XenApp published desktop. The desktop will be shown in the Application view instead of the separate Desktop view.
prefer="application"	Specifies a locally installed application on the Windows client to be used in preference to the published application. The entered application can be one or more words from the local application shortcut or the absolute path (including the executable name) to the application, from the \Start Menu folder.

To assign a keyword to a published application, add the following line in the description field:

```
KEYWORDS:<keyword> [<keyword>]
```

 If you want to assign more than one keyword to a published application, use a space to separate the keywords.

To add Notepad to the featured applications, follow these steps:

1. Open Citrix **AppCenter** on your XenApp Controller Host.

2. View the **application properties** of a published application, like Notepad.

3. Select **Basic | Name** in the left pane.

4. Enter the KEYWORDS featured in the **Application description** textbox and click on **OK**.

5. Log on to the Citrix Receiver and check whether the user can see a **Featured** category on their application list.

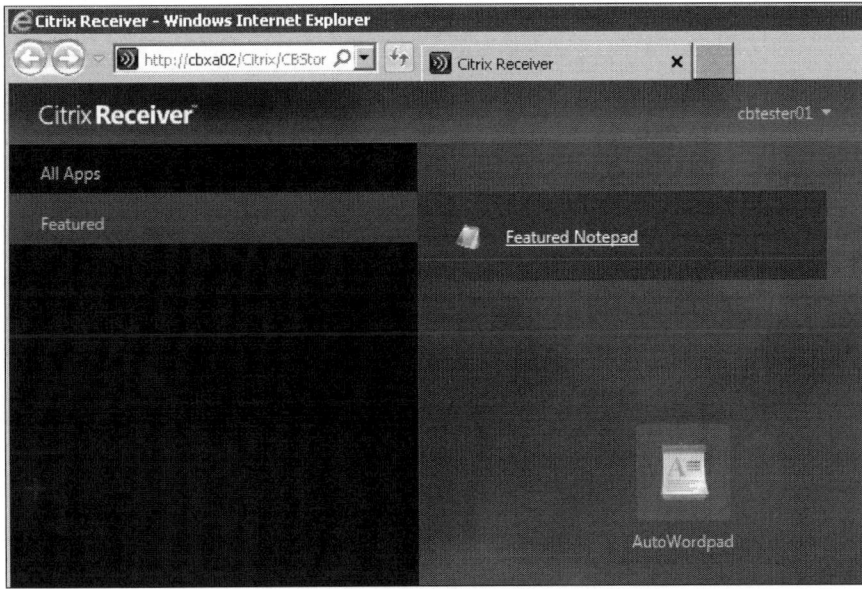

The featured category is shown in the application list as shown in the preceding screenshot.

 When the keyword Auto is used in the application description of a published application in Citrix AppCenter, the application is automatically placed on the user's Apps tab in the Citrix Receiver.

There's more...

You can read more on the different keyword options at Citrix's eDocs at `http://support.` `citrix.com/proddocs/topic/dws-storefront-12/dws-integrate.html` and `http://support.citrix.com/proddocs/topic/dws-storefront-21/dws-plan-` `optimize-ux.html`.

Changing the Server Base URL

This recipe will show you how to change the base URL of the Citrix StoreFront server.

How to do it...

To change the base URL of the Citrix StoreFront server, follow these steps:

1. Open the StoreFront Management Console by navigating to **Start | All Programs | Citrix | Citrix StoreFront**.

2. Select **Server Group** from the left pane.

3. Click on **Change Base URL** in the **Action** pane.

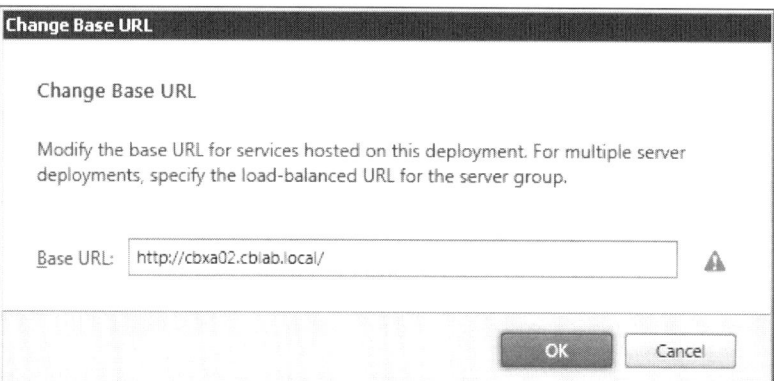

4. Enter the new Base URL and click on **OK**.

There's more...

You can read more on changing the Server Base URL at Citrix's Knowledge Center at `http://support.citrix.com/article/CTX135050`.

Troubleshooting StoreFront Errors

This recipe will show you how to troubleshoot some known errors for CSF.

Getting ready

To troubleshoot your StoreFront configuration, make sure you have enabled logging and/or tracing during your analyzing phase.

Here are some of the default locations for various log files:

Installation	
Interactive	`C:\Windows\Temp\Citrix-DeliveryServicesRoleManager-*.log`
Silent/uninstall	`C:\Windows\Temp\Citrix-DeliveryServicesSetupConsole-*.log`
Interactive/ silent install and uninstall	`C:\Windows\Temp\CitrixMsi-CitrixStoreFront-x64-*.log`
Windows event logs	
Application log	Windows Application log
Citrix log	Applications and Services Logs – Citrix Delivery Services
Windows PowerShell	
Commands	`C:\Program Files\Citrix\Receiver StoreFront\Admin\logs\<PScmd>_*.log`

To keep your log files from growing too rapidly due to the fact that duplicate messages are logged repeatedly, you can adjust the log throttling settings in the `web.config` files of the StoreFront Store and StoreFront Receiver for Web. Adjust the logger element and set the `duplicateInterval` and `duplicateLimit` attributes to configure the maximum number of duplicate messages that will be logged for the specified time interval:

```
<logger duplicateInterval="00:01:00" duplicateLimit="10">
```

To enable tracing, run the following PowerShell commands:

```
Add-PSSnapin Citrix.DeliveryServices.Framework.Commands
Set-DSTraceLevel -All -TraceLevel Verbose
```

To disable tracing, run the following PowerShell commands:

```
Add-PSSnapin Citrix.DeliveryServices.Framework.Commands
Set-DSTraceLevel -All -TraceLevel Off
```

How to do it...

To troubleshoot connection errors to StoreFront, follow these steps:

1. Check the running state of the Citrix Credential Wallet service on the StoreFront server.

2. Check the configured **Authentication Methods** in the StoreFront Management Console. Username and password must be added and enabled.

3. Check whether the LAN client can resolve the FQDN of the StoreFront server mentioned in the URL of the Store by using the following command:

   ```
   ping FQDNServer
   ```

4. Check whether NetScaler can resolve the FQDN of the StoreFront server mentioned in the URL of the Store while using remote access.

5. Check that all required certificates and certificate chains are in place on the NetScaler and StoreFront server.

6. Check whether NetScaler can connect to the XenApp servers and no firewall is blocking communication over port 1494 or 2598 (session reliability).

7. Check the configured STA settings of the virtual server on the NetScaler. At least one STA must be configured and must be showing an UP state.

8. Check whether the Desktop viewer toolbar is disabled for the StoreFront Store.

 The different checks and solutions are discussed in more detail in the following *How it works...* section.

How it works...

Here are some common errors that can occur for Citrix StoreFront and how to solve them.

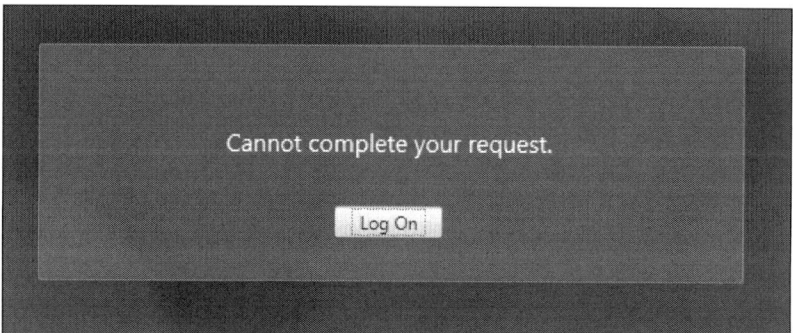

The "cannot complete your request" error can have many different causes. The following are some of the checks you can perform:

1. Ensure the **Citrix Credential Wallet** service is running on the StoreFront server.

2. Ensure the username and password **Authentication** method is added and enabled in StoreFront Management Console.

3. Ensure the internal client can resolve the Server Base URL of the StoreFront Store to the server's local IP address for direct access on the LAN.

While using Remote Access, perform the following checks:

1. Ensure NetScaler can resolve the Server Base URL of the StoreFront Store to the server's local IP address for remote access through the WAN.

2. Ensure all required certificates are installed on the StoreFront server and an internal VIP is created on the NetScaler to support the authentication check from the StoreFront server to the NetScaler.

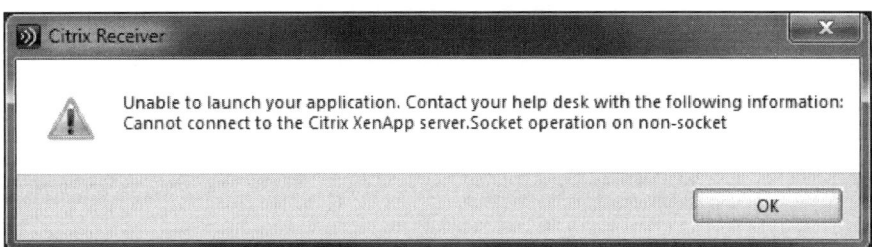

When you receive the preceding error while starting a published application, after you have logged on to StoreFront through Remote Access, check the configured **Secure Ticket Authority** (**STA**) on the Virtual Server configuration of the NetScaler. If no STA is configured or the STA does not report an UP state, NetScaler cannot communicate properly with the XenApp Farm and start the requested application.

Disable the Citrix Desktop Viewer Toolbar

While using StoreFront with Citrix XenApp published desktops and applications, make sure you disable the Desktop Viewer Toolbar that is enabled by default for Receiver for Web.

 The Desktop Viewer Toolbar is developed especially for XenDesktop and is not recommended for use with XenApp.

To disable the toolbar, follow these steps:

1. Edit the `web.config` configuration file for the Receiver for Web (by default, the file is located at `C:\inetpub\wwwroot\Citrix\<sitename>`).

2. Search for the line containing the `showDesktopViewer` attribute.

3. Make sure the following setting is configured:

    `showDesktopViewer="false"`

4. Save the file.

5
The NetScaler Gateway

In this chapter, we will cover the following topics:

- ► Licensing the NetScaler Gateway Enterprise Edition
- ► Configuring the Citrix® Web Interface with a NetScaler Gateway authentication point
- ► Configuring the NetScaler Gateway for the Citrix® Web Interface
- ► Configuring the NetScaler Gateway for Citrix® StoreFront (CSF)
- ► Changing the NetScaler Gateway's logon page theme
- ► Using VLANs on the NetScaler Gateway
- ► Checking the NetScaler Gateway's performance statistics
- ► Recovering the password for the NetScaler Gateway
- ► Saving, restoring, and comparing the NetScaler Gateway configurations

Introduction

A XenApp infrastructure consists of many components to ensure that users can start published desktops or applications. Each Citrix component within the XenApp infrastructure is especially designed to support the entire chain that delivers Windows applications and desktops to the end user. To extend the delivery of the applications and desktops to mobile users and support home workers, the NetScaler appliance can be used to enable remote access to the corporate network resources.

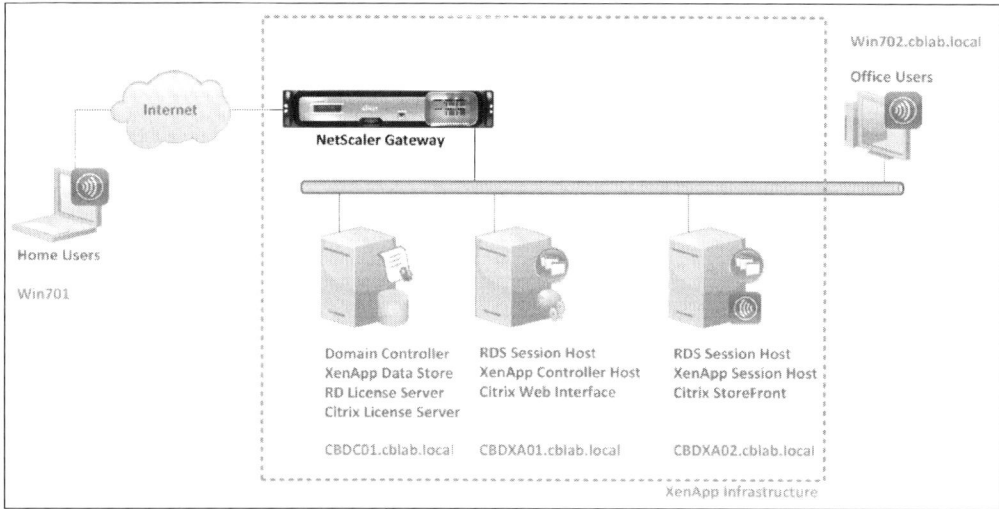

The **Citrix NetScaler** (**CNS**) is not just one product, but an entire product line that offers different NetScaler types and editions, such as the NetScaler Gateway for secure remote access, the NetScaler Branch Repeater for WAN optimization, and the NetScaler AppFirewall for secure access to web applications and shielding websites from malicious attacks. Explaining all the possibilities and what the different NetScalers will offer would require a book of its own.

This chapter will only focus on the NetScaler Gateway functionality that supports remote access to Windows applications and desktops that are published by Citrix XenApp.

All configuration options for this book are tested on a **Citrix NetScaler Gateway** (**CNG**) VPX appliance (Version 10.1 build 118.7.nc) with a NetScaler Gateway Enterprise 90 days evaluation license. The certificates used in the lab environment are based on test certificates, created during setup or by testing tools. Some of the instructions in the following recipes may vary for production environments and different NetScaler Gateway versions.

Licensing the Citrix® NetScaler Gateway Enterprise Edition

This recipe will show you how to license the Citrix NetScaler Gateway Enterprise Edition.

Getting ready

Before assigning a license to the NetScaler Gateway appliance, you are required to enter the basic network information at the console after the first boot of the appliance. When the NetScaler appliance is first started, an IPv4 address must be provided for the NetScaler IP address and the corresponding subnet mask and gateway.

To assign a license to the NetScaler Gateway, a license file must be acquired at the MyCitrix website. When allocating the license to the appliance, the hostname of the appliance must be entered. This hostname will be added to the license file before it can be downloaded.

By default, the hostname for most NetScaler appliances consists of the MAC address of the first **Network Interface Card** (**NIC**), also known as **eth0**. With the NetScaler Gateway, you can enter a name as the hostname.

Make sure the hostname in the license file is identical to the hostname entered during the first configuration of the NetScaler Gateway. The hostname is also case sensitive.

Log on to the MyCitrix site to assign and download the license file for the NetScaler Gateway.

How to do it...

To configure the license for the NetScaler Gateway, perform the following steps:

1. Log on to the Citrix NetScaler Gateway by going to the NetScaler IP address in your Internet browser.

2. Enter the default username and password to log in to the appliance for the first time, as shown in the following screenshot:

3. Select **NetScaler Gateway** as **Deployment Type** and click on **Login**.

 When you log in for the first time, you are asked to provide the basic system configuration information.

4. Provide at least the following information:

    ❑ **NetScaler IP Address (NSIP)**

    ❑ **Subnet IP Address (SNIP)**

    ❑ Netmask and Time Zone

 The different IP addresses that can be configured on the NetScaler are explained in the *How it works* section of this recipe.

5. Enter the optional hostname and DNS (IP Address) information.

6. Select to change the administrator password.

 If you assigned a hostname to the license file, you will need to provide the same hostname (case sensitive) at this step.

7. Click on **Continue** to proceed to the next step of your NetScaler Gateway setup.

8. Check the provided information from the previous step, and click on **Browse** to upload your license file to the appliance.

9. Click on **Continue** when the license file is uploaded successfully.

10. Click on **Done** to finish the setup.

11. Click on **Yes** to confirm the reboot.

The system will reboot. You can log in when the appliance is rebooted.

How it works...

While configuring a NetScaler appliance for the first time, it can be overwhelming to see the different menu options that are available and the different IP address types that are referred to in the available documentation. A NetScaler appliance requires different IP address types to be configured for the different functions it supports. They are as follows:

IP-address type	Explanation
NetScaler IP	This is the management IP address of the NetScaler. This is the IPv4 address that is entered when first configuring the NetScaler and the one used to connect to the management console. Only one NSIP can be configured.
Mapped IP (MIP)	This is the default Subnet IP address used for server-side (backend) connections. Only one MIP address can be configured.
Subnet IP	This is used for multisubnet scenarios to create IP addresses for each subnet that the NetScaler will communicate with to ensure that a route to each subnet is automatically created. More than one SNIP address can be configured. Configuring an SNIP address is optional.
Virtual IP (VIP)	This is assigned to the virtual servers that are created on the NetScaler appliance for Access Gateway, load balancing, or content switching.

A graphical overview of a NetScaler configuration with different subnets and the corresponding NetScaler IP addresses is presented in the following diagram:

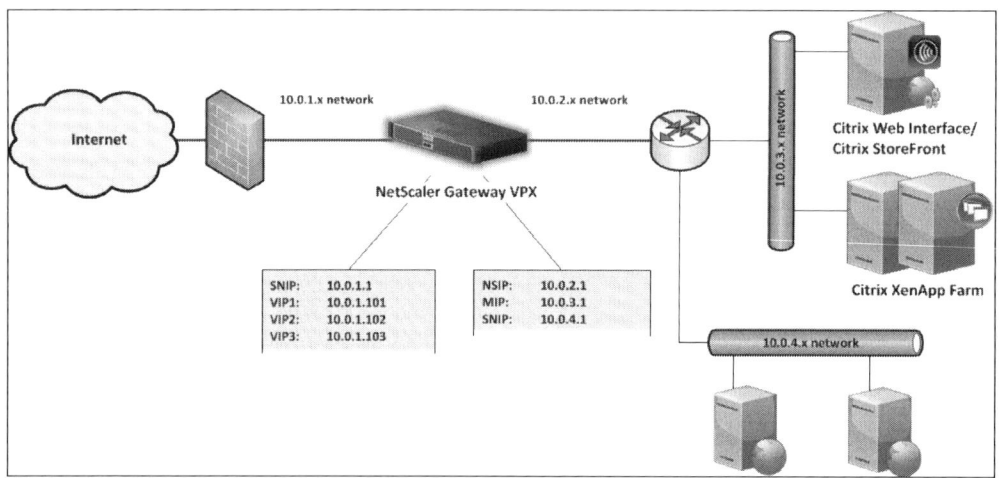

The NetScaler is configured with a NetScaler IP address of **10.0.2.1** that can be used to connect to the management console by browsing `https://10.0.2.1`.

Communications between the XenApp Farm and NetScaler are carried out with the Mapped IP address of **10.0.3.1**, and for communications with the web servers in the second subnet, a Subnet IP address is configured for the **10.0.4.x** subnet. For each connection from the Internet to the internal network, a virtual server is configured with a unique IP address, a so-called Virtual IP address.

Configuring the Citrix® Web Interface with a NetScaler Gateway authentication point

The appliance with the Access Gateway functionality, which was previously known as the Citrix Access Gateway, is now rebranded as the NetScaler Gateway to make it a part of the NetScaler product line.

To ensure that all user authentications are performed at the NetScaler Gateway, the web interface needs to be configured with an Access Gateway authentication point. This authentication point configuration is not described in *Chapter 3, Citrix® Web Interface*, which focused on the **Citrix Web Interface** (**CWI**), and therefore it will be explained prior to the NetScaler Gateway configuration in this chapter.

This recipe will show you how to configure a XenApp website on the Citrix® Web Interface with an Access Gateway authentication point.

How to do it...

To create a XenApp website with an Access Gateway authentication point, perform the following steps:

1. Open the Citrix Web Interface Management console (by navigating to **Start | All Programs | Citrix | Management Consoles | Citrix Web Interface Management**).

2. Select **XenApp Web Sites** from the left pane.

3. Click on **Create Site** in the **Action** pane.

4. Specify the IIS Location settings:

   - ❑ **IIS site**: Default website (default)

   - ❑ **Path**: /Citrix/XenAppNG

   - ❑ **Name**: XenAppNG

   - ❑ **Set as default page for the IIS site**: unselected

5. Click on **Next**.

6. Select **At Access Gateway** as the point of authentication and click on **Next**.

7. Specify the following Access Gateway settings:

   - ❑ **Authentication service URL**: https://<servername>:<port>/ CitrixAuthService/AuthService.asmx

   - ❑ The authentication options are as follows:

     - ❑ **Explicit**: selected

     - ❑ **Prompt users for password**: unselected

     - ❑ **Smart card**: unselected

The authentication service URL connects to the virtual server that is configured as the Access Gateway on the NetScaler. By assigning a certificate to the virtual server, the certificate FQDN is bound to the VIP at the NetScaler. You can enter the certificate FQDN or VIP as the servername in the authentication service URL.

8. Click on **Next**.

9. Check the summary information and click on **Next**.

10. Ensure **Configure this site now** is selected and click on **Next**.

11. Specify the following server Farm settings:

    - ❑ **Farm name**: <XenAppFarmName>

    - ❑ **Servers**: <XenAppControllerHosts>

- ❑ **XML Service Port**: `<XMLport>`
- ❑ **Transport type**: `HTTP` (or `HTTPS`)

12. Click on **Next**.

13. Specify **Logon Screen Appearance (Minimal or Full)** and click on **Next**.

14. Select the **Published Resource Type** as **Online** and click on **Next**.

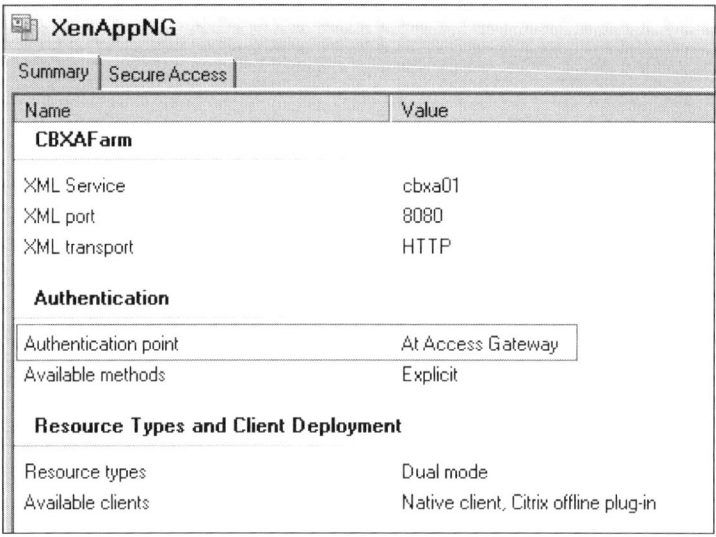

15. Check the summary information and click on **Finish**.

Configuring the NetScaler Gateway for the Citrix® Web Interface

This recipe will show you how to configure the Citrix NetScaler Gateway to connect to the Citrix Web Interface and the XenApp website that was created in the previous recipe.

Getting ready

To configure the NetScaler Gateway for working with the Citrix Web Interface, it must be installed and configured with a XenApp website in your XenApp infrastructure. You can refer to *Chapter 3, Citrix Web Interface*, for recipes on installing and configuring the Citrix Web Interface.

For the NetScaler and Citrix Web Interface to communicate correctly, the XenApp website must be configured to authenticate the Access Gateway. This is explained in the previous recipe.

How to do it...

After configuring the basic system settings and uploading the license file, the next logon to the NetScaler Gateway will start the NetScaler Gateway configuration wizard.

Perform the following steps to configure the NetScaler Gateway to work with the Citrix Web Interface:

1. Click on **Get Started**.

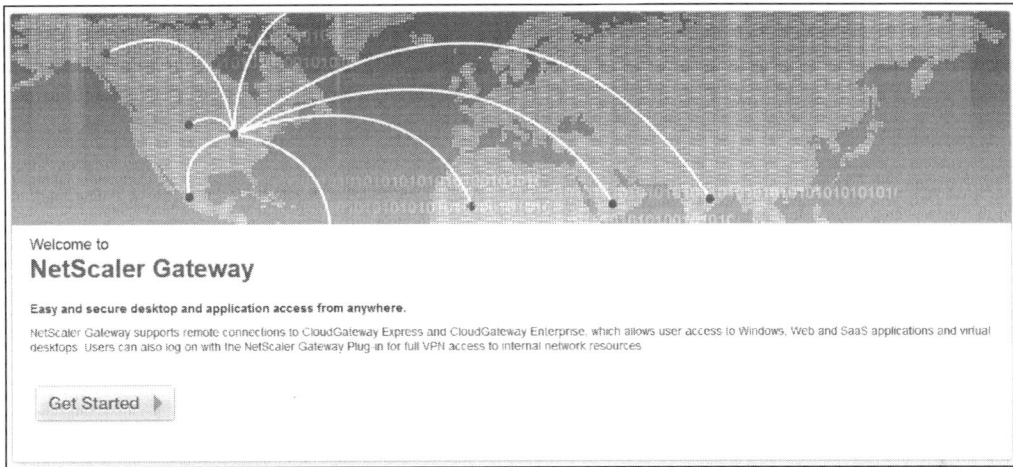

2. Enter the following virtual server information in the **NetScaler Gateway Settings** screen:
   - **Name**: `<VirtualServerName>`
   - **IP-address**: `<VIP>`
   - **Port**: `443` (default)
   - **Redirect request from port 80 to secure port**: unselected

3. Click on **Continue**.

4. Make a certificate selection (choose either **Install** or **Use Test Certificate**) and provide the following certificate information:
   - **Certificate**: Use Test Certificate
   - **Certificate FQDN**: `<certificateFQDN>`

 A self-created test certificate was used in the lab environment. The certificate's FQDN must contain the URL that will be used to connect to the virtual server (both externally and internally).

5. Click on **Continue**.

6. Configure **Authentication Settings** as follows:

   ❏ **Primary Authentication**: LDAP (configure new)

   ❏ **IP-address**: <DomainControllerIP>

   ❏ **Port**: 389 (default)

   ❏ **Time out (seconds)**: 3 (default)

   ❏ **Base DN**: < distinguishedNameUsersOU>

   ❏ **Admin Base DN**: < distinguishedNameAdminAccount>

   ❏ **Server Logon Name Attribute**: sAMAccountName

   ❏ **Password**: <Password>

   ❏ **Secondary Authentication**: None

7. Click on **Continue**.

8. Configure **Enterprise Store Settings** as follows:

   ❏ **XenApp/XenDesktop**: selected

   ❏ **Deployment Type**: Web Interface

   ❏ **XenApp Site URL**: http://<FQDN-CWI>/Citrix/XenApp

   ❏ **XenApp Services Site URL**: http://<FQDN-CWI>/Citrix/PNAgent

   ❏ **Single Sign-on Domain**: <Domain-NetBIOS>

   ❏ **STA URL**: http://<FQDN-XMLService>:<XMLport>

9. Click on **Done**.

The Gateway will automatically be configured with all the required settings to connect the Citrix NetScaler Gateway with the Citrix Web Interface. After the configuration, you will be redirected to the **Home** tab of the NetScaler Management Console.

There's more...

To get the entire chain of components working in the lab environment, additional settings were configured on both the NetScaler Gateway and the Citrix Web Interface to make the logons work with the self-created test certificate.

The additional NetScaler Gateway configurations were as follows:

> ▶ Changed the Subnet IP address for the internal subnet on the NetScaler to a MIP address as advised by the Citrix's Knowledge Center article at `http://support.citrix.com/article/CTX127622`.

> ▶ Added a Dummy VIP for internal use with the same test certificate and LDAP authentication configured in it. This ensures that the CWI can communicate the session tickets to the NetScaler Gateway.

The additional configurations on the internal subnet were as follows:

> ▶ Added a host (AAA) entry on the internal DNS with the FQDN of the NetScaler virtual server. The host record was mapped to the internal VIP of the NetScaler Gateway.

> ▶ Added the test certificate to the CWI (at **Local Computer | physical store | Trusted Root CA**) to support successful communications between the CWI and NetScaler internal VIP.

> ▶ Added the test certificate to the client device (at **Registry | Trusted Root CA**).

Configuring the NetScaler Gateway for Citrix® StoreFront (CSF)

This recipe will show you how to configure the Citrix NetScaler Gateway for using it with CSF to support remote access to Windows published applications and desktops on the corporate network.

Getting ready

To configure remote access with the Citrix NetScaler Gateway and StoreFront, both components need to be set up correctly. The required configuration for Citrix StoreFront can be found in *Chapter 4, Citrix StoreFront*. This recipe assumes that you have followed the provided steps to configure StoreFront accordingly.

How to do it...

Perform the following steps to configure the NetScaler Gateway to work with Citrix StoreFront:

1. Log in to the NetScaler Gateway with the deployment type set as the NetScaler Gateway.

2. Click on the **Home** tab.

3. Click on **+Create New NetScaler Gateway**.

4. Enter the following virtual server information in the **NetScaler Gateway Settings** screen:

    ❑ **Name**: <VirtualServerName>

    ❑ **IP-address**: <VIP>

    ❑ **Port**: 443 (default)

    ❑ **Redirect request from port 80 to secure port**: selected

    ❑ **Gateway FQDN**: <FQDN-VIP>

> The selected redirect request is configured using a load balancing virtual server configuration on NetScaler. This feature is not licensed for the NetScaler Gateway. Therefore, the virtual server is shown with a down state. The redirected URL (advanced setting), however, is functioning and the HTTP requests are redirected to the HTTPS Gateway virtual server.

5. Click on **Continue**.

6. Make a certificate selection (choose either **Install** or **Use Test Certificate**) and provide the certificate information:

    ❑ **Certificate**: Use Test Certificate

    ❑ **Certificate FQDN**: <certificateFQDN>

7. Click on **Continue**.

8. Configure **Authentication Settings** as follows:

    ❑ **Primary Authentication**: LDAP (Configure New)

    ❑ **IP-address**: <DomainControllerIP>

    ❑ **Port**: 389 (default)

    ❑ **Time out (seconds)**: 3 (default)

    ❑ **Base DN**: <distinguishedNameUsersOU>

    ❑ **Admin Base DN**: <distinguishedNameAdminAccount>

    ❑ **Server Logon Name Attribute**: sAMAccountName

    ❑ **Password**: <Password>

    ❑ **Secondary Authentication**: None

9. Click on **Continue**.

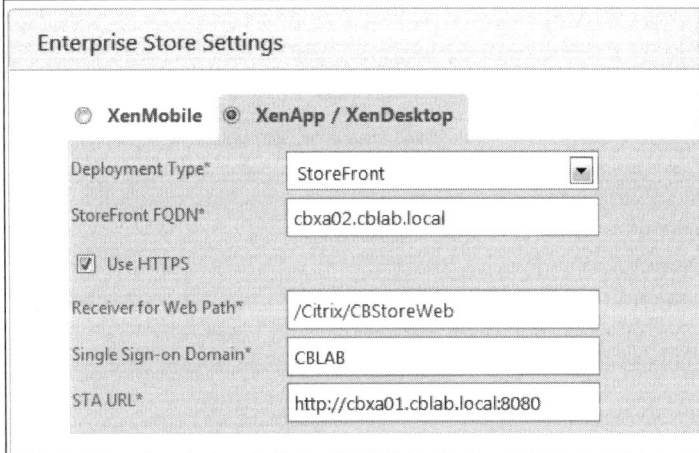

10. Configure **Enterprise Store Settings**:

- [ ] **XenApp/XenDesktop**: selected
- [ ] **Deployment Type**: **StoreFront**
- [ ] **StoreFront FQDN**: <FQDN-CSF>
- [ ] **Use HTTPS**: selected

When selecting HTTPS, a valid certificate must be installed and bound on the **Internet Information Service** (**IIS**), that is running StoreFront. By default, HTTPS is configured for the base URL of StoreFront.

For the lab environment, only self-created certificates were used and StoreFront was configured with a HTTP base URL.

- [ ] **Receiver for Web Path**: /Citrix/StoreWeb (default)
- [ ] **Single Sign-on Domain**: <DomainNetBIOS>
- [ ] **STA URL**: http://<FQDNControllerHost>:<XMLPort>

11. Click on **Done**.

The Gateway will be automatically configured with all the required settings to connect the Citrix NetScaler Gateway with StoreFront. After the configuration, you are redirected to the **Home** tab.

There's more...

To get the entire chain of components working in the lab environment, additional settings were required on both the NetScaler Gateway and StoreFront to make the logons work with the test certificate.

The additional NetScaler Gateway configurations were as follows:

> ▶ Changed the SNIP address for the internal subnet on the NetScaler to an MIP address as advised by the Citrix Knowledge Center article at `http://support.citrix.com/article/CTX127622`.

> ▶ Added a dummy VIP for internal use with the same test certificate and LDAP authentication configured in it. This ensures that StoreFront can communicate the session tickets with the NetScaler.

The additional configurations on the internal subnet were as follows:

> ▶ Added a host (AAA) entry on the internal DNS for FQDN of the NetScaler virtual Server. The host record was mapped to the internal VIP of the NetScaler.

> ▶ Added the test certificate to the StoreFront server (at **Local Computer | physical store | Trusted Root CA**) to support successful communications between StoreFront and the NetScaler internal VIP.

> ▶ Added the test certificate to the client device (at to **Registry | Trusted Root CA**).

Changing the NetScaler Gateway's logon page theme

This recipe will show you how to change the default theme for the logon page of the Citrix NetScaler Gateway to match the same theme that is used by CSF. In this way, the user who logs in is presented with a single consistent look and feel for the remote access and internal access portal.

How to do it...

To change the default theme for the NetScaler Gateway logon page, perform the following steps:

1. Log in to the NetScaler Gateway with the deployment type set as the NetScaler Gateway.
2. Click on the **Configuration** tab.
3. Navigate to **NetScaler Gateway | Global Settings** in the left-hand side pane.
4. Click on **Change global settings** under the **Settings** section in the right-hand side pane.

5. Click on the **Client Experience** tab.

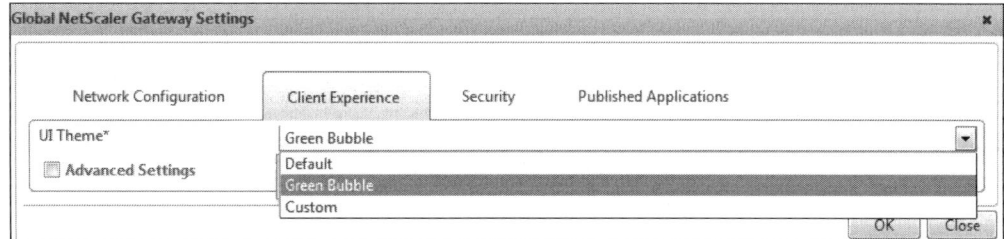

6. Find **UI Theme** and change the setting to **Green Bubble** present in the select box.

7. Click on **OK** to apply the changes.

Using VLANs on the NetScaler Gateway

The Citrix NetScaler Gateway uses the configured **Mapped IP** (**MIP**) and Subnet IP addresses to build its own routing table and determine the different IP subnets that are connected to each network interface of the NetScaler. Each network interface of the NetScaler can be connected to multiple IP subnets.

Assigning VLAN tags directly to the interfaces might prevent the NetScaler from accessing one or more subnets if the VLAN tags are not configured correctly. It is advisable to assign each VLAN to an individually configured **Virtual IP** (**VIP**) address or SNIP address on the NetScaler.

This recipe will show you how to assign VLANs to the configured IP addresses on the CNG.

How to do it...

To assign VLAN IDs to the NetScaler Gateway IP bindings, perform the following steps:

1. Log in to the NetScaler Management Console using the deployment type as the NetScaler Gateway.

2. Click on the **Configuration** tab.

3. Navigate to **System | Network | VLANs**.

4. Click on **Add** and enter the following information:

    ❏   **VLAN ID**: <VLAN-number>

    ❏   **Alias Name**: <VLAN-description>

    ❏   **IPv6 Dynamic Routing**: unselected

    ❏   **IP Binding**: Select the appropriate VIP or SNIP

5. Click on **Create** to finalize the configuration.

Checking the NetScaler Gateway's performance statistics

This recipe will give you a quick rundown on the different statistics and logs that can be viewed on the NetScaler Gateway web interface for diagnostic and troubleshooting activities. It is by no means a complete manual on troubleshooting the NetScaler Gateway as this is beyond the scope of this book.

How to do it...

The NetScaler Management Console offers different sections with statistics and event logs reflecting the performance of the NetScaler Gateway. Here are the instructions for using some of the common statistics that you can check.

The built-in dashboard offers a selection of customizable real-time statistics on the NetScaler performance as well as the latest system log entries. Perform the following steps to check out the current performance statistics on the dashboard:

1. Log in to the NetScaler Management Console using the deployment type as the NetScaler Gateway.

2. Click on the **Dashboard** tab.

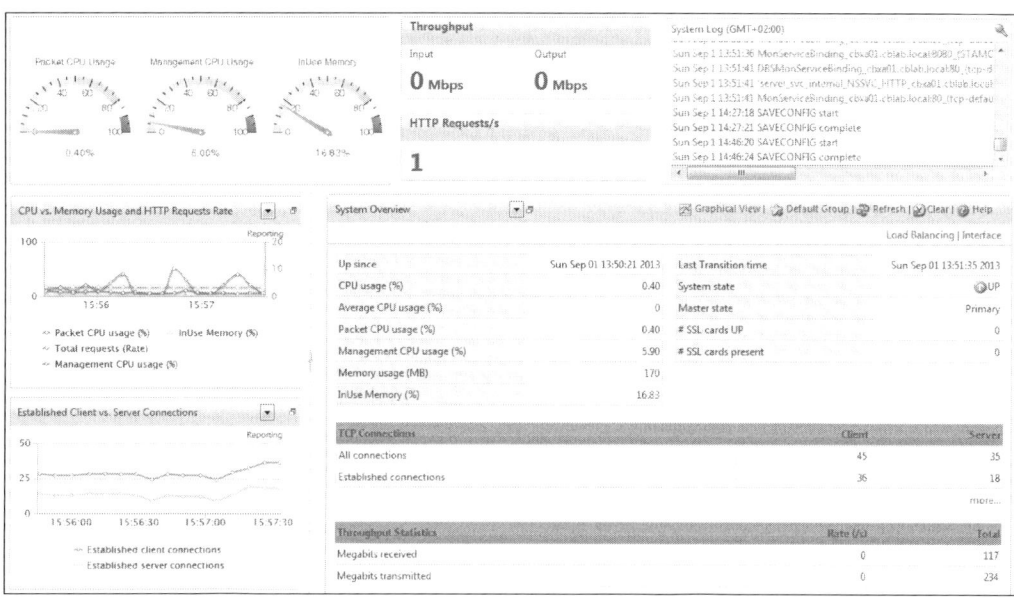

3. Check the current statistics for CPU usage, memory usage, and HTTP requests.

You can use built-in reports to monitor the system, network, SSL, and NetScaler Gateway statistics by performing the following steps:

1. Log in to the NetScaler Management Console using the deployment type as the NetScaler Gateway.

2. Click on the **Reporting** tab.

3. Navigate to **Built-in Reports | System**. Click on **CPU** and **Memory Usage** and **HTTP Requests** in the left pane.

4. The statistics will be shown in the right pane.

To check the current ICA connections hosted by the NetScaler, perform the following steps:

1. Log in to the NetScaler Management Console with the deployment type set as the NetScaler Gateway.

2. Click on the **Configuration** tab.

3. Select **NetScaler Gateway** on the left pane.

4. Click on **ICA Connections** under the **Monitor Connections** section of the right pane.

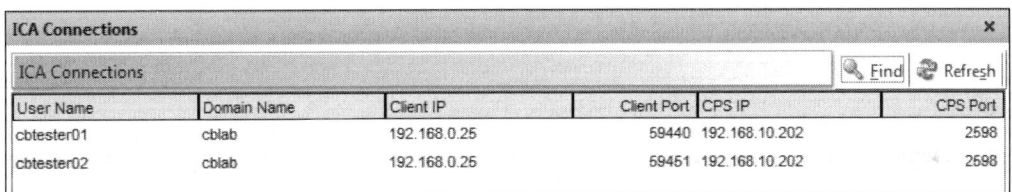

You can find different diagnostic tools and event logs to manage and troubleshoot the NetScaler Gateway by performing the following steps:

1. Log in to the NetScaler Management Console with the deployment type set as the NetScaler Gateway.

2. Click on the **Configuration** tab.

3. Navigate to **System | Diagnostics** in the left pane.

4. Select **Utility**, **Log**, or **Configuration** from the right-hand side pane.

Recovering the password for the NetScaler Gateway

This recipe will show you how to recover a password in case you are locked out of the Citrix NetScaler Gateway (virtual) appliance.

How to do it...

To recover the password for the NetScaler Gateway, perform the following steps:

1. Open the NetScaler Gateway console either using a console cable for the physical appliance or by opening the console on the Hypervisor for the virtual appliance.

2. Restart the NetScaler Gateway and check for the message shown in the following screenshot:

```
Press [Ctrl-C] for command prompt, or any other key to boot immediately.
Booting [/ns-10.1-118.7] in 2 seconds...
```

3. Press *Ctrl + C* to start a command prompt.

4. Start the kernel on a single user mode by entering the following command:
   ```
   boot -s
   ```

5. Press *Enter* when the message shown in the following screenshot appears:

```
Trying to mount root from ufs:/dev/md0c
start_init: trying /sbin/init
Enter full pathname of shell or RETURN for /bin/sh:
```

6. Check disk consistency with the following command:
   ```
   /sbin/fsck /dev/ad0s1a
   ```

7. Display the mounted partitions with the following command:
   ```
   df
   ```

8. Mount the flash drive with the following command:
   ```
   /sbin/mount /dev/ad0s1a /flash
   ```

9. Change to the `nsconfig` directory with the following command:
   ```
   cd /flash/nsconfig
   ```

10. Create a new configuration file with the following command:
    ```
    grep -v "set system user nsroot" ns.conf > new.conf
    ```

11. Create a backup of the existing file with the following command:
    ```
    mv ns.conf old.ns.conf
    mv new.conf ns.conf
    ```

12. Restart the system with the following command:

```
reboot
```

```
Trying to mount root from ufs:/dev/md0c
start_init: trying /sbin/init
Enter full pathname of shell or RETURN for /bin/sh:
\u@/sbin/fsck /dev/ad0s1a
** /dev/ad0s1a
** Last Mounted on /flash
** Phase 1 - Check Blocks and Sizes
** Phase 2 - Check Pathnames
** Phase 3 - Check Connectivity
** Phase 4 - Check Reference Counts
** Phase 5 - Check Cyl groups
104 files, 55937 used, 685382 free (126 frags, 85657 blocks, 0.0% fragmentation)

\u@df
Filesystem 1K-blocks    Used Avail Capacity  Mounted on
/dev/md0c      278510 249180 23760      91%   /
devfs               1      1     0     100%   /dev
\u@/sbin/mount /dev/ad0s1a /flash
\u@cd /flash/nsconfig
\u@grep -v "set system user nsroot" ns.conf > new.conf
\u@
\u@mv ns.conf old.ns.conf
\u@mv new.conf ns.conf
\u@reboot
```

13. You can log in to the appliance with the default `nsroot` credentials after the reboot.

> To change the password after you have logged in, run the
> following command:
>
> `set system user nsroot <password>`

Saving, restoring, and comparing the NetScaler Gateway configurations

This recipe will show you how to save, restore, and compare your Citrix NetScaler Gateway configurations.

How to do it...

The changes that are made to the configuration of the NetScaler Gateway are made to the running configuration that is the active configuration in use while the NetScaler Gateway is up and running. To ensure that the running configuration is preserved and loaded on the next boot of the NetScaler, the configuration must be saved. The running configuration is discarded when the NetScaler shuts down or reboots. While booting, the NetScaler Gateway loads the saved configuration as the current running configuration.

To save your running configuration and make it persistent for NetScaler reboots, perform the following steps:

1. Log in to the NetScaler Management Console with the deployment type set as the NetScaler Gateway.
2. Click on the **Configuration** tab.
3. Select **System** on the left pane.

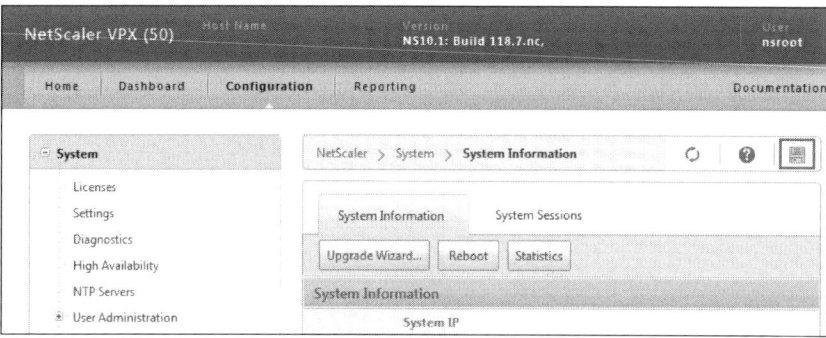

4. Click on the Save icon on the top-right pane.
5. Click on **Yes** in the pop up to confirm the save operation.

To export a saved or running NetScaler Gateway configuration, perform the following steps:

1. Log in to the NetScaler Management Console using the deployment type as the NetScaler Gateway.
2. Click on the **Configuration** tab.
3. Navigate to **System | Diagnostics** on the left pane.
4. Click on **Saved Configuration** or **Running Configuration** in the **View Configuration** section on the right pane.

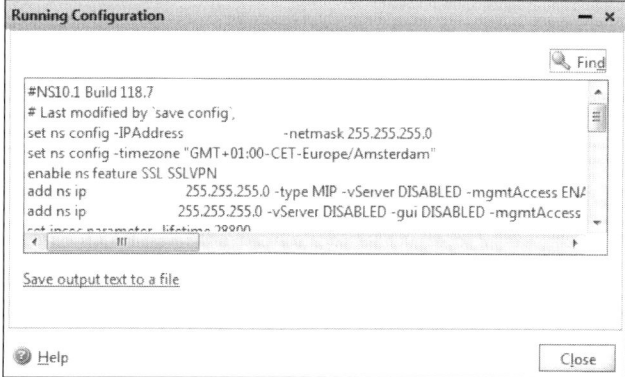

5. Click on **Save output text to a file**.

6. Browse to a folder on your computer, enter a filename, and click on **Save**.

7. Click on **Close**.

To compare the differences between a running and saved configuration, perform the following steps:

1. Log in to the NetScaler Management Console with the deployment type set as the NetScaler Gateway.

2. Click on the **Configuration** tab.

3. Navigate to **System | Diagnostics** on the left pane.

4. Click on **Saved Configuration** and **Running Configuration** present in the **View Configuration** section on the right pane to get an overview of the differences between both the configurations.

5. Click on **Close**.

To restore a previously exported configuration, perform the following steps:

1. Log in to the NetScaler Management Console with the deployment type set as the NetScaler Gateway.

2. Click on the **Configuration** tab.

3. Navigate to **System | Diagnostics** on the left pane.

4. Click on **Clear configuration** in the **Maintenance** section on the right-hand side pane if you want to clear the saved and running configuration of the NetScaler Gateway.

5. Click on **Batch Configuration** in the **Utilities** section on the right-hand side pane.

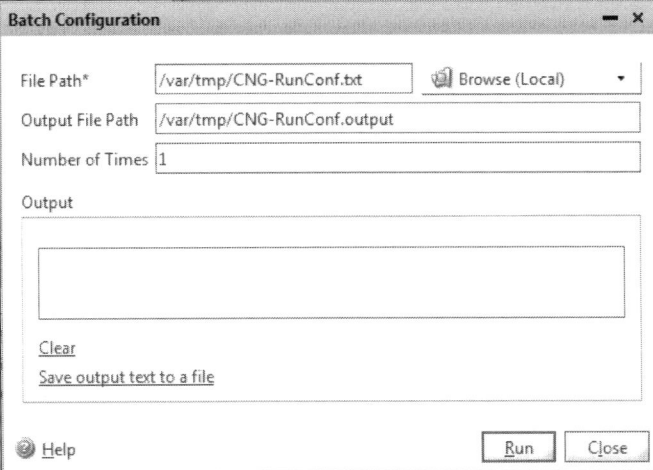

6. Browse to the location of a previously saved file.

7. Click on **Run** to apply the exported configuration.

 Make sure that you save the imported configuration if you want to preserve the settings even when the NetScaler is rebooted. The configuration is only loaded automatically as the running configuration and not as the saved configuration.

8. Click on **Close**.

 The previously described methods are by no means a replacement for any backup and restore procedures for the NetScaler. You can read about these procedures at Citrix's eDocs: `http://support.citrix.com/proddocs/topic/ns-system-10-1-map/ns-system-backup1-tsk.html`.

6

XenApp® Management

In this chapter, we will cover the following topics:

- ▸ Scripting a command-line installation and configuration of the Citrix® XenApp® server
- ▸ Creating custom administrative roles for delegated management
- ▸ Sending a message to one or more logged on XenApp® users
- ▸ Creating a custom Load Evaluator
- ▸ Using Worker Groups to cluster XenApp® servers and configurations
- ▸ Configuring the ICA Listener
- ▸ Configuring the HDX Mediastream Flash Redirection
- ▸ Configuring advanced printing settings
- ▸ Working with print drivers on XenApp® servers
- ▸ Logging administrative changes to a XenApp® Farm
- ▸ Enabling the Windows 7 look and feel desktop theme
- ▸ Implementing the Citrix XenApp® Mobility Pack

Introduction

A XenApp infrastructure consists of many components to ensure that users can start published desktops or applications. Each Citrix component within the XenApp infrastructure is especially designed to support the entire chain that delivers Windows applications and desktops to the end user.

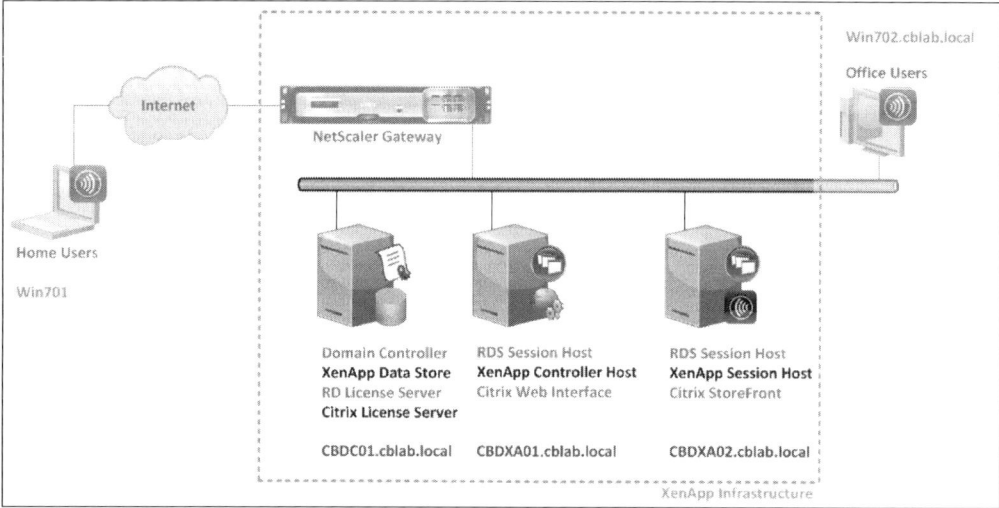

The core of the XenApp infrastructure consists of the XenApp Farm, a collection of XenApp Controller Hosts and Session Hosts that publish Windows desktops and applications to end users based on Microsoft's Remote Desktop Services. The next four chapters of this cookbook will concentrate on **Citrix XenApp** (**CXA**), and provide different recipes for managing, monitoring, reporting, and troubleshooting a XenApp Farm as well as implementing XenApp policies to configure the user experience and session settings.

This chapter will focus on the management of the XenApp Farm and servers.

Scripting a command-line installation and configuration of the Citrix® XenApp® server

This recipe will show you how to build an unattended installation of the CXA Server and configure it. It allows you to create an unattended installation sequence for your XenApp infrastructure deployment.

Getting ready

While using a command-line installation for XenApp, all the prerequisites must be installed on the server.

The prerequisites for **XenApp** are as follows:

- .NET Framework 3.5 SP1
- Windows Server Remote Desktop Services role
- Windows Application Server role
- Microsoft Visual C++ 2005 SP1 redistributable (x64)
- Microsoft Visual C++ 2008 SP1 redistributable (x64)
- IIS role services:
    - Common HTTP Features > Default Document
    - Application Development > ASP.NET, ISAPI Extensions, ISAPI Filters
    - Security > Windows Authentication, Request Filtering

The prerequisites for **AppCenter** (**Management Console**) are as follows:

- Microsoft Windows Group Policy Management Console
- Microsoft Visual C++ 2005 SP1 redistributable (x86)
- Microsoft Visual C++ 2008 SP1 redistributable (x86)
- Microsoft Primary Interoperability Assemblies 2005

The prerequisites for **Enhanced Desktop Experience** are as follows:

- XPS Viewer
- Desktop Experience

You can use the following PowerShell script to install the prerequisites on a Windows 2008 R2 Server:

```
# Turn off Windows Firewall
netsh advfirewall set allprofiles state off
# Import the ServerManager Module
Import-Module ServerManager
# Install .NET Framework 3.5.1
Add-WindowsFeature -Name AS-NET-Framework -LogPath XAPrereqs.log -Restart
# Install RDS Session Host role (reboot required)
Add-WindowsFeature -Name RDS-RD-Server -LogPath XAPrereqs.log -Restart
# Install Windows Application Server role
```

```
Add-WindowsFeature -Name Application-Server -LogPath XAPrereqs.log
-Restart
```

`# Install Microsoft Visual C++ 2005 SP1 Redistributable (x64)`

`D:\Support\vcredist\vc80_vcredist_x64.exe /Q`

`# Install Microsoft Visual C++ 2008 SP1 Redistributable (x64)`

`D:\Support\vcredist\vc90_vcredist_x64.exe /q /l XAPrereqs.log`

`# Install Microsoft required IIS role services`

```
Add-WindowsFeature -Name Web-Default-Doc,Web-Asp-Net,Web-ISAPI-Ext,Web-
ISAPI-Filter,Web-Windows-Auth,Web-Filtering,Web-Mgmt-Compat -LogPath
XAPrereqs.log -Restart
```

`# Install additional components for AppCenter (mgmt console)`

`# Install Windows Group Policy Management Console`

`Add-WindowsFeature -Name GPMC -LogPath XAPrereqs.log -Restart`

`# Install Microsoft Visual C++ 2005 SP1 Redistributable (x86)`

`D:\Support\vcredist\vc80_vcredist_x86.exe /Q`

`# Install Microsoft Visual C++ 2008 SP1 Redistributable (x86)`

`D:\Support\vcredist\vc90_vcredist_x86.exe /q /l XAPrereqs.log`

`# Install Microsoft Primary Interoperability Assemblies 2005`

`D:\Support\vcredist\vs90_piaredist.exe /q`

`# Install additional components for Enhanced Desktop Experience (reboot required)`

```
Add-WindowsFeature -Name Desktop-Experience,XPS-Viewer -LogPath
XAPrereqs.log -Restart
```

 A wizard-based installation will automatically install the prerequisites.

While installing the prerequisites manually, use the software on the installation media so that all the prerequisites will be recognized by the XenApp installer.

How to do it...

With Citrix XenApp 6.5, the installation and configuration of the Citrix XenApp server are separate commands. Installing Citrix XenApp does not determine the server role it will have in the XenApp Farm. The configuration command is run separately and configures the XenApp server to either be a Controller Host or a Session Host in the Farm. Both commands will be handled in this recipe.

To install the Citrix XenApp software on a server using a command-line, follow these steps:

1. Open a command prompt in the **Run as administrator** mode.

2. Run the following command line:

```
XenAppSetupConsole.exe /install:XenApp /exclude:XA_IISIntegration
/Platinum /logfile:XAinstall.log
```

 XenAppSetupConsole.exe can be found on the installation media for Citrix XenApp 6.5 in the \XenApp Server Setup\bin directory.

To configure Citrix XenApp to join an existing XenApp Farm as a Session Host, follow these steps:

1. Open a **Command Prompt** in the **Run As Administrator** mode.

2. Run the following command line:

```
XenAppConfigConsole.exe /ExecutionMode:Join /ImaWorkerMode:True /
DsnFile:<dsnfile> /AuthenticationType:Windows /OdbcUserName:<name>
/OdbcPassword:<password> /CustomXmlServicePort:8080 /AddAnonymousU
sersToRemoteDesktopUserGroup:False /AddUsersGroupToRemoteDesktopUs
erGroup:False /LogFilename:XAconfig.log
```

 The XenAppConfigConsole.exe file can be found in the XenApp installation directory at C:\Program Files (x86)\Citrix\ XenApp\ServerConfig.

A reboot of the server is required to ensure that all the Citrix XenApp services are started correctly and the server is joined to the Farm.

 While joining a server to an existing Farm, you can use the DSN file from an existing XenApp server in the Farm. By default, the mf20.dsn file used by the server can be found at C:\Program Files (x86)\Citrix\ Independent Management Architecture\mf20.dsn.

How it works...

The installation and configuration of Citrix XenApp consists of a separate command-line instruction.

To install the Citrix XenApp software on the Windows Server, the following command can be used:

```
XenAppSetupConsole.exe /install:<items> /exclude:<exclusions> /<edition>
INSTALLDIR="<installdir>" ONLINE_PLUGIN_INSTALLDIR="<plugininstalldir>" /
logfile:<logfile>
```

This command uses the following parameters:

- ▶ `/install`: This provides a comma-separated list of the XenApp items that need to be installed. With no combined server roles, XenApp is the only required item to be installed. It will automatically install the Citrix Console (AppCenter), Receiver for Windows, Citrix Offline plugin, and Windows Desktop Experience Integration.

- ▶ `/exclude`: This provides a comma-separated list of components that need to be excluded from this installation. The valid exclusions are `XA_Console`, `XA_IISIntegration`, and `XenAppEnhancedDesktopExperience`.

- ▶ `/<edition>`: This specifies the XenApp edition. The valid values are Platinum, Enterprise, and Advanced. By default, Platinum is installed.

- ▶ `INSTALLDIR`: This is the installation directory. By default, XenApp is installed in `C:\Program Files (x86)\Citrix`.

- ▶ `ONLINE_PLUGIN_INSTALLDIR`: This is the installation directory for the Citrix Receiver. By default, the Receiver is installed in `C:\Program Files (x86)\Citrix\ICA Client`.

- ▶ `/logfile`: This provides the location for the logfile. By default, the logfile is created in `C:\Windows\Temp`.

 You can find `XenAppSetupConsole.exe` in the `XenApp Server Setup\bin` folder on the installation media.

To configure a XenApp server, run the `XenAppConfigConsole.exe` command from `C:\Program Files (x86)\Citrix\XenApp\ServerConfig`. It is important to distinguish between a new Farm installation performed by the first XenApp server configuration and an existing XenApp Farm to which your XenApp server can be joined. It is also important to specify whether a XenApp server will function as a Controller Host (default), making it a data collector or XML broker or as a Session Host (set the `ImaWorkMode` parameter to `True`), thus enabling it to only host sessions.

To create a new XenApp Farm using an SQL Server database, run the following command:

```
XenAppConfigConsole.exe /ExecutionMode:Create /FarmName:<name> /CitrixAd
ministratorAccount:<admin> /ZoneName:<zone> /AddLocalAdmin:False|True /
DsnFile:<dsnfile> /AuthenticationType:Windows|Sql /OdbcUserName:<name> /
OdbcPassword:<password> /CustomXmlServicePort:<XMLport> /AddAnonymousUser
sToRemoteDesktopUserGroup:True|False /AddAuthenticatedUsersToRemoteDeskto
pUserGroup:False|true /AddUsersGroupToremoteDesktopUserGroup:True|False /
LicenseModel:<licmodel> /LogFilename:<logfile>
```

This command uses the following syntax and parameters:

- ► `/FarmName`: This is required for `ExecutionMode:Create` to specify the XenApp Farm name up to 32 characters.

- ► `/CitrixAdministratorAccount`: This is required for `ExecutionMode:Create` to specify the `domain\user` account that will be the first Citrix administrator in the Farm.

- ► `/ZoneName`: This specifies the zone name. By default, servers are added to the Default Zone.

- ► `/DsnFile`: This specifies the `DSN` file to be used. The file contains information on the SQL server settings.

- ► `/LicenseModel`: This specifies the XenApp license model. The valid values are **XenApp licenses** (**XA**), **XenDesktop concurrent user licenses** (**XDC**), and **XenDesktop user or device licenses** (**XDUD**). By default, XA is configured.

- ► `/LogFilename`: This specifies the logfile to be used. The default logfile location is `C:\Windows\Temp`.

To join a XenApp server to an existing Farm, run the following command:

```
XenAppConfigConsole.exe /ExecutionMode:Join /ZoneName:<zone>
/ImaWorkerMode:False|True /DsnFile:<dsnfile> /
AuthenticationType:Windows|Sql /OdbcUserName:<name> /
OdbcPassword:<password> /CustomXmlServicePort:<XMLport> /AddAnonymousUser
sToRemoteDesktopUserGroup:True|False /AddAuthenticatedUsersToRemoteDeskto
pUserGroup:False|true /AddUsersGroupToRemoteDesktopUserGroup:True|False /
LicenseModel:<licmodel> /LogFilename:<logfile>
```

> The configuration for the License Server and Shadowing can be enforced through Citrix policies and therefore are not included in the provided command line.

There's more...

You can read more on installing Citrix XenApp from the command line at Citrix's eDocs:
`http://support.citrix.com/proddocs/topic/xenapp65-install/ps-install-command-line.html`

You can read more on configuring Citrix XenApp from the command line at Citrix's eDocs:
`http://support.citrix.com/proddocs/topic/xenapp65-install/ps-config-command-syntax-2.html`

Creating custom administrative roles for delegated management

This recipe will show you how to create custom administrative roles for CXA to implement **Role Based Access Control** (**RBAC**) for the XenApp Farm. By creating custom administrative roles for the Citrix XenApp Farm, different administrative tasks can be assigned to different user groups. This way, ServiceDesk engineers can be assigned access to only those tasks that support the user, such as being able to log off a shadow user session without being able to alter the Farm settings. Server Administrators can be assigned access to administrative tasks that will allow them to change Farm settings and configure policies and/or Load Evaluators. And Application Managers can be assigned rights to only adjust the settings for published applications.

How to do it...

To create custom administrative roles, follow these steps:

1. Open the Citrix XenApp management console AppCenter by navigating to **Start** | **Administrative Tools** | **Citrix** | **Management Consoles**.

2. Select **XenApp** | **<FarmName>** | **Administrators** on the left pane.

3. Select **Add Administrator** in the action pane.

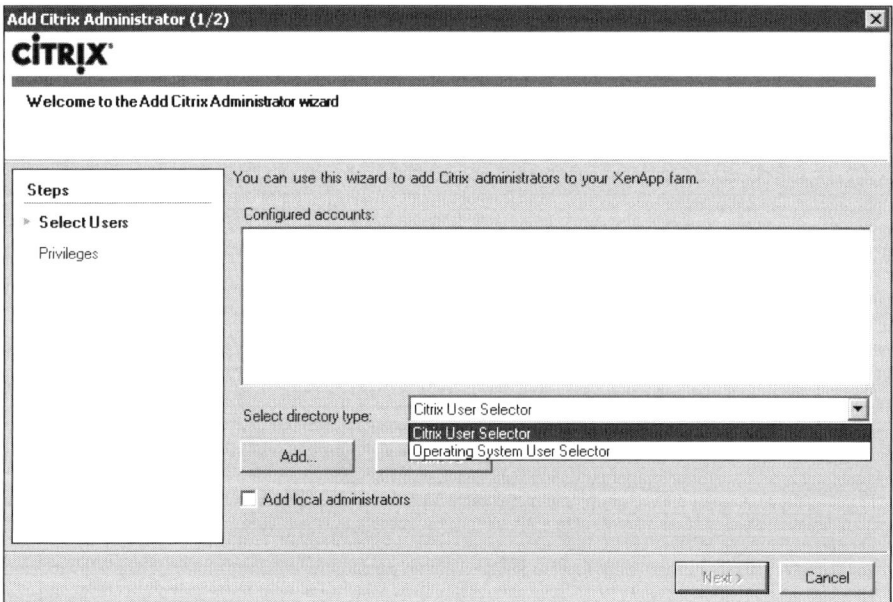

4. Select a directory type and click on **Add**.

5. Select the User or Group you want to add and click on **OK**.

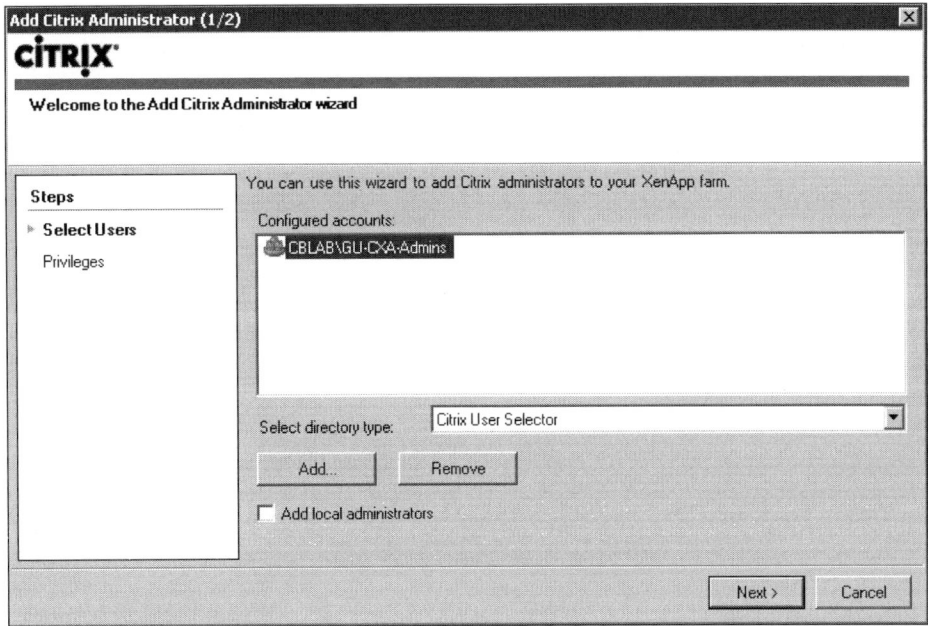

6. Click on **Next**.
7. Set the privilege level to Custom and click on **Next**.

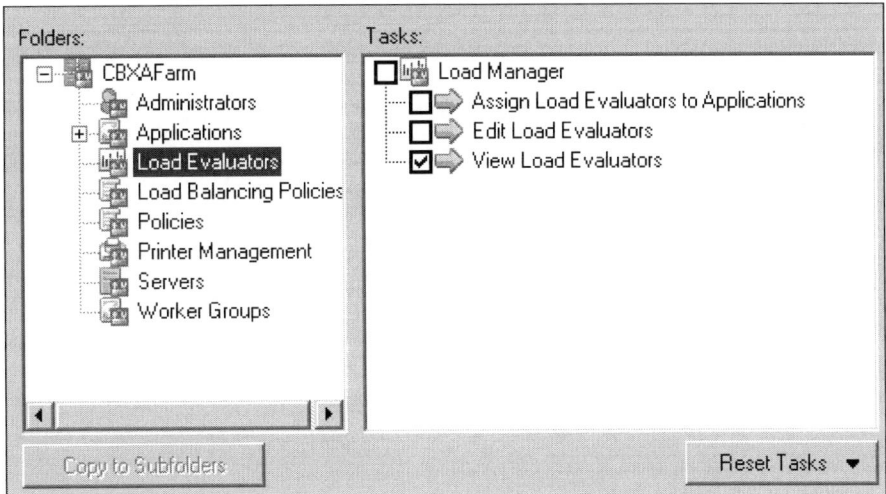

8. Select the tasks that you want to make available by selecting each category in the **Folders** pane and the associated tasks in the **Tasks** pane, and click on **Finish**.

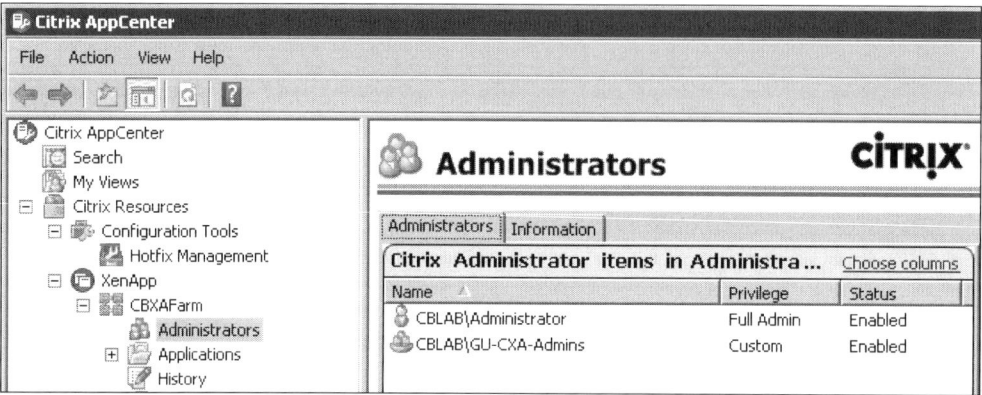

9. The User or Group is added as an administrator for the XenApp Farm with custom privilege.

> The custom administrative privileges for a ServiceDesk engineer (managing user sessions) should contain at least the following settings:
>
> ▸ **Servers folder**: Select View Server Information, Terminate Processes, Session (and all subtasks)
>
> ▸ **Applications folder**: Select View Published Applications and Content, Terminate Processes, Session (and all subtasks)

Sending a message to one or more logged on XenApp® users

This recipe will show you how to send a message to one or more logged on CXA users. With this option, an administrative warning regarding the reboot of a XenApp server or other requests can be sent to a selection of users.

How to do it...

To send a message to one more logged on XenApp users, follow these steps:

1. Open the Citrix XenApp management console AppCenter by navigation to **Start | Administrative Tools | Citrix | Management Consoles**.
2. Select **XenApp | <FarmName> | Servers** on the left pane.

3. Click on the **Users** tab on the middle pane.

4. Select a logged on user account from the list of user sessions.

 You can select more than one user session by holding down the *Ctrl* key.

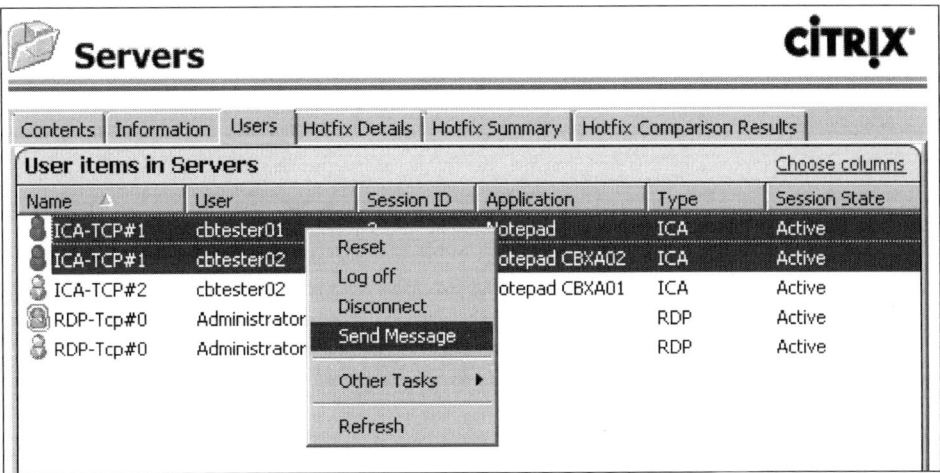

5. Right-click on the selected user session(s) and select **Send Message**.

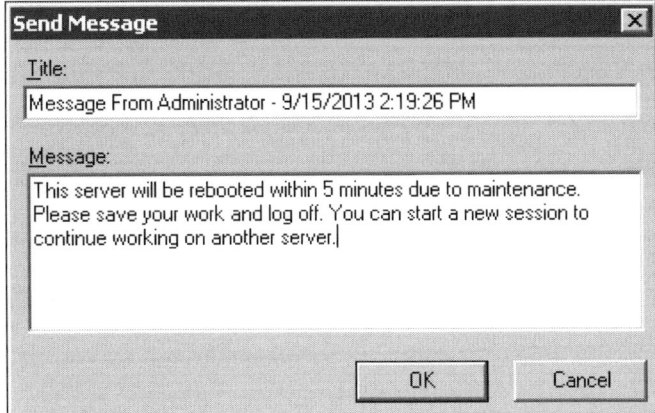

6. Enter a **Title** and **Message** and click on **OK**.

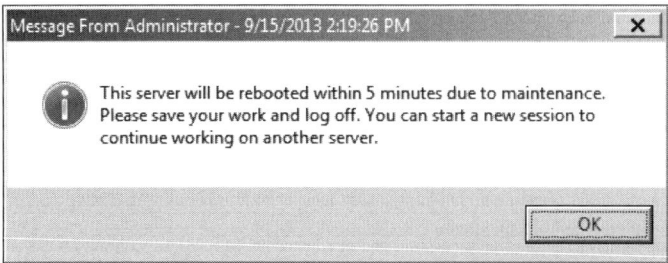

The selected users will immediately get the message shown in their session.

Creating a custom Load Evaluator

This recipe will show you how to create a custom Load Evaluator that can be assigned to a published application or XenApp server.

How to do it...

To create a custom Load Evaluator, follow these steps:

1. Open the Citrix XenApp management console AppCenter by navigation to **Start | Administrative Tools | Citrix | Management Consoles**.

2. Select **XenApp | <FarmName> | Load Evaluators** on the left pane.

3. Select **New | Add load evaluator** on the **Action** pane to the right.

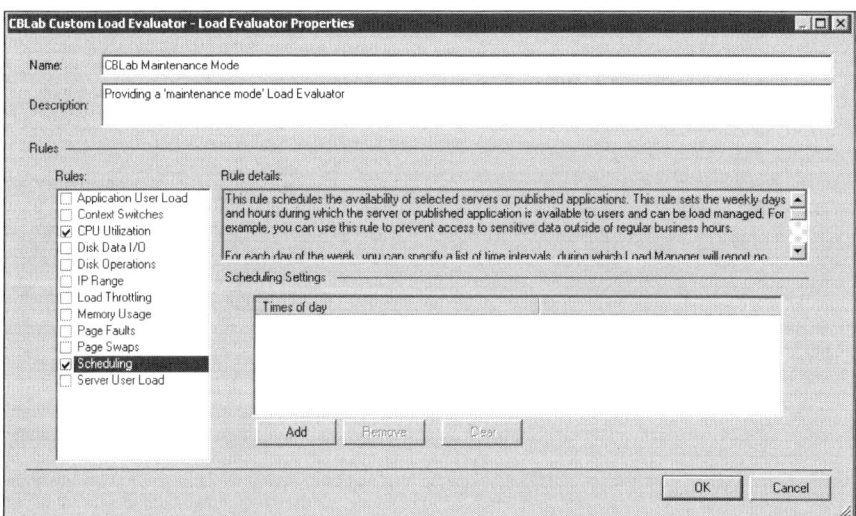

4. Enter **Name** and **Description** for the Load Evaluator that explains its use.

5. Select and configure the rules you want to apply.

6. Click on **OK**.

How it works...

With a Load Evaluator, the XenApp Controller Host knows which calculations to apply to determine a XenApp server or published application load. Based on the rules and outcome, the Controller Host assigns a new session to the XenApp server or published application with the least load (read as: the lowest outcome for the configured rules).

A XenApp Farm comes with two predefined Load Evaluators: default and advanced.

The default Load Evaluator is configured with the following rules:

▶ **Load throttling**: High

▶ **Server user load**: 100

The advanced load evaluator is configured with the following rules:

▶ **CPU utilization**: Full load = 90, No load = 10

▶ **Load throttling**: High

▶ **Memory usage**: Full load = 90, No load = 10

▶ **Page swaps**: Full load = 100, No load = 0

A complete list of the available Load Management Rules can be found at Citrix's eDocs at `http://support.citrix.com/proddocs/topic/xenapp65-admin/lm-rules-list.html`.

Both of the built-in Load Evaluators cannot be changed. You can create a copy of the built-in Load Evaluator and edit the active Load Management Rules, or you can create a custom Load Evaluator from scratch. You cannot add custom Load Management Rules to a Load Evaluator; only the provided rules can be configured.

Load Evaluators are assigned to a XenApp server or published application by using Citrix policies.

Instructions on how to assign the Load Evaluator to a server or application are described in *Chapter 8, XenApp® Policies*, in the *Assigning Load Evaluators to servers and applications* recipe.

As an alternative method to setting a server in a so-called "Maintenance Mode", you can create and assign a custom load evaluator that will always return a full load. With this assigned Load Evaluator, the XenApp server will not receive new user sessions as a Full Load is reported. This allows for the XenApp server to be drained from user sessions without having to change the XenApp server logon control. Prohibiting logons for a server can block RDP connections to the server as well, thus making the server unavailable for administrative connections as well.

To create a Maintenance Mode Load Evaluator, select the following Load Management Rules:

- **Scheduling**: Leave the schedule settings empty (a second rule is required)

- **CPU utilization**: Full load = 1, No Load = 0 (guaranteed full-load configuration)

You can check the assigned Load Evaluator for each XenApp server in the Farm by checking the **Usage by Server** tab of the Load Evaluators window.

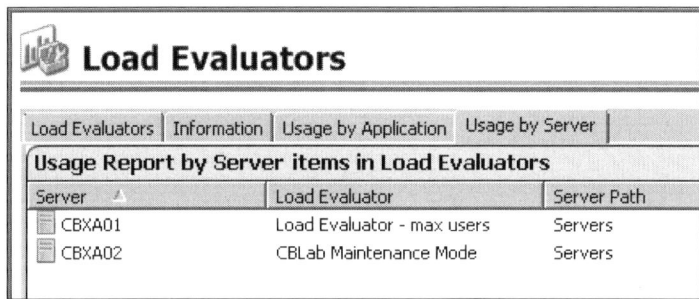

Using Worker Groups to cluster XenApp® servers and configurations

This recipe will show you how to group XenApp servers within a CXA Farm to apply specialized configurations by clustering servers in separate Worker Groups.

How to do it...

To create a Worker Group, follow these steps:

1. Open the Citrix XenApp management console AppCenter by navigating to **Start | Administrative Tools | Citrix | Management Consoles**.

2. Select **XenApp | <FarmName> | Worker Groups** on the middle pane.

3. Select **Create worker group** on the **Action** pane.

4. Enter a **Name** and **Description** for the Worker Group.

5. Select a source to add the XenApp servers manually or based upon Active Directory Group/OU membership.

6. Click on **Add** to either manually add the servers or specify the Active Directory source that dynamically determines the members.

7. Click on **OK**.

To view the members of a Worker Group, follow these steps:

1. Open the Citrix XenApp management console AppCenter by navigating to **Start | Administrative Tools | Citrix | Management Consoles**.

2. Select **XenApp | <FarmName> | Worker Groups** on the middle pane.

3. Expand the **Worker Groups** branch and select a Worker Group.

4. Click on the **Servers** tab on the middle pane to see the current members of the Worker Group.

5. Click on the **Current Settings** tab to view the configuration of the Worker Group.

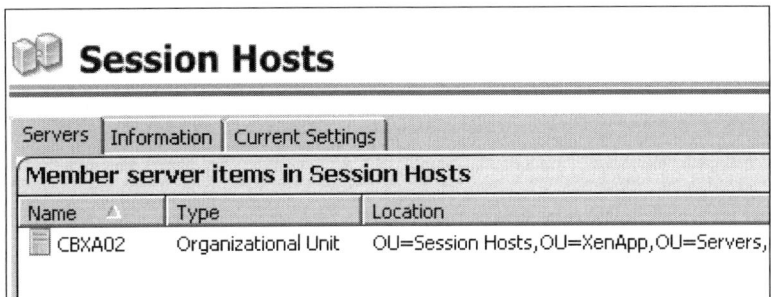

How it works...

Worker Groups can create different XenApp server collections within a XenApp Farm and can be used to assign different Load Evaluators, Citrix policies and published resources to XenApp server collections within the same Farm.

Worker Groups can be configured with three different sources to determine their members:

- Active Directory Containers (OU membership)
- Active Directory Server Groups (Group membership)
- Farm Servers

With Farm Servers, the XenApp servers are added manually to the Worker Group. When Active Directory is selected as the source, Worker Group members are dynamically determined. Based on the configured source, all the XenApp servers that are a member of the specified **Active Directory Group** or **Organizational Unit** (**OU**) are automatically added to the Worker Group.

 Check the Advanced Farm Administration with XenApp Worker Groups white paper for the expected latency of various Worker Group tasks at Citrix's Knowledge Center: `http://support.citrix.com/article/CTX124481`

The following rules apply while working with Worker Groups:

- Worker Groups can only contain XenApp servers from the same XenApp Farm. If an OU or AD Group contains XenApp servers from different Farms, these servers are ignored and not added to the Worker Group.

- Worker Groups can contain multiple XenApp servers or even none if required.

- A XenApp Farm server can be a member of none, one, or more Worker Groups at the same time in the Farm.

You can use Worker Groups to assign published applications, filter policies, or redirect user connections to a different server collection when all the members of the Worker Group are offline.

Publish applications with Worker Groups

Not only can a published application be directly assigned to XenApp servers, but by assigning the application to a Worker Group, you can also create server collections for the published applications. Published applications assigned to a XenApp server can easily be switched by changing the Worker Group membership of the XenApp server without having to edit each application setting individually.

Filter policies with Worker Groups

Each Citrix Policy, whether set through the AppCenter or Group Policy Management Console, can be configured with a filter to specify when the policy applies. Policy filters can select a Worker Group as well.

This allows you to create a special Maintenance Worker Group to use as a policy filter for the assignment of a different Load Evaluator rule or to create an XML service policy rule to assign to a special Controller Host Worker Group.

 You can read more on Citrix policies in *Chapter 8, XenApp® Policies*.

Redirect session connections

To redirect session connections to a different server collection, a Load Balancing policy needs to be created. A Load Balancing policy contains a prioritized Worker Group preference list to determine the server collection that a user session is directed to when logging on. This should not be confused with a Load Evaluator that specifies the calculation rules a Controller Host uses to determine a XenApp server load.

There's more...

You can read more on Worker Groups at Citrix's eDocs at `http://support.citrix.com/proddocs/topic/xenapp65-admin/ps-maintain-worker-groups.html`.

Configuring the ICA Listener

This recipe will show you how to configure the ICA Listener settings on a CXA server. ICA Listener settings can no longer be configured through the Remote Desktop Session Host Configuration Tool, but requires the use of Citrix's ICA Listener Configuration Tool.

How to do it...

To configure the ICA Listener settings, follow these steps:

1. Open the ICA Listener configuration tool by navigating to **Start | Administrative Tools | Citrix | Administrative Tools**.

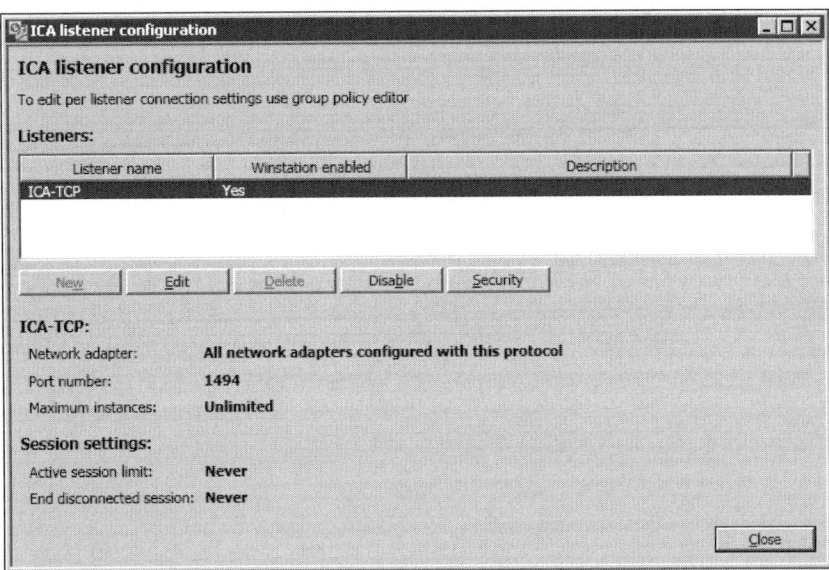

2. Click on **Edit** to change the current configuration.

3. Configure active and disconnected session timeouts on the **Session limits** tab.

4. Configure the Network adapter and ICA connection limit settings on the **Network adapter** tab.

5. Configure an initial program to start on the **Environment** tab.

6. Click on **OK** to apply the changed settings.

7. Click on **Security** to change Permissions for the ICA Listener.

 The changes made with the ICA Listener configuration tool are made at the XenApp server level. The session timeout settings can be centralized using the Microsoft Group Policy settings for the Remote Desktop Session Host.

The following screenshot shows the available **Session Time Limits** policy settings for the **Remote Desktop Session Host**.

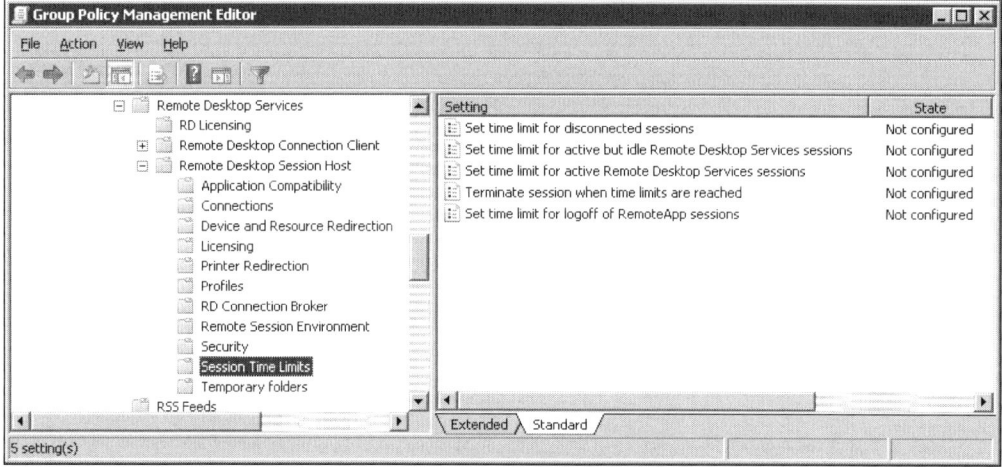

Configuring the HDX MediaStream Flash Redirection

This recipe will show you how to configure both the Windows client and the CXA server to support the HDX MediaStream Flash Redirection (**HDX Flash**).

How to do it...

Configuring the HDX MediaStream Flash Redirection requires the installation of the right Flash Player and additional settings that need to be configured on both the client and the server.

Follow these steps to prepare the client for the HDX MediaStream Flash Redirection:

1. Install the Flash Player for other browsers on the client.
2. Install the Citrix Receiver 3.0 or any higher version on the client.

If the clients are part of the Windows domain and are managed with Group Policies, follow these steps to preconfigure the client settings:

1. Open the Windows Group Policy Management Console by navigating to **Start | Run | gpmc.msc**.
2. Right-click on the **Organizational Unit** (**OU**) that contains the clients.
3. Select **Create a GPO in this domain, and Link it here...**.
4. Enter a **Name** for the new **Group Policy Object** (**GPO**) and click on **OK**.
5. Right-click on the newly created GPO and select **Edit...**.
6. Expand **Computer Configuration | Policies**.
7. Right-click on **Administrative Templates** and select **Add/Remove Templates...**.
8. Click on **Add** to add a policy template.
9. Browse to the location of the HdxFlash-Client.adm template, select the template, and click on **Open** to add the template to the **Current Policy Templates** list.

 By default, the HdxFlash-Client.adm can be found at %Program Files%\Citrix\ICA Client\Configuration\<language> (32-bit) and %Program Files (x86)%\Citrix\ICA Client\Configuration\<language> (64-bit)

10. Click on **Close**.
11. Browse to **Computer Configuration | Policies | Administrative Templates | Classic Administrative Templates | HDX MediaStream Flash Redirection – Client**.
12. Double-click on **Enable HDX MediaStream Flash Redirection on the user device** on the right pane and use the following settings:
    - **Enabled**: Selected
    - **Use HDX MediaStream Flash Redirection**: Always
13. Click on **OK**.
14. Close the Group Policy Management Editor.

The policy setting can also be configured as a User Configuration setting to apply to the logged on Windows user. If the User policy is linked to a computer OU, also enable the Loopback processing policy setting to ensure that the computer settings are applied to all the logged on users.

Follow these steps to prepare the server for the HDX MediaStream Flash redirection:

1. Install the Flash Player for Internet Explorer on the server.
2. Install the HDX MediaStream Hotfix on the server.

At the time of writing this recipe, HDXFlash200WX64003 was the latest HDX MediaStream Hotfix. It can be found at `http://support.citrix.com/article/CTX134426`.

The HDX Flash behavior can be configured through different Citrix policies for the XenApp servers. To configure the required policies, follow these steps:

1. Open the Citrix XenApp Management Console AppCenter by navigating to **Start | Administrative Tools | Citrix | Management Consoles**.
2. Go to **XenApp | <FarmName> | Policies**.
3. Select the **User** tab on the middle pane.
4. Click on **New...** to create a new policy.
5. Enter **Name** and **Description** and click on **Next**.
6. Go to `ICA\Adobe Flash Delivery\Flash Redirection`.
7. Configure the HDX Flash settings that need to differ from the default settings or need to apply for legacy mode Flash support.
8. Use the Flash URL compatibility list to specify the URLs that require a behavior that is different from the behavior applied by default if required.
9. Click on **Next**.
10. Specify a filter if required and click on **Next**.
11. Click on **Create**.
12. Change the **Priority** of the policy with the **Higher** and **Lower** buttons.

To check if the HDX Flash MediaStream Redirection is working, follow these steps:

1. Start a XenApp-published Internet Explorer on the Windows client.
2. Go to a website with Flash content (`http://youtube.com` for instance).

3. Start a video and right-click in the video screen.

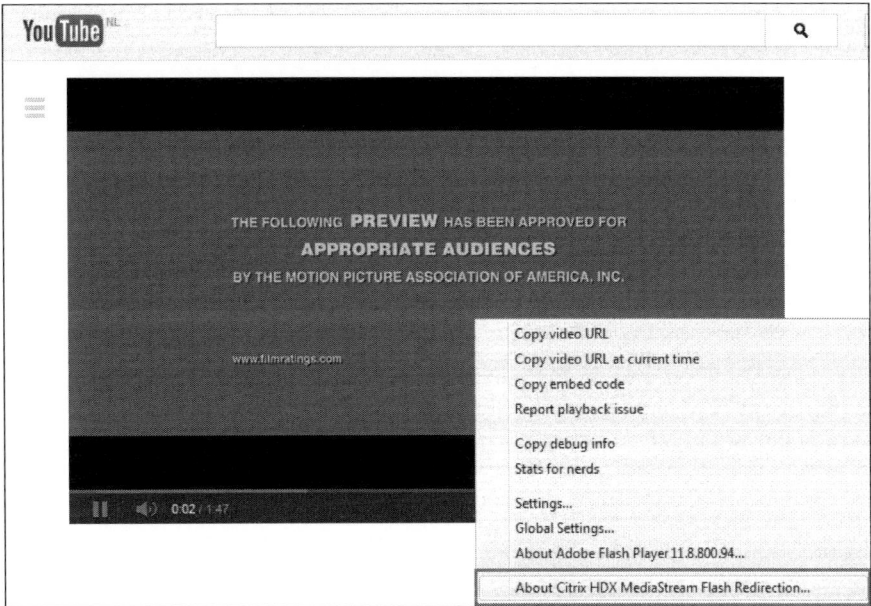

4. Check if the entry **About Citrix HDX MediaStream Flash Redirection** is shown in the context menu.

How it works...

With HDX MediaStream Flash Redirection you can offload Adobe Flash content (animations, video, and applications). When you offload the Flash content to the client device, it is processed by the client's local resources (CPU and RAM) and does not stress out the Citrix XenApp server by claiming its resources. The rendered Flash content on the client device is presented in the XenApp session just as it was rendered on the server. This allows for smooth Flash content presentation without stressing the server and network load.

HDX Flash requires additional settings to be configured and flash components to be installed on both the client and the XenApp server.

To set up the Windows client and XenApp server for HDX Flash, follow the instructions.

Client software requirements

To support HDX Flash using the Windows client, the following software must be installed on the Windows client:

▸ Citrix Receiver for Windows 3.0 and higher versions

▸ Windows Adobe Flash Player for other browsers (the Adobe Flash Player plugin)

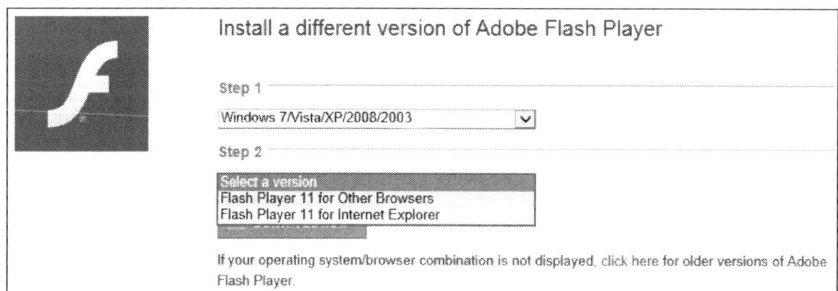

Keep in mind that there are two types of Flash Players.

To use HDX MediaStream for the Flash Content Redirection, the Flash Player for other browsers needs to be installed on the client device while the Flash Player for Internet Explorer needs to be installed on the XenApp server.

In addition to installing the right type of Flash Player on each device, you also need to check the installed version numbers of both players. The Windows client device's Flash Player version must be equal to or higher than the Flash Player version on the XenApp server.

If no additional configurations are applied, users will receive the following message when Flash content is first discovered in a published Internet Explorer.

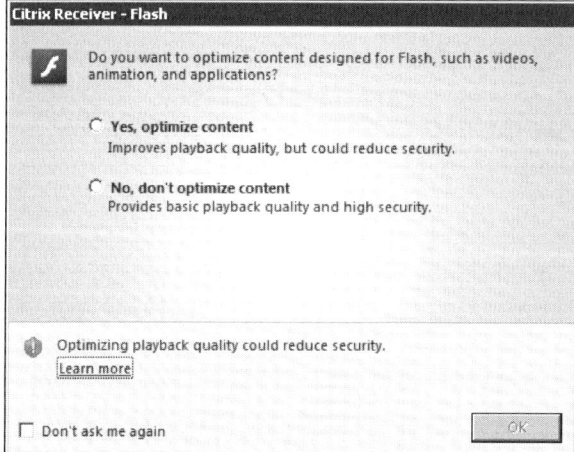

To prevent the message, user preferences regarding HDX Flash can be set through policy settings.

Client policy configuration

To ensure that HDX Flash is used, policy settings can be applied without presenting the user with the above message. You can find the ADM file (Hdxflash-Client.adm) with the required policy settings at the following default locations:

- **32-bit**: %Program Files%\Citrix\ICA Client\ Configuration\<language>
- **64-bit**: %Program Files (x86)%\Citrix\ICA Client\ Configuration\<language>

XenApp server software requirements

To support the HDX Flash MediaStream Redirection using the server, the following software must be installed on the server:

- Internet Explorer 7 and higher versions
- Windows Adobe Flash Player for Internet Explorer (the Adobe Flash Player ActiveX)

XenApp server registry settings

For the use of the HDX Flash MediaStream Redirection with Internet Explorer 9 an additional registry setting is required:

```
HKLM\SOFTWARE\Wow6432Node\Citrix\HdxMediaStreamForFlash
\Server\PseudoServer
Value: IEBrowserMaximumMajorVersion (DWORD)
Data: 00000009
```

Citrix computer policies

To support HDX Flash redirection settings for user sessions, Citrix policies can be configured. You can find the policies in the **ICA | Adobe Flash Delivery | Flash Redirection** category.

There's more...

You can read more on Configuring HDX MediaStream Flash Redirection at Citrix's eDocs at http://support.citrix.com/proddocs/topic/xenapp65-admin/hd-flash-wrapper-ad.html.

Configuring advanced printing settings

Configuring advanced printer settings for Citrix XenApp usually required adjustments to the registry and calculating the right value (DWORD value) for the `DefaultPrnFlags` registry. With Citrix XenApp 6.x, most printer settings can be managed with Citrix policies and the DefaultPrnFlags registry has been removed. In return, we can now adjust six individual registry settings to configure the client printer's behavior.

This recipe will show you how to configure the advanced client printing settings for CXA user sessions.

How to do it...

To configure the advanced printing settings for the client printer creation in a XenApp user session, follow these steps to set the corresponding registry settings:

1. Open the Registry editor by navigating to **Start | Run | regedit**.
2. Create a new registry key at `HKLM\Software\Citrix\Ica\PrintingSettings`.
3. To allow administrators to manage the client printer settings for a user session, add the DWORD value `AdminsCanManageClientPrinters` and set it to 1.
4. To only create printer ports for auto-created client printers, add the DWORD value `CreatePortForAutoCreatedPrintersOnly` and set it to 1.
5. To create both standard and legacy printer ports for each client printer, add the DWORD value `CreateStandardAndLegacyPrinterPorts` and set it to 1.
6. To not auto create network client printers add the DWORD value `DisableNetworkPrinterAutoConnect` and set it to 1.
7. To not allow users to disconnect a client network printer, add the DWORD value `DisableNetworkPrinterDisconnect` and set it to 1.
8. To allow users to manage their client printer settings, add the DWORD value `UsersCanManageClientPrinters` and set it to 1.

How it works...

Advanced printing settings can be configured in two locations: Citrix User policies and the registry. You can configure most printing settings with Citrix User policies. These settings are listed in the `ICA\Printing` category. To configure Citrix policies, you can either use the Citrix Management Console AppCenter or the GPMC plugin to integrate the Citrix policies with Active Directory and Microsoft Group Policies.

You can read all about Citrix XenApp policies in *Chapter 8, XenApp®
Policies*.

The following screenshot shows some of the printer policies that can be configured:

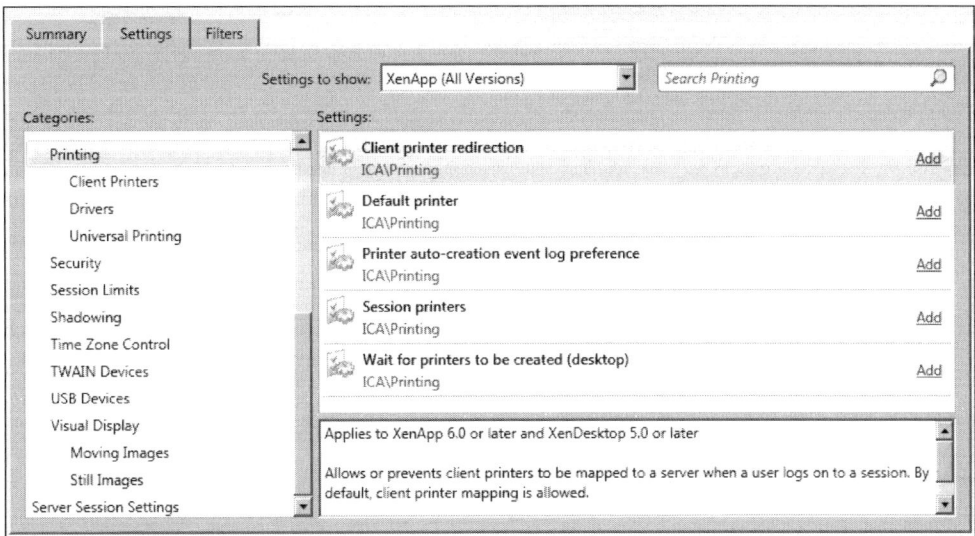

Even though most settings can be managed through Citrix Computer and User policies, there
are still six settings that are configured with registry settings. The registry settings are not
automatically created when installing Citrix XenApp and must be manually added to change
default client printer behavior. To change the default configuration for each setting, follow
these steps:

1. Create a new registry key at `HKLM\Software\Citrix\Ica\PrintingSettings`.

2. Add a DWORD value for the setting that you want to change.

The following screenshot shows each value with the corresponding default setting:

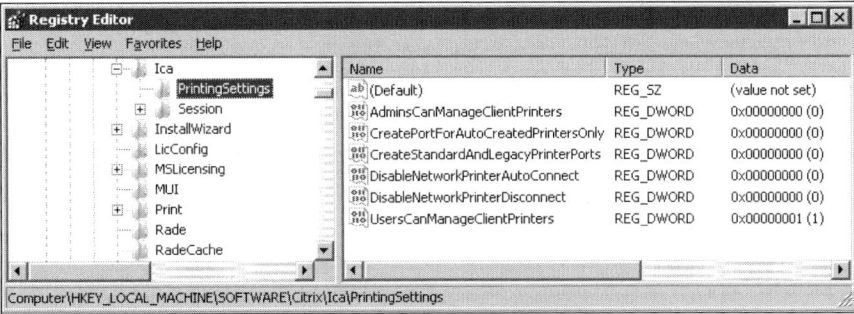

The previous versions of XenApp (Presentation Server 4.5 and XenApp 5) used a DefaultPrnFlags (DWORD) registry key to set various printer settings for session printers located at `HKLM\Software\Citrix\Print`.

As of XenApp 6.5, some of these settings are set using policies and some are set using the new registry location for printing settings. The following table provides an overview of the new location for the DefaultPrnFlags settings:

Setting	DefaultPrnFlags	XenApp 6.5 setting
Create a generic Citrix Universal Printer that is not tied to any specific client printer	0x00000020	▸ **Location**: Citrix User Policy ▸ **Path**: `ICA\Printing\Client Printers`. ▸ **Setting**: Auto-create a generic universal printer
Disable printer properties retention for auto-created printers	0x00003000	▸ **Location**: Citrix User Policy ▸ **Path**: `ICA\Printing\Client Printers` ▸ **Setting**: Printer properties retention
Give administrators access permissions to manage the auto-created printers	0x00004000	▸ **Location**: Registry HKLM ▸ **Path**: `\Software\Ica\ PrintingSettings` ▸ **Setting**: AdminsCanManageClientPrinters
Enable preview on a client as default for the generic Citrix Universal Printer	0x00008000	▸ **Location**: Citrix User Policy ▸ **Path**: `ICA\Printing\Universal Printing` ▸ **Setting**: Universal printing preview preference
Enable preview on a client as default for Citrix Universal auto-created client printers	0x00010000	▸ **Location**: Citrix User Policy ▸ **Path**: `ICA\Printing\Universal Printing` ▸ **Setting**: Universal printing preview preference
Disable the connection of Session Printers during logon and reconnection	0x00400000	▸ **Location**: Registry HKLM ▸ **Path**: `\Software\Ica\ PrintingSettings` ▸ **Setting**: DisableNetworkPrinterAutoConnect

Setting	DefaultPrnFlags	XenApp 6.5 setting
Disable the deletion of Session Printers during logoff	0x00800000	▸ **Location**: Registry HKLM ▸ **Path**: \Software\Ica\ PrintingSettings ▸ **Setting**: DisableNetworkPrinterDisconnect
Instead of creating either legacy style or standard port names, both are created	0x01000000	▸ **Location**: Registry HKLM ▸ **Path**: \Software\Ica\ PrintingSettings ▸ **Setting**: CreateStandardAndLegacyPrinterPorts
Create ports only for auto-created printers rather than for every discovered client printer	0x02000000	▸ **Location**: Registry HKLM ▸ **Path**: \Software\Ica\ PrintingSettings ▸ **Setting**: CreatePortsForAutoCreatedPrintersOnly
Suppresses 1106 errors that are being written to the event log	0x08000000	▸ **Location**: Citrix User Policy ▸ **Path**: ICA\Printing ▸ **Setting**: Printer auto-creation event log preference
Disable the Universal Print Driver for Specific Print Drivers	0x10000000	▸ **Location**: Citrix User Policy ▸ **Path**: ICA\Printing\Client Printers ▸ **Setting**: Printer driver mapping and compatibility
Give Users print permissions for auto-created printers	0x20000000	▸ **Location**: Registry HKLM ▸ **Path**: \Software\Ica\ PrintingSettings ▸ **Setting**: UsersCanManageClientPrinters
Disable the use of auto-retained and auto-restored printers	0x80000000	▸ **Location**: Citrix User Policy ▸ **Path**: ICA\Printing\Client Printers ▸ **Setting**: Retained and restored client printers

There's more...

You can find the DefaultPrnFlags Reference Document at Citrix's Knowledge Center: `http://support.citrix.com/article/CTX119684`

You can read more on the new registry settings and location for advanced printing settings at Citrix's Knowledge Center: `http://support.citrix.com/article/CTX124885`

Working with print drivers on Citrix® XenApp®

This recipe will show you how to manage printer drivers on **Citrix XenApp** (**CXA**) servers.

How to do it...

To replicate printer drivers between XenApp servers, follow these steps:

1. Install the printer server role with the following PowerShell commands:

   ```
   Import-Module ServerManager

   Add-WindowsFeature RSAT-Print-Services
   ```

2. Open the Print Management console on the source XenApp server by navigating to **Start | Run | printmanagement.msc**.

3. Select **Print Management |Print Servers | <Server name>** on the left pane.

4. Select **More Actions | Export printers to a file ...**.

5. Click on **Next**.

6. Select a file location and click on **Next**.

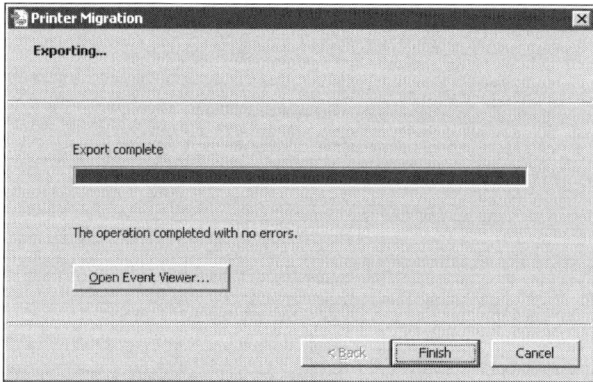

7. Click on **Finish**.

Follow these steps to import printer drivers:

1. Open the Print Management console on the destination XenApp server by navigating to **Start | Run | printmanagement.msc**.

2. Select **Print Management | Print Servers | <Server name>** on the left pane.

3. Select **More Actions | Import printers from a file ....**

4. Select the file location and click on **Next**.

5. Review the list of items and click on **Next**.

6. Select import options:

   ❑ **Import Mode**: Keep the existing printers.

   ❑ **List in the directory**: Don't list any printers.

   ❑ **Convert LPR Ports to Standard Port Monitors**: Unselected.

7. Click on **Next**.

8. Click on **Finish**.

How it works...

Printer management on XenApp servers has changed for XenApp 6.5. Most session-related printer configurations are set with Citrix policies. You can configure printer redirection, creation, and preferences for each XenApp user session using the corresponding policies.

> Configuring and maintaining printers through Citrix policies is discussed in detail in *Chapter 8, XenApp® Policies*.

Older versions of XenApp offered a management console to control the installed printer drivers and replication on each XenApp server in the Farm. This management console is no longer available for Citrix XenApp 6.5.

On XenApp 6.5 servers printer drivers are managed by the Windows 2008 R2 Print Management console (part of the Print and Document Services Tools feature). The Print Management console can be installed without installing the Print Server role.

Install the Print Management Console

To install the Print Server role, run the following PowerShell command:

```
# Import the Server Manager module with corresponding cmdlets
Import-Module ServerManager
# Add the Print Management Console
Add-WindowsFeature RSAT-Print-Services –LogPath <log.txt> -Restart
```

Replicate printer drivers

To replicate printer drivers on Windows Server 2008 R2, the Print Management console can be used. No direct replication actions are provided, but using the export and import function will work to replicate printer drivers between servers.

 In addition to the printer drivers, the export file also contains printer and port information for each printer while using the Print Management console. To export only printer drivers you can use the `printBRM.exe` command-line tool. Or read all about Misja Geuskens' solution in his blogpost: `http://blog.misjageuskens.nl/2013/05/26/how-to-keep-your-printerdrivers-in-sync-at-your-xenapp-6-x-farm/`

With these options, the existing drivers are not changed; only new drivers are added to the XenApp server.

There's more...

In addition to using the Print Management console, PowerShell can also be used to replicate and even auto-replicate printer drivers between XenApp servers. *Chapter 10, PowerShell and Command-line Tooling*, offers a detailed recipe, *Replicating printer drivers with PowerShell for XenApp®*.

For those that prefer to use a GUI-based solution, check out the XenApp Printer Driver Manager tool created by Gourami: `http://www.gourami.eu/products/xenapp-printer-driver-manager`

See also

▶ The *Replicating printer drivers with PowerShell* recipe in *Chapter 10, PowerShell and Command-line Tooling*

Logging administrative changes to a XenApp Farm

This recipe will show you how to configure CXA Configuration Logging to keep track of all administrative changes made to the XenApp Farm configuration.

Getting ready

To configure Citrix XenApp Configuration Logging, an SQL database must be created in advance with a corresponding service account that is configured with the `db_owner` role membership.

How to do it...

To configure Configuration Logging, follow these steps:

1. Open the Citrix XenApp management console AppCenter by navigation to **Start | Administrative Tools | Citrix | Management Consoles**.

2. Right-click on **XenApp | <FarmName>** and select **Farm properties**.

3. Select **Configuration Logging** on the left pane.

4. Click on **Configure Database...** on the right pane.

5. Provide the connection type settings and click on **Next**.

6. Select the database from the select box and click on **Next**.

7. Change connection options and pooling if required and click on **Next**.

 Change the **Use encryption** setting to `No` if you are not using SSL to connect to the SQL database. By default, the **Use encryption** is set to `Yes` and a certificate is required.

8. Select **Test Database Connection**.

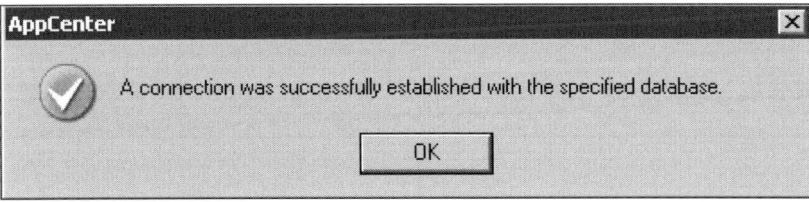

9. Click on **OK** and click on **Finish**.

10. Select **Log administrative tasks** to the Configuration Logging database.

11. Deselect **Allow changes to the farm when logging database is disconnected** if you do not want to allow changes to the Farm without proper logging.

12. Select **Require administrators to enter database credentials before clearing the log** to ensure that the logged entries cannot accidentally be cleared.

13. Click on **OK** to apply and activate Configuration Logging.

To view the logged entries, follow these steps:

1. Open the Citrix XenApp management console AppCenter by navigation to **Start** | **Administrative Tools** | **Citrix** | **Management Consoles**.

2. Select **XenApp** | **<FarmName>** | **History** on the left pane.

3. Click on **Set filter...** on the **History** pane.

4. Configure the filter to apply.

 To prevent excessive resource usage while viewing logged entries, configure the log filter to narrow the log query results and returned log entries.

5. Click on **OK**.

6. Right-click on the **History** pane and select **Get** log.

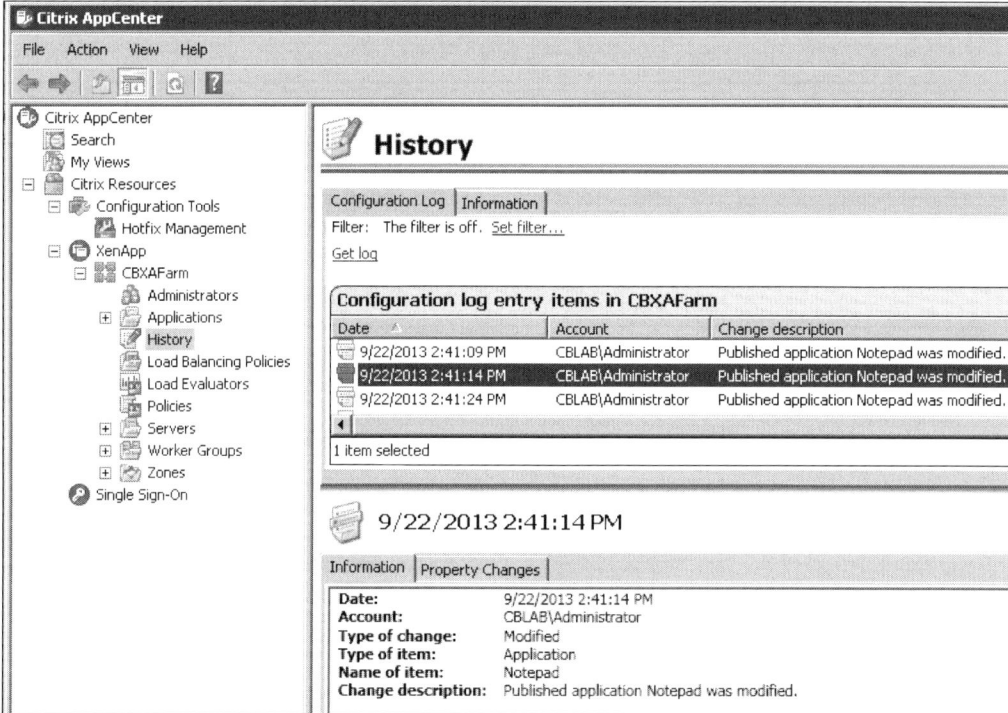

A list of configuration log entry items is shown. While selecting an item, more details are provided in the bottom half of the pane. Even though textual changes may not always be logged, details are provided for changed properties, relationships, and so on.

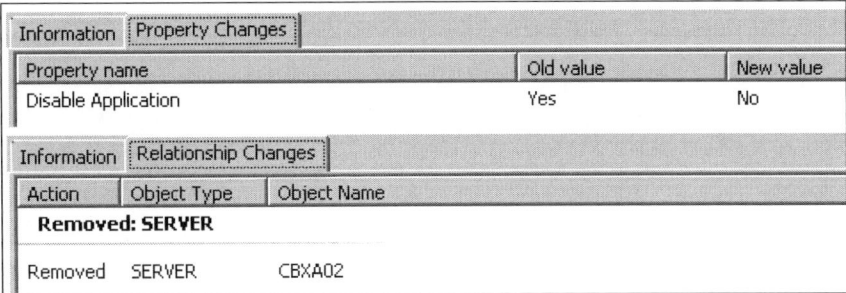

There's more...

A detailed step-by-step instruction to set up a Configuration Logging database is provided on the Citrix blog at `http://blogs.citrix.com/2012/03/01/how-to-set-up-a-configuration-logging-database-for-xenapp-6-5/`.

Enabling the Windows 7 look and feel desktop theme

This recipe will show you how to enable the Windows 7 look and feel desktop theme for published desktops on CXA Servers. By default, the Windows 7 look and feel desktop theme is not enabled on Windows Server 2008 R2 Servers.

Getting ready

To enable the Windows 7 look and feel theme for published desktops, both Windows features and XenApp-installed components are required.

To enable the Windows 7 look and feel theme for Windows Server 2008 R2 servers, the Desktop Experience feature must be installed. You can check if the feature is installed by running the following PowerShell command:

```
# Import the Server Manager module with corresponding cmdlets
Import-Module ServerManager
# Show the feature setting for Desktop Experience
```

```
Get-WindowsFeature desk*
```

To install the Desktop Experience feature, run the following PowerShell commands:

```
# Import the Server Manager module with corresponding cmdlets
Import-Module ServerManager
# Add the Desktop-Experience feature
Add-WindowsFeature Desktop-Experience –LogPath <log.txt> -Restart
```

The Windows Desktop Experience Integration component also needs to be installed during the XenApp installation. This component is installed by default.

Check the installation of the Windows Desktop Experience Integration through Citrix XenApp server Roles (**Start | Administrative Tools | Citrix | XenApp Server Role Manager**) through the add or remove server roles option.

How to do it...

With all the prerequisites in place, a published desktop user is by default presented with the Windows Classic theme.

To import Citrix's specialized Desktop Experience Group Policies, follow these steps:

1. Run Windows PowerShell as **Administrator**.

2. Change the directory to `C:\Program Files (x86)\Citrix\App Delivery Setup Tools`.

3. Type `.\New-CtxManagedDesktopGPO.ps1` to install the corresponding GPOs.

```
Administrator: Windows PowerShell
Windows PowerShell
Copyright (C) 2009 Microsoft Corporation. All rights reserved.

PS C:\Users\administrator.CBLAB> cd 'C:\Program Files (x86)\Citrix\App Delivery Setup Tools'
PS C:\Program Files (x86)\Citrix\App Delivery Setup Tools> .\New-CtxManagedDesktopGPO.ps1
Creating the Group Policy objects for the Enhanced Desktop Experience feature.
Validating install and GPO backup paths provided.
Changing working directory C:\Program Files (x86)\Citrix\App Delivery Setup Tools\.
Testing if GPOs (CtxPersonalizableUser, CtxRestrictedUser, CtxRestrictedComputer, and CtxStartMenuTaskbarUser.) can be c
reated.
Importing GPO  to CtxStartMenuTaskbarUser
Created New GPO CtxStartMenuTaskbarUser.
Created New GPO CtxRestrictedUser.
Created New GPO CtxRestrictedComputer.
Created New GPO CtxPersonalizableUser.

.................................................
The Group Policy objects, which manage a user's desktop configuration, have been successfully created.
The following GPOs will need to be linked to the appropriate OUs:
CtxPersonalizableUser, CtxRestrictedUser, CtxRestrictedComputer, and CtxStartMenuTaskbarUser
PS C:\Program Files (x86)\Citrix\App Delivery Setup Tools> _
```

4. Check if the GPOs are created with the Group Policy Editor.

5. Link the Desktop Experience policies that you want to apply to the XenApp servers OU:

   □ `CtxStartMenuTaskbarUser`: This changes the look and feel of the pinned shortcuts and Start menu to a Windows 7 theme

   □ `CtxPersonalizableUser`: This allows users to change the applied desktop wallpaper

   □ `CtxRestrictedUser`: This prevents users from changing the wallpaper, start menu, and taskbar settings

   □ `CtxRestrictedComputer`: This prevents users from accessing Task Manager, Administrative Tools, Windows Update, Help and Support, and removable drives

6. Run `gpupdate /force` on the XenApp server.

When a user starts a new desktop session, an initialization script is run to enable the user settings that are run first. After the script is completed, the look and feel is changed from the default classic theme to a Windows 7 look and feel.

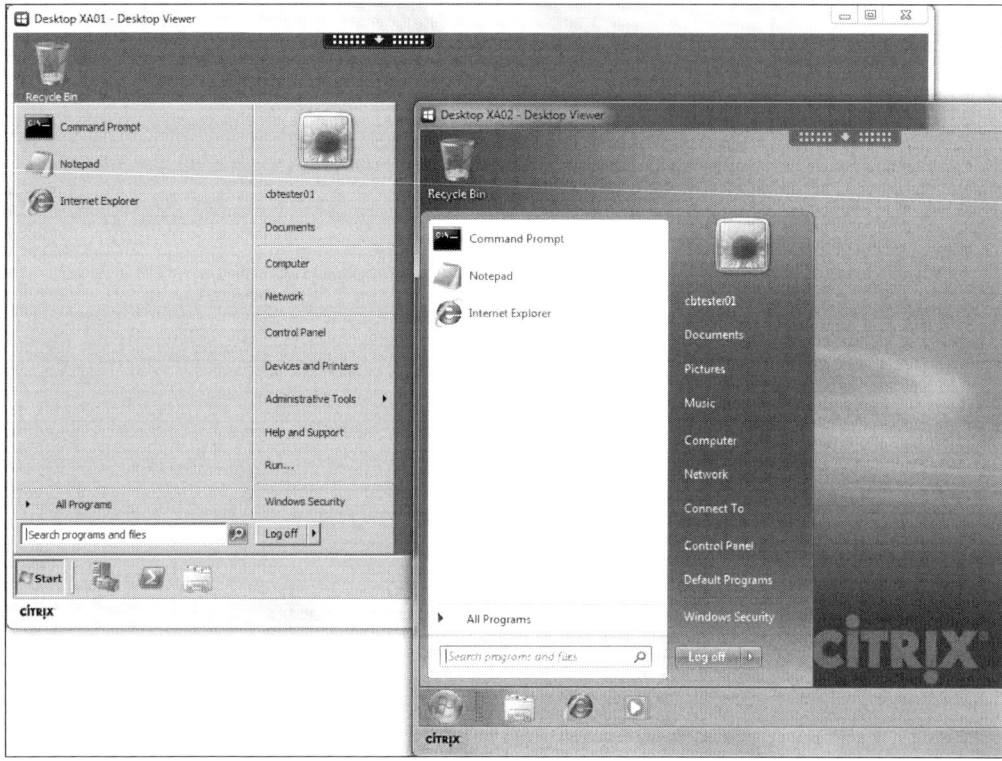

The preceding screenshot shows the default Windows Classic theme on the left-hand side and the new Windows 7 look and feel theme on the right.

There's more...

You can read more on the Windows 7 look and feel theme at Citrix's eDocs at `http://support.citrix.com/proddocs/topic/xenapp65-admin/ps-csp-win7-desktop-experience.html` and Citrix's Knowledge Center at `http://support.citrix.com/article/CTX133429`.

Implementing the Citrix® XenApp® Mobility Pack

This recipe will show you how to implement the CXA Mobility Pack for mobile devices.

How to do it...

The Citrix XenApp 6.5 Mobility Pack is also known as Hotfix XA650W2K8R2X64025, which can be downloaded from Citrix's Knowledge Center at `http://support.citrix.com/article/CTX132912`.

 This Hotfix is now part of Hotfix Rollup Pack 2 for Citrix XenApp 6.5 for Microsoft Windows Server 2008 R2 that was released in June 2013.

Part of the Mobility Pack installation is the installation of additional policy settings for mobile devices. To install the Mobility Pack, it is advised to install Hotfix Rollup Pack 2 by performing the following steps:

1. Download Hotfix Rollup Pack 2 from Citrix's Knowledge Center at `http://support.citrix.com/article/CTX136248`.

2. Log on to the XenApp Controller Host with an administrator account and run the installation.

3. Reboot your XenApp server (a reboot is required).

 Run the installation on the additional Controller Host servers of the XenAppFarm first before running it on the Session Host servers.

Configure the mobile device settings with the additional policies by following these steps:

1. Open the Citrix XenApp management console AppCenter by navigating to **Start | Administrative Tools | Citrix | Management Consoles**.

2. Select **XenApp | <FarmName> | Policies** on the left pane.

3. Select the **User** tab on the **Policies** pane.

4. Click on **New...** to add a new policy.

5. Enter **Name** and **Description** and click on **Next**.

6. Select the **ICA\Mobile Experience** or **ICA\Client Sensors\Location** category.

7. Configure the policy settings and click on **Next**.

8. Configure a filter to apply and click on **Next**.

9. Click on **Create**.

How it works...

The Citrix Mobility Pack focuses on improving the user experience for the Citrix Receiver connections from mobile devices for XenApp-published desktops and applications.

The Mobility Pack offers the following features for mobile devices:

▸   Support for mobile device controls.

▸   Automatic display of the device keyboard.

▸   Touch-optimized desktop with:

□   Start button and touch-friendly menus to navigate to the applications and documents.

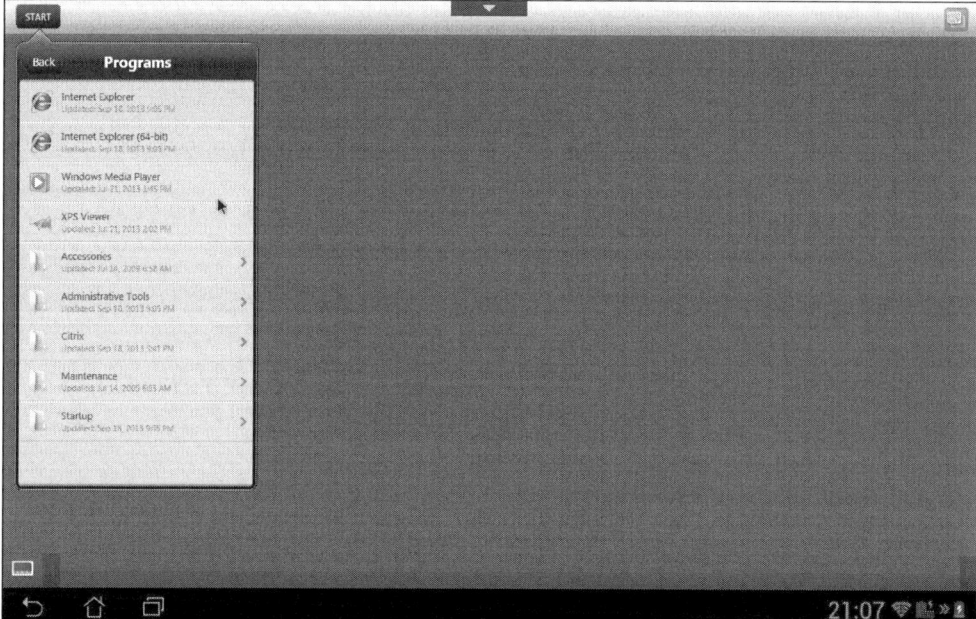

❑   Switch from the touch-optimized desktop to the Windows desktop (the bottom-left icon) and back again (the top-right icon):

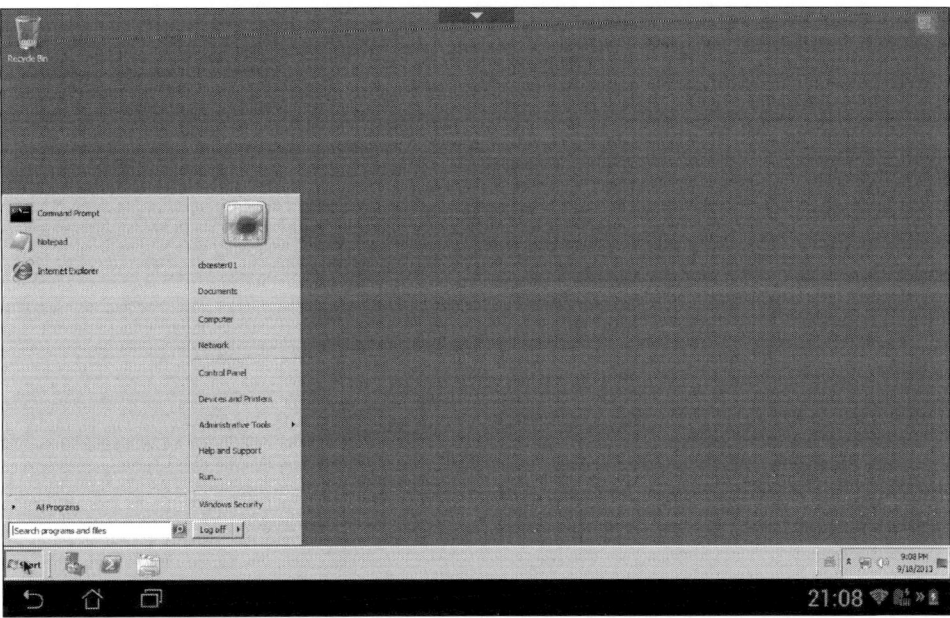

You can use the following additional policy settings to configure Mobility Pack features:

Policy location	Policy
ICA\Client Sensors\ Location	▸ Allows applications to use the physical location of the client device ▸ The setting is allowed or prohibited ▸ Determines if applications run in the XenApp session can use the physical location of the device
ICA\Mobile Experience	▸ Automatic keyboard display ▸ The setting is allowed or prohibited ▸ Determines whether the keyboard is automatically displayed or users must manually open the keyboard
ICA\Mobile Experience	▸ Launches the touch-optimized desktop ▸ The setting is allowed or prohibited ▸ Determines whether a touch-friendly interface or the Windows interface is used

Policy location	Policy
`ICA\Mobile Experience`	▸ Remote the combo box ▸ The setting is allowed or prohibited ▸ Determines whether the device-native combo box or the Windows combo box is shown

There's more...

You can read more on the Best Practices for Citrix XenApp Hotfix Rollup Pack Installation and Deployment at Citrix's Knowledge Center at `http://support.citrix.com/article/CTX120842`.

You can read more on the Citrix XenApp Mobility Pack at Citrix's eDocs at `http://support.citrix.com/proddocs/topic/receiver/mobility-pack-wrapper.html`.

7

XenApp® Maintenance and Monitoring

In this chapter, we will cover the following topics:

- ▶ Monitoring live session information with AppCenter
- ▶ Installing hotfixes and rollup packages
- ▶ Validating the integrity of the XenApp® Farm Data Store database
- ▶ Maintaining the XenApp® Farm Data Store
- ▶ Preparing for XenApp® imaging and provisioning
- ▶ Monitoring XenApp® with Performance Monitor
- ▶ Monitoring XenApp® server status with EdgeSight
- ▶ Monitoring XenApp® with Health Monitoring and Recovery
- ▶ Managing XenApp® resource allocation
- ▶ Configuring XenApp® reboot schedules for maintenance
- ▶ Monitoring user sessions with Desktop Director for XenApp® 6.5

Introduction

A XenApp infrastructure consists of many components to ensure that users can access published desktops or applications. Each Citrix component within the XenApp infrastructure is especially designed to support the entire chain that delivers Windows applications and desktops to the end user.

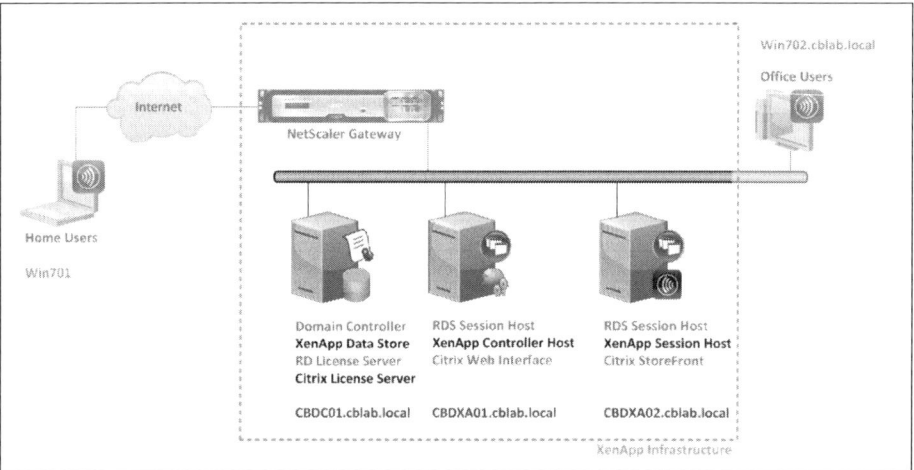

The core of the XenApp infrastructure consists of the XenApp Farm, a collection of XenApp Controller and Session Hosts that publish Windows desktops and applications to end users, based upon Microsoft's Remote Desktop Services.

This chapter will focus on the maintenance and monitoring of the XenApp Farm and servers.

Monitoring live session information with AppCenter

This recipe will show you how to monitor user session information with Citrix XenApp's management console AppCenter.

How to do it...

To live monitor user sessions on the XenApp servers with AppCenter, follow these steps:

1. Open the Citrix XenApp management console AppCenter by navigating to **Start** | **Administrative Tools** | **Citrix** | **Management Consoles**.

2. Select **XenApp** | **<FarmName>** | **Servers** in the left pane.

3. Click on the **Users** tab in the **Servers** pane

4. Select a user session to see more detailed information on the session, such as CPU and memory usage, running processes, and others.

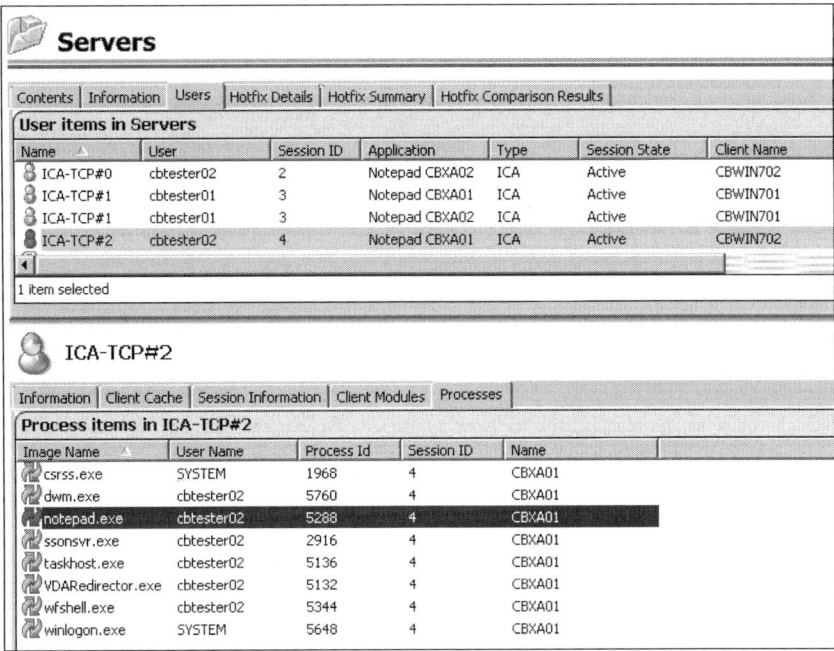

5. Add additional columns to the process information to view extra information, such as the Working Set Size and %CPU Load when required.

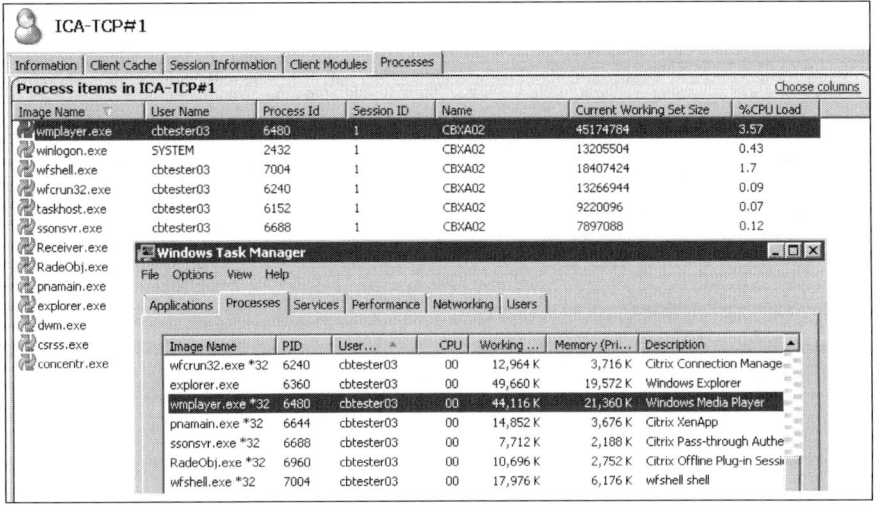

An overview of the running processes in a remote user session is provided, similar to the process overview in the local Windows Task Manager on the XenApp server for the logged-on user.

 You can also select the **Applications** node or a specific application or server to see the user sessions currently running the published application or logged on to the server.

Installing hotfixes and rollup packages

This recipe will show you how to install **Citrix XenApp** (**CXA**) Hotfixes and Rollup Packs on the XenApp servers.

How to do it...

To install a Citrix XenApp hotfix, follow these steps:

1. Check for available XenApp 6.5 hotfixes at Citrix's Knowledge Center at `http://support.citrix.com/product/xa/v6.5_2008r2/`.
2. Download the required hotfixes.
3. To install the hotfix unattended you can use the following command:

   ```
   msiexec /update <hotfixfile> /qn /log <logfile> /norestart
   ```

To uninstall a Citrix XenApp hotfix, follow these steps:

1. Retrieve the product code for XenApp 6.5 with the following command:
   ```
   cpatch /s /r
   ```

2. Retrieve the patch code for the hotfix with the following command:
   ```
   cpatch /s /l <ProductCode> |more
   ```

3. Uninstall the hotfix with the following command:

   ```
   msiexec /uninstall <PatchCode> /package <ProductCode> /qn /log
   <logfile> /norestart
   ```

How it works...

To ensure a stable XenApp infrastructure it is important to maintain XenApp servers, by regularly installing the released Citrix XenApp hotfixes and rollup packs. This also ensures support from Citrix for your running configuration.

Citrix recommends thorough testing and evaluating of hotfix rollup packs on a test server or farm. Make sure you cover every-day-user activity and administrative tasks simulations during the test period to mimic everyday usage of the XenApp Farm.

You can check the available Hotfixes and Rollup Packs for XenApp 6.5 at Citrix's Knowledge Center: `http://support.citrix.com/product/xa/v6.5_2008r2/hotfix/general/`

All the public hotfixes are shown and a link to each Knowledge Center article and hotfix download is provided. By signing in with your MyCitrix account, you can also see limited release hotfixes if required.

At the time of writing this book, Hotfix Rollup Pack 3 (release date December 2013) was the latest major release.

The rollup packs contain multiple hotfixes and supersede many individual hotfixes. When installing a rollup pack, make sure you read the release notes and check the **Replaced Hotfixes** section.

It is a good practice to install all hotfixes marked as **Critical Updates**, these usually include the Hotfix Rollup Packs. Otherwise, only install public hotfixes when the related problems are actually experienced in your XenApp infrastructure.

To install a hotfix or Hotfix Rollup Pack, use the following directives to apply the recommended installation order for a hotfix (rollup pack) in the XenApp Farm:

Always install and test the hotfix in a test environment before performing the installation of any hotfix in a production environment

1. Before installing the hotfix follow these directives:
    - When installing the hotfix ensure no user sessions are run on the server.
    - Check if the **Citrix Independent Management Architecture** (**IMA**) service is running on the server.
    - Always backup the Data Store database before installing a hotfix. Some hotfixes have an impact on the Data Store by adding additional tables and/or columns to the database.

❑ Ensure all servers in the XenApp Farm are running the same hotfix level even though it is possible to run servers with different hotfix levels in the same XenApp Farm. To run a stable and uniform environment, the time period for running a mixed hotfix server level must be kept as short as is possible.

Running different hotfix levels in the same XenApp farm can alter the Data Collector election results. The order used with the election is: 1. Highest IMA version, 2. Election Preferences, 3. Highest Host ID. This can promote a XenApp server Controller Host with a higher hotfix level to become the Data Collector for the XenApp Farm.

2. Download the hotfix from the Citrix Knowledge Center website.

3. First update the Data Collector for a zone.

   You can check the current Data Collector for a zone by selecting the zone in the left pane of **Citrix AppCenter** and selecting the **Information** tab in the middle pane. Only Controller Hosts can act as the Data Collector for a zone.

4. Update all other Controller Host servers in the zone.

5. Update all Session Hosts servers in the zone.

6. Repeat steps 3 to 5 for each zone that is configured in the XenApp Farm.

To install the hotfix unattended you can use the following command line:

```
msiexec /update <hotfixfile> /qn /log <logfile> /norestart
```

To uninstall a hotfix unattended with the `msiexec.exe` executable, the patch code and product code for the hotfix must be provided. You can use the Citrix Patch Handling Utility to retrieve the codes for the hotfix, which is automatically installed during the XenApp installation and located at `C:\Program Files (x86)\Common Files\Citrix\System32` by default.

To retrieve the product code, use the following command line:

```
cpatch /s /r
```

You can find the product code in the output as shown in the following screenshot:

```
Administrator: Command Prompt

C:\Temp>cpatch /s /r

*******************Product Information*******************
ProductName = Citrix XenApp 6.5
ProductCode = {1471A89F-8CAB-4C46-89AB-942432D1DD3D}
ProductLanguage = 1033
ProductVersion = 6.5.0.0

C:\Temp>_
```

To retrieve the patch code for the specified hotfix, use the following command line:

```
cpatch /s /l <ProductCode> |more
```

 The product code is the same for all Citrix XenApp 6.5 hotfix installations, the patch code will differ for each hotfix.

You can find the patch code in the output as shown in the following screenshot:

```
C:\> Administrator: Command Prompt

C:\Temp>cpatch /s /l {1471A89F-8CAB-4C46-89AB-942432D1DD3D} |more
********************Hotfix Information********************
HotfixName = XA650W2K8R2X64R02
HotfixLocalPackage = C:\Windows\Installer\20c6989.msp
PatchCode = {B1CF9796-DC5D-2498-CA8D-E03BF20DDD70}
ProductName = Citrix XenApp 6.5
ProductVersion= 6.5.0.0
ProductCode= {1471A89F-8CAB-4C46-89AB-942432D1DD3D}
ProductLanguage= 1033
InstalledBy = CBLAB\Administrator
InstallDate = 20130918
InstalledOn = 1379529940
Install Date = Sep 18, 2013
Install Time = 20:45:40
HotfixSequence = 6.5.7000.1
MoreInfoURL = http://support.citrix.com/article/CTX136248
CreationTimeUTC = 6/13/2013 10:22:57 AM
Classification = HRP
PatchState = 1
```

With all the codes retrieved, we can use the following command to uninstall the hotfix:

```
msiexec /uninstall <PatchCode> /package <ProductCode> /qn /log <logfile>
/norestart
```

 To uninstall Citrix XenApp 6.5 Hotfix Rollup Pack 2, you would use the following command:

```
msiexec /uninstall {B1CF9796-DC5D-2498-CA8D-
E03BF20DDD70} /package {1471A89F-8CAB-4C46-89AB-
942432D1DD3D} /qb /log c:\temp\uninstallHFRP2.log /
norestart
```

There's more...

You can read all about the best practices for Citrix XenApp Hotfix Rollup Pack installation and deployment at Citrix's Knowledge Center: http://support.citrix.com/article/CTX120842

You can read more on the recommended hotfixes for XenApp 6.5 at Citrix's Knowledge Center: `http://support.citrix.com/article/CTX129229`

You can read more on the different command line options for the Citrix Patch Handling Utility at Citrix's Knowledge Center: `http://support.citrix.com/article/CTX105646`

Validating the integrity of the XenApp® Farm Data Store database

This recipe will show you how to validate the integrity of the Citrix XenApp (CXA) Farm Data Store by using the *dscheck* utility.

How to do it...

To check the integrity of the XenApp Data Store database with the dscheck utility, follow these steps:

Run the following command:

`C:\Program Files (x86)\Citrix\system32\dscheck.exe`

How it works...

With the installation of XenApp 6.5, a small collection of Citrix utilities is placed in the installation folder. One of these tools is the Data Store Validation Utility (dscheck.exe), which can be used to check the integrity of the Data Store database. To check the integrity, run the following command:

`C:\Program Files (x86)\Citrix\system32\dscheck.exe`

When no errors are detected, the following output is shown:

To clean the database of inconsistent data, you can add the /Clean parameter to the command:

```
dscheck /Clean
```

 Always create a backup of the Data Store database, before running the **/Clean** option, to support a rollback scenario to restore the previous situation.

There's more...

You can read more on the dscheck utility at Citrix's eDocs: http://support.citrix. com/proddocs/topic/xenapp65-admin/ps-commands-dscheck.html

For those who are more comfortable using tools that provide a **Graphical User Interface** (**GUI**), check out the DSCheck Maintenance Assistant, which offers a GUI for DSCHECK that can be used by administrators to run all dscheck.exe commands against the Data Store by simply clicking on the appropriate command button. The DSCheck Maintenance Assistant can be downloaded at Citrix's Knowledge Center: http://support.citrix.com/article/ CTX137608

Maintaining the XenApp® Farm Data Store

This recipe will show you how to perform maintenance tasks on the CXA Data Store by using the *dsmaint* utility.

How to do it...

You can run different maintenance tasks on the XenApp Farm Data Store with the dsmaint utility. Dsmaint supports tasks such as backing up, migrating, and compacting the database for both the Data Store and Streaming Offline database.

To migrate the data store to a new database server, follow these steps:

1. Prepare the new database server with a copy or backup of the current database.

2. Create a DSN file for the new database server.

3. Run dsmaint migrate on the XenApp servers that already have an active data store connection and need to be rerouted to the new database server:

   ```
   dsmaint migrate /srcdsn:<sourcedsn> /srcuser:<sourceuser> /
   srcpwd:<pwd> /dstdsn:<destdsn> /dstuser:<destuser> /dstpwd:<pwd>
   ```

4. Run `dsmaint config` on the XenApp servers without existing data store connections that need to connect to the new database server:

```
dsmaint config [/rade] [/user:<username>] [/pwd:<password>] [/
dsn:<dsnfile>]
```

Each XenApp server runs a copy of the Data Store configuration in a **Local Host Cache** (**LHC**) database. To verify and recreate the LHC, follow these steps:

1. Verify the integrity of the LHC.

```
dsmaint verifylhc
```

2. Stop the IMA service.

3. Recreate the LHC.

```
dsmaint recreatelhc
```

4. Start the IMA service.

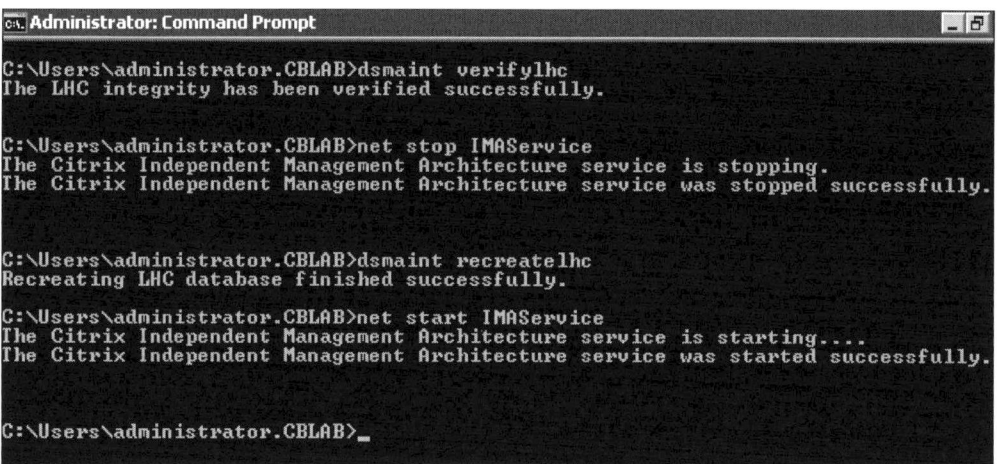

How it works...

You can run different maintenance tasks on the XenApp Farm Data Store with the `dsmaint` utility.

To perform the different maintenance tasks, run the following command:

```
dsmaint <option> <parameters>
```

Each option uses different parameters. The following options and corresponding parameters are available:

Option	Parameters
CONFIG	Changes the parameters used by IMA to connect to the data store.
	`dsmaint config [/rade] [/user:<username>] [/pwd:<password>] [/dsn:<dsnfile>]`
MIGRATE	Migrates the database from one data source to another.
	`dsmaint migrate [{/srcdsn:<dsn1> /srcuser:<user1> / srcpwd:<pwd1>}] [{/dstdsn:<dsn2> /dstuser:<user2> / dstpwd:<pwd2>}]`
SQL Server options	
PUBLISHSQLDS	Publishes a SQL Server data store so that it can be replicated.
	`dsmaint publishsqlds {/user:<username> / pwd:<password>}`
SQL Server Express options	
BACKUP	Creates a backup copy of the SQL Server Express deployment data store.
	`dsmaint backup <destinationpath>`
RECOVER	Recovers local data store from the last known good backup data. Used in combination with the backup option for the SQL Express deployment data store.
	`dsmaint recover`
Local host cache options	
COMPACTDB	Compacts the LHC or RADE database file.
	`dsmaint compactdb [/lhc]`
RECREATELHC	Recreates the local host cache database.
	`dsmaint recreatelhc`
VERIFYLHC	Verifies integrity of MS Access LHC.
	`dsmaint verifylhc [/autorepair]`
Offline data store options	
RECREATERADE	Recreates the application streaming offline database.
	`dsmaint recreaterade`

There's more...

You can read more on the DSMAINT utility at Citrix's eDocs: http://support.citrix.com/proddocs/topic/xenapp65-admin/ps-commands-dsmaint-v2.html

Preparing for XenApp® imaging and provisioning

This recipe will show you how to prepare a Citrix XenApp server installation for imaging and provisioning. Provisioning enables you to stream a single XenApp server image to multiple XenApp servers (both physical and virtual), thus reducing the need to change different server configurations within a single XenApp Farm, while reducing maintenance to a single (master) image. To ensure that no server specific settings are retained in the master image, a XenApp server needs to be prepared for imaging and/or provisioning.

 To read more on provisioning, you can check out the book *Getting Started with Citrix Provisioning Services 7.0*, by *Puthiyavan Udayakumar*, published by Packt Publishing.

How to do it...

To prepare a XenApp server that is already joined to the XenApp Farm for imaging and provisioning, follow these steps:

1. Install and configure the XenApp server role.

2. Install and configure the required applications and settings.

3. Check each application for the required method to prepare it for imaging and provisioning and perform the advices actions.

 There are a lot of client/server applications that require additional actions to prepare the agent software for imaging, like virus scanners, Microsoft System Center, automation software agents, and others.

Check your application software for instructions on preparing it for imaging and provisioning.

4. Prepare the XenApp server for imaging with the following command:

```
"C:\Program Files (x86)\Citrix\XenApp\ServerConfig\
XenAppConfigConsole.exe" /ExecutionMode:ImagePrep /
RemoveCurrentServer:True /ClearLocalDatabaseInformation:False /
LogFilename:<logfile>
```

5. Run Microsoft `sysprep` as the final preparation step for server imaging.

There's more...

You can read more on preparing for XenApp imaging and provisioning at Citrix's eDocs: `http://support.citrix.com/proddocs/topic/xenapp65-install/ps-image-prep.html`

Monitoring XenApp® with Performance Monitor

This recipe will show you how to monitor a XenApp server with Windows Performance Monitor.

How to do it...

To use Windows Performance Monitor, we'll start by creating a Data Collector Set that contains the counters we want to monitor.

To create a Data Collector Set, follow these steps:

1. Start Windows Performance Monitor by navigating to **Start | Run | perfmon**.

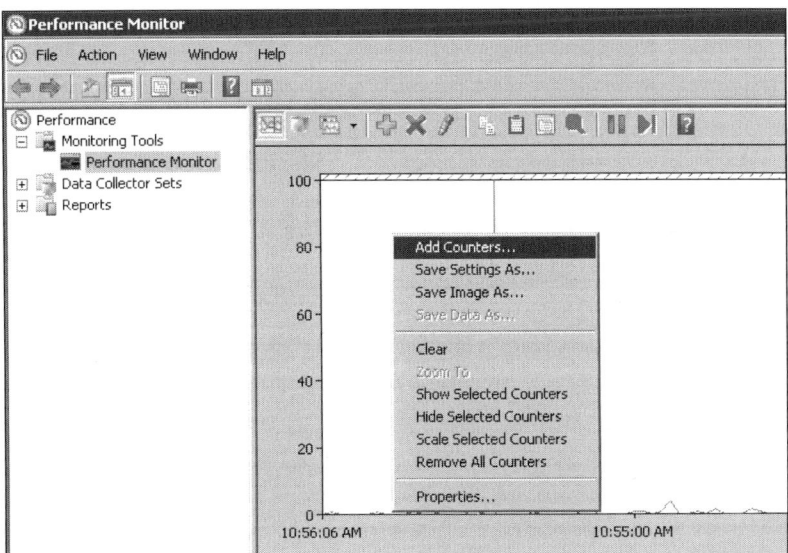

2. Right-click on the graph in the right pane and select **Add Counters**.

3. Add the following Windows counters to check the performance of the Windows server:

Category	Counter	Description
Memory	% Committed Bytes in use	The amount of virtual memory in use.
	Available Mbytes	The amount of physical memory available for running processes.
	Pages/sec	The rate at which pages are read from or written to disk to resolve hard page faults.
Network Interface	Bytes Total/sec	The rate at which bytes are sent and received over each network adapter.
	Output Queue Length	The length of the output packet queue, in packets.
Paging File	% Usage	The amount of the Page File instance in use.
Physical Disk	% Idle Time	The time the disk was idle.
	Average Disk Queue Length	The number of I/O operations that are waiting for the hard drive to become available.
	Disk Reads/sec	The average time to read data from the disk.
	Disk Writes/sec	The average time it takes to write data to the disk.
Processor	% Interrupt Time	The time the processor spends receiving and servicing hardware interruptions.
	% Processor Time	The elapsed time the processor spends in executing a non-idle thread.
	% User Time	The elapsed time the processor spends in user mode.
System	Processor Queue Length	The number of threads in the processor queue.

4. Check the measured values for the different counters.

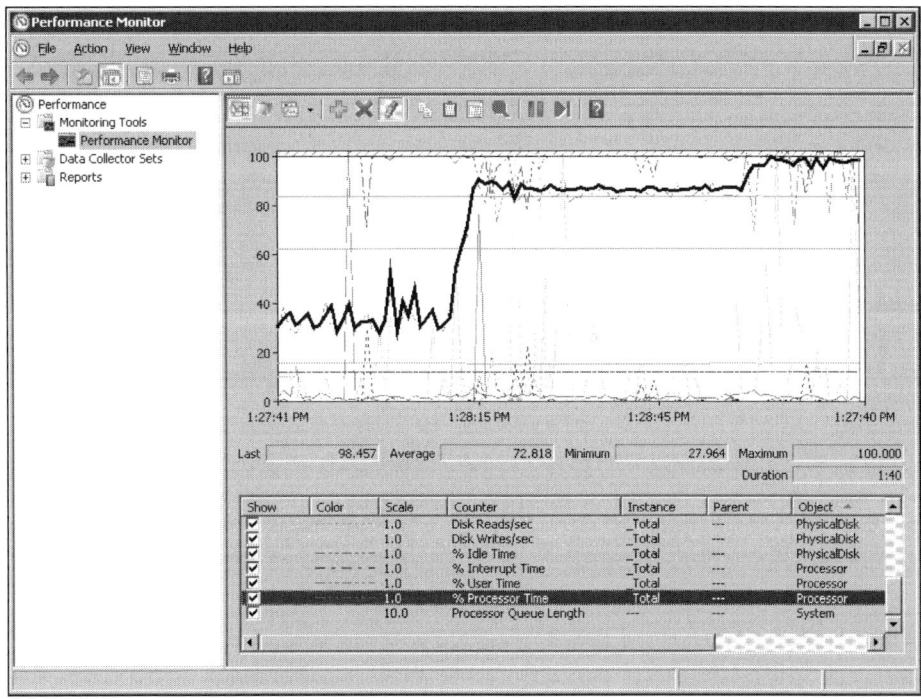

5. You can add the following Citrix counters to check the performance of the XenApp processes and user session specific performance on the server:

Category	Counter	Description
Citrix CPU Utilization Mgmt User	CPU Usage	The CPU resource consumed by a user at a given time, averaged over a few seconds.
Citrix IMA Networking	Network Connections	The number of active IMA network connections to other IMA servers.
Citrix Licensing	License Server Connection Failure	The number of minutes that the XenApp server has been disconnected from the License Server.
Citrix MetaFrame Presentation Server	Cumulative Server Load	The combined processor utilization and connected XenApp user session loads for this server.
	Data Store Connection Failure	The number of minutes that the XenApp server has been disconnected from the data store.

Category	Counter	Description
	Zone Elections	The number of zone elections.
ICA Session	Input HDX Mediastream for Flash Data bandwidth	The bandwidth used when streaming flash data in an HDX-enabled session.
	Input Session Bandwidth	The bandwidth used from client to server for a session.
	Latency - Session Average	The average client latency over the lifetime of a session.
	Output Session Bandwidth	The bandwidth used from server to client for a session.
Secure Ticket Authority	STA Bad Data Request Count	The total number of unsuccessful ticket validation and data retrieval requests during the lifetime of the STA.
Terminal Services	Active Sessions	The total number of active sessions.
	Total Sessions	The total number of sessions (Active and Disconnected).

6. The user session specific metrics can allocate user sessions that are consuming excessive resources, as is shown in the following screenshot, for the first ICA session:

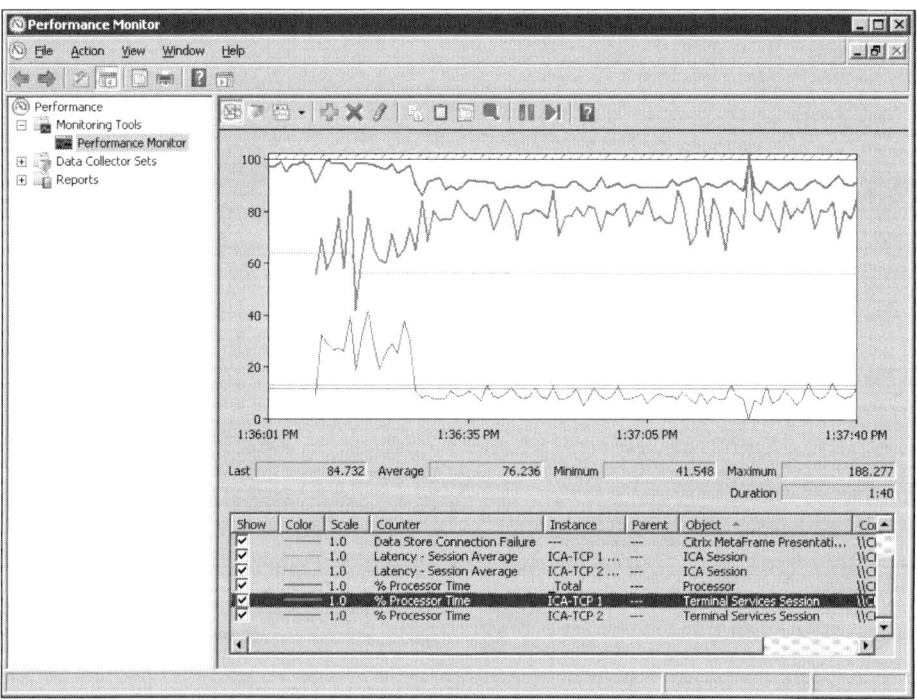

There's more...

You can read more on Citrix XenApp Performance Benchmarking and Analysis with Perfmon at Citrix's Knowledge Center: `http://support.citrix.com/article/CTX133593`

You can read more on key counters for Windows server at Microsoft's TechNet: `http://technet.microsoft.com/nl-nl/magazine/2008.08.pulse(en-us).aspx`

Monitoring XenApp® server status with EdgeSight

This recipe will show you how to use Citrix EdgeSight for XenApp to monitor the CXA Farm and servers health. EdgeSight licenses are included with the Citrix XenApp platinum licenses.

Getting started

This recipe assumes the required EdgeSight infrastructure is installed and configured as well as the local installation of the EdgeSight Agents on the XenApp servers.

 You can find all updates, technotes and documentation on Citrix EdgeSight for XenApp 5.4 at Citrix's Knowledge Center: `http://support.citrix.com/product/es/xav5.4`

How to do it...

To monitor the XenApp servers with EdgeSight, follow these steps:

1. Log on to the EdgeSight website.
2. Select the **Monitor** tab.
3. Select **Dashboard** in the left menu.

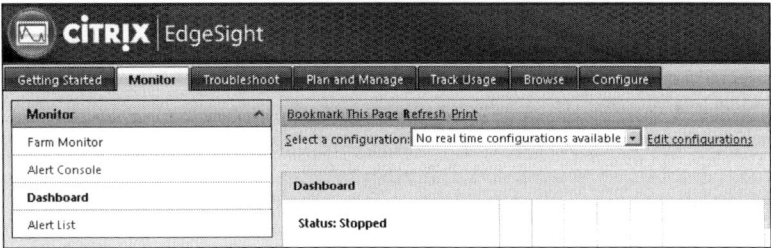

4. Click on **Edit configurations** to create a new configuration.

5. Click on **New Real Time Configuration**.

6. Enter a Configuration Name and click on **Create the Configuration**.

7. Add the XenApp server devices to the Configuration Members box and click **Next**.

8. Configure the **Performance Counters** you want to monitor (only 8 counters are allowed per configuration) and click on **Next**.

9. Click **Finish**.

10. Click on the created Configuration to return to the **Dashboard**.

11. Click on **Start Updating** to start monitoring.

12. You can select a device to see more detailed information for each counter.

There's more...

You can read more on Citrix EdgeSight for XenApp 5.4 at Citrix's Knowledge Center: `http://support.citrix.com/product/es/xav5.4`

You can read more on Citrix EdgeSight 5.4 at Citrix's eDocs: `http://support.citrix.com/proddocs/topic/edgesight54/es-54-landing-page.html`

Monitoring XenApp® with Health Monitoring and Recovery

This recipe will show you how to configure XenApp Health Monitoring and Recovery policies to monitor the Citrix XenApp server.

How to do it...

To use the Health Monitoring and Recovery feature of Citrix XenApp to monitor the server, follow these steps:

1. Open the Citrix XenApp management console **AppCenter** by navigating to **Start | Administrative Tools | Citrix | Management Consoles**.
2. Select **XenApp | <FarmName> | Policies** in the left pane.
3. Click on **New** in the **Computer** tab in the right pane.
4. Enter a **Name** and **Description** for the policy and click on **Next**.
5. Select **Server Settings | Health monitoring and Recovery** in the left pane.

6. Configure the corresponding computer policy settings for **Health monitoring**, **Health monitoring tests**, and **Maximum percent of servers with logon control** in the right pane and click on **Next**.

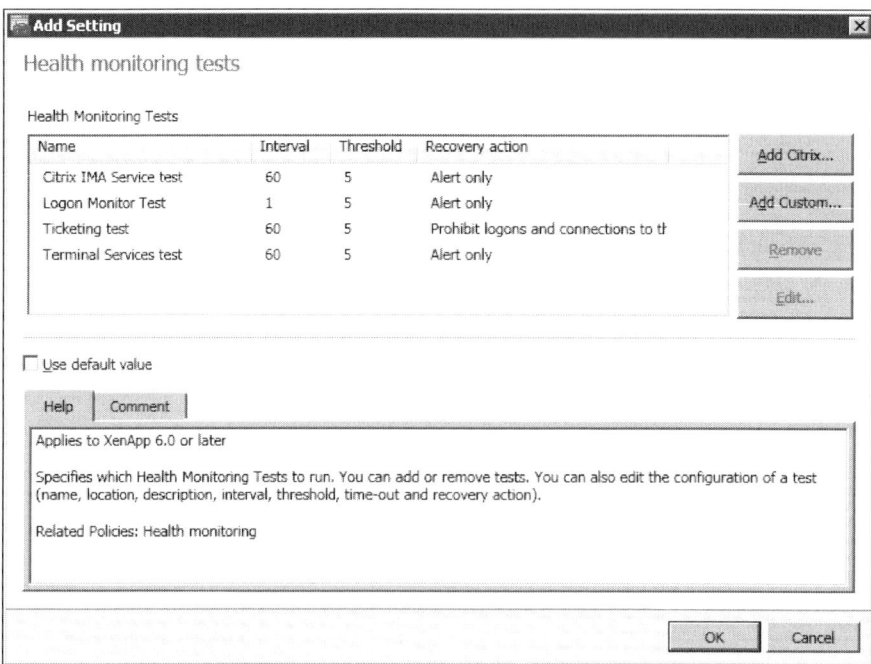

7. Configure a policy filter if one is required and click on **Next**.
8. Click on **Create**.

 The policy changes will be active after a server reboot or `gpupdate /force` command is issued.

There's more...

You can read more on Health Monitoring and Recovery at Citrix's Knowledge Center at `http://support.citrix.com/article/CTX131352`, or the available Citrix tests at Citrix's eDocs at `http://support.citrix.com/proddocs/topic/xenapp65-admin/ps-maintain-monitor-server-perf.html`.

Managing XenApp® resource allocation

This recipe will show you how to manage the allocation of CXA server resources, such as CPU and RAM.

How to do it...

To manage memory and CPU usage for the XenApp servers, follow these steps:

1. Open the Citrix XenApp management console **AppCenter** by navigating to **Start | Administrative Tools | Citrix | Management Consoles**.

2. Select **XenApp | <FarmName> | Policies** in the left pane.

3. Click on **New** in the **Computer** tab in the right pane.

4. Enter a **Name** and **Description** for the policy and click on **Next**.

5. Select **Server Settings | Memory/CPU** in the left pane.

6. Configure the different policy setting in this section for CPU and Memory optimization and click on **Next**.

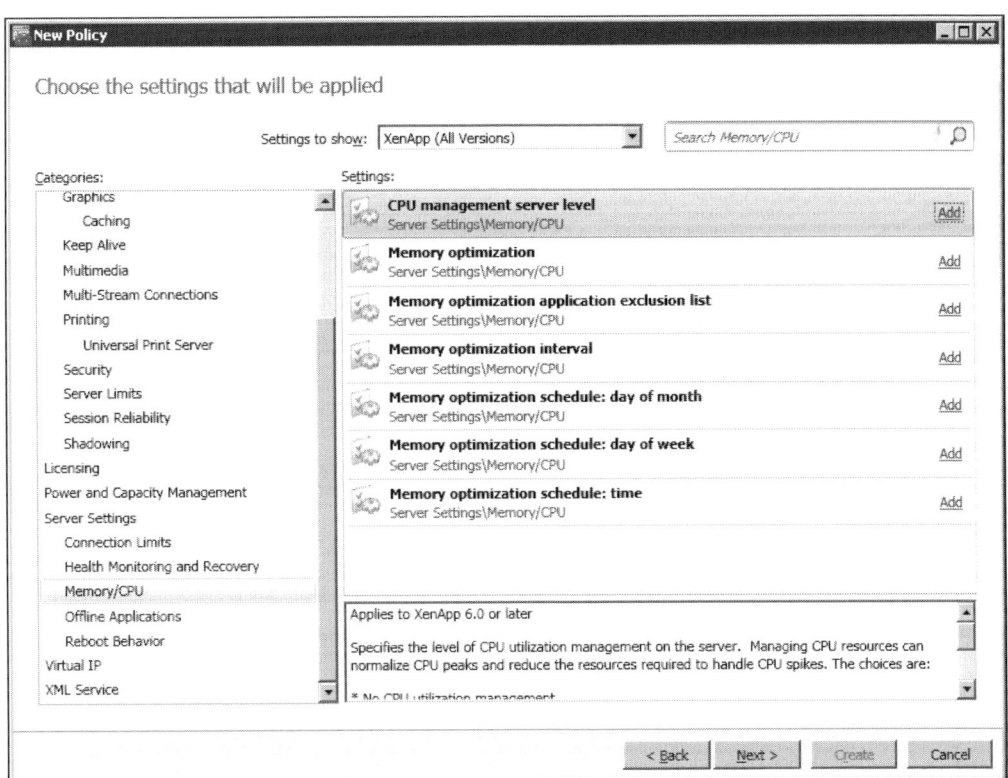

7. Configure a policy filter if one is required and click on **Next**

8. Click on **Create**.

9. Turn off **Dynamic Fair Share Scheduling** (**DFSS**) by changing the following registry key to `0` on the XenApp server:

```
HKLM\SYSTEM\CurrentControlSet\Control\Session Manager\Quota
System\EnableCpuQuota
```

How it works...

Citrix XenApp offers special policies to manage the allocation of resources to users running sessions on the XenApp servers.

Citrix offers the CPU utilization management feature to improve the way a XenApp farm normalizes CPU peaks when CPU-intensive processes are run by logged on users.

CPU utilization Management can be set to:

▶ No CPU utilization management: disables CPU utilization management

▶ Fair sharing of CPU between sessions: ensures CPU resources are equally shared between users

▶ Preferential Load Balancing ensures that the CPU resources are shared based upon user and/or application importance level

When the CPU utilization is configured for fair sharing, the available CPU resources are equally shared between the user sessions on a XenApp server by providing the CPU reservation and CPU shares.

The CPU reservation ensures that a percentage of the server's CPU resource is available for each user. The server will reserve up to 20% of the CPU resources on a server for the local system account, which shall not be made available to users.

The CPU shares are used to allocate a percentage of the available CPU time (or cycles) for each user. The available CPU time is equally divided between the user sessions on the server.

When the CPU utilization is configured for the Preferential Load Balancing users and applications can be assigned an importance level (Low, Normal, or High) to allocate more CPU resources to a user and/or application. By default, each user and application is set with a Normal importance level.

The importance level for users is configured through a Citrix user policy setting, while applications are configured through the **Limits** section of their properties.

Citrix CPU Utilization Management is incompatible with **Dynamic Fair Share Scheduling** (**DFSS**), a Windows Remote Desktop Services component. Ensure DFSS is disabled on each server when CPU Utilization Management is enabled. As configuring DFSS through Group Policy is known to cause problems, it is advised to use the dedicated DFSS registry key.

Citrix offers memory optimization by creating shared DLLs for applications that are run in more than one user session on a XenApp server. Memory optimization is disabled by default. In addition to enabling memory optimization, you also need to provide the schedule information to determine when the server will check for DLLs that can be shared. You can configure the settings with Citrix Computer policy settings.

There's more...

You can read more on disabling DFSS at Citrix's Knowledge Center at `http://support.citrix.com/article/ctx127135`

You can read more on Memory and CPU policy settings at Citrix's eDocs at `http://support.citrix.com/proddocs/topic/xenapp65-admin/ps-ref-policies-memory-cpu.html`

Configuring XenApp® reboot schedules for maintenance

This recipe will show you how to configure a scheduled reboot schema for a CXA.

How to do it...

To configure a reboot schedule, follow these steps:

1. Open the Citrix XenApp management console **AppCenter** by navigating to **Start | Administrative Tools | Citrix | Management Consoles**.
2. Select **XenApp | <FarmName> | Policies** in the left pane.
3. Click on **New** in the **Computer** tab in the right pane.
4. Enter a Name and Description for the policy and click on **Next**.

5.   Select **Server Settings | Reboot Behavior** in the left pane.

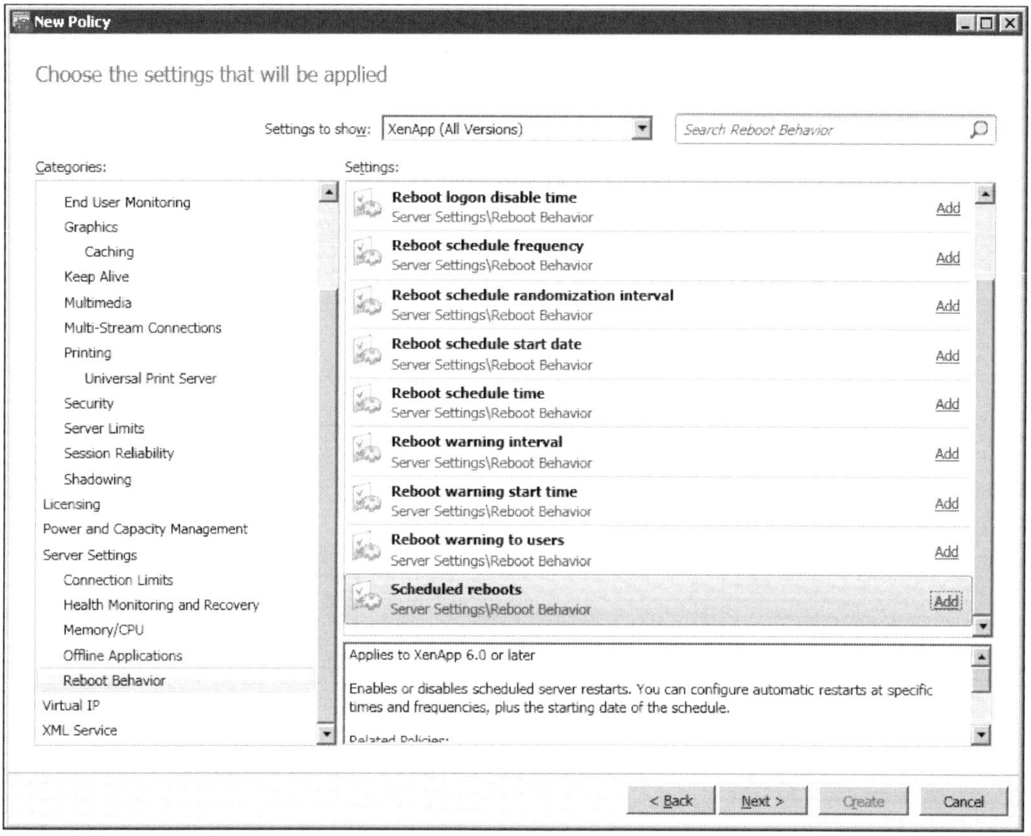

New Policy — □ ×

Choose the settings that will be applied

Settings to show: [XenApp (All Versions) ▼]   [*Search Reboot Behavior* 🔍]

Categories:

- End User Monitoring
- Graphics
  - Caching
- Keep Alive
- Multimedia
- Multi-Stream Connections
- Printing
  - Universal Print Server
- Security
- Server Limits
- Session Reliability
- Shadowing
- Licensing
- Power and Capacity Management
- Server Settings
  - Connection Limits
  - Health Monitoring and Recovery
  - Memory/CPU
  - Offline Applications
  - Reboot Behavior
- Virtual IP
- XML Service

Settings:

Reboot logon disable time Server Settings\Reboot Behavior	Add
Reboot schedule frequency Server Settings\Reboot Behavior	Add
Reboot schedule randomization interval Server Settings\Reboot Behavior	Add
Reboot schedule start date Server Settings\Reboot Behavior	Add
Reboot schedule time Server Settings\Reboot Behavior	Add
Reboot warning interval Server Settings\Reboot Behavior	Add
Reboot warning start time Server Settings\Reboot Behavior	Add
Reboot warning to users Server Settings\Reboot Behavior	Add
Scheduled reboots Server Settings\Reboot Behavior	Add

Applies to XenApp 6.0 or later

Enables or disables scheduled server restarts. You can configure automatic restarts at specific times and frequencies, plus the starting date of the schedule.

Related Policies:

[< Back] [Next >] [Create] [Cancel]

---

6.   Configure the different policy settings to apply the desired reboot schedule time and corresponding user messages and click on **Next**.

7.   Configure a policy filter if one is required and click on **Next**.

8.   Click on **Create**.

It is best practice to regularly reboot a Citrix XenApp or Remote Desktop Session Host server due to memory leaks that can occur on Windows servers. A weekly reboot schedule is configured in most production environments. Feel free to adjust this schedule when performance metrics are indicating that a more frequent reboot schedule is required.

How it works...

The Citrix XenApp reboot schedules are now configured through the Citrix Computer policy settings. To apply different reboot schedules to different XenApp server groups, you can configure a policy Worker Group filter. This way, the policy is only applied to XenApp servers that are a member of the Worker Group.

The downfall to configuring the reboot schedule through policies is that only one policy can be actively applied to a XenApp server, as only one configured reboot schedule is applied.

This means that we can configure a weekly reboot schedule for a XenApp server by configuring the reboot schedule start date to a day of the week and set the reboot schedule frequency to 7 days. But we cannot configure a XenApp server to have both a weekly Tuesday and a weekly Friday scheduled reboot, as only one of the reboot schedule policies would be applied. Depending on the highest priority, the reboot schedule for either Tuesday or Friday would be applied.

There's more...

You can read more on creating a staggered Scheduled Reboot Policy at Citrix's Knowledge Center: http://support.citrix.com/article/CTX126043

Monitoring user sessions with Desktop Director for XenApp® 6.5

Desktop Director was originally designed to offer support desks a website for monitoring XenDesktop user sessions and session information. It also offers basis administrator tasks that can be performed. In additional to Citrix XenDesktop, Desktop Director is also available for Citrix XenApp 6.5 to monitor user session information. This recipe will show you how to monitor a user session with Desktop Director for XenApp 6.5.

Getting started

This recipe assumes Desktop Director is installed. To install Desktop Director 2.1 for XenApp 6.5, you can follow the see directions at Citrix's Knowledge Center: http://support.citrix.com/article/CTX135849

How to do it...

To monitor a user session with Desktop Director, follow these steps:

1. Go to the **Desktop Director** website by navigating to **Start** | **All Programs** | **Citrix**.

2. Log in with a user account that has been granted access.

3. Enter a (partial) username in the search box, and click on the appropriate username to retrieve session information.

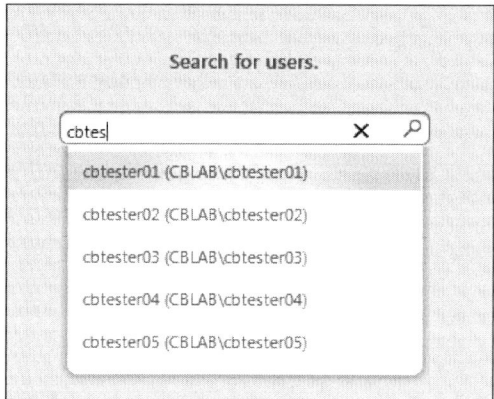

4. You can perform basic administrative tasks with the **Session Control** and **Send Message** buttons in the **Session Details** pane.

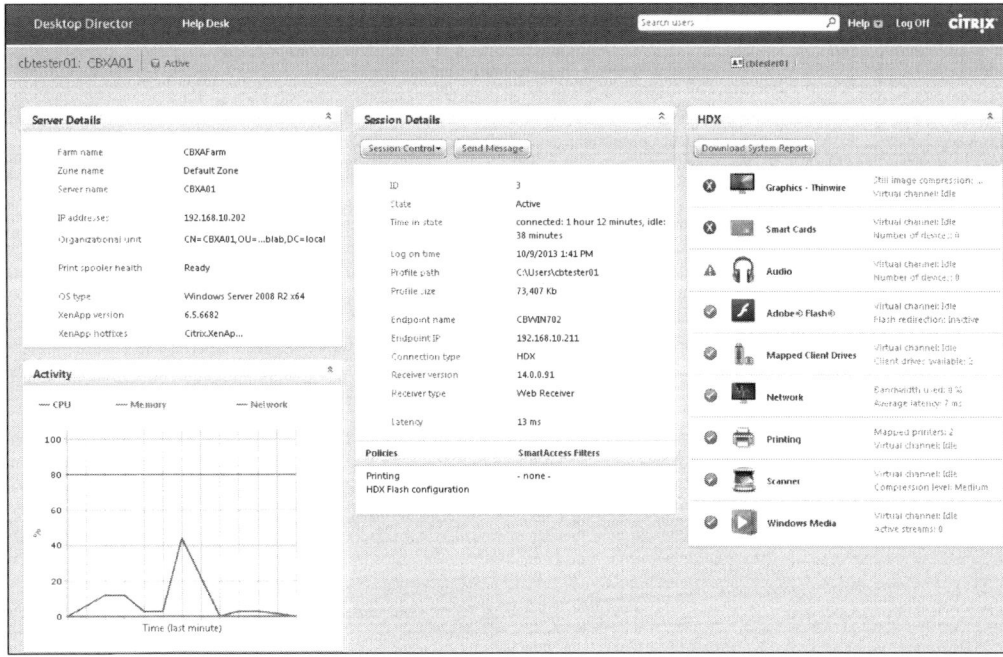

The information shown by Desktop Director represents real-time performance information on the current user session and XenApp server.

If you are just using XenApp or a combination of XenDesktop and XenApp with Desktop Director you need to search for the user. No dashboard will be shown after you have logged on. You will only see real-time information for the selected user, if it has a published application running. If the user does not have any application running, no information is shown.

8

XenApp® Policies

In this chapter, we will cover the following topics:

- ► Creating a XenApp Computer or User policy
- ► Adding filters to a policy
- ► Comparing XenApp policies and templates
- ► Simulating connection scenarios with Citrix® policies
- ► Configuring policy priorities and exceptions
- ► Configuring and maintaining XenApp printing
- ► Enabling shadowing
- ► Assigning Load Evaluators to servers and applications
- ► Enhancing user experience with HDX
- ► Redirecting the client drives of the user device
- ► Configuring session pre-launch and lingering options

Introduction

A XenApp infrastructure consists of many components to ensure users can start published desktops or applications. Each Citrix component within the XenApp infrastructure is specially designed to support the entire chain that delivers Windows applications and desktops to the end user.

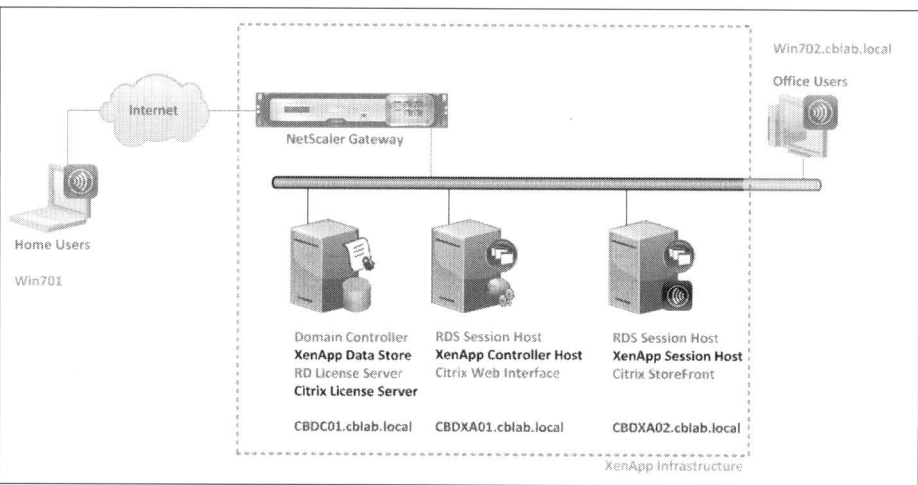

The core of the XenApp infrastructure consists of the XenApp Farm, a collection of XenApp Controller, and Session Hosts that publish Windows desktops and applications to end users, based on Microsoft's Remote Desktop Services. This chapter will focus on the Citrix policies that are available to configure Computer and User settings for the XenApp Farm and servers. Using policies, many of the settings can be centrally configured, which will apply to the filtered set of XenApp servers or user sessions. Policies also ensure that newly added servers or user sessions receive the same preset configuration and uniformity is applied across the XenApp Farm.

Policies can be configured either by using Microsoft's **Group Policy Management Console** (**GPMC**) or by using Citrix's AppCenter. When using Microsoft's GPMC, you will need to install an additional hotfix to ensure the Citrix policies are integrated in the GPMC. Check Citrix Support for the latest hotfixes for Citrix XenApp 6.5 available at `http://support.citrix.com/product/xa/v6.5_2008r2/hotfix/general/`.

As most of the recipes in this chapter zoom in on the different Citrix policies that can be set, the instructions in the *How to do it...* section will look similar for some of the recipes. Details on the policy settings are addressed in the *How it works...* section of each recipe. The policies in the recipes of this chapter are configured using Citrix AppCenter.

Creating a XenApp® Computer or User policy

This recipe will show you how to create policies in general to configure Computer and User settings for Citrix XenApp.

Getting ready

Before configuring computer and user policies, you have to decide which tool to use to create and configure Citrix policies. As of Citrix XenApp 6.x, you can use both the Microsoft Group Policy Management Console (GPMC) as Citrix's AppCenter to create policies. Policies can be managed from only one of the consoles as policies created with GPMC are not visible in AppCenter and vice versa.

When using GPMC, a public hotfix must be installed on the machine that is running on the management console. The latest version can be found at Citrix's Knowledge Center: `http://support.citrix.com/product/xa/v6.5_2008r2/hotfix/general/public/`.

How to do it...

To create a Citrix policy that is applied to the XenApp servers with AppCenter, follow these steps:

1. Open the Citrix XenApp Management Console AppCenter (**Start | Administrative Tools | Citrix | Management Consoles**).

2. Navigate to **XenApp | <FarmName> | Policies** in the left pane.

3. Click on the **Computer** tab in the **Policies** pane.

4. Click on **New** to create a new policy.

5. Enter values in the **Name** and **Description** fields for the policy and click on **Next**.

6. Select a category in the left pane.

7. Add a policy setting by clicking on **Add** in the right pane for each setting.

8. Configure the policy setting and click on **OK**.

9. Repeat steps 6 to 8 to add more policy settings.

10. Click on **Next** when all policy settings are configured.

11. Configure the filter settings and click on **Next**.

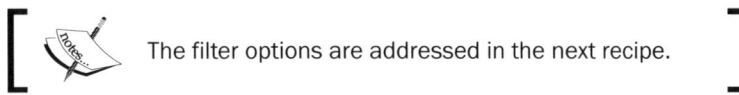 The filter options are addressed in the next recipe.

12. Ensure the **Enable this policy** option is selected and click on **Create**.

Computer policies are applied to XenApp servers when the server is started or when policy updates are applied to the XenApp server. To force the policies to be applied immediately to the XenApp server, run the following command on the server:

```
gpupdate /force
```

To create a Citrix policy that is applied to the XenApp user session with AppCenter, follow these steps:

1. Open the Citrix XenApp management console AppCenter (**Start | Administrative Tools | Citrix | Management Consoles**).

2. Navigate to **XenApp | <FarmName> | Policies** in the left pane.

3. Click on the **User** tab in the **Policies** pane.

4. Click on **New** to create a new policy.

5. Enter values in the **Name** and **Description** fields for the policy and click on **Next**.

6. Select a category in the left pane.

7. Add a policy setting by clicking on **Add** in the right pane for each setting.

8. Configure the policy setting and click on **OK**.

9. Repeat steps 6 to 8 to add more policy settings.

10. Click on **Next** when all policy settings are configured.

11. Configure the filter settings and click on **Next**.

 Filter options are addressed in the next recipe.

12. Ensure the **Enable this policy** option is selected and click on **Create**.

 Just like Windows User policies, Citrix User policies are applied when the user session starts.

There's more...

You can read more on creating Citrix policies at Citrix's eDocs at `http://support.citrix.com/proddocs/topic/xenapp65-admin/ps-admin-publishing-policies-create-all.html`.

See also

- ▶ The *Adding filters to a policy* recipe
- ▶ The *Comparing XenApp® policies and templates* recipe
- ▶ The *Simulating connection scenario's with Citrix® policies* recipe
- ▶ The *Configuring policy priorities and exceptions* recipe

Adding filters to a policy

This recipe will show you how to add filters to a policy to apply the policy to a selective group of XenApp servers or user sessions. Policies that are not configured with a filter apply to all XenApp servers in the farm and to all logged on users for a XenApp session. This will have the same effect as using the default unfiltered computer or user policy that cannot have a filter applied to it.

How to do it...

You can apply different policy filters to computer or user policies. To add filters to a Citrix Computer policy follow these steps:

1. Create a new policy by following steps 1 to 10 from the previous recipe.
2. Click on **Add** to configure the **Organizational Unit (OU)** or **Worker Group** filter.

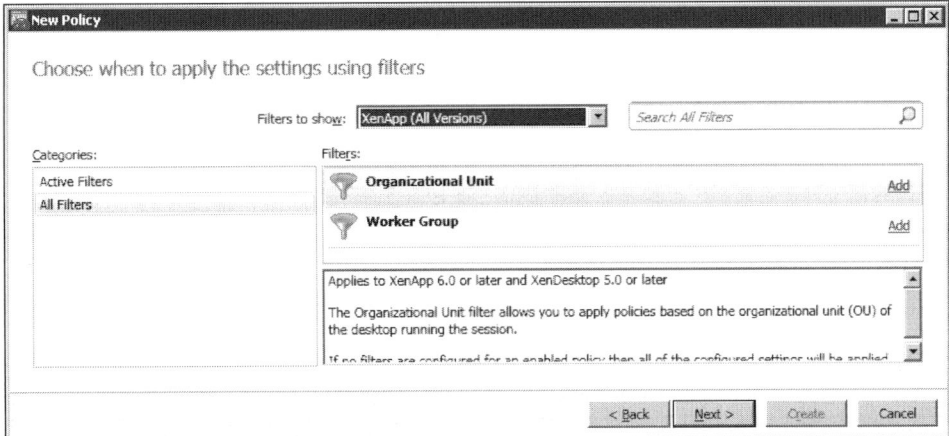

3. Click on **Add** to configure a filter element.
4. Configure the mode (allow or deny) and use **Browse** to find the correct worker group or OU.

5. Click on **OK** to add the filter element.

6. Repeat steps 3 to 5 to add more filter elements.

7. Click on **OK** to add the filter to the policy.

8. Repeat steps 2 to 7 to configure multiple filters for the policy.

9. Click on **Next**.

10. Ensure the **Enable this policy** option is selected and click on **Create**.

To add filters to a Citrix User policy follow these steps:

1. Create a new policy by following the steps 1 to 10 from the previous recipe.

2. Click on **Add** to configure **Access Control**, **Branch Repeater**, **Client IP Address**, **Client Name**, **Organizational Unit** (OU), **User or Group**, or **Worker Group filter**.

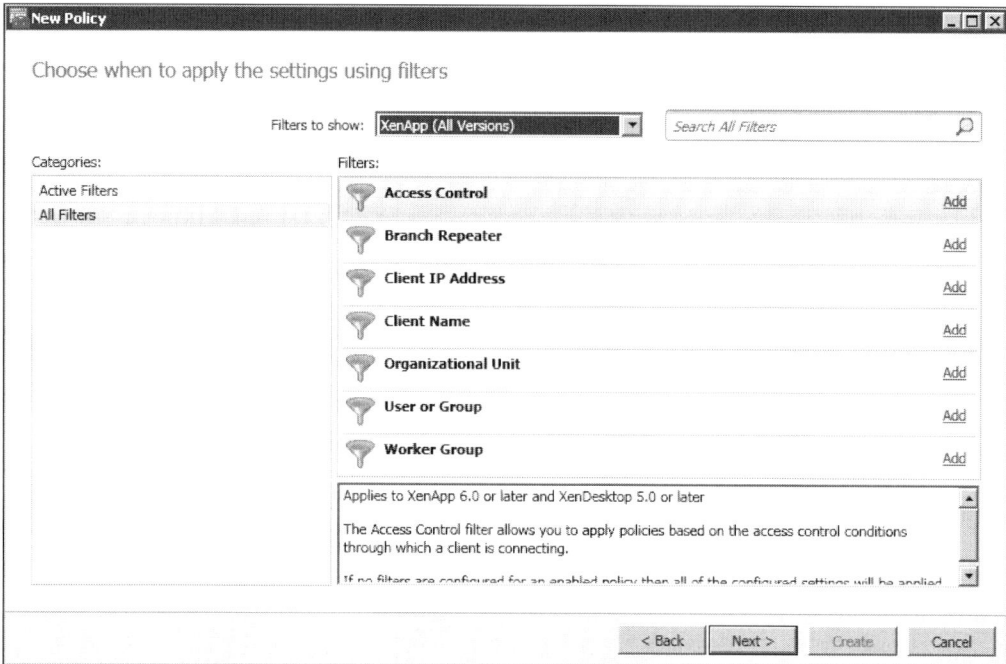

3. Click on **Add** to configure a filter element.

4. Configure the mode (allow or deny) and use **Browse** to find the correct OU, **User or Group**, or **Worker Group**, or enter filter-specific settings for **Client IP Address**, **Name**, **Access Control**, or **Branch Repeater**.

5. Click on **OK** to add the filter element.

6. Repeat steps 3 to 5 to add more filter elements.

7. Click on **OK** to add the filter to the policy.

8. Repeat steps 2 to 7 to configure multiple filters for the policy.

9. Click on **Next**.

10. Ensure the **Enable this policy** option is selected and click on **Create**.

See also

▸ The _Creating a XenApp® Computer or User policy_ recipe

▸ The _Comparing XenApp® policies and templates_ recipe

▸ The _Simulating connection scenarios with Citrix® policies_ recipe

▸ The _Configuring policy priorities and exceptions_ recipe

Comparing XenApp® policies and templates

This recipe will show you how to compare policy settings with other policies or policy templates by using Citrix's management console AppCenter to see if policies contain similar settings, contradicting settings, or have no correlation whatsoever.

How to do it...

To compare policies with templates in AppCenter, follow these steps:

1. Open the Citrix XenApp management console AppCenter (**Start | Administrative Tools | Citrix | Management Consoles**).

2. Navigate to **XenApp | <FarmName> | Policies** in the left pane.

3. Click on the **Templates** tab in the **Policies** pane.

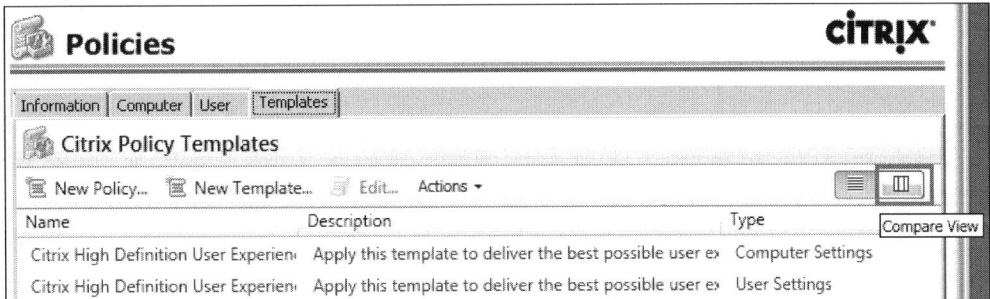

4. Click on the **Compare View** icon on the right-hand side of the menu bar.

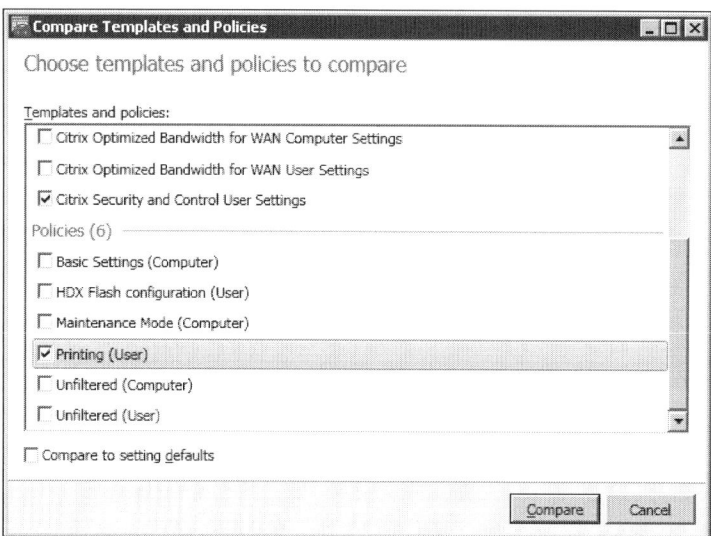

5. Select the policies that you want to compare and click on **Compare**.

To check the configured policy settings against default policy settings for the XenApp Farm, select a policy, and select the **Compare to setting defaults** option.

The policy settings from the selected policies are shown and can easily be compared.

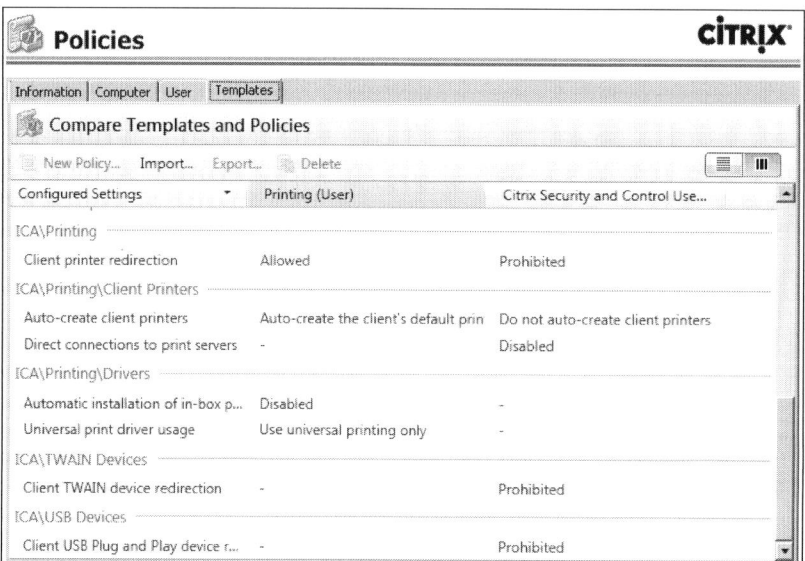

To add additional policies to the comparison or check all available policy settings, click on **Configured Settings** and select either **Add/Remove Columns** or **Show All Settings**.

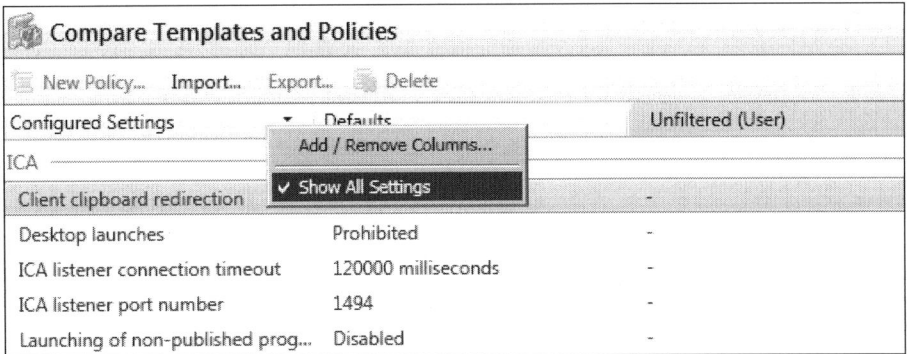

There's more...

You can read more about comparing policies and templates at Citrix's eDocs: `http://support.citrix.com/proddocs/topic/xenapp65-admin/ps-policies-templates-compare.html`.

See also

- ▶ The *Creating a XenApp® Computer or User policy* recipe
- ▶ The *Adding filters to a policy* recipe
- ▶ The *Simulating connection scenarios with Citrix® policies* recipe
- ▶ The *Configuring policy priorities and exceptions* recipe

Simulating connection scenarios with Citrix® policies

This recipe will show you how to generate a report on the applied policies for a user or computer by running a simulation with the Citrix Group Policy Modeling Wizard.

How to do it...

To check the applied policy settings by simulating a user session with AppCenter, follow these steps:

1. Open the Citrix XenApp Management Console AppCenter (**Start | Administrative Tools | Citrix | Management Consoles**).

2. Navigate to **XenApp** | **<FarmName>** | **Policies** in the left pane.

3. Click on the **Run the modeling wizard** option in the **Actions** pane.

4. Click on **Next**.

5. Configure the following options:

   ❑ Show DCs in this domain: `<domain>`

   ❑ Process the simulation on this DC: Any available DC...

6. Click on **Next**.

7. Configure the User and/or Computer information for the simulation and click on **Next**.

8. Configure filter selections you want to apply to the simulation and click on **Next**.

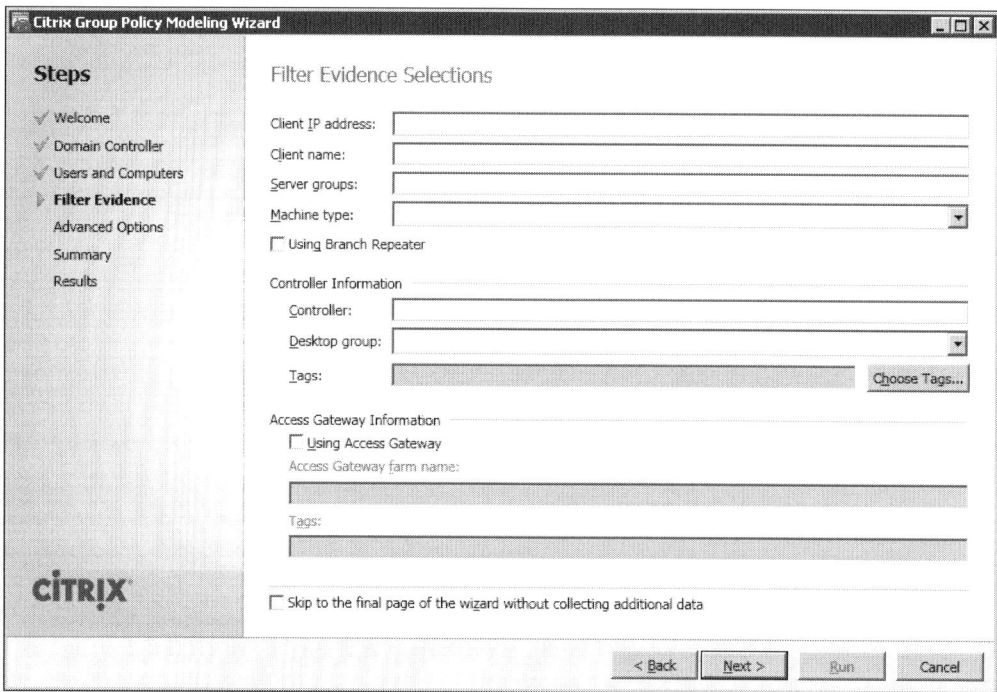

9. Configure the **Advanced Simulation Options** and click on **Next**.

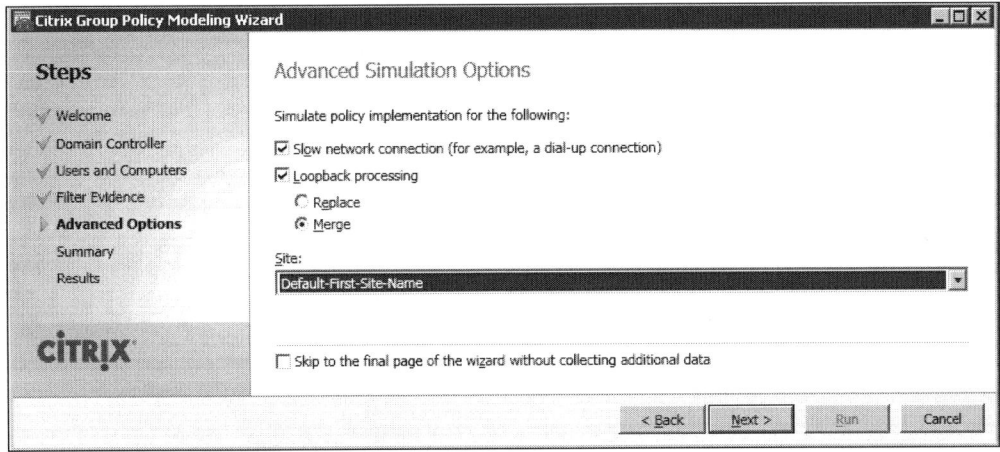

10. Select the **Summary of Selections** options and click on **Run**.

11. Click on **Close** after the simulation is run to close the wizard and view the results.

You are taken to the **Modeling Results** tab. This tab shows a report of the Citrix policies that are and are not applied. For each Computer and User policy, the settings are listed with the resulting value and the winning policy responsible for the setting.

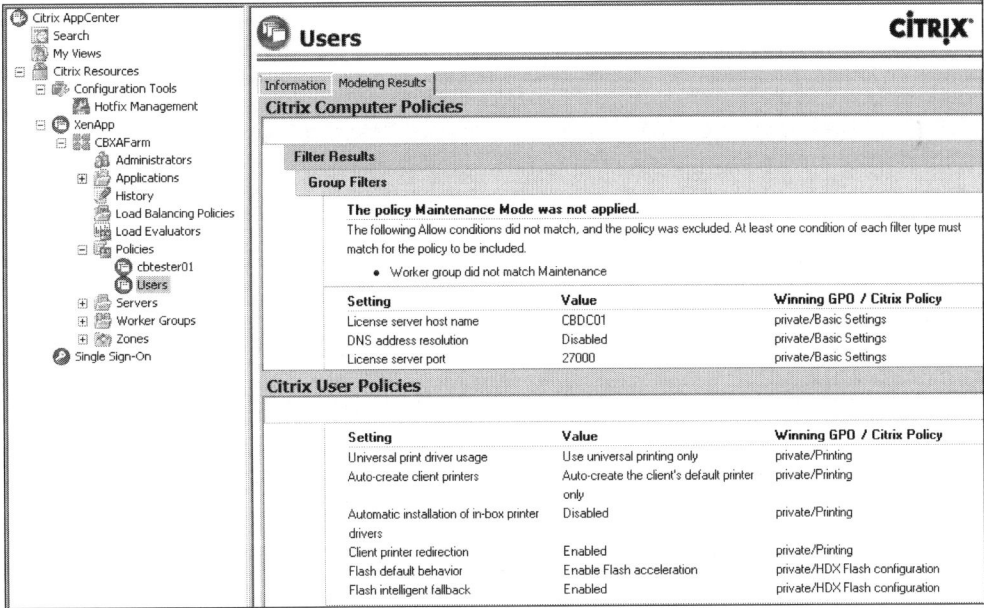

See also

- ▸ The *Creating a XenApp® Computer or User policy* recipe
- ▸ The *Adding filters to a policy* recipe
- ▸ The *Comparing XenApp® policies and templates* recipe
- ▸ The *Configuring policy priorities and exceptions* recipe

Configuring policy priorities and exceptions

This recipe will show you how to change policy priorities and exceptions with the Citrix management console AppCenter.

How to do it...

To change the priority of a policy with AppCenter, follow these steps:

1. Open the Citrix XenApp management console AppCenter (**Start | Administrative Tools | Citrix | Management Consoles**).
2. Navigate to **XenApp | <FarmName> | Policies** in the left pane.
3. Click on the **Computer** or **User** tab in the **Policies** pane.
4. Select a policy and use **Higher** and **Lower** to change the priority of the policy. The value 1 represents the highest priority.

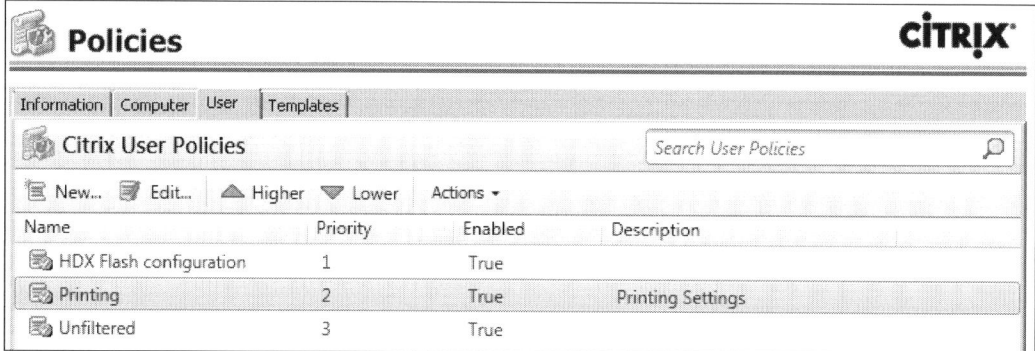

To create an exception for a policy with AppCenter, follow these steps:

1. Open the Citrix XenApp Management console AppCenter (**Start | Administrative Tools | Citrix | Management Consoles**).

2. Navigate to **XenApp** | **<FarmName>** | **Policies** in the left pane.

3. Click on the **Computer** or **User** tab in the **Policies** pane.

4. Select a policy and use **Edit** to change the policy settings.

5. Click on the **Filters** tab and click on **Add** or **Edit** to change the filter configuration.

6. Click on **Add** or **Edit** to change the filter element configuration.

7. Set the **Mode** to deny ensuring the policy settings are not applied for the configured **User, (Worker) Group** or **Organizational Unit**, thus creating an exception for the policy.

8. Click on **OK** to apply the filter element configuration.

9. Click on **OK** to apply the filter configuration.

10. Click on **OK** to apply the policy configuration.

How it works...

Each configured Citrix policy is given a priority to determine the order in which policies are applied when multiple policies are configured. By default each newly created policy is given the lowest priority (or highest priority number). The policy with priority number 1 has the highest priority.

When a user logs on to a Citrix session, all policies that match the configured filters for the connection, the client device and the user are determined and are applied in the order of their priority. Settings are merged according to the priority and whether a setting is disabled or enabled.

  ► When multiple policies contain the same settings, the policy with the highest priority determines the active setting

  ► When multiple policies contain the same setting, a policy setting set to disabled overrides the same policy setting set to enabled in a policy with a lower priority

For example:

  ► Policy A (prio = 2) contains a setting for the XML Service port to 8080

  ► Policy B (prio = 1) contains a setting for the XML Service port to 80

These policies result in a setting for the XML service on the Citrix XenApp server to port 80, as is shown in the following screenshot:

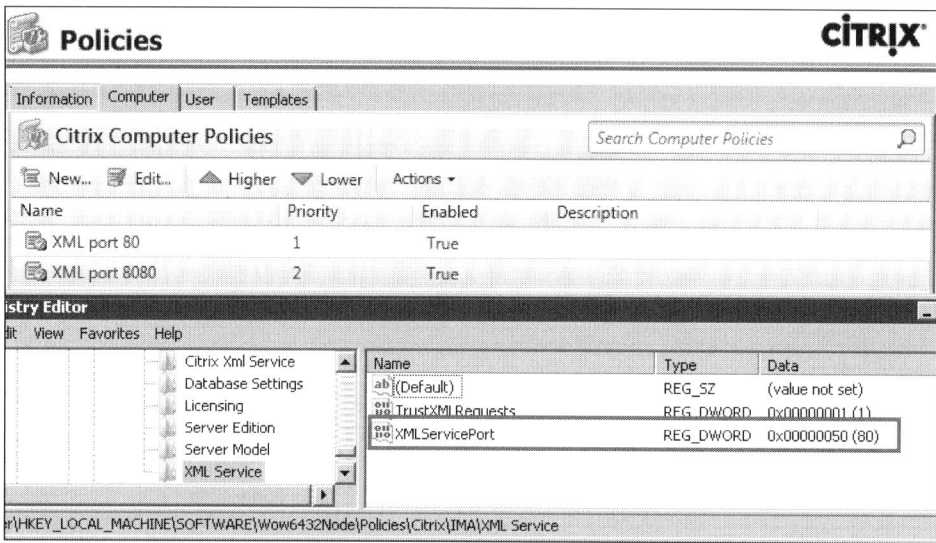

▸ Policy A (prio = 2) disables local drive redirection
▸ Policy B (prio = 1) enables local drive redirection

These policies result in a setting for the drive redirection to be enabled, as is illustrated in the following screenshot:

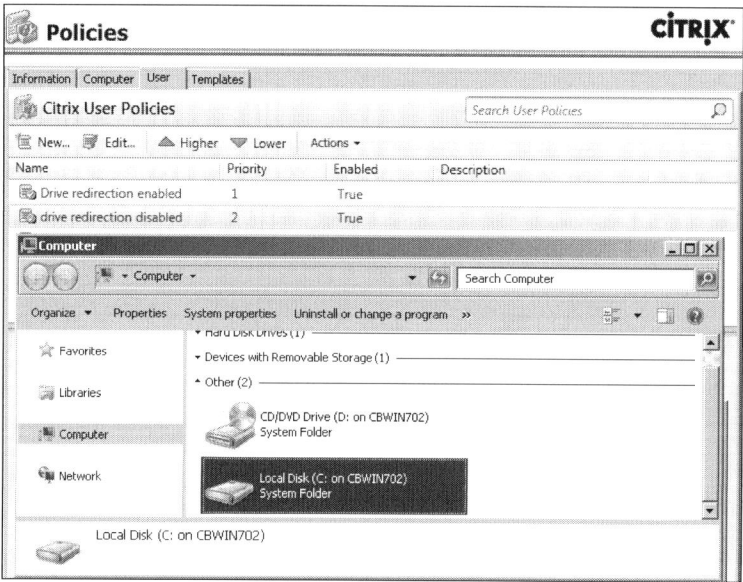

There's more...

You can read more on policy priorities and exceptions at Citrix's eDocs: `http://support.citrix.com/proddocs/topic/xenapp65-admin/ps-admin-policies-priority-exceptions-all.html`.

See also

▸ The *Creating a XenApp® Computer or User policy* recipe

▸ The *Adding filters to a policy* recipe

▸ The *Comparing XenApp® policies and templates* recipe

▸ The *Simulating connection scenario's with Citrix® policies* recipe

Configuring and maintaining XenApp® printing

This recipe will address the policies you can configure to enable XenApp printing settings. With Citrix XenApp (CXA), you can configure printing settings for the Citrix Universal Print Server with Computer policies and client printing with User Policies. The Citrix Universal Print Server policies will not be addressed in detail this recipe.

How to do it...

To set policies for XenApp printing with AppCenter, follow these steps:

1. Open the Citrix XenApp Management Console AppCenter (**Start | Administrative Tools | Citrix | Management Consoles**).

2. Navigate to **XenApp | <FarmName> | Policies** in the left pane.

3. Click on the **User** tab to configure the session printing policies.

4. Click on **New** to create a new policy.

5. Enter **Name** and **Description** for the policy and click on **Next**.

6. Navigate to the **ICA | Printing** category in the left pane to configure basic client printing settings, such as printer behavior and session printers.

7. Navigate to **ICA | Printing | Client Printers** to configure client printer settings.

8. Navigate to **ICA | Printing | Drivers** to configure printer driver settings.

9. Navigate to **ICA | Printing | Universal Printing** to configure universal printing settings.

10. Add a policy setting by clicking on **Add** in the right pane for each setting.

11. Configure the policy setting and click on **OK**.

12. Repeat steps 6 to 11 to add more policy settings.

13. Click on **Next** when all policy settings are configured.

14. Configure the filter settings and click on **Next**.

[ The filter options are addressed in the *Adding filters to a policy* recipe.]

15. Ensure that the **Enable this policy** option is selected and click on **Create**.

How it works...

To decide upon the policy settings to configure for client printing, the configurable settings are listed per printing category.

The following policy settings can be configured for **Printing**:

Policy setting	Explanation
Client printer redirection	This allows or prevents client printers to be mapped to a server when a user logs on to a session. The default value is: Allowed.
Default printer	This specifies how the client's default printer is established in an ICA session. It sets the default printer to the client's default printer.
Printer auto-creation event log preference	This specifies which events are logged during the printer autocreation process. You can choose to log no errors or warnings, only errors, or errors and warnings. The default value is: Log errors and warnings.
Session printers	This lists the network printers to be autocreated in an ICA session.

The following policy settings can be configured for **Client printers**:

Policy setting	Explanation
Auto-create client printers	This specifies which client printers are autocreated. This setting overrides default client-printer autocreation settings. The default value is: Autocreate all client printers.
Auto-create generic universal printer	This enables or disables autocreation of the Citrix Universal Printer generic printing object for sessions with a UPD capable client. The default value is: Disabled.
Client printer names	This selects the naming convention for autocreated client printers. The default value is: Standard printer names.

Policy setting	Explanation
Direct connections to print servers	This enables or disables direct connections from the host to a print server for client printers hosted on an accessible network share. The default value is: Enabled.
Printer driver mapping and compatibility	This lists driver substitution rules for autocreated client printers.
Printer properties retention	This specifies whether and where to store printer properties. The default value is: Held in profile only if not saved on client.
Retaining and restoring client printers	This enables or disables the retention and re-creation of client printers. The default value is: Allowed.

The following policy settings can be configured for **Drivers**:

Policy setting	Explanation
Auto install of in-box printer drivers	This enables or disables the automatic installation of printer drivers from the Windows in-box driver set or from driver packages which have been staged onto the host using pnputil.exe /a. The default value is: Enabled.
Universal driver preference	This specifies the order in which XenApp attempts to use Universal Printer drivers.
Universal print driver usage	This specifies when to use universal printing. The default value is: Use universal printing only if the requested driver is unavailable.

The following policy settings can be configured for **Universal printing**:

Policy setting	Explanation
Universal printing EMF processing mode	This controls the method of processing the EMF spool file on the Windows client machine. The default value is: Spool directly to printer.
Universal printing image compression limit	This defines the maximum quality and the minimum compression level available for images printed with the Universal Printer driver. The default value is: Best quality (lossless compression).
Universal printing optimization defaults	This specifies the default settings for the Universal Printer when it is created for a session.
Universal printing preview preference	This specifies whether to use the print preview function for autocreated or generic universal printers. The default value is: Do not use print preview for autocreated or generic universal printers.
Universal printing print quality limit	This specifies the maximum dots per inch (dpi) available for generating printed output in the session. The default value is: No Limit.

There's more...

You can read more about Printing Policy settings at Citrix's eDocs: `http://support.citrix.com/proddocs/topic/xenapp65-admin/ps-console-policies-rules-printing.html`.

See also

▸ The *Enabling shadowing* recipe

▸ The *Assigning Load Evaluators to servers and applications* recipe

▸ The *Enhancing user experience with HDX* recipe

▸ The *Redirecting the client drives of the user devices* recipe

▸ The *Configuring session pre-launch and lingering options* recipe

Enabling shadowing

This recipe will show you how to configure shadowing policy settings to allow support and help desk personnel to interact with an active user session and offer assistance.

Getting ready

To enable shadowing of user sessions and allowing help desk personnel to interact with the user session, the shadowing feature must be selected during the initial configuration of the XenApp server. The feature is configured when installing and configuring the first XenApp server (Controller Host) and applies for all the servers in the XenApp Farm. If you prohibit shadowing and want to allow it at a later stage, you will need to reinstall the XenApp software and reconfigure the XenApp Farm settings.

Allowing shadowing does not automatically enable the feature for each user. Additional settings, through policies, are required to configure shadowing options for support and help desk personnel.

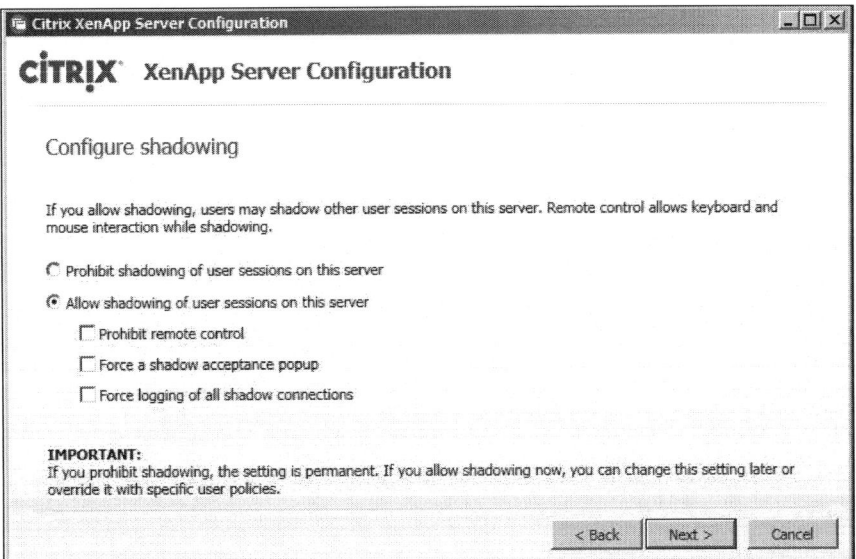

How to do it...

To allow support and Service Desk engineers the option to shadow an existing user session, follow these steps:

1. Open the Citrix XenApp management console AppCenter (**Start | Administrative Tools | Citrix | Management Consoles**).

2. Navigate to **XenApp | <FarmName> | Policies** in the left pane.

3. Click on the **User** tab to configure the session printing policies.

4. Click on **New** to create a new policy.

5. Enter values in the **Name** and **Description** fields for the policy and click on **Next**.

6. Navigate to the **ICA | Shadowing** category in the left pane to configure all shadowing policy settings.

7. Add a policy setting by clicking on **Add** in the right pane for each setting.

8. Configure the policy setting and click on **OK**.

9. Repeat steps 6 and 7 to add more policy settings.

10. Click on **Next** when all policy settings are configured.

11. Configure the filter settings and click on **Next**.

 Filter options are addressed in the *Adding filters to a policy* recipe.

Ensure the **Enable this policy** option is selected and click on **Create**.

How it works...

To decide upon the policy settings to configure for shadowing, the configurable settings are listed per printing category.

The following policy settings can be configured for **shadowing**:

Policy setting	Explanation
Input from shadow connections	This allows or prevents shadowing users to take control of the keyboard and mouse of the user being shadowed during a shadowing session.
	Default: Allowed.
Log shadow attempts	This allows or prevents recording of attempted shadowing sessions in the Windows event log.
	Default: Enabled.
Notify user of pending shadow connections	This allows or prevents shadowed users to receive notification of shadowing requests from other users. When a user receives a shadowing request, the user can accept or deny the request.
	Default: Enabled.
Users who can shadow other users	This specifies the users or groups who can shadow other users.
Users who cannot shadow other users	This specifies the users or groups who cannot shadow other users.

There's more...

You can read more on shadowing policy settings in Citrix's eDocs at `http://support.citrix.com/proddocs/topic/xenapp65-admin/ps-console-policies-rules-workspace-shadowing-v2.html`.

Keep in mind that shadowing is not supported when multiple monitors are used as is explained at Citrix's Knowledge Center at `http://support.citrix.com/article/CTX125693`.

You can read more on how to configure Windows Remote Assistance in Citrix XenApp 6.5 for multi-monitor shadowing in a blogpost by Lal Mohan at `http://lalmohan.co.nz/2013/07/02/configure-windows-remote-assistance-in-citrix-xenapp-6-5-for-multi-monitor-shadowing/`.

See also

▶ The *Configuring and maintaining XenApp® printing* recipe

▶ The *Assigning Load Evaluators to servers and applications* recipe

▶ The *Enhancing user experience with HDX* recipe

▶ The *Redirecting the client drives of the user devices* recipe

▶ The *Configuring session pre-launch and lingering options* recipe

Assigning Load Evaluators to servers and applications

This recipe will show you how to assign a Load Evaluator to a XenApp server or published application in the Citrix XenApp (CXA) Farm.

Getting ready

To be able to assign a custom Load Evaluator to a server or application, the load evaluator must exist. Instructions on how to create a custom Load Evaluator can be found in the *Creating a custom Load Evaluator* recipe in *Chapter 6, XenApp® Management*.

How to do it...

To assign a Load Evaluator to a XenApp server by using policy settings, follow these steps:

1. Open the Citrix XenApp management console AppCenter (**Start | Administrative Tools | Citrix | Management Consoles**).

2. Navigate to **XenApp | <FarmName> | Policies** in the left pane.

3. Click on the **Computer** tab to configure the session printing policies.

4. Click on **New** to create a new policy.

5. Enter values in the **Name** and **Description** fields for the policy and click on **Next**.

6. Select the **Server Settings** category in the left pane.

7. Add the Load Evaluator Name policy settings by clicking on **Add** in the right pane.

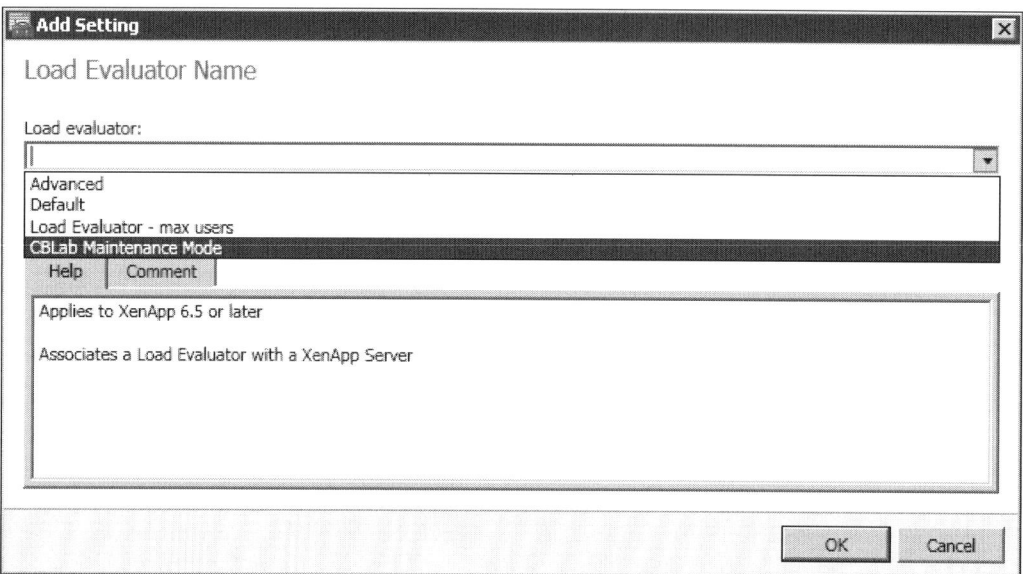

8. Select the appropriate Load Evaluator from the drop-down box and click on **OK**.

9. Click on **Next**.

10. Configure the filter settings to determine the XenApp servers the selected load evaluator needs to apply to and click on **Next**.

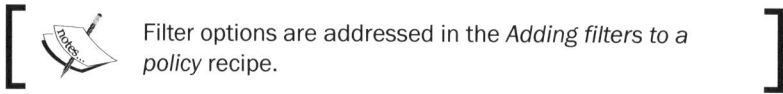

Filter options are addressed in the *Adding filters to a policy* recipe.

11. Ensure the **Enable this policy** option is selected and click on **Create**.

Load Evaluators can only be assigned to servers when using policies. To assign a Load Evaluator to an application, follow these steps:

1. Open the Citrix XenApp management console AppCenter (**Start | Administrative Tools | Citrix | Management Consoles**).

2. Navigate to **XenApp | <FarmName> | Applications | <ApplicationName>** in the left pane.

3. Right-click on the published application and navigate to **Other Tasks | Attach application to load evaluator**.

4. Select the Load Evaluator you want to apply to the application and click on **OK**.

See also

▸ The *Configuring and maintaining XenApp® printing* recipe

▸ The *Enabling shadowing* recipe

▸ The *Enhancing user experience with HDX* recipe

▸ The *Redirecting the client drives of the user devices* recipe

▸ The *Configuring session pre-launch and lingering options* recipe

Enhancing user experience with HDX

This recipe will show you how to enhance the user experience with HDX policy settings. **HDX** (**High Definition User Experience**) refers to a collection of enhancements for the virtual desktop provided by either XenDesktop or XenApp. The policies described in this recipe focus on HDX MediaStream.

How to do it...

To enhance the user experience with HDX technology, different policy settings can be configured for audio, video, display, and flash.

Follow these steps to configure the available HDX Computer policy settings with AppCenter:

1. Open the Citrix XenApp management console AppCenter (**Start | Administrative Tools | Citrix | Management Consoles**).

2. Navigate to **XenApp | <FarmName> | Policies** in the left pane.

3. Click on the **Computer** tab to configure the HDX policies.

4. Click on **New** to create a new policy.

5. Enter values in the **Name** and **Description** fields for the policy and click on **Next**.

6. Navigate to **ICA | Multimedia** in the left pane to configure all Windows Media policy settings.

7. Add a policy setting by clicking on **Add** in the right pane for each setting.

8. Configure the policy setting and click on **OK**.

9. Repeat steps 6 to 8 to add more policy settings.

10. Click on **Next** when all policy settings are configured.

11. Configure the filter settings and click on **Next**.

 Filter options are addressed in the *Adding filters to a policy* recipe.

12. Ensure the **Enable this policy** option is selected and click on **Create**.

Follow these steps to configure the available HDX User policy settings with AppCenter:

1. Open the Citrix XenApp management console AppCenter (**Start | Administrative Tools | Citrix | Management Consoles**).

2. Navigate to **XenApp | <FarmName> | Policies** in the left pane.

3. Click on the **User** tab to configure the HDX policies.

4. Click on **New** to create a new policy.

5. Enter values in the **Name** and **Description** fields for the policy and click on **Next**.

6. Navigate to the **ICA | Adobe Flash Delivery | Legacy Server Side Optimizations** category in the left pane.

7. Click on **Add** for the Flash quality adjustment settings.

8. Configure the policy setting and click on **OK**.

9. Navigate to **ICA | Visual Display | Still Images** category in the left pane.

10. Add a policy setting by clicking on **Add** in the right pane for each setting.

11. Configure the policy setting and click on **OK**.

12. Repeat steps 9 to 11 to add more policy settings.

13. Click on **Next** when all policy settings are configured.

14. Configure the filter settings and click on **Next**.

 Filter options are addressed in the *Adding filters to a policy* recipe.

15. Ensure the **Enable this policy** option is selected and click on **Create**.

How it works...

To decide upon the policy settings to configure and enhance the user experience through HDX settings, the configurable settings are listed as per HDX category.

The following policy settings can be configured for optimizing **Audio and Video playback**:

Policy setting	Explanation
Windows Media Redirection	This controls and optimizes the way XenApp servers deliver streaming audio and video to users. Default: Allowed.
Windows Media Redirection Buffer Size	This specifies a buffer size from 1 to 10 seconds for Windows Media Redirection. Default: 5 seconds.
Windows Media Redirection Buffer Size Use	This specifies whether the system uses the buffer size specified in the "Windows Media Redirection Buffer Size" setting or uses its own built-in default buffer size. Default: Disabled.

The following policy settings can be configured for optimizing **Flash delivery**:

Policy setting	Explanation
Flash quality adjustments	This adjusts quality of the Flash content rendered on session hosts to improve performance. Default: Optimize Adobe Flash animation options for low bandwidth connections only.

The following policy settings can be configured for optimizing **Throughput of image files**:

Policy setting	Explanation
Lossy compression level	This specifies the degree of lossy compression used on images. For improved responsiveness with bandwidth-intensive images, use high compression. Default: Medium.
Lossy compression threshold value	This specifies the maximum bandwidth in kilobits per second for a connection to which lossy compression is applied. Compression is applied only to client connections under this bandwidth.
Progressive compression level	This provides a less detailed but faster initial display than lossy compression. Use very-high or ultra-high compression for improved viewing. For progressive compression to be effective, its compression level must be higher than the lossy compression level setting. Default: None.

See also

▶ The *Configuring and maintaining XenApp® printing* recipe

▶ The *Enabling shadowing* recipe

▶ The *Assigning Load Evaluators to servers and applications* recipe

▶ The *Redirecting the client drives of the user devices* recipe

▶ The *Configuring session pre-launch and lingering options* recipe

Redirecting the client drives of the user device

This recipe will show you how to configure access to user device resources, such as client drives, USB devices, and printers by configuring Citrix User policy settings with Citrix's Management Console AppCenter.

How to do it...

To configure client drives and user device policies with AppCenter, follow these steps:

1. Open the Citrix XenApp management console AppCenter (**Start | Administrative Tools | Citrix | Management Consoles**).
2. Navigate to **XenApp | <FarmName> | Policies** in the left pane.
3. Click on the **User** tab to configure the session printing policies.
4. Click on **New** to create a new policy.
5. Enter **Name** and **Description** for the policy and click on **Next**.
6. Navigate to the **ICA | Client Sensors | Location** category in the left pane.
7. Click on **Add** for the **Allow applications to use the physical location of the client device** settings.
8. Configure the policy setting and click on **OK**.
9. Navigate to the **ICA | File Redirection** category in the left pane.
10. Add a policy setting by clicking on **Add** in the right pane for each setting.
11. Configure the policy settings and click on **OK**.
12. Repeat steps 9 to 11 to add more policy settings.
13. Navigate to the **ICA | USB Devices** category in the left pane.
14. Add a policy setting by clicking on **Add** in the right pane for each setting.
15. Configure the policy setting and click on **OK**.

16. Repeat steps 13 to 15 to add more policy settings.

17. Click on **Next** when all policy settings are configured.

18. Configure the filter settings and click on **Next**.

[ Filter options are addressed in the *Adding filters to a policy* recipe.]

19. Ensure that the **Enable this policy** option is selected and click on **Create**.

How it works...

To decide upon the policy settings to configure and determine the interaction with client device resources from the user's Citrix XenApp session, the configurable settings are listed next as per the category.

The following policy settings can be configured for optimizing **Client sensors**:

Policy setting	Explanation
Allow applications to use the physical location of the client device	This enables or disables the ability for applications to use the physical location of the client device. The default value is: Disabled.

The following policy settings can be configured for optimizing **File redirection**:

Policy setting	Explanation
Auto connect client drives	This allows or prevents automatic connection of client drives when the users log on. The default value is: Enabled.
Client drive redirection	This enables or disables file (drive) redirection to and from the client. When enabled, users can save files to their client drives. When disabled, all file redirection is prevented, regardless of the state of the individual file redirection settings such as Client floppy drives and Client network drives. The default value is: Allowed.
Client <type> drives	The types of this setting are fixed, floppy, network, optical, and removable. This allows or prevents users from accessing or saving files to fixed/floppy/network/optical/removable drives on the user device. Default: Allowed.

Policy setting	Explanation
Read-only client redirection	When enabled, files/folders on mapped client drives can only be accessed in read-only mode. When disabled, files/folders on mapped client drives can be accessed in regular read/write mode. Default: Disabled.

The following policy settings can be configured for optimizing **USB devices**:

Policy setting	Explanation
Client USB device redirection	This enables or disables redirection of USB devices to and from the client (workstation hosts only). Default: Prohibited.
Client USB device redirection rules	This lists redirection rules for USB devices.
Client USB Plug and Play device redirection	This allows or prevents plug-n-play devices such as cameras or point-of-sale (POS) devices to be used in a client session. Default: Allowed.

See also

▸ The *Configuring and maintaining XenApp® printing* recipe

▸ The *Enabling shadowing* recipe

▸ The *Assigning Load Evaluators to servers and applications* recipe

▸ The *Enhancing user experience with HDX* recipe

▸ The *Configuring session pre-launch and lingering options* recipe

Configuring session pre-launch and lingering options

This recipe will show you how to apply policy settings to support session pre-launch and lingering options.

Getting ready

When configuring session pre-launch policy settings, a pre-launch application must exist. You can read instructions on creating a pre-launch application in Citrix's eDocs at `http://support.citrix.com/proddocs/topic/xenapp65-publishing/ps-pub-prelaunch.html`.

How to do it...

To configure policies for pre-launch sessions, follow these steps:

1. Open the Citrix XenApp management console AppCenter (**Start** | **Administrative Tools** | **Citrix** | **Management Consoles**).

2. Navigate to **XenApp** | **<FarmName>** | **Policies** in the left pane.

3. Click on the **User** tab to configure the session printing policies.

4. Click on **New** to create a new policy.

5. Enter values in the **Name** and **Description** fields for the policy and click on **Next**.

6. Navigate to the **ICA** | **Session Limits** category in the left pane.

7. Click on **Add** for the **Pre-launch Disconnect Timer Interval** settings.

8. Configure the policy setting and click on **OK**.

9. Click on **Add** for the **Pre-launch Terminate Timer Interval** settings.

10. Configure the policy setting and click on **OK**.

11. Click on **Next** when both policy settings are configured.

12. Configure the filter settings and click on **Next**.

 Filter options are addressed in the *Adding filters to a policy* recipe.

13. Ensure the **Enable this policy** option is selected and click on **Create**.

To create a pre-launch application, follow these steps:

1. Open the Citrix XenApp management console AppCenter (**Start | Administrative Tools | Citrix | Management Consoles**).

2. Navigate to **XenApp | <FarmName> | Applications** in the left pane.

3. Right-click on the application that you want to pre-launch and navigate to **Other Tasks | Create pre-launch application**.

The pre-launch application is automatically created and added to the `applications` folder.

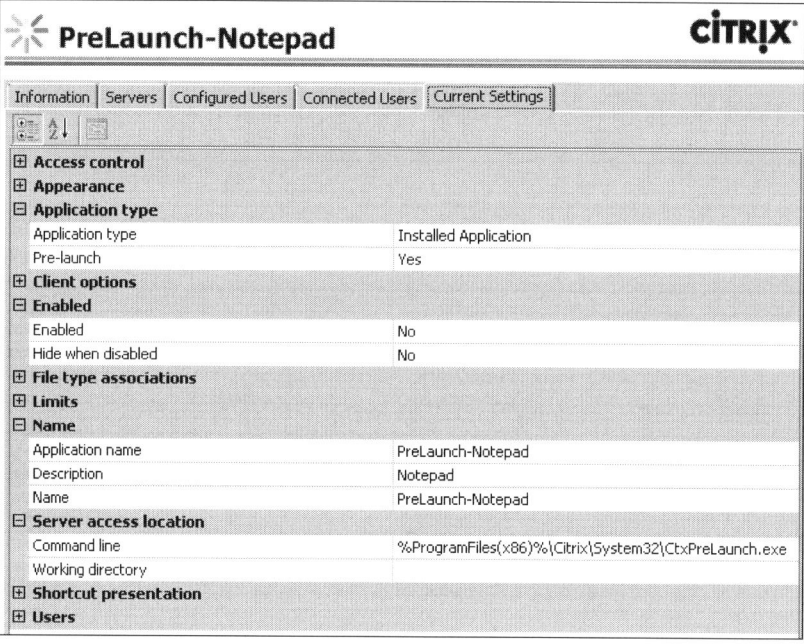

To configure policies for lingering sessions, follow these steps:

1. Open the Citrix XenApp management console AppCenter (**Start | Administrative Tools | Citrix | Management Consoles**).

2. Navigate to **XenApp | <FarmName> | Policies** in the left pane.

3. Click on the **User** tab to configure the session printing policies.

4. Click on **New** to create a new policy.

5. Enter values in the **Name** and **Description** fields for the policy and click on **Next**.

6. Navigate to the **ICA | Session Limits** category in the left pane.

7. Click on **Add** for the **Linger Disconnect Timer Interval** settings.

8. Configure the policy setting and click on **OK**.

9. Click on **Add** for the **Linger Terminate Timer Interval** settings.

10. Configure the policy setting and click on **OK**.

11. Click on **Next** when both policy settings are configured.

12. Configure the filter settings and click on **Next**.

> Filter options are addressed in the *Adding filters to a policy* recipe.

13. Ensure the **Enable this policy** option is selected and click on **Create**.

> Lingering settings apply to user sessions and do not require additional application creations or settings to become active. The policy settings determine the behavior of user sessions when a user logs off.

How it works...

The session pre-launch feature enables the ability to reduce the application launch time by creating a pre-launch session when a user logs on to the Citrix Receiver. Even though no published application is yet started by the user, a Citrix session is already created in the XenApp Farm by only running the default `ctxprelaunch.exe` process. When a user starts a published application by clicking on the corresponding icon in the Citrix Receiver, the application process is started within the pre-launch session and the application can be started immediately without the normal delays that occur when starting a Remote Desktop session on the Citrix XenApp server. The user desktop environment has already been started.

> Pre-launch sessions are supported when using the Citrix Receiver only. No pre-launch sessions are created when the Citrix Receiver for Web is used to start an application.

CBXA01

Information	Users	Sessions	Processes	Published Applications	Hotfix Details	Hotfix Summary	Hotfix Comparison

User items in CBXA01

Name ▲	User	Session ID	Application	Type	Ses...	Application State
ICA-TCP#2	cbtester01	3	PreLaunch-Notepad	ICA	Active	Pre-launch

The following policy settings can be configured for **pre-launch sessions**:

Policy setting	Explanation
Pre-launch Disconnect Timer Interval	This disconnects an existing pre-launch session after the specified number of minutes. Once disconnected, the XenApp license is released. If the user launches an application before the timer expires, it is launched in the existing session.
	Default: 60 (minutes)
Pre-launch Terminate Timer Interval	This terminates an existing Pre-launch session after the specified number of minutes. If the user launches an application before the timer expires, the session is reconnected if necessary. The application will then launch in the session. If the timer interval is set to zero, the pre-launched session terminates immediately.
	Default: 60 (minutes)

When applications are started by published applications and not from within a published desktop, the Session Linger feature might enhance performance.

Normally when a user starts a published application, a remote desktop session is started in the background on the XenApp server; this starts the application and the application window is presented to the user (instead of the full desktop). If the user closes the application window, the remote desktop session is ended for that user as well. If the user commits a mistake and restarts the same application within seconds, it might take longer to show the application again, as the remote desktop session needs to be recreated first.

Session Lingering keeps the user session active on the XenApp server for a predefined time when the published application is closed. This way, restarting the application does not take the extra time to recreate the user session, as the application is started in the user session that was still running in the background. The published application can be presented more quickly to the user.

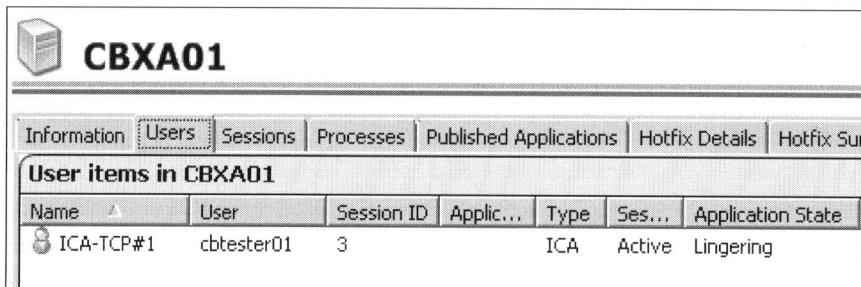

The following policy settings can be configured for **Session Lingering**:

Policy setting	Explanation
Linger Disconnect Timer Interval	This disconnects an existing session the specified number of minutes after the last application exits. If the user launches an application before the timer interval expires, the Linger Disconnect timer will reset. If not configured or set to zero, lingering sessions will not disconnect before logging off. Default: 0 (minutes)
Linger Terminate Timer Interval	This terminates an existing session the specified number of minutes after the last application exits. If the user launches an application before the timer interval expires, the Linger Terminate timer is reset. If not configured or set to zero, session lingering will be disabled. Default: 60 (minutes)

To get Session Pre-launch working with Citrix Receiver 4.x and StoreFront, ensure the Receiver is installed with a command line that includes the ENABLEPRELAUNCH=true option as described in Citrix's eDocs at http://support.citrix.com/proddocs/topic/receiver-windows-40/receiver-windows-session-pre-launch.html.

There's more...

You can read more on Session Pre-Launch and Lingering at the Citrix Blog at http://blogs.citrix.com/2012/02/10/a-field-guide-to-xenapp-session-pre-launch/.

You can read more on configuring the Citrix Receiver to support Session Pre-launch at Citrix's eDocs at http://support.citrix.com/proddocs/topic/receiver-windows-40/receiver-windows-session-pre-launch.html.

See also

▶ The *Configuring and maintaining XenApp® printing* recipe
▶ The *Enabling shadowing* recipe
▶ The *Assigning Load Evaluators to servers and applications* recipe
▶ The *Enhancing user experience with HDX* recipe
▶ The *Redirecting the client drives of the user devices* recipe

9
XenApp® Troubleshooting

In this chapter, we will cover the following topics:

- ▶ Starting AppCenter more rapidly
- ▶ Troubleshooting the Protocol Driver error message
- ▶ Troubleshooting the IMA service
- ▶ Troubleshooting pass-through authentication with Web Interface
- ▶ Troubleshooting XenApp® policies for Worker Groups
- ▶ Using HDX Monitor to check user experience
- ▶ Getting a full desktop instead of the published application
- ▶ Troubleshooting printer drivers on XenApp® servers
- ▶ Retaining client printer settings in user profile
- ▶ Mapping client printers does not work when connecting through Web Interface 5.4
- ▶ Troubleshooting client clipboard issues
- ▶ Using Citrix® Auto Support to troubleshoot a XenApp® Server

Introduction

After designing and implementing a XenApp infrastructure the real fun starts. You are now responsible for managing a XenApp 6.5 production environment that will provide majority of the users with business applications to support them in their daily tasks. A well designed and implemented XenApp infrastructure can run without disturbances for a long time, but it is inevitable that you will be faced with irradical behavior from time to time. It does require a good understanding of the infrastructure design, the XenApp principles, and the entire stack from published application to user to troubleshoot incidents and find solutions to reported problems in your production environment.

This chapter offers some basic tooling and troubleshooting guidelines for common problems that may occur in a XenApp production environment. Troubleshooting can sometimes mean you quickly find the cause and need to apply a fix, or it can mean you have to follow an (improvised) checklist to check step-by-step which setting might be causing problems. Both situations have been addressed by the recipes of this chapter. Some offer step-by-step instructions to apply a fix for a commonly known issue, others offer step-by-step instructions for checking each configuration item to find the cause.

Starting AppCenter more rapidly

This recipe will show you how to speed up the Citrix XenApp Management Console AppCenter and have it start more rapidly.

How to do it...

To automatically start Citrix AppCenter more rapidly, follow these steps:

1. Open the Citrix XenApp management console AppCenter (**Start | Administrative Tools | Citrix | Management Consoles**).

2. An informational pop-up window might be shown:

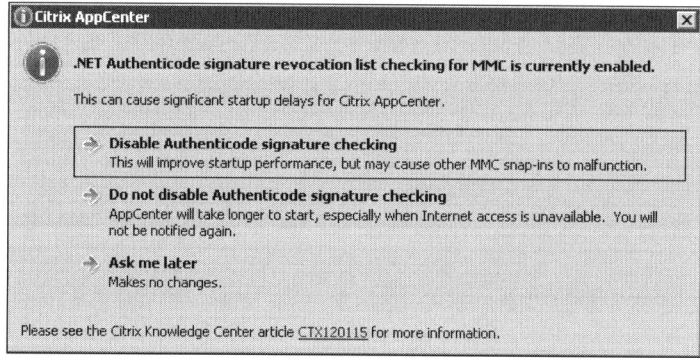

3. Select **Disable Authenticode signature checking** in the pop-up window.

 By selecting **Disable Authenticode signature checking**, the `mmc.exe.config` file (explained in the manual steps) is automatically created.

To manually speed up Citrix AppCenter, follow these steps:

1. Open Windows Explorer and browse to `C:\Windows\SysWOW64`.

2. Create a new file called `mmc.exe.config`.

3. Edit the file and add the following text:

```
<?xml version="1.0" encoding="utf-8"?>
<configuration>
runtime>
<generatePublisherEvidence enabled="false" />
</runtime>
</configuration>
```

Now, when you start Citrix AppCenter, it will appear more rapidly as the Authenticode signature check is disabled with the preceding file and code.

How it works...

Citrix AppCenter is a Microsoft .NET Framework 2.0 managed application that has an Authenticode signature. Each time the application is started, the signature is checked by a so-called **Certificate Revocation List** (**CRL**) lookup. During this process, the .NET runtime tries to access the Microsoft Certificate Revocation List servers to verify the Authenticode assembly, which requires Internet access as Microsoft's servers are on the Internet. If the system running the application does not have Internet access, the CRL lookup is re-tried for up to 15 seconds before it will time out.

To speed up the start of the application, the Authenticode signature checking can be disabled, so the check is not performed and no idle waiting for a time-out will occur.

Microsoft offers a fix to add the `generatePublisherEvidence` configuration setting to the .NET Framework 2.0 as explained in Knowledge Base article KB936707.

This article describes the procedure to manually create an application configuration file:

> To create an application configuration file that contains this configuration setting, follow these steps:
>
> 1. Create a file, and then name the file the *<ApplicationName>*.exe.config file.
> 2. In a text editor, open the file that you created in step 1.
> 3. Add the following code to the file.
>
>    ```
>    <?xml version="1.0" encoding="utf-8"?>
>    <configuration>
>          <runtime>
>                  <generatePublisherEvidence enabled="false"/>
>          </runtime>
>    </configuration>
>    ```
>
> 4. Save the changes to the file.

There's more...

You can read more on the earlier mentioned fix at Microsoft's Support at `http://support.microsoft.com/kb/936707/en-us`.

Troubleshooting the Protocol Driver error message

This recipe will show you how to troubleshoot the Protocol Driver Error messages that users may receive when they are unable to launch a published application from XenApp 6.5.

How to do it...

The Protocol Driver error message can have more than one cause, so let's run a step-by-step analysis of the entire route from client to server to find the specific reason.

1. Ensure the latest ICA client is installed on the client device, including the Online Plug-in.

    1. Find the Citrix Receiver icon in the system tray on the Windows client.

    2. Right-click on the icon and select **About**.

3. Click on **Support Info** to see the Receiver version, installed plug-ins, and Online Plug-in version:

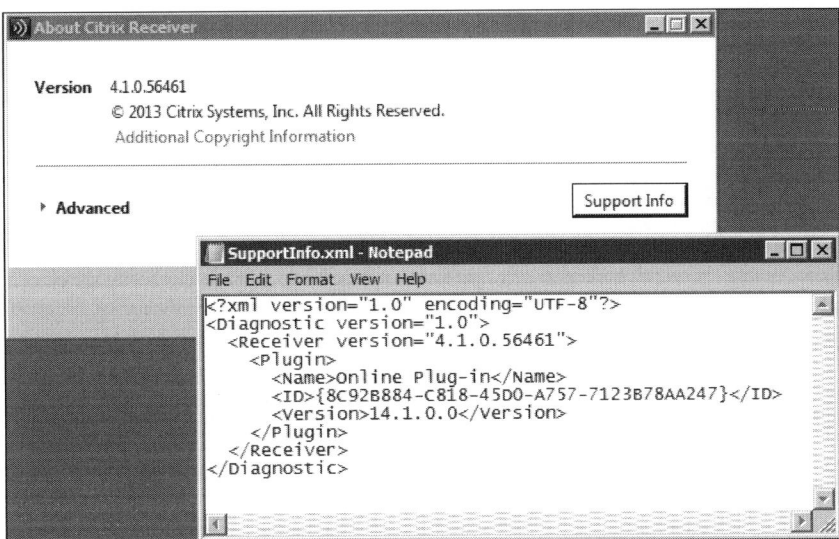

2. Ensure the Citrix Web Interface site is added to the local intranet or trusted sites in Internet Explorer:

    1. Select **Tools | Internet Options** from the menu.

    2. Click on the **Security** tab.

    3. The active zone for the site is selected, this should either be local intranet or trusted sites.

 To add the site to the **Trusted sites** zone, select the zone and click on **Sites** to add the URL of the site to the zone.

3. Save the `launch.ica` file to check the connection settings to the XenApp Farm.

 The `launch.ica` file is by default stored in the temporarily Internet files, but deleted directly after it is run by the Citrix Receiver. By enabling the ICA logfile, you can track the ICA settings that were applied. Only enabling logging during troubleshooting activities. If no connection can be made, the `launch.ica` file will not be logged.

Enable the ICA logfile settings in the registry, by editing these registry keys:

32-bit: HKLM\SOFTWARE\Citrix\ICA Client\Engine\Configuration\Advanced\Modules\Logging

64-bit: HKLM\SOFTWARE\Wow6432Node\Citrix\ICA Client\Engine\Configuration\Advanced\Modules\Logging

ab LogFile	REG_SZ	C:\temp\icalog.log
ab LogICAFile	REG_SZ	true

4. If the published application cannot be started and no logging is made, check the Citrix Computer policy for the **Trust XML requests** setting in the XenApp Farm. See if changing the setting to `Enabled` (less secure) fixes the problem. When the Trust XML requests setting is set to `Disabled`, the following error is shown in the Citrix Web Interface:

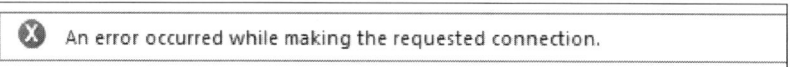

An error occurred while making the requested connection.

5. Check whether the ICA logfile contains the **CGPAddress** setting. When Session Reliability is enabled with the Citrix Computer policy **Session reliability connections** setting, the **CGPAddress** setting is added to the ICA file that starts the published application or desktop. Different configurations for the ICA file are shown in the following screenshot.

6. Check the **Address** setting of the ICA logfile. If the **Fully Qualified Domain Name** (**FQDN**) of the XenApp Session Host is shown, the Citrix Computer policy **DNS Address resolution** setting is enabled. Else an IP address is shown.

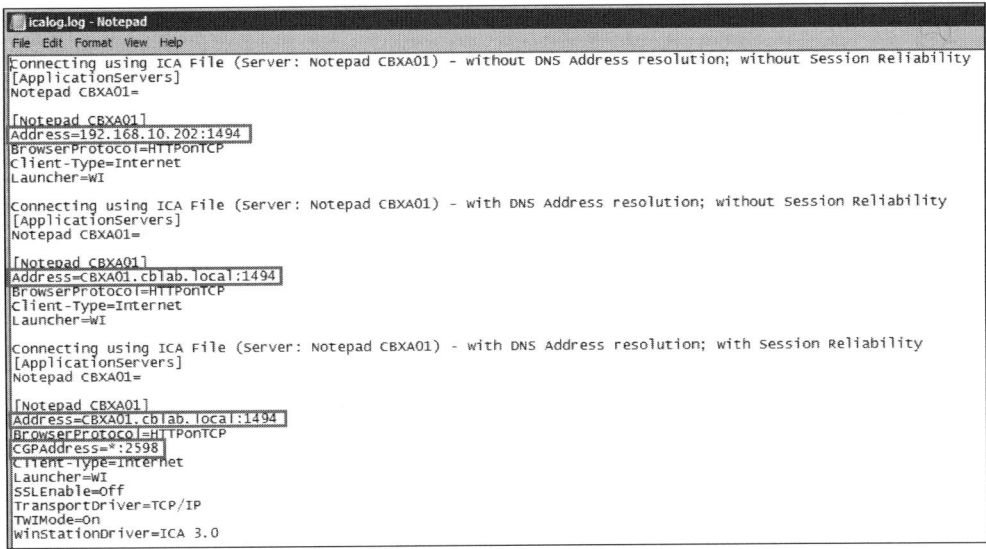

7. When the FQDN of the XenApp Session Host cannot be resolved by the client, the published application cannot be started and an error is shown.

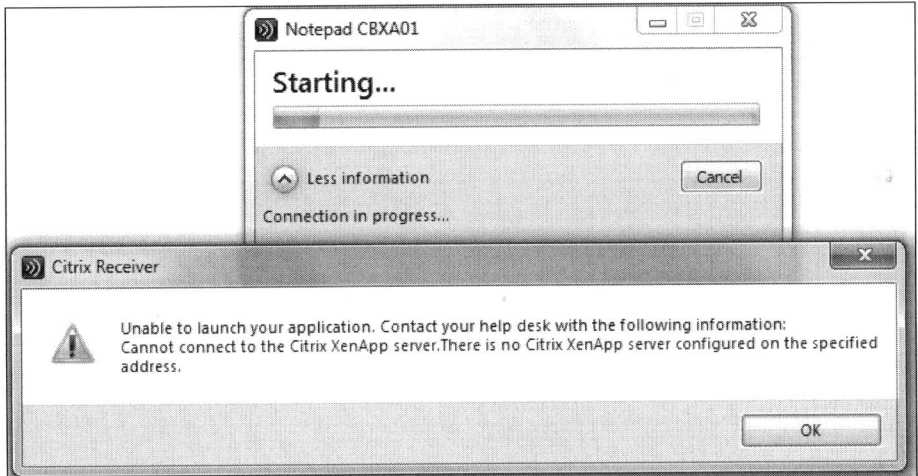

8. Check the client DNS settings, or disable the Citrix Computer policy **DNS address resolution** setting to fix the problem.

9. Check to see if the published application has available Citrix Session Host servers configured, if the following error is shown:

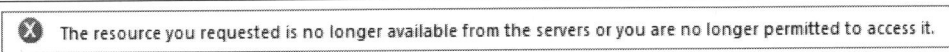

There's more...

You can read more troubleshooting tips at Citrix's Knowledge Center at `http://support.citrix.com/article/CTX128115`.

XenApp servers that are configured with more than one network adapter are called multihomed servers. Always check the ICA listener settings and network bindings for these servers as they can cause connection problems as well.

You can read more on Application Launch Requests might fail on a XenApp 6.5 multihomed server at Citrix's Knowledge Center at `http://support.citrix.com/article/CTX131554`.

Troubleshooting the IMA service

This recipe will show you how to troubleshoot a XenApp server when the Citrix **Independent Management Architecture** (**IMA**) service is not started. The IMA service is the core component of the XenApp server and provides the connection to the Data Store, sends status updates to the Controller Host, supports Load Evaluations and user sessions. If the IMA Service is not running, no sessions can be hosted by the server.

How to do it...

To troubleshoot the IMA Service, follow these steps:

1. The IMA Service takes a long time to start. An event is logged by the Service Control Manager stating the IMA service didn't start. If the IMA service does start eventually the message can be ignored.

 The Service Control Manager has a default timeout of six minutes. If the IMA Service doesn't update the localhost cache from the database in time, an event is logged by the Service Control Manager. You can change the Service Control Manager timeout, by increasing the following registry setting (decimal value in milliseconds): `HKLM\SYSTEM\CurrentControlSet\Control\ServicesPipeTimeout`

2. If the IMA Service is not starting, check the following registry key:

    `HKLM\SOFTWARE\Wow6432Node\Citrix\IMA\RUNTIME`

    `Value: CurrentlyLoadingPlugin (REG_SZ)`

    - **No data**: IMA Service could not connect to the datastore or the localhost cache is missing/corrupt
    - **Data**: The failing IMA Service subsystem is logged

If the data lists `ImaLicSs.dll`, it might indicate that another server is on the network using the same NetBIOS name or IP address.

3. If the IMA Service is not starting check the following registry key:

    `HKLM\SOFTWARE\Wow6432Node\Citrix\IMA\RUNTIME`

    `Value: PSRequired (REG_DWORD)`

    - ❏ Change the value to `0` and restart the IMA Service as it will stop from recreating the localhost cache

 If the value is set to `1`, the IMA Service will try to recreate the localhost cache from the Data Store when it is started. This might trigger the Service Control Manager time-out, and leave the IMA Service in a unresponsive starting state.

4. If manually starting the IMA Service results in an error code of 2147483649 the local system account might be missing a temp directory (required for the IMA service to run).

    - ❏ Manually create a temp directory, and check if the TMP and TEMP system environment variables are pointing to this directory

5. If manually starting the IMA Service results in an error code of 2147483647, the used service account may not have the required permissions.

    - ❏ The service account used for the IMA service requires "Log on as a service" permissions

6. If a service account is used to start the IMA Service that relies on a roaming profile, check the size of the profile or error messages indicating the profile cannot be loaded. Test with a local user profile or a small roaming profile account to see if the problem is fixed.

7. Check if the Print spooler service is running and configured with the Local System Account. The IMA service depends on it.

8. Test the connection to the Data Store with an ODBC test utility and the used DSN file to ensure the connection string, username, and password are correct.

    - ❏ The DSN file used by the IMA Service can be found in the following registry key:

      `HKLM\SOFTWARE\Wow6432Node\Citrix\IMA\DataStoreName`

The username and password used by the IMA Service for the Data Store connection can be changed by using the dsmaint command. The DSMAINT command will be addressed in *Chapter 10, PowerShell and Command-line Tooling*.

9. If the IMA Service fails to start due to a corrupt localhost cache. You can recreate the localhost cache with the dsmaint recreatelhc command. For the command to work, a connection must be made with the Data Store.

10. You can check if the Data Store itself is corrupt with the dscheck command.

 The dscheck command will be addressed in *Chapter 10, PowerShell and Command-line Tooling*.

There's more...

You can read more on troubleshooting the IMA Service at Citrix's Knowledge Center at http://support.citrix.com/article/CTX105292.

You can read more on the IMA Service unresponsive starting state and Data Store corruption at Citrix's Knowledge Center at http://support.citrix.com/article/CTX131631.

Troubleshooting pass-through authentication with Web Interface

This recipe will show you how to troubleshoot pass-through authentication from a domain joined Windows client through the Citrix Web Interface.

How to do it...

To troubleshoot pass-through authentication, follow these steps:

1. Open the task manager on the client device (**Start | Run | taskmgr.exe**).

2. Check if the process **ssonsvr.exe** is running in the task manager:

    ❑ Ensure the Citrix Receiver was installed with the following command line and that the client device was rebooted afterwards:

    ```
    CitrixReceiver.exe /includeSSON ENABLE_SSON=Yes
    ```

3. Open the registry on the client device (**Start | Run | regedit**).

4. Check if the registry value **Enable** is set to `true` for the following registry key:

   `32-bit: HKLM\SOFTWARE\Citrix\ICA Client\SSON`

   `64-bit: HKLM\SOFTWARE\Wow6432Node\Citrix\ICA Client\SSON`

5. Check if the site is added to the local intranet or trusted sites zone.

   ❑ In the Internet Explorer menu click on **Tools | Internet Options | Security tab**

   ❑ Select the local intranet zone and click on **Sites | Advanced**

   ❑ Enter the URL and click on **Add**, **Close**, and **OK**

   ❑ Click on **Custom level** at the **Security level for this zone** section

   ❑ Scroll to the bottom of **Settings**, and select **Automatic logon with current user name and password** for the **User Authentication | Logon option**

   ❑ Click on **OK** (confirm if asked) and **OK**

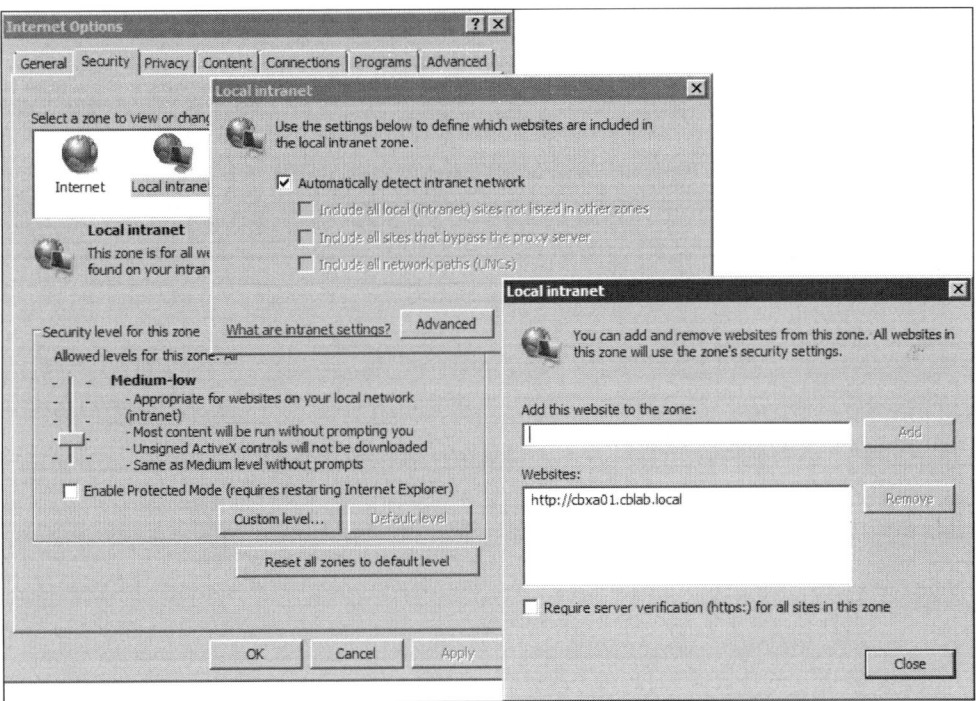

6. Check if the required computer policy settings are configured to enable pass-through authentication for the client device and Web Interface authentication ticket:

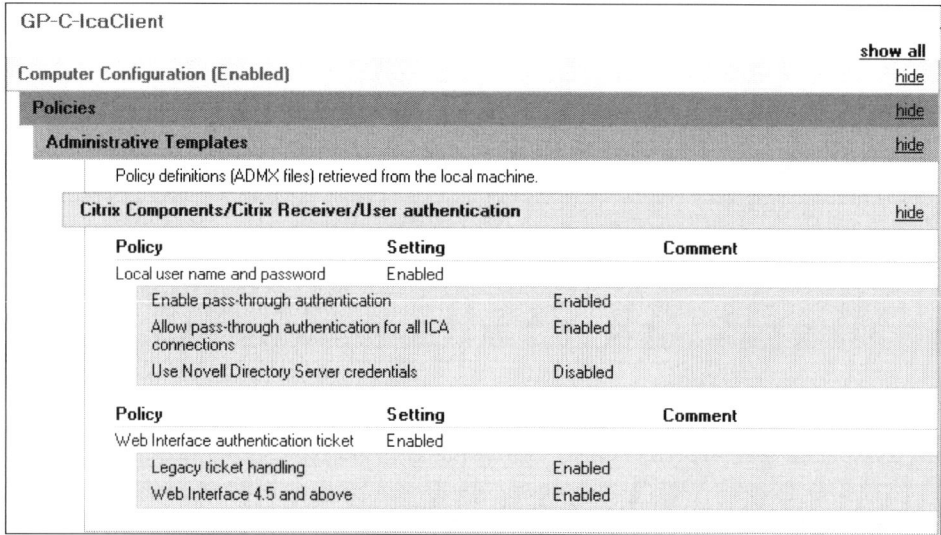

7. Open the Citrix Web Interface Management console on the Web Interface server (**Start | All Programs | Citrix | Management Consoles**).

8. Select **XenApp Web Sites** in the left pane.

9. Select the configured **XenApp Web Site** in the middle pane and click on **Authentication Methods** in the **Action** pane.

10. Ensure pass-through is selected as available method.

11. Click on **Properties**.

12. Select **Automatic Logon** in the left pane and ensure that the **Enable automatic logon by default** option is selected.

13. Select **Kerberos Authentication** in the left pane and ensure that the **Use Kerberos authentication to connect to server** option is not selected.

14. Click on **OK**.

15. Browse to the Web Interface on the client device.

Pass-through should now be working, and the user is automatically logged on to the Citrix Web Interface with the logged on Windows account.

There's more...

You can read more on installing the Citrix Receiver from the command line on Citrix's eDocs at `http://support.citrix.com/proddocs/topic/receiver-windows-34/receiver-windows-cfg-command-line.html`.

You can read more on configuring the Citrix Receiver for pass-through with StoreFront at Citrix's Knowledge Center at `http://support.citrix.com/article/CTX133855`.

Troubleshooting XenApp® policies for Worker Groups

This recipe will show you how to troubleshoot the XenApp policies, when they are not applied correctly to the Worker Group that is configured in the policy filter.

How to do it...

To troubleshoot XenApp policies filtered for Worker Groups, follow these steps:

1. Open the Citrix XenApp management console AppCenter (**Start | Administrative Tools | Citrix | Management Consoles**).

2. Select **XenApp | <FarmName> | Policies** in the left pane.

3. Click on the **Computer** tab in the **Policies** pane.

4. If a policy uses a Worker Group filter, check if the XenApp server is a member of the filtered Worker Group.

5. Run `gpupdate /force` to immediately apply the latest policy settings to the XenApp server.

6. Check the Worker Groups the XenApp server is a member of by running the following PowerShell command:

    ```
    Get-XAWorkerGroup | ServerName <XenAppServerName>
    ```

> To run the preceding PowerShell command, the XenApp 6.5 Server SDK needs to be installed. You can download the SDK at `https://www.citrix.com/downloads/xenapp/sdks/powershell-sdk.html`. You can read more on PowerShell commands and scripts for XenApp in the next chapter.

7. Check the Worker Groups that the XenApp server is a member of, by checking the following registry setting on the XenApp server:

`HKLM\SOFTWARE\Wow6432Node\Policies\Citrix\Evidence`

Name	Type	Data
ab (Default)	REG_SZ	(value not set)
ab ServerGroup	REG_MULTI_SZ	Maintenance

8. Make sure the Worker Group in the filter has the exact same name as the one mentioned in the registry key. Worker Group names are case sensitive.

 Worker Group names in filters can differ due to the renaming of a Worker Group, which does not automatically change the used Worker Group name in the policy filter.

9. Check the applied Citrix computer policy settings at the following registry key and subkeys in the registry of the XenApp server:

`HKLM\SOFTWARE\Wow6432Node\Policies\Citrix`

There's more...

You can read more on not applied policies to XenApp Worker Groups at Citrix's Knowledge Center at `http://support.citrix.com/article/CTX135148`.

You can read more on not applied XenApp Policies on XenApp 6.5 at Citrix's Knowledge Center at `http://support.citrix.com/article/CTX134961`.

Using HDX Monitor to check user experience

This recipe will show you how to use the HDX monitor to check the user experience statistics of an active Citrix XenApp user session. The HDX Monitor is a very powerful tool to get a quick overview of all the statistics for an active user session, which can be very helpful while troubleshooting reported incidents and problems by users.

 HDX Monitor relies on WMI counters to track the user session performance, which might have an impact on the XenApp servers overall performance. While HDX Monitor is a great tool for troubleshooting individual user sessions, it is not suited for performance monitoring.

Getting ready

To use HDX Monitor, you can install the 3.x version on any management server or desktop that is part of the same domain as the XenApp servers you are diagnosing.

 You can read more on the download instructions at Citrix's Knowledge Center at http://support.citrix.com/article/CTX135817.

While using the HDX Monitor to remotely target the XenApp servers, make sure the XenApp server is configured for Windows Remote Management. This can be done by checking the Connection Requirements on the **About** screen for remote targeting a XenApp server.

About

Version Information

You are running HDX Monitor version 3.2.4862.28379

Learn more about this version

Connection Requirements

1. Make sure you are targeting a server, (XenDesktop VDA or a XenApp Server) not a client.
2. This computer should be in the same domain as that of the target machine.
3. For remote targeting using Winrm (see Settings/Monitor/Access Type), execute the following command on the target system once (RunAs Admin): "winrm quickconfig". This step is required for XenApp.
4. The target machine may-be turned off or in process of rebooting. In the latter case, please wait for a little while and "Try Again".
5. To access Event logs remotely, the target machine's firewall must allow the Remote Event Log Management feature for the Domain.

How to do it...

To monitor HDX configuration settings for XenApp user sessions with HDX Monitor live, follow these steps:

1. Open the HDX Monitor (**Start | All Programs | Citrix**).
2. Select **System** as your **Select Target**, enter a server name and click on **Open**.

3. An overview is automatically given of the Citrix ICA session with the lowest ID. The discovered errors and/or warnings are shown with a corresponding icon per section:

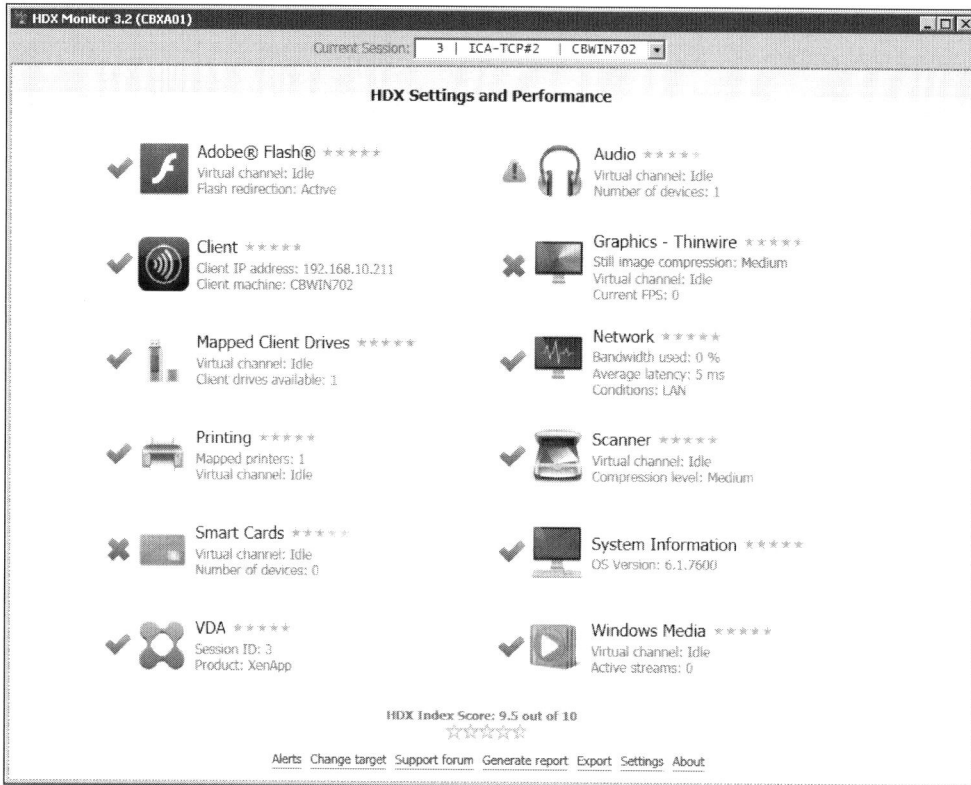

4. Switch between the user sessions by selecting a different **Current Session** from the selection box in the top center of the HDX Monitor.

5. Zoom in on detailed information for each section, by clicking on that section. Each detailed section pane shows an overview of the recorded attributes and WMI values as well as errors, warnings, and tips that are identified by the HDX Monitor. Click on **more details...** to open the corresponding Citrix Knowledge Center articles:

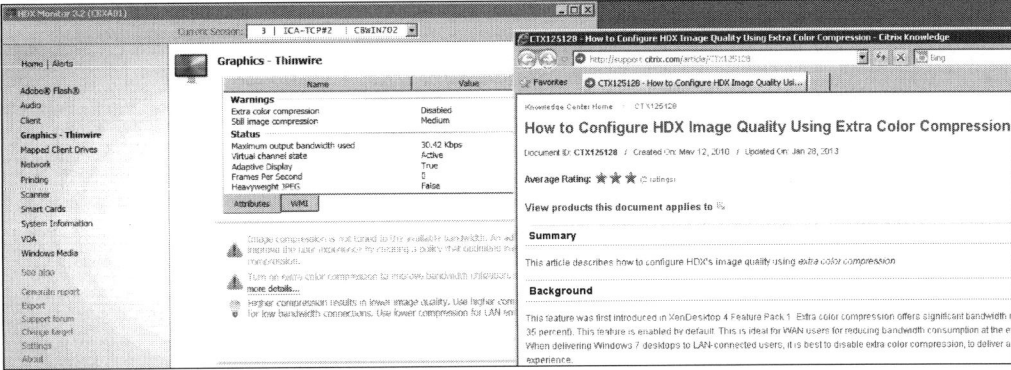

6. Click on **Generate Report** to create a report on the current session HDX settings:

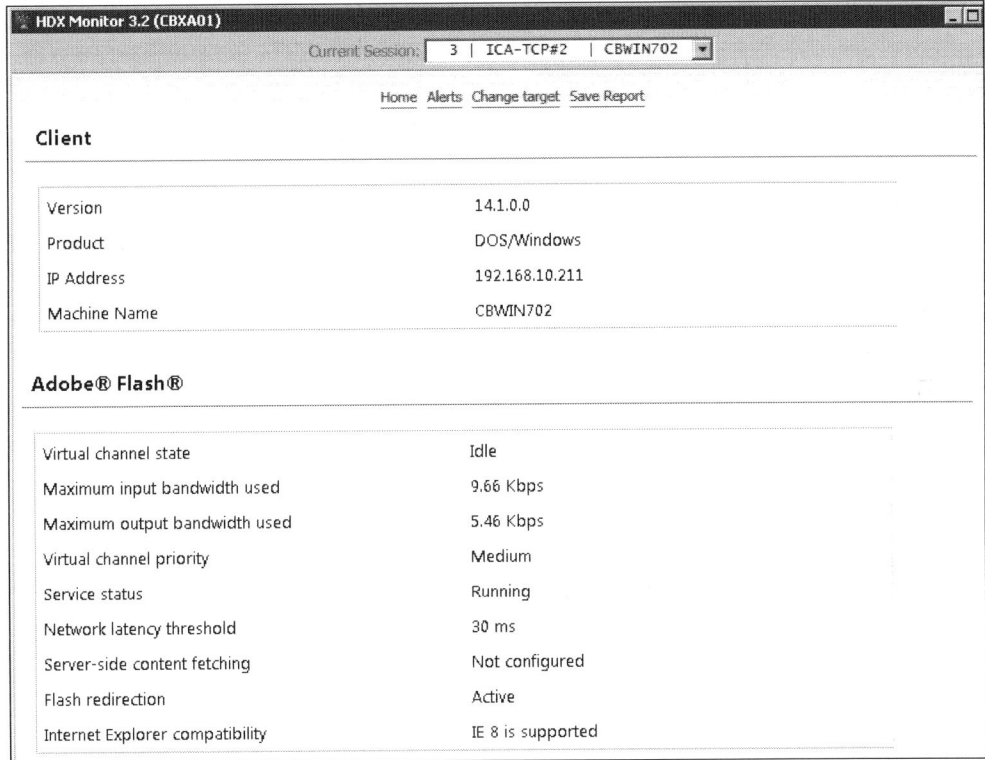

7. You can save the report by clicking on **Save Report**, and save the current session statistics as an HTML page.

8. Click on **Export** to save the current session statistics as an XML file.

 Use the **Export** option to store a baseline for your (test) user settings, which can be imported for future reference and comparison at a later stage. Simply import an exported file in the HDX Monitor by selecting **Import** as your **Select Target** and browsing to the XML file on the startup screen.

9. Click on **Alerts** for an overview of all Errors, Warnings, and/or Tips/Hints created by HDX Monitor:

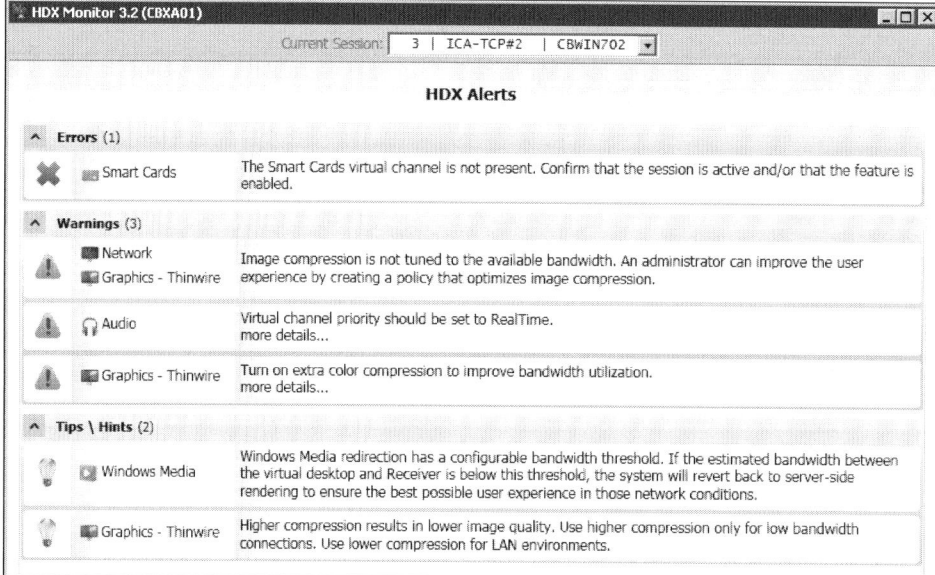

10. Check the network settings by clicking on **Network** to get an overview of the **Network conditions** for the user session. The **Network conditions** will give you a good indication on the latency experienced by a user and discover network performance problems.

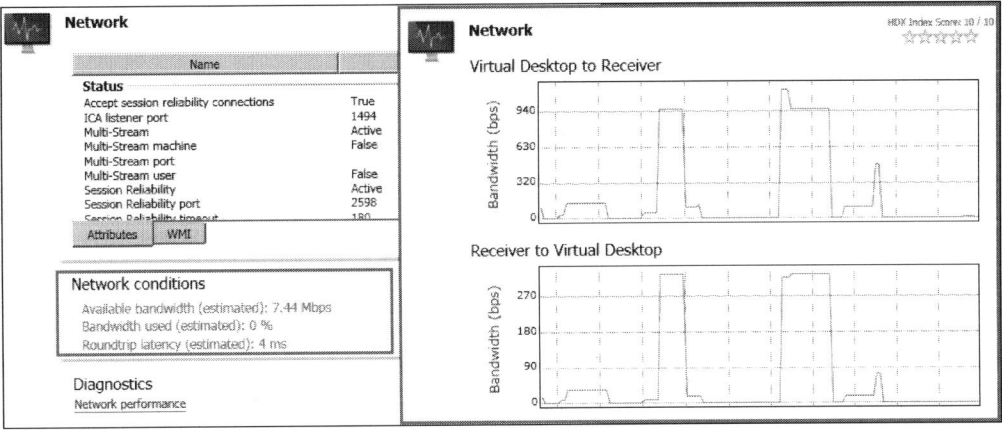

11. Check the current output and input session bandwidth by clicking on **Network Performance** under **Diagnostics** to see a graphical representation of the bandwidth counters.

Getting a full desktop instead of the published application

This recipe will show you how to resolve the known issue on a Windows Server 2008 R2 Server, where a full desktop session starts instead of the published application that was selected.

How to do it...

A common issue that can be encountered, when a user clicks on a published application, is that a full desktop is started. To troubleshoot the problem, follow these steps:

> The behavior can be linked to the seamless or windowed setting of the application, so ensure switching between both application appearances does not differ. The different application behavior for windowed and seamless appearances are explained in the following Citrix Knowledge Center article at http://support.citrix.com/article/CTX138775.

1. Open the Remote Desktop Session Host Configuration management console (**Start | Run | tsconfig.msc**).

2. Double-click on the **ICA-TCP connection**.

3. Select the **Environment** tab.

4. Check if the option to start a program when the user logs on, is not set with an empty program path and filename:

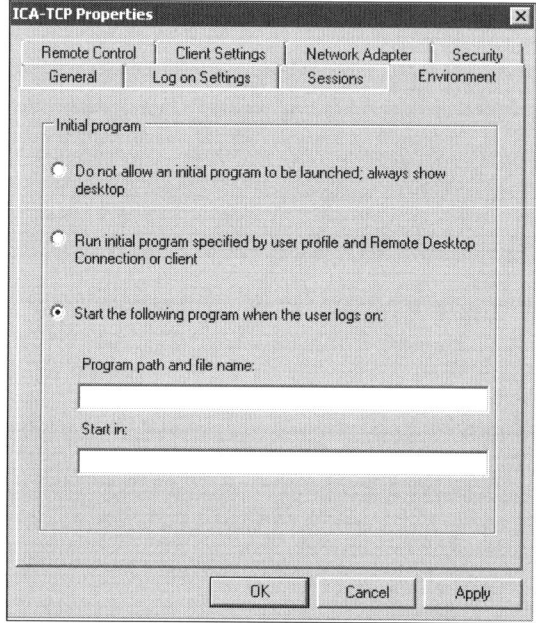

5. Open the **Group Policy Management Configuration** (**GPMC**) management console (**Start | Run | gpmc.msc**).

6. Check whether a policy is set to **Start a program on connection** as either a **Computer Configuration** or a **User Configuration** with an empty program path and filename:

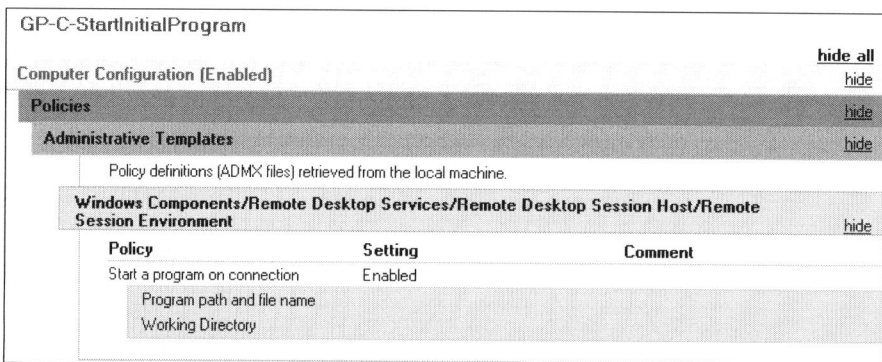

7. Open the registry on the XenApp server (**Start | Run | regedit**).

8. Check whether the `AppSetup` value for the `Winlogon` key contains at least the following data:

   `HKLM\SOFTWARE\Microsoft\Windows NT\CurrentVersion\Winlogon`

   `Value: AppSetup (REG_SZ)`

   `Data: CtxHide.exe UsrLogon.Cmd,cmstart.exe`

9. If no Service Pack is installed on the Windows Server 2008 R2 XenApp server, make sure Microsoft **Fix316926** is installed on the XenApp server. You can download the required Microsoft hotfix at `http://support.microsoft.com/kb/969851/en-us`.

Troubleshooting printer drivers on XenApp® servers

The printer driver is one of the most important and challenging things of a XenApp server configuration, as a lot of printing issues are printer driver related. Even though printer drivers on Windows Server 2003 were more troublesome, it is still important to only implement signed Windows printer drivers on Windows Server 2008 R2 Servers. It is still possible for a bad printer driver to claim excessive server resources; thus, influencing server and session performance for all logged on users.

This recipe will show you how to troubleshoot printer drivers on Citrix XenApp servers.

How to do it...

To retrieve information on each installed print driver on the XenApp server, follow these steps:

1. Download Print Detective from the Citrix Knowledge Center at `http://support.citrix.com/article/CTX116474`.

2. Unzip the file to a folder on the XenApp server.

3. Run `PrintDetective.exe`:

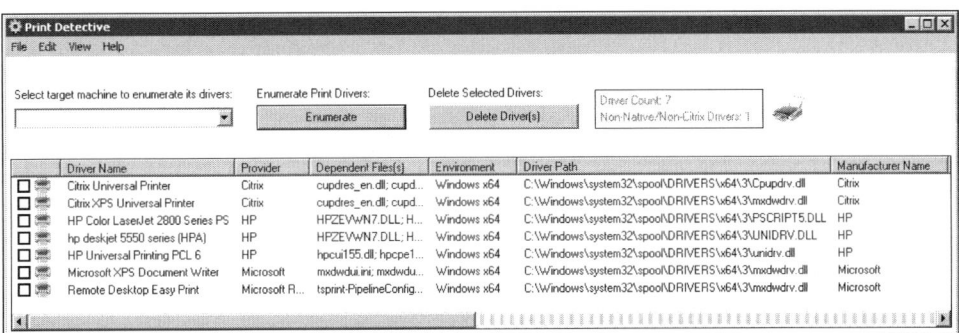

4. Select **View | non-Native/Non-Citrix Drivers Only** to only view the non-native drivers:

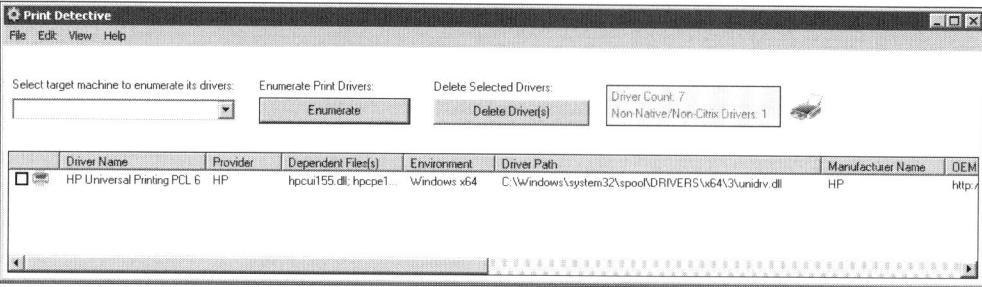

5. Select **View | Reset View** to see all drivers.

6. Select a print driver and click on **Delete Driver(s)** to delete a print driver from the XenApp server.

To run a stress test for a print driver on the XenApp server, follow these steps:

1. Download StressPrinters from the Citrix Knowledge Center at `http://support.citrix.com/article/CTX109374`.

2. Unzip the file to a folder on the XenApp server.

3. Install the print drivers to test on the XenApp server.

4. Run `StressPrinters64.exe`:

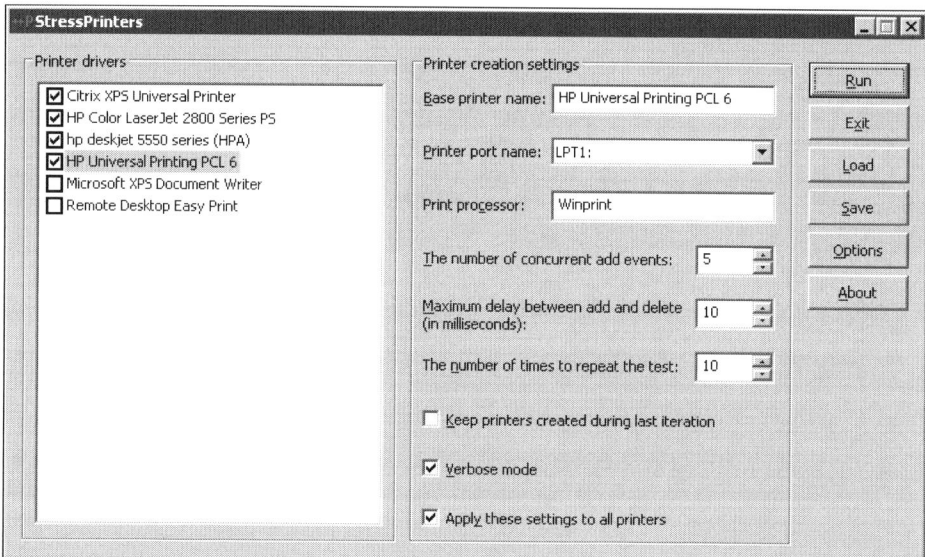

5. Select one or more printer drivers and configure the printer creation settings.

   ❑ Use the Microsoft's Print Management console to verify if the printer port LPT1 is free on the server

   ❑ Choose a representative number for the number of concurrent add events, maximum delay between add and delete (in milliseconds), and number of times to repeat the test

   ❑ Select **Verbose mode** to keep track of the progress

   ❑ Select **Apply these settings to all printers** to re-use the configuration for all selected print drivers

6. Click on **Run** to start the stress test:

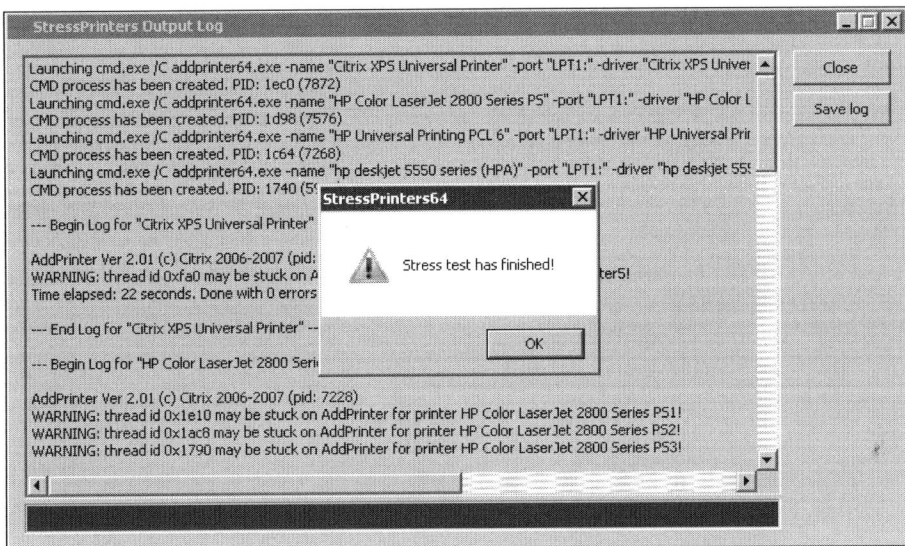

7. Depending on the configuration, StressPrinters can take a while to run.

8. Check the output log for any error and warning messages.

9. Click on **Save log** to save the test results for later reference.

10. Logged errors indicate an unstable printer driver and installing it on a XenApp server should be avoided.

How it works...

Print Detective distinguishes between native/inbox drivers and non-native/manufacturer drivers. A native driver is included in the Windows Operating System, and has been tested for high performance and stability by Microsoft. A non-native driver is provided by the manufacturer through a support website and might not be subject to the same testing standards.

To distinguish between drivers, you can check the registry settings for each driver, which can be found at:

```
HKLM\SYSTEM\CurrentControlSet\Control\Print\Enviromments\<WindowsOS>\
Drivers\Version-3\<DriverName>
```

Each driver contains a `MinInboxDriverVerVersion` value with a version number. If the version number is 0.0.0.0, it is a non-native driver. If an actual version number is shown, it is a native driver:

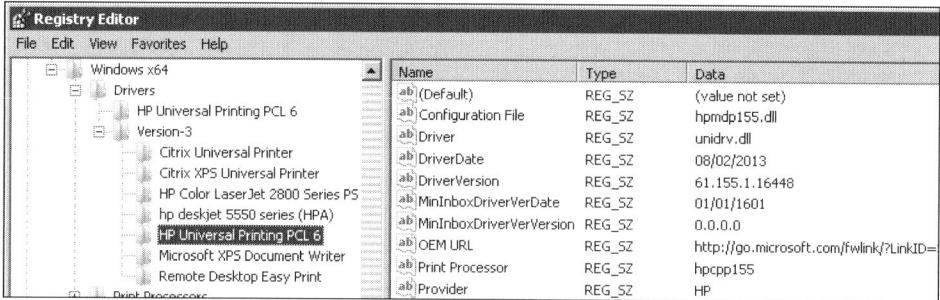

Stress Printers provides a stress test tool for printer drivers by simulating the user session printer creation process on a XenApp server. During the test, StressPrinters will rapidly create and delete printers based upon the selected printer driver(s). By stressing the printer drivers and their behavior during the creation and deletion of session printers, the stability of the print driver and multi-user support can be tested. This way, ill performing print drivers can be detected during the test and installation of such printer drivers in a production environment can be prevented.

There's more...

You can read more on the Citrix Universal print drivers at Citrix's eDocs at `http://support.citrix.com/proddocs/topic/xenapp65-admin/ps-configuring-universal-printer-all.html`.

You can read more on the installed printer drivers at Citrix's Knowledge Center at `http://support.citrix.com/article/CTX128594`.

You can read more on distinguishing native and non-native drivers at Citrix's Knowledge Center at `http://support.citrix.com/article/CTX126093`.

You can read more on StressPrinters at Citrix's Knowledge Center at `http://support.citrix.com/article/CTX109374`.

Retaining client printer settings in user profile

This recipe will show you how to check for client-printer settings retention in the user profile.

Getting ready

To retain the printer settings for future user sessions, the following aspects must be met:

- The printer driver (driver name, version, and devmode) on the client and server side must be an exact match

- The `<PrinterDriverName>` registry key on the client and server side must be an exact match. The key can be found at:

  `HKLM\SYSTEM\CurrentControlSet\Control\Print\Environments\Windows`
  `x64\Drivers\Version-3\<PrinterDriverName>`

- Changes to printer preferences must be made through the (published) `Printers` and `Faxes` folder

How to do it...

To ensure client-printer settings are retained in the user profile, follow these steps:

1. Open the Citrix XenApp management console AppCenter (**Start | Administrative Tools | Citrix | Management Consoles**).

2. Select **XenApp | <FarmName> | Policies** in the left pane.

3. Click on the **User** tab in the Policies pane.

4. Click on **New** to create a new policy.

5. Enter **Name** and **Description** for the policy and click on **Next**.

6. Select **ICA | Printing | Client Printers**.

7. Configure the **Printer properties retention** setting with the **Retained in user profile only** option and click on **OK**.

8. Click on **Next**.

9. Configure the filter settings and click on **Next**.

 Filter options are addressed in *Chapter 8, XenApp® Policies, Adding filters to a policy* recipe.

10. Ensure the **Enable this policy** option is selected and click on **Create**.

To ensure the session printer settings are not deleted when a user logs off, follow these steps:

1. Open the registry on the XenApp server (**Start | Run | regedit**).

2. Create the following DWORD:

    ```
    HKLM\SOFTWARE\Citrix\ICA\Printing Settings
    Value: DisableNetworkPrinterDisconnect (REG_DWORD)
    Data: 1
    ```

 By default network printers are always deleted at logoff, unless the preceding registry key is set.

To check if the printer settings are retained, follow these steps:

1. Create a new user session by starting the published `Printer` and `Faxes` folder.

2. Check the creation of the following user registry keys and values:

    ❑ Retained Session Printer properties:

    ```
    HKCU\Software\Citrix\PrinterProperties
    ```

3. Change the printer settings on the printer preferences **General** tab.

4. Log off the user session.

5. Start a new user session and check to see if the printer settings are restored.

Make sure the preceding registry keys are stored by a user profile solution when the Hybrid or Mandatory profiles are used.

There's more...

Read more on How to Retain Printer settings at Citrix's Knowledge Center at `http://support.citrix.com/article/CTX119691`.

Mapping client printers does not work when connecting through Web Interface 5.4

When using Web Interface 5.4 to start a published application or desktop, it can occur that no client printers are mapping in the Citrix XenApp user session, regardless of the policies that are correctly configured. This recipe will show you how to fix this issue.

How to do it...

To fix the issue, that no client printers are mapped when a published application or desktop is launched through Web Interface 5.4, follow these steps:

1. Open the Citrix Web Interface Management console (**Start | All Programs | Citrix | Management Consoles**).

2. Select **XenApp Web Sites** in the left pane.

3. Select the configured **XenApp Web Site** in the middle pane, and click on **Session Settings** in the **Action** Pane.

4. Select **Connection Performance** in the left pane.

5. Select the **Enable printer mapping** option in the **Bandwidth Profile** section and click on **OK**:

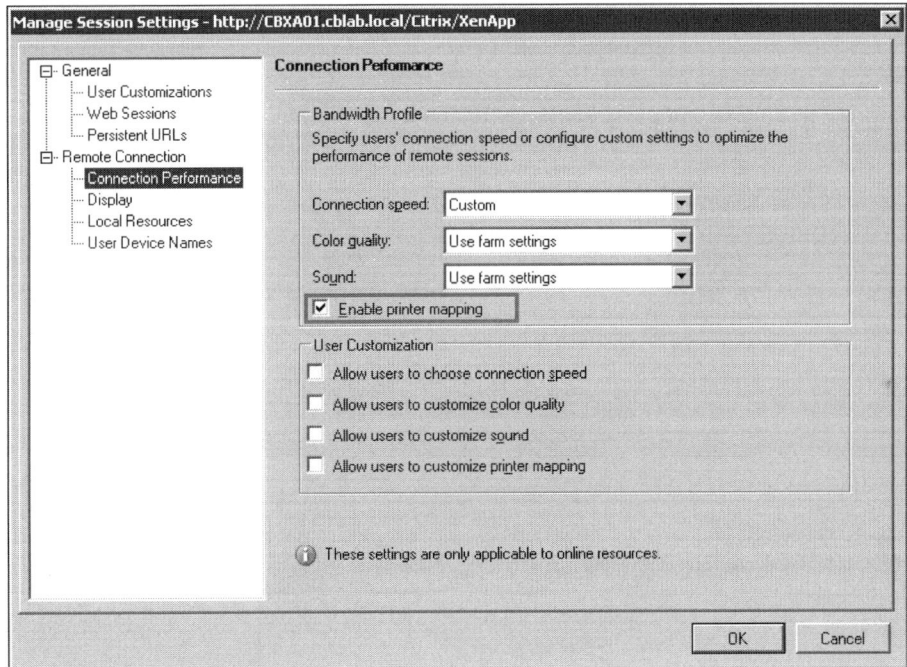

6. Check if the client printer is correctly mapped in a new user session, started through Web Interface 5.4.

Troubleshooting client clipboard issues

This recipe will show you how to troubleshoot the client clipboard issues that prevent a user from copying and pasting between the client device and the Citrix XenApp user session.

How to do it...

To fix a broken clipboard, follow these steps:

1. Open the Remote Desktop Session Host Configuration console (**Start | Run | tsconfig.msc**).

2. Double-click on the **ICA-TCP Connection** and select the **Client Settings** tab:

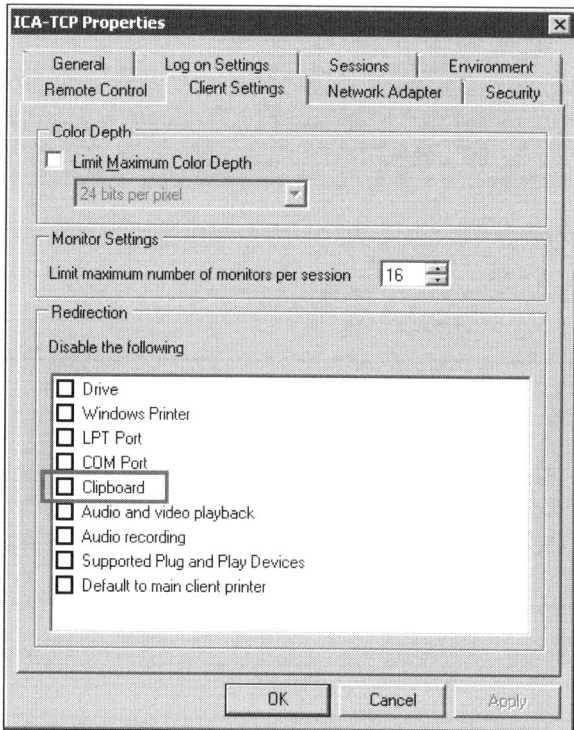

3. Ensure **Clipboard** is not selected in the **Redirection** section to be disabled.

4. Click on **OK**.

5. Double-click on the **RDP-TCP Connection** and select the **Client Settings** tab.

6. Ensure **Clipboard** is not selected in the **Redirection** section to be disabled.

7. Click on **OK**.

8. Open the Citrix XenApp management console AppCenter (**Start | Administrative Tools | Citrix | Management Consoles**).

9. Select **XenApp | <FarmName> | Servers** in the left pane.

10. Click on the **Users** tab in the **Servers** pane.

11. Select the user session where the broken clipboard is reported and click on the **Processes** tab.

12. Check if the process `wfshell.exe` is running in the user session.

13. Check if the following registry key and values exist:

    `HKLM\SYSTEM\CurrentControlSet\Control\Citrix\wfshell\Virtual Clipboard`

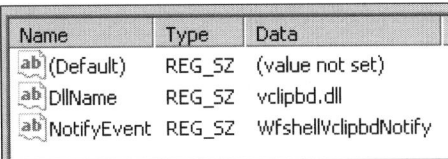

Name	Type	Data
(Default)	REG_SZ	(value not set)
DllName	REG_SZ	vclipbd.dll
NotifyEvent	REG_SZ	WfshellVclipbdNotify

14. Check if `vclipbd.dll` exists on the XenApp server (by default located in `C:\Program Files (x86)\Citrix\system32`).

15. Open the `default.ica` file on the Citrix Web Interface server in Notepad and search for the `ClipboardAllowed=Off` setting within the `[WfClient]` or `[<App Server>]` section. If no entry is found, the default setting is to allow Clipboard (the `default.ica` file is stored by default in `C:\inetpub\wwwroot\Citrix\XenApp\conf`).

To temporarily restore the clipboard functionality, run the RepairCBDChain tool on the local device and/or within the XenApp user session. The tool is available at Citrix's Knowledge Center at `http://support.citrix.com/article/CTX106226`.

Using Citrix® Auto Support to troubleshoot a XenApp® server

This recipe will show you how to use Citrix Auto Support to analyze a XenApp server logfile generated by the preferred Citrix Scout tool.

Getting ready

To use the online Citrix Auto Support you must have a MyCitrix account to log on and upload a logfile. You can create a MyCitrix account for free.

How to do it...

To use Citrix Auto Support, follow these steps:

1. Download Citrix Scout from Citrix's Knowledge Center at `http://support.citrix.com/article/CTX130147`.

2. Unzip the downloaded file to a folder on the XenApp server.

3. Double-click `run.exe` to start Scout (click on **Run** if any security warning is shown).

4. Select **Config | Settings** from the menu and configure the collection settings, such as report folder, events to collect, max log size, and max number of machines for data collection:

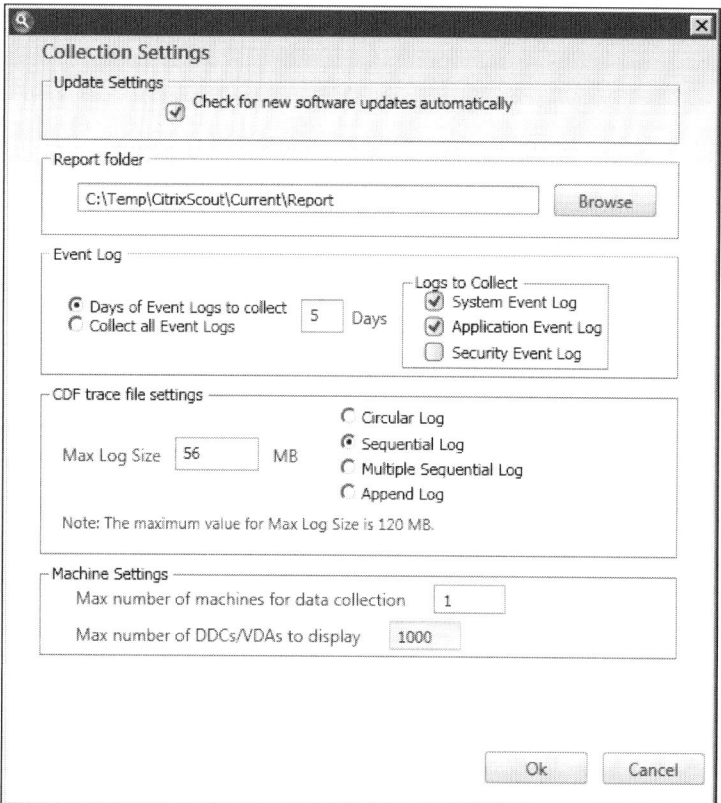

5. Click on **OK**.

6. Click on **Collect & Upload**.

7. Select the machines for data collection and click on **Continue** (progress is shown in the status bar of the tool).

8. Click on **Save** to save the scan results to a `.zip` file.

9. Enter your MyCitrix credentials and click on **Upload**.

10. Accept the agreement.

11. Click on **View Analysis on Citrix Auto Support** to browse to
    `https://taas.citrix.com`.

12. Log on to Citrix Auto Support with your MyCitrix credentials.

13. Click on **Get Started**.

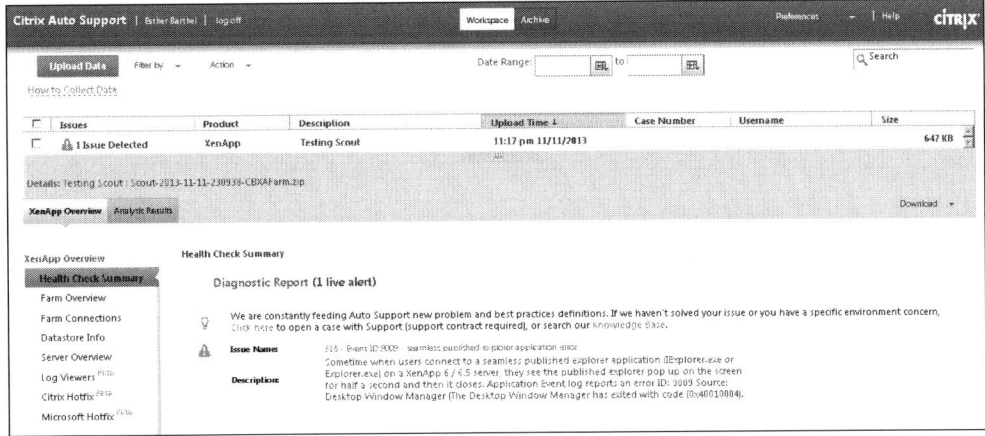

14. A dashboard is shown with the results of the last data collection and any issues that may have been detected.

15. By clicking on the **Issue Name** link, the corresponding Event ID, resolutions, and recommendations are shown. These might include a link to a corresponding Citrix Knowledge Center article as shown in the following screenshot:

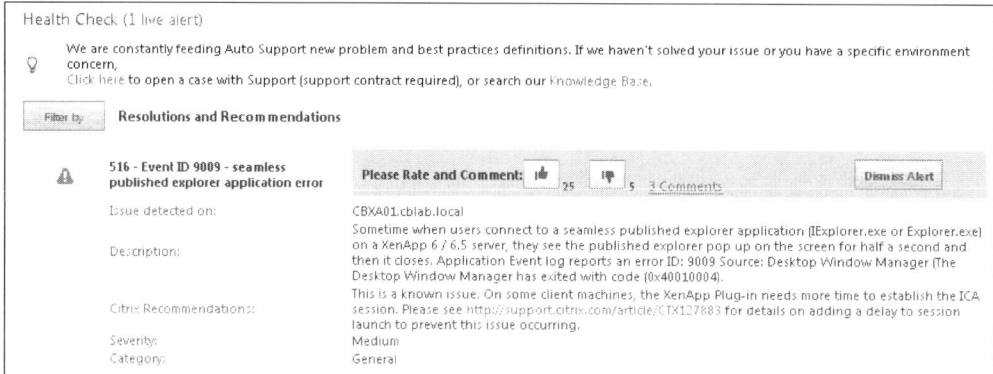

Test each recommended resolution and/or recommendation in a test environment before applying them to a Citrix XenApp production environment. Always verify whether the provided solution is solving a problem.

10
PowerShell and Command-line Tooling

In this chapter, we will cover the following topics:

- ▶ Retrieving the XenApp® Farm information with QUERY
- ▶ Diagnosing the XenApp® load-balancing rules with LBDIAG
- ▶ Performing data store maintenance with DSMAINT and DSCHECK
- ▶ Installing the XenApp® 6.5 PowerShell SDK
- ▶ Replicating printer drivers with PowerShell
- ▶ Creating Citrix® policies with PowerShell
- ▶ Changing the XenApp® product edition with PowerShell
- ▶ Creating a basic XenApp® inventory report with PowerShell
- ▶ Managing Farm administration roles with PowerShell
- ▶ Checking the XenApp® server load with PowerShell
- ▶ Monitoring the Citrix® License Server with PowerShell

Introduction

In addition to the standard management console that is included in the XenApp installation, Citrix offers command-line tools for diagnosis and administration tasks as well. Some tools are included in the installation while others are provided as additional downloads from the Citrix Knowledge Center.

With Windows Server 2008, Microsoft introduced Windows PowerShell, a task-automation and configuration-management framework consisting of a command-line shell and associated scripting language built in the .NET framework. The basic set of cmdlets and providers included in the default installation of PowerShell can easily be extended with application-specific cmdlets and providers from third parties, allowing PowerShell to manage not only the Windows components but other applications as well. Citrix offers a XenApp 6.5 PowerShell SDK that includes a complete set of cmdlets to manage a XenApp Farm with PowerShell commands and scripts.

This chapter will focus on some of the common command-line tools and PowerShell scripts that will help in managing a XenApp Farm.

The scripts provided in this chapter act as examples of how PowerShell can be used to create reports or configure settings for a Citrix XenApp Farm. I created and tested the scripts in my own lab with the limited PowerShell knowledge that I have. So, feel free to improve and optimize the sample scripts from this book and share them with the community.

Retrieving the XenApp® Farm information with QUERY

This recipe will show you how to use the QUERY command to retrieve the Citrix XenApp Farm information and report on the health of the Farm, server, users, sessions, and processes. The QUERY command is part of Windows **Remote Desktop Services** (**RDS**) with an additional extension for Citrix XenApp to support Farm information retrieval as well. The Citrix extension uses its own `qfarm.exe` command.

The `query.exe` command can be found at `C:\Windows\System32`.

The `qfarm.exe` command can be found at `C:\Program Files (x86)\Citrix\system32`.

How to do it...

To retrieve live information on the XenApp Farm statistics, perform the following steps:

1. Open a command prompt by navigating to **Start | Run | cmd.exe**.

2. Run the following command to display the common Farm information:

   `query farm`

   ```
   C:\Users\administrator.CBLAB>query farm

   Server                  Transport  Network Address
   ----------------------  ---------  ----------------------
   CBXA01*                 TCP/IP     192.168.10.202 D
   CBXA02                  TCP/IP     192.168.10.203
   ```

3. Run the following command to display the current server load and logon mode:

   `query farm /load`

   ```
   C:\Users\administrator.CBLAB>query farm /load

   Server Name        Server Load    Load Throttling Load   Logon Mode
   -----------------  -----------    --------------------   ------------------
   CBXA01             800            OFF                    AllowLogons
   CBXA02             4237           0                      ProhibitLogonsOnly
   ```

4. Run the following command to check for offline servers:

   `query farm /offline`

   ```
   C:\Users\administrator.CBLAB>query farm /offline

   Server Name          Zone Name
   -------------------  -----------------
   CBXA02               DEFAULT ZONE
   ```

5. Run the following command to display the available published applications and the current application load (if applicable):

   `query farm /app`

   ```
   C:\Users\administrator.CBLAB>query farm /app
                                                            App       Server
   Application Name                          Server Name    Load      Load
   --------------------------------------    -----------    -----     ------
   Desktop XA01                              CBXA01         200       800
   Notepad CBXA02                            CBXA02                   6314
   Notepad CBXA01                            CBXA01                   800
   IE-HDX                                    CBXA01                   800
   Desktop XA02                              CBXA02                   6314
   Explorer                                  CBXA01                   800
   Printers                                  CBXA01                   800
   ```

6. The output of `query user /SERVER:CBXA01` is as follows:

```
C:\Users\administrator.CBLAB>query user /SERVER:CBXA01
 USERNAME              SESSIONNAME        ID  STATE   IDLE TIME  LOGON TIME
 administrator         rdp-tcp#0           2  Active          .  11/17/2013 10:45 AM
 cbtester01            ica-tcp#1           3  Active          9  11/17/2013 12:29 PM

C:\Users\administrator.CBLAB>query user /SERVER:CBXA02
 USERNAME              SESSIONNAME        ID  STATE   IDLE TIME  LOGON TIME
 administrator         rdp-tcp#0           2  Active          3  11/17/2013 1:21 PM
 cbtester03            ica-tcp#1           4  Active          5  11/17/2013 5:41 PM
```

7. Run the following command to check the running processes for a logged on user:

```
query process cbtester03 /SERVER:CBXA02
```

```
C:\Users\administrator.CBLAB>query process cbtester03 /SERVER:CBXA02
 USERNAME              SESSIONNAME        ID     PID  IMAGE
 cbtester03            ica-tcp#1           4    5688  taskhost.exe
 cbtester03            ica-tcp#1           4   15940  dwm.exe
 cbtester03            ica-tcp#1           4   16156  wfshell.exe
 cbtester03            ica-tcp#1           4   11820  notepad.exe
```

How it works...

The QUERY command offers detailed information about the current XenApp Farm settings including Farm, process, server, session, and user. To retrieve detailed information on one of the topics, you need to specify the topic you want to zoom in on, as shown in the following screenshot:

```
Administrator: Command Prompt

C:\Users\administrator.CBLAB>query /?
QUERY { FARM | PROCESS | SERVER | SESSION | TERMSERVER | USER }

C:\Users\administrator.CBLAB>_
```

Each query topic offers parameters that can be set for that specific topic to get the detailed information on the current settings for the Farm, session, or user. To get an overview of XenApp Farm, start with the `query farm` command as shown in the following screenshot:

```
Administrator: Command Prompt

C:\Users\administrator.CBLAB>query farm /?
Display information about servers on the local farm.

QUERY FARM [server [/ADDR ¦ /APP ¦ /APP AppName ¦ /LOAD ¦ /LTLOAD]]
    [/TCP] [/IPX] [/NETBIOS] [/CONTINUE]
    [/APP ¦ /APP AppName ¦ /DISC ¦ /LOAD ¦ /LTLOAD ¦ /OFFLINE ¦
     /OFFLINE ZoneName ¦ /ONLINE ¦ /ONLINE ZoneName ¦ /PROCESS ¦ /ZONE ¦
     /ZONE ZoneName ¦ /ZONEAPP ¦ /ZONEAPP AppName¦ /ZONELOAD ¦ /SERVERS]

    /TCP            Display TCP/IP data.
    /IPX            Display IPX data.
    /NETBIOS        Display NetBIOS data.

    /ADDR           Display address data on selected server.
    /APP            Display application names and server load.
    /DISC           Display disconnected session data.
    /LOAD           Display server load and logon mode.
    /LTLOAD         Display server and load throttling load.
    /OFFLINE        Display offline servers.
    /ONLINE         Display online servers including servers with logons disabled.
    /SERVERS        Display server names and IP addresses.
    /PROCESS        Display active processes.
    /ZONE           Display zones and data collectors.
    /ZONEAPP        Display application names and server load of local zone.
    /ZONELOAD       Display server load of local zone.

    /CONTINUE       Don't pause after each page of output.

C:\Users\administrator.CBLAB>query farm

Server                  Transport Network Address
--------------------------------------------------
CBXA01*                 TCP/IP    192.168.10.202 D
CBXA02                  TCP/IP    192.168.10.203

C:\Users\administrator.CBLAB>_
```

A good start is to use the `/load` switch to see the calculated value for each server's load (based on the assigned load evaluator) and to check whether or not the server prohibits logons. Check the following table for common load values:

Value	Explanation
0 to 9998	Normal range of load values
10000	Full load (100 percent) on the server
20000	Incorrect XenApp server edition license mismatch / the server is unavailable
99990	Insufficient rights to run query farm (or `qfarm.exe`)
99999	No load evaluator assigned/configured

To check if any server is offline, not responding to ICA requests, use the `/offline` switch. A few examples of this output can be seen in the following screenshot:

```
Administrator: Command Prompt

C:\Users\administrator.CBLAB>query farm /load

Server Name           Server Load   Load Throttling Load   Logon Mode
CBXA01                800           OFF                    AllowLogons
CBXA02                7951          0                      AllowLogons

C:\Users\administrator.CBLAB>query farm /load

Server Name           Server Load   Load Throttling Load   Logon Mode
CBXA01                800           OFF                    AllowLogons
CBXA02                10000         OFF                    AllowLogons

C:\Users\administrator.CBLAB>query farm /load

Server Name           Server Load   Load Throttling Load   Logon Mode
CBXA01                800           OFF                    AllowLogons
CBXA02                10000         OFF                    ProhibitLogonsOnly

C:\Users\administrator.CBLAB>query farm /load

Server Name           Server Load   Load Throttling Load   Logon Mode
CBXA01                800           OFF                    AllowLogons

C:\Users\administrator.CBLAB>query farm /offline

Server Name           Zone Name
CBXA02                DEFAULT ZONE

C:\Users\administrator.CBLAB>
```

To retrieve information on the currently logged on users in the XenApp Farm, use the `query user` command:

```
Administrator: Command Prompt

C:\Users\administrator.CBLAB>query user /?
Display information about users logged on to the system.

QUERY USER [username | sessionname | sessionid] [/SERVER:servername]

    username            Identifies the username.
    sessionname         Identifies the session named sessionname.
    sessionid           Identifies the session with ID sessionid.
    /SERVER:servername  The server to be queried (default is current).


C:\Users\administrator.CBLAB>query user
 USERNAME              SESSIONNAME        ID  STATE   IDLE TIME  LOGON TIME
>administrator         rdp-tcp#0           2  Active        .    11/17/2013 10:45 AM
 cbtester01            ica-tcp#1           3  Active        4    11/17/2013 11:05 AM

C:\Users\administrator.CBLAB>query user /server:CBXA02
 USERNAME              SESSIONNAME        ID  STATE   IDLE TIME  LOGON TIME
 cbtester03            ica-tcp#1           3  Active        2    11/17/2013 11:53 AM

C:\Users\administrator.CBLAB>
```

The `query user` command will show you information on the logged on users per server.

 To get an overview of all user sessions in the Farm, use the `query farm` or `qfarm` command.

To retrieve information on the sessions running on a server, use the `query session` command:

```
Administrator: Command Prompt

C:\Users\administrator.CBLAB>query session /?
Display information about Remote Desktop Sessions.

QUERY SESSION [sessionname | username | sessionid]
              [/SERVER:servername] [/MODE] [/FLOW] [/CONNECT] [/COUNTER] [/VM]

  sessionname        Identifies the session named sessionname.
  username           Identifies the session with user username.
  sessionid          Identifies the session with ID sessionid.
  /SERVER:servername  The server to be queried (default is current).
  /MODE              Display current line settings.
  /FLOW              Display current flow control settings.
  /CONNECT           Display current connect settings.
  /COUNTER           Display current Remote Desktop Services counters information.
  /VM                Display information about sessions within virtual machines.


C:\Users\administrator.CBLAB>query session /counter
 SESSIONNAME       USERNAME              ID  STATE   TYPE      DEVICE
 services                                0  Disc
 console                                 1  Conn
>rdp-tcp#0          Administrator         2  Active  rdpwd
 ica-tcp#1          cbtester01            3  Active  wdica
 ica-tcp                             65536  Listen
 rdp-tcp                             65537  Listen
Total sessions created: 5
Total sessions disconnected: 1
Total sessions reconnected: 0

C:\Users\administrator.CBLAB>query session /counter /server:CBXA02
 SESSIONNAME       USERNAME              ID  STATE   TYPE      DEVICE
 services                                0  Disc
 console                                 1  Conn
 ica-tcp#1          cbtester03            3  Active  wdica
 ica-tcp                             65536  Listen
 rdp-tcp                             65537  Listen
Total sessions created: 4
Total sessions disconnected: 1
Total sessions reconnected: 0

C:\Users\administrator.CBLAB>_
```

The `query session` command will show you the information on all the running sessions per server. These include console, RDP and ICA sessions, and the ICA and RDP listeners. To list the Remote Desktop Services counters for the queried server, use the `/counter` switch.

To retrieve detailed information on the processes running in a user session on a XenApp server, use the `query process` command as shown in the following screenshot:

```
Administrator: Command Prompt

C:\Users\administrator.CBLAB>query process /?
Displays information about processes.

QUERY PROCESS [* | processid | username | sessionname | /ID:nn | programname]
    [/SERVER:servername]

    *                    Display all visible processes.
    processid            Display process specified by processid.
    username             Display all processes belonging to username.
    sessionname          Display all processes running at sessionname.
    /ID:nn               Display all processes running at session nn.
    programname          Display all processes associated with programname.
    /SERVER:servername   The Remote Desktop Session Host server to be queried.

C:\Users\administrator.CBLAB>query process cbtester03 /server:CBXA02
 USERNAME              SESSIONNAME           ID    PID  IMAGE
 cbtester03            ica-tcp#1              3    9752  taskhost.exe
 cbtester03            ica-tcp#1              3   10004  dwm.exe
 cbtester03            ica-tcp#1              3   10136  wfshell.exe
 cbtester03            ica-tcp#1              3    9720  notepad.exe

C:\Users\administrator.CBLAB>_
```

There's more...

You can read more on the Terminal Server QUERY command at Microsoft Support at `http://support.microsoft.com/kb/186592`.

You can read more on the QFARM command at Citrix's eDocs at

`http://support.citrix.com/proddocs/topic/xenapp65-admin/ps-commands-query-farm-v2.html`.

Diagnosing the XenApp® load balancing rules with LBDIAG

This recipe will show you how to diagnose load balancing rules that are applied to a logged on user with the LBDIAG command.

How to do it...

To diagnose load balancing with LBDIAG, perform the following steps:

1. Download the LBDIAG tool from the Citrix's Knowledge Center at `http://support.citrix.com/article/CTX124446`.
2. Unzip the files to a local folder on the XenApp server.
3. Open a command prompt by navigating to **Start | Run | cmd.exe**.

4. Navigate to the folder that contains `lbdiag.exe` with the `cd` command.

5. Run the following command to diagnose the current load-balancing rules for the Notepad application in XenApp Farm:

```
lbdiag <ApplicationName> /USER <user> /PASS <password> /DOMAIN
<DomainName> /CLIENTNAME <ClientName> /CLIENTIP <ip-address>
```

```
C:\Temp\LBDIAG>lbdiag "Notepad" /USER cbtester03 /PASS ******** /DOMAIN CBLAB /CLIENTNAME Win702 /CLIENTIP 192.168.10.211
User CBLAB\cbtester03 is a member of the following groups:
      CBLAB\cbtester03
      CBLAB\Domain Users
      *CITRIX_BUILTIN*\*CITRIX_USERS*
      CBXA01\Users
      0X0/NI/*CITRIX_BUILTIN*/S-1-5-32-555
      CBXA01\Remote Desktop Users
      CBLAB\GU-RDS-Users

No load balancing policy contains a worker group preference list for the
specified user.

The user will connect to the least-loaded of the following servers:
      Server Name        Server Load  Server Address
      ----------         -----------  --------------
      CBXA01             800          CBXA01.cblab.local
      CBXA02             10000        CBXA02.cblab.local
```

How it works...

LBDiag is a command-line tool that will simulate the load-balancing process for a user starting a published application. It provides a report on the current user configuration, the policies that are applied, and the servers it can connect to.

```
Administrator: Command Prompt

C:\Temp\LBDIAG>lbdiag /?
XenApp Load Balancing Diagnostics Utility

LBDIAG AppName [/POLICY PolicyName ! [/GROUPS Group1 [Group2...] !
      /USER UserName [/PASS Password] /DOMAIN Domain]
      /CLIENTNAME ClientName /CLIENTIP ClientIP] [/QUICK]

    AppName        Browser name of an application.  This is the field labelled
                   "Application Name" in the management console.
    /POLICY        Simulates a user with the specified load balancing policy.
    /GROUPS        Simulates a user belonging to one or more groups, in
                   DOMAIN\GROUPNAME format.
    /USER          Simulates a user by credentials.  Requires the /PASS and
                   /DOMAIN options.
    /PASS          Specifies the password for the simulated user.  If not
                   provided, a password prompt will appear.
    /DOMAIN        Specifies the domain for the simulated user.
    /CLIENTNAME    Specifies the user's client name.  Required unless /POLICY is
                   provided.
    /CLIENTIP      Specifies the client's IPv4 address in dotted notation.
                   Required unless /POLICY is provided.
    /QUICK         Skips the server address and app installation checks.
```

There's more...

You can read more about LBDiag at Citrix's Knowledge Center `http://support.citrix.com/article/CTX124446`.

Performing data store maintenance with DSMAINT and DSCHECK

This recipe will show you how to use the `dsmaint.exe` and `dscheck.exe` command-line tools to perform maintenance tasks on the Data Store and **Local Host Cache** (**LHC**) of a XenApp Farm.

The dsmaint.exe command can be found at

`C:\Program Files (x86)\Citrix\system32\Citrix\Ima`

The dscheck.exe command can be found at

`C:\Program Files (x86)\Citrix\system32`

How to do it...

To perform maintenance tasks on the Data Store and Local Host Cache, perform the following steps:

1. Open the command prompt by navigating to **Start | Run | cmd.exe**.

2. Change the connection settings to the Data Store hosted on an SQL server with the following commands:

   ```
   net stop IMAService /y
   dsmaint config /user:<dbuser> /pwd:<dbpassword> /dsn:"<dsnfile>"
   net start IMAService
   ```

3. To check the consistency of the Data Store itself and automatically fix any encountered errors, run the following command:

   ```
   dscheck /clean
   ```

Citrix recommends that you perform regular Data Store backups and also perform a Data-Store backup before using the `dscheck /clean` option.

4. To verify the integrity of the Local Host Cache, run the following command:

   ```
   dsmaint verifylhc
   ```

5. To rebuild the Local Host Cache on the XenApp server, run the following commands:

```
net stop IMAService /y
dsmaint recreatelhc
net start IMAService
```

 You are automatically prompted to run the `dsmaint recreatelhc` command if the Local Host Cache is found to be corrupt by the `dsmaint verifylhc` command. It is also advised that you run the command after `dscheck` is run and errors are fixed on the data store.

An example of the output of the `dsmaint` command is shown in the following screenshot:

```
Administrator: Command Prompt

C:\Users\administrator.CBLAB>net stop imaservice /y
The following services are dependent on the Citrix Independent Management Architecture service.
Stopping the Citrix Independent Management Architecture service will also stop these services.

   Citrix WMI Service

The Citrix WMI Service service is stopping..
The Citrix WMI Service service was stopped successfully.

The Citrix Independent Management Architecture service is stopping.
The Citrix Independent Management Architecture service was stopped successfully.

C:\Users\administrator.CBLAB>dsmaint recreatelhc
Recreating LHC database finished successfully.

C:\Users\administrator.CBLAB>net start imaservice
The Citrix Independent Management Architecture service is starting...
The Citrix Independent Management Architecture service was started successfully.
```

 Check out `DsCheckMaintAssist.exe` at `http://support.citrix.com/article/CTX137608` if you prefer a user interface and not the command-line options for DSMAINT and DSCHECK.

How it works...

DSMAINT is a powerful command installed by the XenApp installation to perform maintenance and configuration tasks on the Citrix XenApp data store.

To change the connection settings from a XenApp server to the data store, run the following command:

```
dsmaint config /user:<dbuser> /pwd:<dbpassword> /dsn:"<dsnfile>"
```

The DSN file currently in use by the XenApp server is stored in the following registry key:

`HKLM\SOFTWARE\Wow6432Node\Citrix\IMA\DataSourceName`

Name	Type	Data
(Default)	REG_SZ	(value not set)
DatabaseDriver	REG_SZ	ImaSql.dll
DataSourceName	REG_SZ	C:\Program Files (x86)\Citrix\Independent Management Architecture\mf20.dsn

To create a new DSN file, you can use the following options:

▶ Create a copy of the `mf20.dsn` file in use, and edit it with Notepad by changing the values to the new data store's location.

▶ Create a new DSN file with the **Data Sources** (ODBC) tool from **Administrative tools** on the XenApp server.

▶ Create a new DSN file in Notepad based on the following sample:

  ❑ A DSN file from a server connection to a remote SQL Server instance will look as follows:

```
[ODBC]
DRIVER=SQL Server
DATABASE=<dbname>
APP=Citrix IMA
UID=Administrator
SERVER=<SQLServer>\<InstanceName>,<port>
Trusted_Connection=Yes
```

When a SQL Server Express database is used, you can run the following backup parameter for the `dsmaint` executable, or use the `recover` parameter to restore the database to its last known good state:

```
dsmaint backup <destination>
dsmaint recover
```

To check the consistency of the local cache, you can run the following command:

```
dsmaint verifylhc
```

You can even add the `/autorepair` switch to automatically have the local cache on the XenApp server repaired when errors are detected.

To recreate the local cache, run the following command:

```
dsmaint recreatelhc
```

For maintenance of the data store, you can use DSCHECK to execute commands directly on the data store. DSCHECK is often run after DSMAINT is used to ensure that both the data store and the Local Host Cache are consistent. While DSCHECK can run different tests to check the data store's consistency, it is mostly used without switches to run a consistency check.

To only run a consistency check, use the following command:

`dscheck`

To check for consistency and fix errors, add the following switch:

`dscheck /clean`

There's more...

You can read more on DSMAINT at Citrix's eDocs at `http://support.citrix.com/proddocs/topic/xenapp65-admin/ps-commands-dsmaint-v2.html`

You can read more on DSCHECK at Citrix's eDocs at `http://support.citrix.com/proddocs/topic/xenapp65-admin/ps-commands-dscheck.html`

If you are more comfortable with using a tool that provides a graphical user interface for the `dsmaint config` command, check out the IMA Helper tool at Citrix's Knowledge Center at `http://support.citrix.com/article/CTX133983`.

Installing the XenApp® 6.5 PowerShell SDK

This recipe will show you how to install the XenApp 6.5 PowerShell SDK to perform XenApp-specific PowerShell commands and scripts.

How to do it...

To install the XenApp SDK, perform the following steps:

1. Download the XenApp 6.5 PowerShell SDK from Citrix's downloads: `https://www.citrix.com/downloads/xenapp/sdks/powershell-sdk.html`.
2. Unzip the file to a local folder on the XenApp server.
3. Run `XASDK6.5.exe` to start the installation.
4. Accept the terms of the license agreement and click on **Next**.

5. Select the **Update the execution policy** option and click on **Next**.

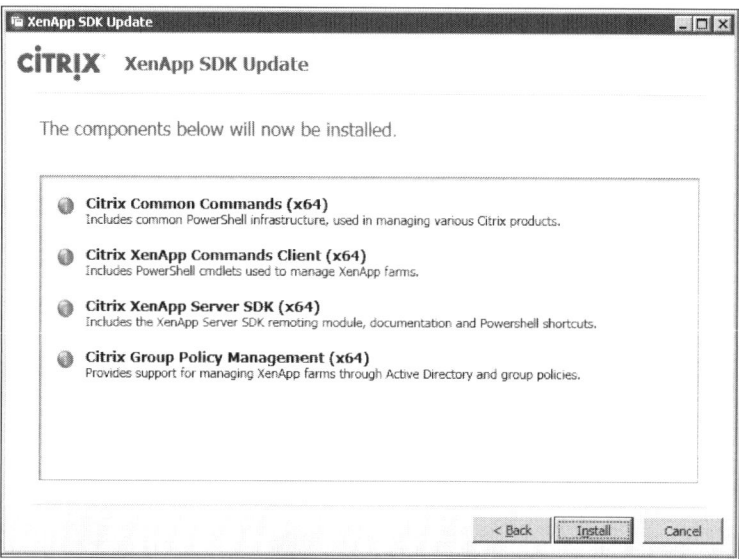

6. Click on **Install**.

7. Click on **Finish**.

8. Start Windows PowerShell with Citrix XenApp 6.5 SDK by navigating to **Start | All Programs | Citrix | XenApp 6.5 Server SDK**.

 The required PowerShell snap-ins are automatically loaded when the **Windows PowerShell with Citrix XenApp 6.5 SDK** shortcut is started.

The following screenshot shows the snap-ins that are automatically loaded when the Windows PowerShell with Citrix XenApp 6.5 SDK shortcut is used from the **Start** menu:

```
Administrator: Windows PowerShell with Citrix XenApp 6.5 Server SDK
Windows PowerShell
Copyright (C) 2009 Microsoft Corporation. All rights reserved.

Loading Citrix.Common.Commands snapin...
Loading Citrix.XenApp.Commands snapin...
Loading Citrix.Common.GroupPolicy snapin...

To list all the Citrix commands: Get-CtxCommand
To list the Citrix commands related to a specific topic: Get-CtxCommand *topic*
To display all the help for a command: Get-Help command -Full
To see about XenApp topics: Get-Help about_XenApp*
To see about Citrix topics: Get-Help about_Citrix*

PS C:\Users\Administrator> _
```

Replicating printer drivers with PowerShell

This recipe will show you how to replicate printer drivers between XenApp servers using PowerShell commands.

Getting ready

To use the provided PowerShell commands, the XenApp PowerShell SDK needs to be installed.

 Check **Installing the XenApp 6.5 PowerShell SDK** for the installation instructions.

Ensure that the required PowerShell execution mode is set. To check the execution mode, run the following PowerShell command:

```
Get-ExecutionPolicy
```

If the mode is set to restricted, change it to the required mode with the following command:

```
Set-ExecutionPolicy RemoteSigned
```

How to do it...

To replicate printer drivers with PowerShell, perform the following steps:

1. Open Windows PowerShell with Citrix XenApp 6.5 Server SDK by navigating to **Start | All Programs | Citrix | XenApp 6.5 Server SDK**.

2. Run the following PowerShell command to get an overview of the installed print drivers on the XenApp server that will be used as the source:

   ```
   Get-XAPrinterDriver -Servername CBXA01 | Format-Wide -Property
   DriverName
   ```

 You need to provide the full printer driver name with the replication commands; so, note down the full driver name for future reference.

3. Run the following PowerShell command to manually replicate a printer driver:

```
Start-XAPrinterDriverReplication -DriverName "hp deskjet 5550
series (HPA)" -TargetServerName CBXA02
```

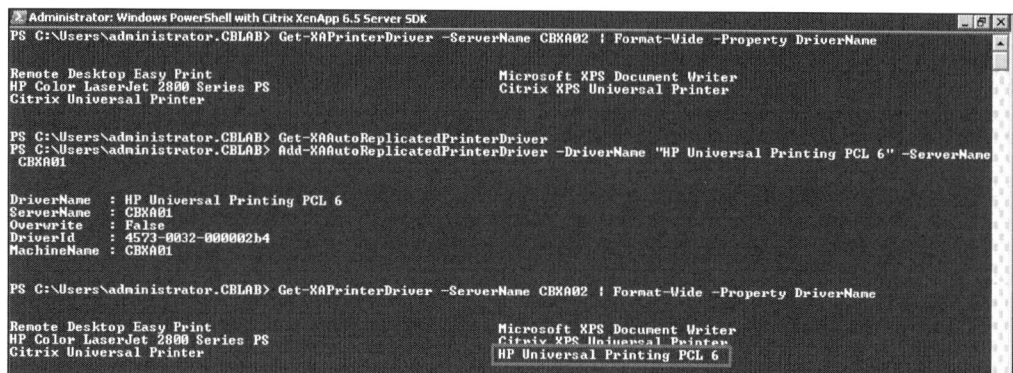

4. Retrieve all the autoreplicated printer drivers with the following command:

```
Get-XAAutoReplicatedPrinterDriver
```

5. Run the following PowerShell command to add a printer driver to the autoreplication list, and have it automatically replicated to the XenApp servers in the Farm:

```
Add-XAAutoReplicatedPrinterDriver -DriverName "HP Universal
Printing PCL 6" -ServerName CBXA01
```

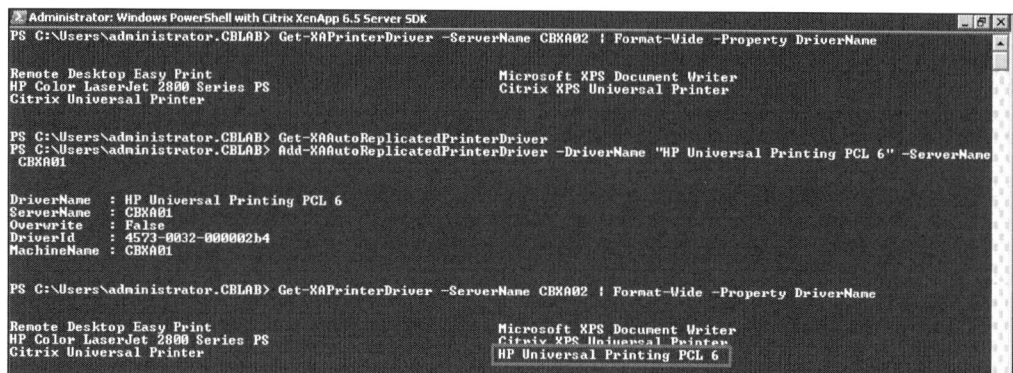

6. To remove a printer driver from the autoreplication list, run the following command:

```
Remove-XAAutoReplicatedPrinterDriver -DriverName "HP Universal
Printing PCL 6" -ServerName CBXA01
```

Keep in mind that it might take a few minutes before the printer driver is replicated and shown as an installed driver on the destination XenApp server. Removing a printer driver from the replication list does not remove it from the XenApp servers in the Farm.

There's more...

You can read more about printer driver replication with PowerShell at Citrix's Knowledge Center at http://support.citrix.com/article/CTX126125.

Creating Citrix® policies with PowerShell

A lot of Citrix XenApp 6.5 features and settings are managed through Citrix policies. This recipe will show you how to create Citrix policies with PowerShell commands and scripts.

Getting ready

To use the provided PowerShell commands, the XenApp PowerShell SDK needs to be installed.

Check **Installing the XenApp 6.5 PowerShell SDK** for the installation instructions.

Ensure that the required PowerShell execution mode is set. To check the execution mode, run the following PowerShell command:

```
Get-ExecutionPolicy
```

If the mode is set to restricted, change it to the required mode with the following command:

```
Set-ExecutionPolicy RemoteSigned
```

How to do it...

To create a Citrix policy, perform the following steps:

1. Open Windows PowerShell with Citrix XenApp 6.5 Server SDK by navigating to **Start | All Programs | Citrix | XenApp 6.5 Server SDK**.

The PowerShell scripts in this recipe assume that policies are created and managed with AppCenter and not with Microsoft's Group Policy Management Console.

2. Create a new Citrix computer policy with the following command:

```
New-Item 'LocalFarmGpo:\Computer\Basic XenApp Settings'
```

3. Configure the common policy settings with the following commands:

```
# Navigate to policy settings:
cd 'LocalFarmGpo:\Computer\Basic Settings\Settings\'
# Set DNS address resolution:
Set-ItemProperty '.\ServerSettings\DnsAddressResolution' -Name
State -Value Enabled
# Set License server host name:
Set-ItemProperty '.\Licensing\LicenseServerHostName' -Name Value
-Value CBDC01
# Set License server port:
Set-ItemProperty '.\Licensing\LicenseServerPort' -Name Value
-Value 27000
# Set Load Evaluator Name:
Set-ItemProperty '.\ServerSettings\LoadEvaluator' -Name Value
-Value 'Load Evaluator - max users'
# Set XenApp product edition:
Set-ItemProperty '.\ServerSettings\ProductEdition' -Name Value
-Value Platinum
# Set XenApp product model:
Set-ItemProperty '.\ServerSettings\ProductModel' -Name Value
-Value XenAppCCU
# Set XML Service Port:
Set-ItemProperty '.\XMLService\XmlServicePort' -Name Value -Value
8080
```

4. If a policy setting needs to be removed, use the following command:

```
Set-ItemProperty '.<PathToPolicySetting>' -Name State -Value
NotConfigured
```

5. To set a policy setting to `Disabled`, use the following command:

```
Set-ItemProperty '.<PathToPolicySetting>' -Name State -Value
Disabled
```

6. To set a policy setting to `Enabled`, use the following command:

```
Set-ItemProperty '.<PathToPolicySetting>' -Name State -Value
Enabled
```

How it works...

The Citrix XenApp 6.5 SDK offers a `Citrix.Common.GroupPolicy` snap-in that enables you to create and configure Citrix policies on a XenApp server. This snap-in uses a `LocalFarmGpo` PowerShell drive to navigate through the Citrix policies and manage the settings.

To create a new Citrix computer policy, use the following command:

```
New-Item 'LocalFarmGpo:\Computer\<PolicyName>'
```

To check a policy setting, run the following command:

```
Get-ItemProperty ".\Computer\Basic Settings\Settings\<PathToSetting>"
```

 The returned state will indicate whether the setting is enabled or not.

To edit a policy setting, use the following command:

```
Set-ItemProperty LocalFarmGpo:\Computer\<PolicyName>\
Settings\<PathToSetting> -Name Value -Value <NewValue>
```

A small selection of the Citrix computer policy categories and settings that can be configured with the `LocalFarmGpo` PowerShell drive, are shown in the following table:

Category	Subcategory	Settings
ICA	It doesn't have a subcategory	`IcaListenerPortNumber` and `IcaListenerTimeout`
	`Graphics`	`DisplayDegradePreference`, `DisplayDegradeUserNotification`, `DisplayMemoryLimit`, `ImageCaching`, and `MaximumColorDepth`
	`ServerLimits`	`IdleTimerInterval`
	`SessionReliability`	`SessionReliabilityConnections`, `SessionReliabilityPort`, and `SessionReliabilityTimeout`
	`Shadowing`	`Shadowing`
Licensing	It doesn't have a subcategory	`LicenseServerHostName` and `LicenseServerPort`

Category	Subcategory	Settings
ServerSettings	It doesn't have a subcategory	`DnsAddressResolution`, `FullIconCaching`, `InitialZone`, `LoadEvaluator`, `ProductEdition`, and `ProductModel`
	`DatabaseSettings`	`InitialDatabaseName`, `InitialDatabaseServerName`, and `InitialFailoverPartner`
XMLService	It doesn't have a subcategory	`TrustXmlRequests` and `XmlServicePort`

Use *Tab* to autocomplete the path to each policy setting. A complete list of the available group policy settings can be found in the `Citrix XenApp 6.5 Server SDK Help` file.

Changing the XenApp® product edition with PowerShell

With Citrix XenApp 6.5, the product edition for each Citrix XenApp server is set with a Citrix Computer policy. The product edition of a XenApp server must match with the product edition from the license file to ensure that a license is allocated for each logged on user or device. This recipe will provide the required PowerShell commands and scripts to change the XenApp product edition by creating that Citrix Computer policy.

Getting ready

To use the provided PowerShell commands, the XenApp PowerShell SDK needs to be installed.

Check **Installing the XenApp 6.5 PowerShell SDK** for the installation instructions.

Ensure that the required PowerShell execution mode is set. To check the execution mode, run the following PowerShell command:

```
Get-ExecutionPolicy
```

If the mode is set to restricted, change it to the required mode with the following command:

```
Set-ExecutionPolicy RemoteSigned
```

How to do it...

To change the XenApp 6.5 product edition with PowerShell, perform the following steps:

1. Open Windows PowerShell with Citrix XenApp 6.5 Server SDK by navigating to **Start |
   All Programs | Citrix | XenApp 6.5 Server SDK**.

2. Configure the product edition with the following command:

   ```
   # Navigate to Unfiltered policy settings:
   cd 'LocalFarmGpo:\Computer\Unfiltered\Settings\'
   # Set XenApp product edition:
   Set-ItemProperty '.\ServerSettings\ProductEdition' -Name Value
   -Value Platinum
   ```

3. Ensure that the policy setting is enabled with the following command:

   ```
   Set-ItemProperty '.\ServerSettings\ProductEdition' -Name State
   -Value Enabled
   ```

> You can find the configured product edition of the XenApp server in the
> registry at HKLM\SYSTEM\CurrentControlSet\Control\Citrix.

Name	Type	Data
ab (Default)	REG_SZ	(value not set)
ab ProductFeature	REG_SZ	PLT
ab ProductName	REG_SZ	Citrix Presentation Server
ab ProductVersion	REG_SZ	6.50
011 110 ProductVersionNum	REG_DWORD	0x00000610 (1552)
011 110 Version	REG_DWORD	0x00000003 (3)

Creating a basic XenApp® inventory report with PowerShell

This recipe will show you how to display the basic XenApp Farm information in a simple HTML report using a PowerShell script.

Getting ready

To use the provided PowerShell commands, the XenApp PowerShell SDK needs to be installed.

 Check **Installing the XenApp 6.5 PowerShell SDK** for the installation instructions.

Ensure that the required PowerShell execution mode is set. To check the execution mode, run the following PowerShell command:

```
Get-ExecutionPolicy
```

If the mode is set to restricted, change it to the required mode with the following command:

```
Set-ExecutionPolicy RemoteSigned
```

How to do it...

To create an HTML report with basic XenApp Farm information, perform the following steps:

1. Open Windows PowerShell with Citrix XenApp 6.5 Server SDK by navigating to **Start | All Programs | Citrix | XenApp 6.5 Server SDK**.

2. Create the HTML report by running the following PowerShell script:

```
$Farm = Get-XAFarm | ConvertTo-HTML FarmName,ServerVersion,Session
Count -Fragment

$Servers = Get-XAServer | ConvertTo-HTML ServerName,ZoneName,Elect
ionPreference,OSVersion,OSServicePack,CitrixVersion,CitrixEdition,
CitrixServicePack,LogOnMode -Fragment

$Applications = Get-XAApplication | ConvertTo-HTML ApplicationType
,DisplayName,Description,Enabled,PreLaunch -Fragment

$Output = "<h3>XenApp Farm Inventory</h3>$Farm"

$Output += "<p>$Servers</p>"

$Output += "<p>$Applications</p>"

ConvertTo-HTML -Body $Output -Title "XenApp Farm Report" | Out-
File C:\temp\XAFarmReport.htm

Invoke-Item C:\temp\XAFarmReport.htm
```

 The preceding script is a small example of how PowerShell can aid in reporting on XenApp Farm settings. To document all XenApp Farm settings for future reference, I recommend that you use Carl Webster's script that will be discussed in *Chapter 12, Citrix® Community*.

A sample of the generated HTML report is shown in the following screenshot:

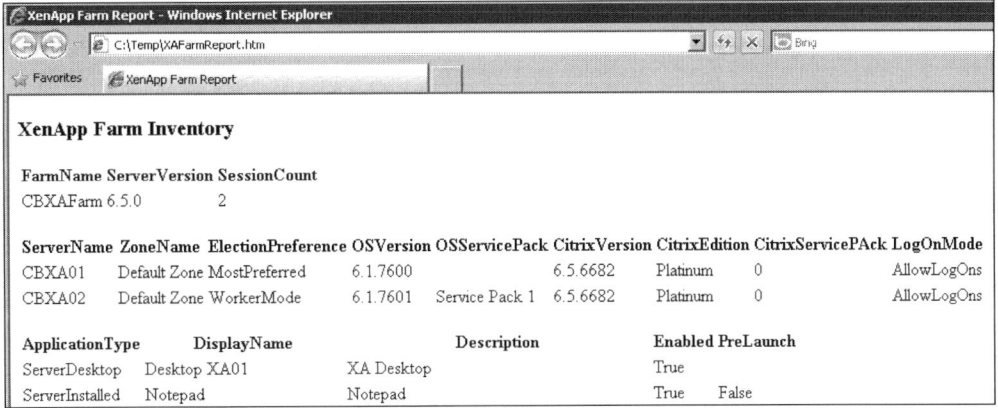

Managing Farm administration roles with PowerShell

This recipe will show you how to manage the administrators of Citrix XenApp Farm with PowerShell commands.

Getting ready

To use the provided PowerShell commands, the XenApp PowerShell SDK needs to be installed.

 Check **Installing the XenApp 6.5 PowerShell SDK** for the installation instructions.

Ensure that the required PowerShell execution mode is set. To check the execution mode, run the following PowerShell command:

```
Get-ExecutionPolicy
```

If the mode is set to restricted, change it to the required mode with the following command:

```
Set-ExecutionPolicy RemoteSigned
```

How to do it...

To manage the XenApp Farm administrators with PowerShell, perform the following steps:

1. Open Windows PowerShell with Citrix XenApp 6.5 Server SDK by navigating to **Start | All Programs | Citrix | XenApp 6.5 Server SDK**.

2. Check the current Farm administrators by running the following PowerShell script:

   ```
   Get-XAAdministrator
   ```

3. Create a new Farm administrator with the following command:

   ```
   New-XAAdministrator CBLAB\cbtester05 -AdministratorType Custom
   -Enabled False -FarmPrivileges ViewFarm,ViewPrinterDrivers
   ```

4. Set `FolderPrivileges` for the newly created administrator with the following command:

   ```
   Set-XAAdministratorFolder CBLAB\cbtester05 -Folderpath
   Applications  -FolderPrivileges ViewApplications,EditApplications,
   ViewSessions,ConnectSessions,SendMessages,LogOffSessions,Disconnec
   tSessions
   ```

5. Check the newly created administrator and custom privileges with AppCenter:

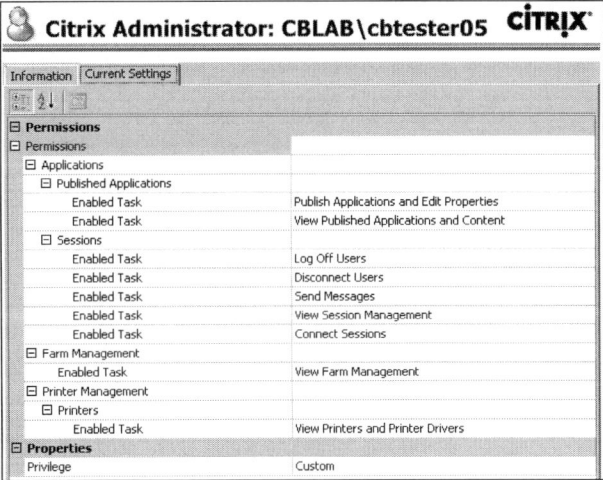

How it works...

The XenApp 6.5 PowerShell SDK offers commands to manage the Farm administrators with PowerShell. To add a new administrator to the Farm, use the following command:

```
New-XAAdministrator <account> -AdministratorType <admintype> -Enabled
<Boolean> -FarmPrivileges <privileges>
```

This command uses the following syntax and parameters:

- ▶ `account`: This represents a full Active Directory user account or a group, prefixed with the domain name
- ▶ `-AdministratorType`: This specifies the administrative type; this can be `ViewOnly`, `Full`, or `Custom`
- ▶ `-Enabled`: This specifies whether the Farm administrator is enabled (`True`) or not (`False`)
- ▶ `-FarmPrivileges`: This specifies the administrative privileges set for the XenApp Farm

The following Farm privileges can be set:

Folders	Tasks
Farm	ViewFarm, EditZone, EditConfigurationLog, and EditFarmOther
Administrators	ViewAdmins, LogOnConsole, and LogOnWIConsole
Load Evaluators	ViewLoadEvaluators, AssignLoadEvaluators, and EditLoadEvaluators
Load Balacing Policies	ViewLoadBalancingPolicies and EditLoadBalancingPolicies
Printer Management	ViewPrinterDrivers and ReplicatePrinterDrivers

In addition to setting FarmPrivileges, an administrator can also receive folder privileges. These privileges can be set with the following command:

```
Set-XAAdministratorFolder <account> -Folderpath <path> –FolderPrivileges <privileges>
```

This command uses the following syntax and parameters:

- account: This is a full Active Directory user account or a group prefixed with a domain name.
- -Folderpath: This specifies the full path to the folder.
- -FolderPrivileges: This specifies the administrative privileges set on the available folders.

The available folder privileges that can be set are as follows:

Folders	Tasks
Applications	ViewApplications, EditApplications, ViewSessions, ConnectSessions, SendMessages, LogOffSessions, DisconnectSessions, ResetSessions, and TerminateProcessApplication
Servers	AssignApplicationsToServers, ViewSessions, ConnectSessions, SendMessages, LogOffSessions, DisconnectSessions, ResetSessions, ViewServers, EditOtherServerSettings, RemoveServer, and TerminateProcess
Worker Groups	ViewWorkerGroups and AssignApplicationsToWorkerGroups

Checking the XenApp® server load with PowerShell

This recipe will show you how to check the current XenApp server load with PowerShell.

Getting ready

To use the provided PowerShell commands, the XenApp PowerShell SDK needs to be installed.

 Check **Installing the XenApp 6.5 PowerShell SDK** for the installation instructions.

Ensure that the required PowerShell execution mode is set. To check the execution mode, run the following PowerShell command:

```
Get-ExecutionPolicy
```

If the mode is set to restricted, change it to the required mode with the following command:

```
Set-ExecutionPolicy RemoteSigned
```

How to do it...

To create an HTML report with the basic XenApp server load information, perform the following steps:

1. Open Windows PowerShell with Citrix XenApp 6.5 Server SDK by navigating to **Start | All Programs | Citrix | XenApp 6.5 Server SDK**.

2. Create the HTML report by running the following PowerShell script:

```
$XAServerInfo = Get-XAServer | Select-Object
ServerName,ZoneName,LogOnMode,@{Name='LoadEvaluator';Expression
={Get-XALoadEvaluator -ServerName $_.ServerName | Select-Object
-ExpandProperty LoadEvaluatorName}},@{Name='Load';Expression={Get-
XAServerLoad -ServerName $_.ServerName | Select-Object
-ExpandProperty Load}} | ConvertTo-HTML -Fragment

ConvertTo-HTML -Body $XAServerInfo -Title "XenApp Load Report" |
Out-File C:\temp\XALoadReport.htm

Invoke-Item C:\temp\XALoadReport.htm
```

 The script is a small example of how PowerShell can aid in reporting on actual XenApp server load values.

The following screenshot shows an example of the HTML report which was generated by the provided PowerShell script:

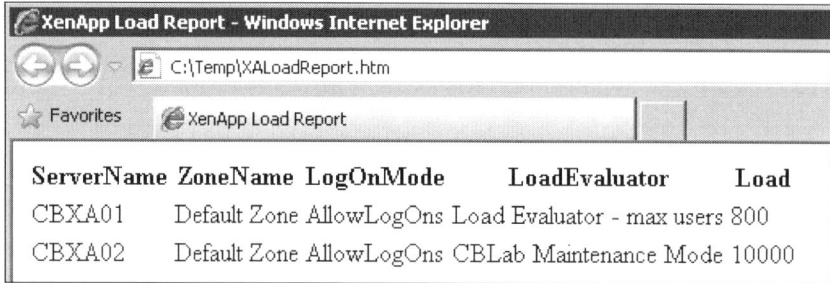

Monitoring the Citrix® License Server with PowerShell

This recipe will show you how to monitor the Citrix License Server and the percentage of available licenses with PowerShell.

How to do it...

To check the percentage of free licenses on the Citrix License Server, perform the following steps:

1. Start Windows PowerShell by navigating to **Start | All Programs | Accessories | Windows PowerShell**.

2. Check the available licenses by running the following PowerShell script:

```
# Get Citrix License info

$licensePool = Get-WmiObject  -Class "Citrix_GT_License_Pool"
-ComputerName "CBDC01" -Namespace "root\CitrixLicensing"

$licinfo=($licensePool | Select-Object @{n="Product";e={$_.
PLD}},@{n="LicenseType";e={$_.LicenseType}},@{n="Installed";e={$_.
Count}},@{n="Used";e={$_.InUseCount}},@{n="Free";e={$_.
PooledAvailable}},@{n="Used%";e={[Math]::Round((($_.InUseCount/$_.
Count)*100),2)}} | Sort-Object Product)

# Output

$licinfo | Format-Table -auto

# Get Total license count

$tcAvailable=0

$tcInstalled=0
```

```
foreach ($item in $licinfo)
{
  $tcAvailable=$tcAvailable + $item.Free
  $tcInstalled=$tcInstalled + $item.Installed
}
$perFree = [Math]::Round(($tcAvailable/$tcInstalled)*100,1)
#Return info as text
Write-Host "Total Installed: $tcInstalled"
Write-Host "Total Available: $tcAvailable"
Write-Host "Total Free (%): $perFree%"
```

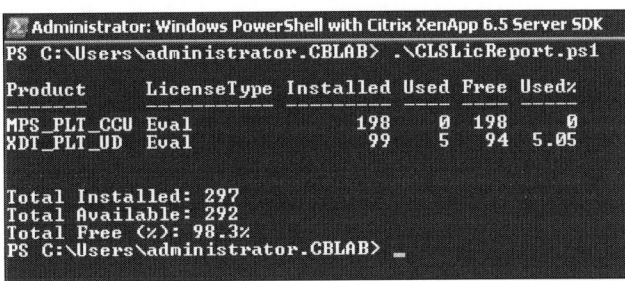

The preceding screenshot shows an example of the output of the PowerShell script. The lab environment used for this book only contains evaluation licenses, both XenApp Concurrent User licenses and XenDesktop Named User/Device licenses, which are clearly listed in the shown results. As only a few accounts were used, there are more than enough licenses available.

Unfortunately, none of the Citrix License Server specific PowerShell commands are included in the XenApp 6.5 PowerShell SDK; so, we need to rely on WMI queries to retrieve license information.

11
XenApp® Infrastructure Best Practices

In this chapter, we will cover:

- ► Administrating XenApp® Farms Best Practices
- ► Implementing XenApp® Virtualization Best Practices
- ► Implementing Citrix XenApp® recommendations
- ► Optimizing guide for XenApp® 6.5 Computer settings
- ► Optimizing guide for XenApp® 6.5 User settings
- ► Printing recommendations for Citrix® XenApp®
- ► Configuring Citrix policies Best Practices
- ► Designing user profile Best Practices for XenApp®
- ► Configuring Citrix® guidelines for antivirus software
- ► Planning XenApp® High Availability
- ► Migrating from Citrix® Web Interface to StoreFront Best Practices

Introduction

The previous chapters of this book focused on the many components that build a XenApp infrastructure, and provided recipes to automate, manage, maintain, and troubleshoot each component. These chapters addressed the most common configuration options and known errors that can occur in every production environment. There is, however, one question not yet answered and that question concerns the most optimal configuration settings for a XenApp infrastructure; and the optimal configuration of XenApp servers and XenApp Farms in particular.

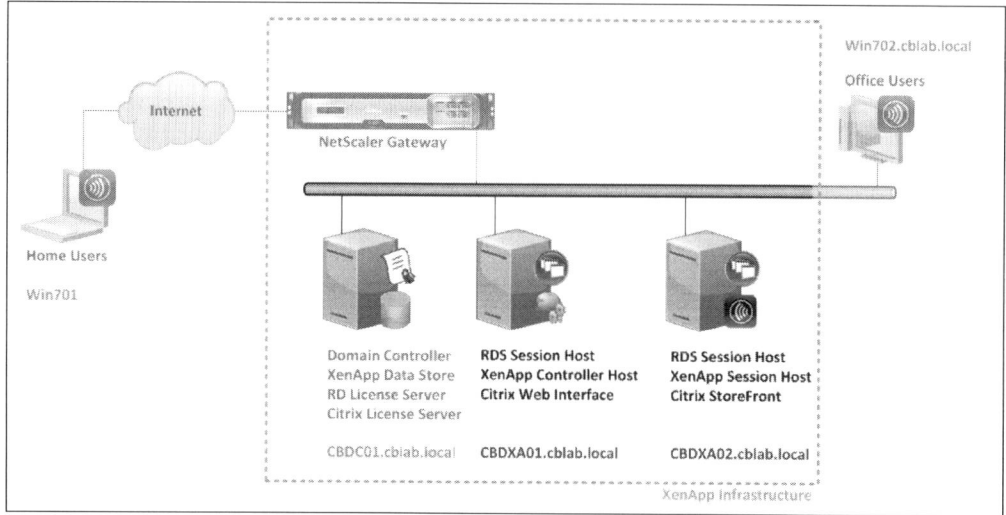

This chapter will focus on the various best practices guides provided by Citrix at the Citrix Knowledge Center to improve the performance and stability of a XenApp infrastructure.

Administrating XenApp® Farms Best Practices

This recipe will address the top 10 best practices for XenApp administrators as provided by Citrix.

You can read the Best Practices for XenApp Administrators at Citrix's Knowledge Center at http://support.citrix.com/article/ CTX127574.

How to do it...

To apply the top 10 best practices for XenApp administrators, follow these guidelines:

1. Back up the Farm Data Store on a regular basis:

    ❑ Check the Database Server documentation for backup and restore recommendations.

2. Build at least one test XenApp environment/farm:

    ❑ Ensure all changes to the production environment are tested in a separate (production resembling) environment before implementing them onto the production farm.

Use DTAP where and when possible!

DTAP (Development, Testing, Acceptance, and Production) ensures no changes are directly applied to a production environment before first being developed, tested, and accepted in a separate environment that closely represents the actual production environment. This ensures that a production change is fully tested and the outcome of the change is known.

3. Keep current with updates and hotfixes:

    ❑ Check available hotfixes and updates at Citrix's Knowledge Center at `http://support.citrix.com/product/xa/v6.5_2008r2/hotfix/general/`

    ❑ Always apply hotfixes marked as critical (such as Hotfix Rollup Packs)

    ❑ Public hotfixes need to be applied if they actually provide a fix for known production farm problems

    ❑ Apply recommended hotfixes for XenApp 6.0 and later, on Windows Server 2008 R2 at `http://support.citrix.com/article/CTX129229`

Applying service packs and hotfixes is highly recommended to keep a stable and secure XenApp Farm. Always apply Service Packs/Hotfix Rollup Packs and fixes marked as critical; public hotfixes should be applied on an "as needed" basis only. "Don't fix it if it ain't broken".

4. Implement a Change Management plan:

    ❑ Manage changes that need to be applied to the farm

    ❑ Keep track of all applied changes to the XenApp Farm (implement configuration logging)

5. Avoid non-native / third-party printer drivers:

    ❑   Most printer problems are related to non-native installed drivers that are not tested or designed to support multiuser server-based environments

    ❑   Use these Citrix tools to determine if you have printer driver related issues:

    ❑   **Print Detective**: `http://support.citrix.com/article/CTX116474`.

    ❑   **StressPrinters**: `http://support.citrix.com/article/CTX109374`.

6. Get familiar with common tools:

    ❑   Check `http://support.citrix.com/article/CTX126294` for a complete list of Citrix Support Troubleshooting tools

7. Know the types of memory dumps:

    ❑   Check `http://support.microsoft.com/kb/254649/en-us` for the different dump types available on Windows Server 2008 R2

8. Understand zones and data collectors:

    ❑   Understand the impact of multiple zones on the XenApp Farm and required server roles

    ❑   Understand the additional features that are supported by the XenApp controller host

    ❑   Read the guidelines at Citrix's eDocs at `http://support.citrix.com/proddocs/topic/xenapp65-install/ps-config-prep.html`

9. Monitor XenApp Farm health:

    ❑   Use EdgeSight or Citrix scout to monitor the farm

    ❑   Implement health monitoring with Citrix Policies

    ❑   Regularly check event logs for errors

    ❑   Implement third-party monitoring tools, such as Microsoft System Center Operations

10. Review Plugin/Receiver considerations:

    ❑   Ensure users are connecting to the XenApp Farm with a supported Citrix Receiver and the required plugins

Implementing XenApp® Virtualization best practices

This recipe will address the best practices for virtualizing Citrix XenApp servers based upon the guidelines provided by Citrix.

 You can read the XenApp Planning Guide – Virtualization Best Practices at Citrix's Knowledge Center at `http://support.citrix.com/article/CTX129761`.

How to do it...

To apply the best practices for virtualized XenApp servers, follow these guidelines:

1. Use the following guidance to estimate the user density based upon the number of physical cores available:

Number of sockets	Users per physical core		
	Light	Normal	Heavy
Dual	18	12	6
Quad	15	10	5

2. Use the following guidance to estimate the required RAM per virtual server:
   - [#Light users] x 341 MB
   - [#Medium users] x 512 MB
   - [#Heavy users] x 1024 MB

 Only use the above values for planning estimates. Always plan performance and load tests before taking the XenApp servers into production as processor speed, processor architecture, application set, usage patterns, and the number of idle users will influence the maximum supported capacity.

3. Align the virtual machine specifications with the application requirements and usage expectations.

4. Plan sufficient host machine resources to allow for maintenance outage for one or more hosts and VM migrations to different hosts.

5. Take Microsoft license costs into account.

Microsoft offers a Windows Server 2008 R2 Virtualization Calculator at `http://www.microsoft.com/windowsserver2008/en/us/ server-calculator/default.aspx` to help determine the license costs.

6. Consider the following recommendations:

Decision	Best practice	Hypervisor
Overcommit CPU: No	Experience has shown that greater levels of scalability are achieved by not overcommitting CPU.	Hyper-V XenServer vSphere
Utilize hyper-threading: Yes	Utilizing hyper-threading in a XenApp environment has been shown to improve user density. It is recommended to NOT enable CPU pinning for VMs when hyper-threading is enabled.	Hyper-V XenServer vSphere
Disable ASLR: No	It is advisable to keep **Address Space Layout Randomization** (**ASLR**) enabled, which is the default setting. This functionality is included with Windows 2008, Windows 2008 R2, Windows Vista, and Windows 7.	Hyper-V XenServer vSphere
Disable DEP: Turn on for all programs and services except those selected	**Data Execution Prevention** (**DEP**) helps protect against damage from viruses and other security threats. It can, however, create strange errors and require a process exclusions. The instructions to configure DEP and create exclusions can be found at `http://www.winserverhelp. com/2011/02/add-dep-exception-program- application-windows-server-core/`.	Hyper-V XenServer vSphere
Enable Transparent Page Sharing: Depends	Enabling or disabling Transparent Page Sharing has not been shown to either help or hurt performance on newer systems (Windows 2008, Windows 2008 R2, Windows Vista, and Windows 7).	vShpere
Optimize for XenApp:	Since the release of the Nehalem processors, much of the functionality has been placed on the hardware, so this particular XenServer setting can be ignored.	XenServer
Memory allocation: Fixed	It is advisable to set fixed values for memory reservations for XenApp virtual machines.	Hyper-V XenServer vSphere

Decision	Best practice	Hypervisor
Host swapping: No	Swapping out memory from one XenApp host will degrade performance for all virtual machines as the memory is being transferred to/from disk.	vSphere
Dynamic power savings: No	Hypervisors might not be able to adjust the BIOS settings to allow for full power when required. This results in resources not being fully utilized.	Hyper-V XenServer vSphere

Implementing Citrix® XenApp® recommendations

This recipe offers recommendations for implementing a XenApp infrastructure based upon the best practices guide provided by Citrix.

 You can download the XenDesktop and Citrix XenApp Best Practices Reference Guide at Citrix's Knowledge Center at `http://support.citrix.com/article/CTX132799`.

How to do it...

To implement the Citrix XenApp best practices, follow these guidelines:

1. Consider the following general recommendations:

Area	Best practice
Application compatibility	Verify application compatibility as soon as possible and calculate sufficient time to analyze and fix application problems that can occur.
Separation of components	Plan key XenApp components and services on dedicated servers to enhance security, redundancy, and support.
Test environment	Use an isolated test infrastructure to implement and verify each change before it is implemented in production. Ensure the test environment mirrors the production environment as closely as possible.

Area	Best practice
Hotfixes and Service Packs	Hotfixes and updates for Windows, applications, and Citrix components should be kept up-to-date to ensure optimal performance, stability, and security. For Citrix specific hotfixes the following recommendations apply: ▸ Service Packs and Hotfix Rollup Packs should always be installed ▸ Security Fixes and hotfixes marked as critical should always be installed ▸ General public hotfixes and limited release hotfixes should be installed on an "as needed" basis only Follow the Best Practices for Citrix XenApp Hotfix Rollup Pack Installation and Deployment at Citrix's Knowledge Center at `http://support.citrix.com/article/CTX120842`.
Dedicated management servers	Implement dedicated XenApp-based management servers (in controller host mode to support local management) that host the required tools and applications to support Citrix management.

2. Consider the following XenApp Controller recommendations:

Area	Best practice
Number of Farms	Follow the planning guidelines at Citrix's eDocs at `http://support.citrix.com/proddocs/topic/xenapp65-planning/ps-planning-number-farms-v2.html`.
Number of zones	Follow the planning guidelines at Citrix's eDocs at `http://support.citrix.com/proddocs/topic/xenapp65-planning/ps-planning-zones-wans-v2.html`.

Area	Best practice
Dedicated Controller Host/ XML broker	Follow these recommendations: ▸ For XenApp Farms with more than 10 servers, implement a dedicated XenApp Controller Host with a zone election preference "Most Preferred" and not hosting any applications. ▸ For XenApp Farms with more than 20 servers, implement an additional dedicated XenApp Controller Host with a zone election preference "Preferred" and not hosting any applications. ▸ For XenApp Farms with more than 2,000 concurrent users, add two dedicated XML brokers with a default zone election preference and not hosting any applications. These XML brokers are used for Web Interface to Farm communications.
Session-only mode	When dedicated Controller Hosts are used in the XenApp Farm, all application hosting servers should be configured as session hosts.
Configuration logging	Use the configuration logging feature when multiple administrators apply changes to the XenApp Farm.

3. Consider the following SQL Server database recommendations:

Area	Best practice
SQL DB redundancy	When the XenApp server loses its connection to the Data Store, users can still connect to the farm as the information needed to establish a connection is stored in the **Local Host Cache** (**LHC**) on the XenApp server. If the Data Store is unavailable, administrators will be unable to use the Citrix AppCenter Console or other Citrix query-based utilities and no configuration changes can be applied. ▸ To support disaster recovery scenarios and implement SQL database redundancy, follow the recommendations for using SQL database mirroring at Citrix's Knowledge Center at `http://support.citrix.com/article/CTX111311`.
SQL DB backups	Back up the XenApp databases on a regular basis to support quick restore plans and reduce the size of the SQL transaction log.

Always check the Supported Databases for Citrix Products matrix for database features that are supported for Citrix XenApp 6.5 at `http://support.citrix.com/article/CTX114501.`

4. Consider the following License Server recommendations:

Area	Best practice
Citrix License Server redundancy	With a 30-days grace period for a connection loss to the Citrix License Server, a single Citrix License Server is sufficient.
Citrix License Server scalability	A single Citrix License Server (2 cores/2 GB RAM) can issue approximately 170 licenses per second or 306,000 licenses per 30 minutes.
Microsoft License Server redundancy	Implement two RDS License Servers with evenly divided CALs for redundancy.

5. Consider the following Active Directory recommendations:

Area	Best practice
Active Directory configurations	Citrix recommends the following configuration for XenApp server farms with Active Directory: ▸ XenApp servers are in their own **Organizational Units** (**OUs**) ▸ Create OUs for Worker Groups (application silos), keeping servers from different Worker Groups organized in their own OUs ▸ The server farm domain has no trust relationships with non-Active Directory domains, as this can affect operations requiring trusted domains ▸ All servers reside in the same domain ▸ The server farm is in a single Active Directory forest
Loopback policy	Citrix recommends using the "Group Policy Loopback Processing Mode". This mode allows user configurations to be applied via GPOs that are linked to the OU of the computer object rather than the user object. The loopback policy setting is located at: Computer Configuration—**Administrative Templates | System | Group Policy**.

Area	Best practice
Assigning permissions	Whenever possible, permissions (such as user rights, administrative access, or application assignment) should be assigned to user groups rather than individual users.

6. Consider the following Web Interface recommendations:

Area	Best practice
Web Interface redundancy	At least two Web Interface servers should be deployed to prevent this component from becoming a single point of failure. Follow the recommendations for Web Interface Best Practices Avoiding Major Production Outages at Citrix's Knowledge Center at `http://support.citrix.com/article/CTX125715`.
Web Interface load balancing	Multiple Web Interface servers should be load-balanced by means of an intelligent load balancing appliance (Citrix NetScaler), that is able to verify the availability of the Web Interface service on a constant basis. Instructions on Load Balacing Web Interface with NetScaler can be found at Citrix's Knowledge Center at `http://support.citrix.com/article/CTX128563`.
XenApp XML broker redundancy	Each Web Interface server should point to two or more XML Brokers for reasons of redundancy, which can be implemented with the following two recommended methods: ▸ Use an industry-proven load balancer with built-in XML monitors and session persistency, such as Citrix NetScaler ▸ If a load balancer is not available, each Web Interface server should be configured with the address of at least two XML brokers in each farm. It is recommended to disable the automatic load balancing of the XML brokers within the Web Interface properties, and configure at least a second XML broker address for redundancy reasons.
Secure HTTP/ XML traffic	Encrypt HTTP traffic between the user devices and the Web Interface servers, as well as the XML traffic between the Web Interface servers and the XenApp Farm to prevent usernames/domain information from being transferred in clear text, and passwords from being transferred using weak encryption.

Area	Best practice
Secure Ticket Authority	When a NetScaler Gateway is used, configure at least two Citrix **Secure Ticket Authorities** (**STAs**) to prevent this component from becoming a single point of failure. To prevent failed logons and to optimize logon times, ensure that the STAs specified within the NetScaler Gateway match the STAs specified within the Web Interface, including the order specified.
Scalability	Assign sufficient resources to the Web Interface server to ensure that it does not become a bottleneck during periods of peak activity. Citrix has performed internal testing on the scalability of the Web Interface and found that a dual 2.2 GHz CPU server running Web Interface 5.4 can handle more than 30,000 sessions per hour.
Two-factor authentication	For reasons of security, two-factor authentication should be integrated into the NetScaler Gateway and Web Interface solution for all untrusted networks (Internet). Two-factor authentication requires the presentation of two "factors": ▸ "Something the user has" (Hardware Token) ▸ "Something the user knows" (Pin) This authentication mode decreases the risk of unauthorized persons accessing the environment by impersonating internal employees.
Certificate Revocation Checking	For scenarios where Web Interface servers are not connected to the internet, it is recommended to disable the **Certificate Revocation Check** (**CRC**) functionality. Instructions for disabling the CRC are described in the *Speeding up the Web Interface first logon time* recipe in *Chapter 3, Citrix® Web Interface*.

There's more...

You can read more on Provisioned XenApp Servers Stop Accepting Connections that are Restarted when the License Server is Unavailable at Citrix's Knowledge Center at http://support.citrix.com/article/CTX131202.

You can read more on Advanced Farm Administration with XenApp Worker Groups at Citrix's Knowledge Center at http://support.citrix.com/article/CTX124481.

You can read more on Loopback processing of Group Policy at Microsoft's Support at `http://support.microsoft.com/kb/231287/en-us`.

Optimizing Guide for XenApp® 6.5 Computer settings

This recipe will show you how to optimize XenApp 6.5 Server settings based upon the guide provided by Citrix.

 You can download the Windows 2008 R2 Optimization Guide at Citrix's Knowledge Center at `http://support.citrix.com/article/CTX131577`.

How to do it...

To apply optimizations for XenApp 6.5 Servers, perform the following steps:

1. Open the Group Policy Management Console (**Start | Run | gpmc.msc**).
2. Browse to the **Organization Unit** (**OU**) that contains the XenApp servers.
3. Create a new GPO and link it to the OU.
4. Enter a name and click on **OK**.
5. Right click on the newly created GPO and click on **Edit**.
6. Navigate to **Computer Configuration | Policies | Administrative Templates | Windows Components** and configure the following components:

Item	Windows component	Setting
Error Reporting	Windows Error Reporting	Disable Windows Error Reporting: Enabled
Windows Update	Windows Updates	Configure Automatic Updates: Disabled
RDP Listener—Printer mapping	**Remote Desktop Services	Remote Desktop Session Host	Printer Redirection**	Do not allow client printer redirection: Enabled

7. Navigate to **Computer Configuration | Policies | Administrative Templates | System** and configure the following components:

Item	System	Setting
CEIP	**Internet Communication Management	Internet Communication Settings**	Turn off Windows Customer Experience Improvement Program: Enabled
System Restore	System Restore	Turn off System Restore: Enabled

8. Navigate to **Computer Configuration | Preferences | Windows Settings | Registry** and add the following registry settings:

   `HKLM\System\CurrentControlSet\Control`

Item	Registry path	Setting (decimal)
Hide System Hard Error Messages	\Windows	"ErrorMode"=00000002
Spooler Warning Events	\Print\Providers	"EventLog"=00000001

9. Navigate to **Computer Configuration | Preferences | Windows Settings | Registry** and add the following registry settings:

   `HKLM\System\CurrentControlSet\Control\Session Manager`

Item	Registry path	Setting (decimal)
Paging of the Executive	\Memory Management	"DisablePagingExecutive"=00000001
Write Cache (Operating System)	\Configuration Manager	"RegistryLazyFlushInterval"=00000060
Worker Threads	\Executive	"AdditionalCriticalWorkerThreads"=00000064

10. Navigate to **Computer Configuration | Preferences | Windows Settings | Registry** and add the following registry settings:

`HKLM\System\CurrentControlSet\Services\LanmanWorkstation`

Item	Registry path	Setting (decimal)
SMB 2.x client tuning on XenApp server	\Parameters	"DisableBandwidthThrottling"=00000001 "DisableLargeMtu"=00000000

11. Navigate to **Computer Configuration | Preferences | Windows Settings | Registry** and add the following registry settings:

`HKEY_USERS\.DEFAULT\Control Panel`

Item	Registry path	Setting (decimal)
Disable Logon Screensaver	\Desktop	"ScreenSaveActive"="0"

12. Navigate to **Computer Configuration | Preferences | Windows Settings | Registry** and add the following registry settings:

`HKLM\SOFTWARE\Microsoft\Windows\CurrentVersion\Policies`

Item	Registry path	Setting (decimal)
SMB 2.x client tuning on XenApp server	\Explorer	NoRemoteRecursiveEvents"=00000001

13. Navigate to **Computer Configuration | Preferences | Windows Settings | Registry** and add the following registry settings:

`HKLM\SOFTWARE\Microsoft\Windows\CurrentVersion`

`HKLM\Software\Wow6432Node\Microsoft\Windows\CurrentVersion`

Item	Registry path	Setting (decimal)
Run and RunOnce	\Run \RunOnce	Remove settings for these keys

14. Navigate to **Computer Configuration | Preferences | Control Panel Settings**. Right click on **Power Options**, select **New Power Plan (Windows Vista and later)**, and configure the following settings:

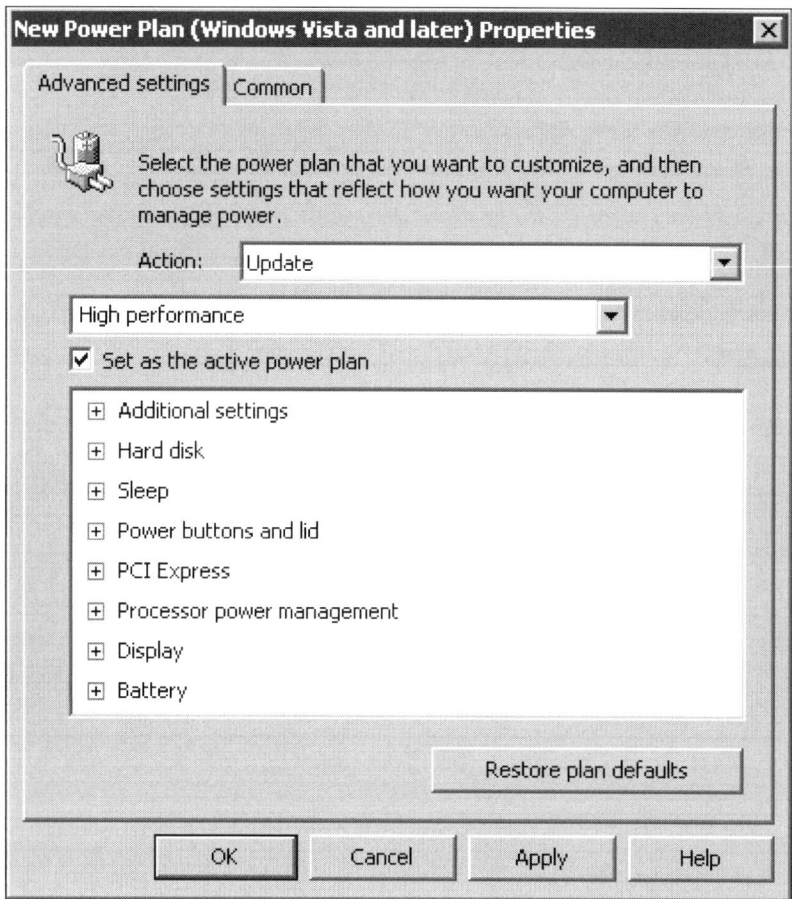

15. Open the system properties (**Start | Control Panel | System and Security | System | Advanced system settings**).

16. Select the **Advanced** tab and click on **Settings** in the **Performance** section.

17. Select the **Advanced** tab and click on **Change** in the **Virtual memory** section.

18. Optimize the Page File on the XenApp server by setting the recommended page file size as the **Custom size Initial** and **Maximum size**:

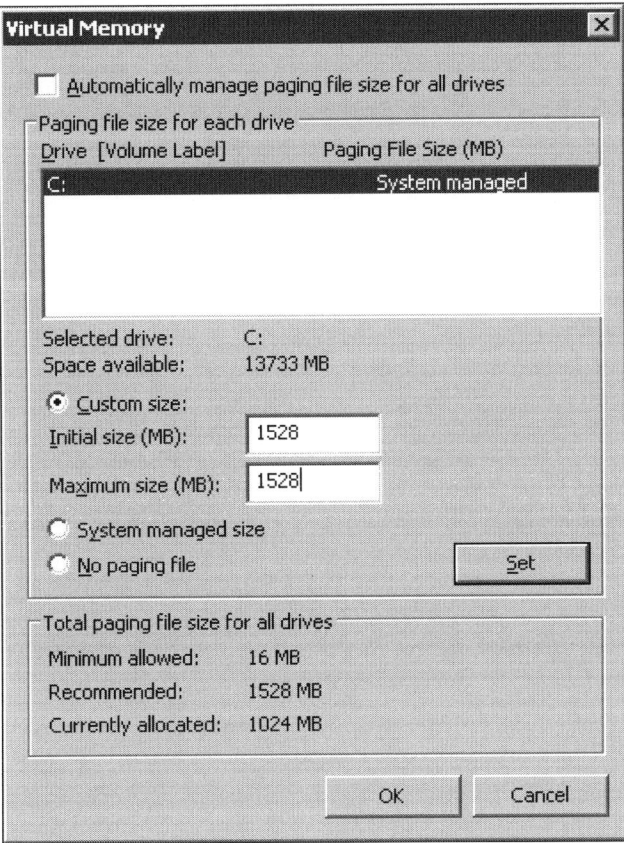

19. Click on **Set** and then click on **OK** to apply the new setting (a reboot is required).

20. Open the task scheduler on the XenApp server (**Start | All Programs | Administrative Tools**).

21. Navigate to **Task Scheduler Library | Microsoft | Windows** and disable the following scheduled tasks:

Category	Schedule
Application Experience	AitAgent ProgramDataUpdater
Autochk	Proxy

Category	Schedule
Customer Experience Improvement Program	Consolidator KernelCeipTask UsbCeip
Customer Experience Improvement Program	ServerCeipAssistant ServerRoleCollector ServerRoleUsageCollector
Disk diagnostic	Microsoft-Windows-DiskDiagnosticDataCollector Microsoft-Windows-diskDiagnosticResolver
Power Efficiency Diagnostics	AnalyzeSystem
Server Manager	ServerManager
Windows Error Reporting	QueueReporting

22. Run the following command on a XenApp server to disable the Boot Animation:

```
bcdedit /set bootux disabled
```

23. Disable all application's auto-update (Jave, Adobe Reader, and so on).

24. Disable the following Windows Services:

Service	Setting
Desktop Windows Manager Session Manager	Optional (depends on usage of Aero theme)
Network List Service	Disable
Network Location Awareness	Disable
Themes	Disable
Windows Defender	Disable
Windows Update	Optional (depends on Windows Update implementation)

25. Configure the BIOS Power Scheme for maximum performance when possible.

26. Run defragmentation on a regular basis.

Optimizing Guide for XenApp® 6.5 User settings

This recipe will show you how to optimize XenApp 6.5 user settings based upon the guide provided by Citrix.

 You can download the Windows 2008 R2 Optimization Guide at Citrix's Knowledge Center at `http://support.citrix.com/article/CTX131577`.

How to do it...

To apply the optimizations for XenApp 6.5 user sessions, perform the following steps:

1. Open the Group Policy Management Console (**Start | Run | gpmc.msc**).
2. Browse to the **Organization Unit** (**OU**) that contains the XenApp servers.
3. Create a new GPO and link it to the OU.
4. Enter a name and click on **OK**.
5. Right click on the newly created GPO and click on **Edit**.
6. Navigate to **User Configuration | Policies | Administrative Templates | Windows Components** and configure the following components:

Item	Windows Component	Setting
Disable Recycle Bin	**Windows Components	Windows Explorer**	Do not move deleted files to the Recycle Bin: Enabled
Disable Screen Saver	**Control Panel	Personalization**	Enable Screen Saver: Disable
Document History	Start Menu and Taskbar	Do not keep history of recently opened documents: Enable Remove Balloon Tips on Start Menu items: Enable Remove frequent program list from Start Menu: Enable
Background Spell Checking	Disable using Group Policy	Load required ADMX files

7. Configure the following registry settings: Navigate to **User Configuration |
Preferences | Windows Settings | Registry** and add the following registry settings:

`HKCU\Control Panel`

Item	Windows Component	Setting
Reduce Menu show delay	\Desktop	"MenuShowDelay"="150"
Auto End Tasks	\Desktop	"AutoEndTasks"= "1" "WaittoKillAppTimeout"= "20000"
Disable Visual Effects	\Desktop\WindowMetrics	"MinAnimate"="0"
	\Desktop	"FontSmoothing"="0" "UserPreferencesMask"=90,12,01,80 ,10,00,00,00

> Ensure that the Auto End Tasks setting does not conflict with a desktop management tool such as RES Workspace Manager or AppSense DesktopNow. These tools might run their own cleanup processes when a user logs off the session. These cleanup processes can be terminated before they are completed as all processes are terminated at logoff when AutoEndTasks is set to 1 and the timeout period is reached.

8. Navigate to **User Configuration | Preferences | Windows Settings | Registry** and add the following registry settings:

`HKCU\Software\Microsoft\Windows\CurrentVersion\Explorer`

Item	Windows Component	Setting
Disable all Visual Effects except "Use common tasks in folders" and "Use visual styles on windows and buttons"	\VisualEffects	"VisualFXSetting"= 00000003
	\Advanced	"ListviewAlphaSelect"=00000000 "TaskbarAnimations"=00000000 "ListviewWatermark"=00000000 "ListviewShadow"=00000000

9. Navigate to **User Configuration | Preferences | Windows Settings | Registry** and add the following registry settings:

   `HKCU\Software\Microsoft\Internet Explorer`

Item	Windows Component	Setting
Internet Explorer | Force Offscreen Composition	\Main	"Force Offscreen Composition"=00000001

10. Navigate to **User Configuration | Preferences | Windows Settings | Registry** and add the following registry settings:

    `HKCU\AppEvents\Schemes\Apps\.Default`

Item	Windows Component	Setting
Disable Windows Logon notification sounds	\WindowsLogon\.Current	"(Default)"=""
Disable Windows Logoff notification sounds	\WindowsLogoff\.Current	"(Default)"=""

11. Configure the following Citrix User Policies:

Category	Setting
Desktop UI	Desktop wallpaper: Prohibited Menu animation: Prohibited View window content while dragging: Prohibited
Visual Display—Moving Images	Progressive compression level: Low (min. setting)
Printing—Drivers	Automatic Installation of in-box drivers: Disabled

Printing recommendations for Citrix® XenApp®

This recipe will provide guidelines for printer configurations in Citrix XenApp infrastructures as provided by Citrix. Approximately 90 percent of most printing issues are related to printer drivers. The other 10 percent can be related to the Microsoft print spooler (`spoolsv.exe`) or the Citrix Print Manager service (`cpsvc.exe`).

You can read the Printing Recommendations for a XenApp/Terminal Server Environment at Citrix's Knowledge Center at `http://support.citrix.com/article/CTX136332`.

You can read the XenDesktop and XenApp Printing – Planning Guide at Citrix's Knowledge Center at `http://support.citrix.com/article/CTX134943`.

How to do it...

To apply printing recommendations for XenApp, follow these guidelines:

1. The print server OS should match the OS of the XenApp server (Windows 2008 R2 for XenApp 6.5). Keep the bit version of the OS in mind as well (64-bits for XenApp 6.5).

2. Ensure printer drivers match not only by name, but also by version number. Even a small difference between the version numbers might cause printer connection failures.

3. Use the Universal Print Driver as much as possible for client printers.

4. Use the Universal Print Server for network printers where possible.

5. If every feature and function of the printer is required and this is not supported by the Universal Printer Driver, use a manufacturer driver. Otherwise, stick to Universal Printer Drivers as much as possible. Some manufacturers also offer a Universal Print Driver that supports most of their printers and features.

Keep the following situations in mind with regard to printer driver isolation mode:

▶ Some print drivers can share processes, others cannot. Check with the manufacturer whether the print driver is suited for process sharing or not.

▶ Having every print driver running in "Shared Mode" is similar to running all drivers in "None" mode. Each driver can still crash the process (`printisolationhost.exe`) shared by all print drivers.

▶ Test each driver before installation onto each XenApp server to determine which driver needs to be isolated and which driver can share a single process.

Use the StressPrinters tool to test each print driver's stability. StressPrinters is addressed in the *Troubleshooting printer drivers on XenApp servers* recipe in *Chapter 9, XenApp® Troubleshooting*.

▶ Do not use drivers that require isolation, unless absolutely necessary. A driver requiring isolation is a strong indicator it will cause problems.

▶ When problematic print drivers are encountered, contact the manufacturer to request an alternative driver or recommended replacement driver. Only install a problematic print driver as a last resort or temporary situation, and strive to replace it with a fixed or stable driver.

For Citrix XenApp printing policies, follow these recommendations:

1. In environments where a large number of client printers are configured per user only, auto-create the default printer for each user to limit the total amount of mapped client printers per XenApp server.

2. Use Session Printers in the following situations:

   ❏ Users roam between locations while using a single device or laptop for all locations

   ❏ Thin clients are used that cannot connect to network printers directly

3. Use the following diagram, provided by Citrix, to determine the print job routing configuration settings:

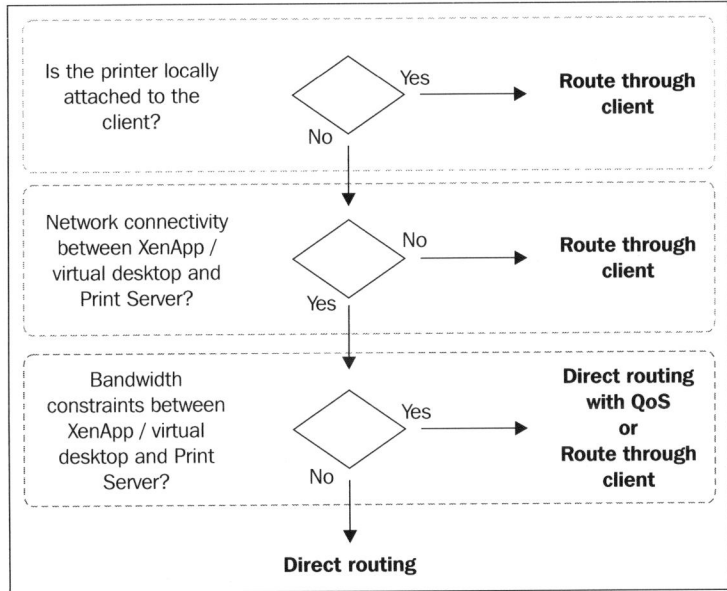

© Citrix Systems, Inc. All Rights Reserved.

4. Use the Universal Printer in the following situations:

   ❏ User logon performance is a priority, and the "Start this application without waiting for client printers" option cannot be used due to application compatibility.

   ❏ Users expect that all printouts will be sent to the local default printer by default.

5. Disable the automatic installation of printer drivers.

6. Installation of kernel mode (type 2) drivers must be avoided. Always test if the Citrix Universal Printer Driver can be used alternatively to support basic printing functionality.

7. When the Citrix Universal Printer Driver cannot be used, use printer driver mapping to keep the amount of the installed printer drivers on a XenApp server to a minimum.

8. Use Printer Driver replication for small environments where no image management or software deployment tool is used.

9. The Citrix Universal Printer Driver should be used whenever possible to reduce the number of installed printer drivers.

10. Set the Citrix EMF Universal Printer Driver as the Universal Driver preference whenever possible.

11. Usage of the Citrix Universal Print Server is highly recommended for network printers as it enables administrators to keep the number of print drivers installed on a XenApp server to a minimum. When the Citrix Universal Print Server is used, all network printers on the XenApp server will leverage the Citrix Universal Printer Driver.

How it works...

Even though it was more difficult with Windows 2003 than it is with Windows 2008 R2 to have a stable printing environment, you still need to be aware of the problems that one bad printer driver can cause. Especially on a XenApp server where, more than one user session is simultaneously accessing printer drivers and print spoolers.

When it is stated that a printer driver "is not signed", it is actually stating that the printer driver is not tested for usage in a multiuser environment such as Remote Desktop Services and Citrix XenApp. Even though it might perform perfectly on a desktop with only one user making printer calls, it's unknown how it will act on a XenApp server.

To prevent situations where one printer driver can crash the print spooler and cause mayhem for all other users of that spooler, Windows 2008 R2 introduces printer driver isolation options. This ensures each printer driver can be run in isolation mode. Isolation mode offers a couple of options:

- **Shared Mode**: The print driver is run in a separate process from the spooler. Other printers can share this process.

- **Isolated Mode**: The print driver is run in its own isolated process. No other printers can share this process.

- **None Mode**: This is the normal operation mode, where the print driver is run directly by the print spooler process.

Driver isolation depends on the following situations:

► Whether the manufacturer has the driver marked as compatible with isolation in the `INF` file.

► Whether the group policy setting "Override print driver execution compatibility setting reported by print driver" is enabled.

If neither is true, a driver is loaded into the spooler process as with previous Windows versions, thus running the driver in the previously mentioned "None" mode.

Drivers marked for isolation are, by default, loaded in one single process, thus running in the previously mentioned "Shared mode". An administrator can change the isolation mode of the driver with the **Print Management Console** (**PMC**), by right-clicking on a driver and setting the isolation mode manually.

There's more...

You can read more on Printer Driver Isolation at Microsoft's MSDN at `http://msdn.microsoft.com/en-us/library/windows/hardware/ff560836(v=vs.85).aspx`.

Configuring Citrix® policies Best Practices

This recipe will address the best practices guidelines for configuring Citrix XenApp policies as provided by Citrix.

 You can read the Planning Guide – Citrix XenApp and XenDesktop Policies at Citrix Knowledge Center at `http://support.citrix.com/article/CTX134081`.

How to do it...

To apply the best practices for Citrix XenApp policies, follow these guidelines:

1. If a single policy management tool is preferred, configure Citrix policies through Active Directory group policies using Citrix ADMX files.

2. If Citrix administrators do not have access to AD policies or filtering mechanisms such as Smart Access are required, use AppCenter to configure Citrix policies.

Citrix policies must be managed by either Group Policy Management Console or by AppCenter as both consoles cannot be used simultaneously. Configured policies are only shown in the management console used to configure the policies and are not visible in the other console. The chosen management console must be used consistently to avoid confusion and corruption of Citrix policies.

3. Configuring policies at the highest common denominator to simplify the process of understanding the **Resultant Set of Policies** (**RSoP**) and troubleshooting policy configurations.

4. Apply a loopback policy, which is a computer configuration policy that forces the computer to apply the assigned user configuration policy of the OU to any user who logs into the server or virtual desktop, regardless of the user's location within Active Directory.

5. Use the Active Directory policy filtering to specify specific users or groups of users to which the policy is applied. Policy filtering is accomplished using the security properties of each target policy.

6. Keep in mind that with Active Directory and Citrix policies, the following is the order in which the policies are applied:

   ❑ **First** (lowest precedence): Local server policies

   ❑ **Second**: Citrix policies created using the Citrix AppCenter

   ❑ **Third**: Site-level AD policies

   ❑ **Fourth**: Domain-level AD policies

   ❑ OU based AD policies

     Fifth: Highest-level OU in domain

     Sixth and subsequent: Next-level OU in domain

     Last (highest precedence): Lowest-level OU containing object

7. Apply the following Citrix user policy settings to configure a policy baseline:

 The settings in the following table are those settings that differ from the policy settings that are active by default. Only the deviations are mentioned.

ICA\Adobe Flash Delivery\Flash Redirection	
Flash acceleration	Enabled
Flash default behavior	Enable Flash Acceleration

ICA\Adobe Flash Delivery\Flash Redirection	
Flash error logging	Enabled
Flash intelligent fallback	Enabled
Flash latency threshold	30 milliseconds

ICA\Adobe Flash Delivery\Legacy Server Side Optimization	
Flash quality adjustment	Allow

ICA\Audio	
Audio Plug N Play	Allow
Audio quality	Medium
Client audio redirection	Allow
Client microphone redirection	Prohibit

If enough bandwidth is available and audio is required for the XenApp session, set the quality to High. The Medium or Low settings are used to maximize the number of user sessions per server or for low-bandwidth connections.

ICA\File Redirection	
Client floppy drive	Prohibit
Client optical drive	Prohibit
Host to client redirection	Disable
Preserve client driver letters	Disable
Read-only client driver access	Disable
Use asynchronous writes	Disable

ICA\Port Redirection	
Auto connect client COM ports	Disable
Auto connect client LPT ports	Disable
Client COM port redirection	Disable
Client LPT port redirection	Disable

ICA\Printing	
Client printer redirection	Allow
Default printer	Set to client's main printer
Printer auto creation log preference	Errors
Wait for printers to be created (desktop)	Disabled

ICA\Printing\Client Printers	
Automatic installation of in-box printer drivers	Disabled
Universal driver usage	Use Universal Printing only if requested driver is unavailable

ICA\Printing\Universal Printing	
Universal printing EMF processing mode	Spool to printer
Universal printing image compression limit	Best Quality
Universal printing optimization defaults	Standard Quality Caching of embedded images Caching of embedded fonts
Universal printing preview preference	Used for auto-generated and generic printing

ICA\Session Limits	
Linger Disconnect Timer Interval	5 minutes
Linger Terminate Timer Interval	10 minutes
Pre-Launch Disconnect Timer Interval	15 minutes
Pre-Launch Terminate Timer Interval	30 minutes
Session connection timer	Disabled

ICA\Shadowing	
Log shadow attempts	Allow
Notify user of pending shadow connections	Allow
Users who can shadow other users	<ShadowUsersGroup>

ICA\Time Zone Control	
Estimate local time for legacy clients	Enable
Use local time of client	Use Client time zone

ICA\Visual Display\Moving Images	
Moving Image Compression	Enabled

Server Session Settings	
Session importance	Normal
Single Sign-on	Disabled

8. Apply the following Citrix computer policy settings to configure a policy baseline:

ICA	
ICA listener connection timeout	120000 ms
ICA listener port number	1494

ICA\Auto Client Reconnect	
Auto client reconnect	Allow
Auto client reconnect logging	Disabled

ICA\End User Monitoring	
ICA round trip calculation	Enable
ICA round trip calculations for idle connections	Disable

ICA\Graphics	
Display memory limit	32768 KB
Display mode degrade preference	Degrade color depth first
Dynamic Windows preview	Enabled
Image caching	Enabled
Maximum allowed color depth	32 bit
Notify user when display mode is de-graded	Disabled
Queuing and tossing	Enabled

ICA\Graphics\Caching	
Persistent Cache Threshold	3000000 Kbps

ICA\Keep Alive	
ICA keep alive timeout	60 seconds
ICA keep alines	Enabled

ICA\Multimedia	
Windows Media Redirection	Allowed
Windows Media Redirection Buffer Size	10 seconds
Windows Media Redicrection Buffer Size Use	Enabled

ICA\Session Reliability	
Session reliability connections	Prevent

ICA\Shadowing	
Shadowing	Allow

Licensing	
License server host name	<CLSHostname>
License server port	27000 (default)

Designing User Profile Best Practices for XenApp®

This recipe will provide guidelines for designing a user profile solution for XenApp environments as provided by Citrix.

 You can read the User Profile Best Practices for XenApp at Citrix's Knowledge Center at http://support.citrix.com/article/CTX120285.

How to do it...

To design a good user profile strategy for XenApp, perform the following steps:

1. Define profile requirements, based upon these questions:

Question	Consideration
Do users need to save their settings?	Folder redirection can be used with all profile types.
Do applications store settings in the registry?	When HKCU is not used, consider mandatory profiles.
How will printers be made available?	Use XenApp policies to enable printers and set retention options.
	If properties can be contained on the client device, consider mandatory profiles.
How is the XenApp Farm designed?	Roaming profiles suffer from "last write wins" when multiple application silos are used.

2. In addition to the answers from the previous questions, use the following profile comparison table to decide on the User Profile type for the XenApp Farm:

Profile type	Benefits	Disadvantages
Local profile	▸ Fast Logon ▸ No centralized repository required for profile storage ▸ No corrupt profile	▸ Settings are inconsistent across servers and sessions ▸ Consumes local disk space

Profile type	Benefits	Disadvantages
Roaming profile	▸ Accessible from any XenApp server ▸ User settings are saved across sessions	▸ Slow login ▸ "Last write wins" can lead to loss of settings with application silos
Mandatory profile	▸ Fast Logon ▸ No corrupt profile	▸ User settings are not saved across sessions
Multiple profiles	▸ Combines benefits of mandatory and roaming profiles without the disadvantages	▸ Requires additional file server space ▸ Complex to implement ▸ Requires administrative expertise and maintenance
Hybrid profile (user profile management)	▸ Fast logon ▸ Most control over settings ▸ Addresses "last write wins" issue ▸ Minimal space requirements	▸ Requires administrative effort and skills to implement and maintain

3. Use Active Directory Group policies to configure the following options for mandatory and roaming profiles:

   ❑ Folder redirection

   ❑ Folder exclusion

   ❑ Delete locally cached profiles on logoff

4. Use Active Directory Group policies to configure the following options for multiple profiles:

   ❑ Set the user profile path to `%profilepath%\%username%`, and assign a unique environment variable value (with policy preferences) for each application silo to distinguish between profile paths

   ❑ Only allow local user profiles for application silos to ensure the roaming profile is not loaded on the application silo servers

   ❑ Set the path for RDS roaming user profile setting to set a unique user profile path per application silo server

5. Use a user profile management tool to define each file and/or registry key that needs to be saved at logoff and loaded at logon for each user.

There's more...

You can read more on Citrix Profile Management at Citrix's eDocs at `http://support.citrix.com/proddocs/topic/user-profile-manager-kib/upm-wrapper-kib.html`.

Configuring Citrix® guidelines for antivirus software

This recipe will provide guidelines for configuring antivirus software in Citrix XenApp infrastructures as provided by Citrix.

> You can read the Citrix Guidelines for Antivirus Software Configuration at Citrix Knowledge Center at `http://support.citrix.com/article/CTX127030`.

How to do it...

To implement the antivirus guidelines for Citrix XenApp, follow these recommendations:

1. Consider the following general antivirus scanning recommendations:

    - Scan excluded files and folders on a regular basis using scheduled scans. Perform scheduled scans during non-business or off-peak hours to mitigate any potential performance impact.

    - The integrity of excluded files and folders should be maintained at all times. Consider File Integrity Monitoring or Host Intrusion Prevention to protect the integrity of files and folders which have been excluded from real-time or on-access scanning.

> Database and logfiles should not be included in this type of data integrity monitoring because these files are expected to change.

    - Folders that are excluded from real-time or on-access scanning should be monitored closely for the creation of new files in these folders.

2. Consider these XenApp optimization and exclusion recommendations:

    - Scan on write events or only when files are modified, to keep the performance impact to a minimum

❏ Scan local drives or disable network scanning

❏ Exclude the following files and folders from being scanned:

pagefile(s)

Print Spooler directory

❏ Exclude specific files and folders within the `\Program Files\Citrix` directory or subdirectories that are accessed heavily or modified frequently by Citrix processes:

Local Host Cache: This file is located at `\Independent Management Architecture\imalhc.msb`

Application Streaming offline db: This file is located at `\Independent Management Architecture\RadeOffline.mdb`

Local Resource Manager Summary db: This file is located at `\Citrix Resource Manager\LocalDB\RMLocalDatabase.mdb`

Application Streaming: This file is located at `\RadeCache and \Deploy folders`

❏ Remove any unnecessary antivirus related entries from the `Run` key in the following Registry setting:

HLKM\Software\Microsoft\Windows\Current Version\Run

❏ When the pass-through authentication is being used, exclude the XenApp Online Plugin bitmap cache directory (`%AppData%\ICAClient\Cache`)

❏ When the streamed user profile feature of Citrix Profile management is used, ensure the antivirus solution is configured to be aware of **Hierarchical Storage Manager** (**HSM**) drivers

Read more on HSM drivers at Citrix's eDocs at `http://support.citrix.com/proddocs/topic/user-profile-manager-kib/upm-secure-antivirus.html`.

3. When Citrix Provisioning Services is used, check the Provisioning Services Antivirus Best Practices at Citrix's Knowledge Center at `http://support.citrix.com/article/CTX124185`.

4. Check Microsoft's Virus scanning recommendations for enterprise computers at Microsoft Support at `http://support.microsoft.com/kb/822158/en-us`.

Planning XenApp® High Availability

This recipe will show you how to plan Citrix XenApp High Availability based upon the guide provided by Citrix.

 You can download the High Availability for Citrix XenDesktop and Citrix XenApp – Planning Guide at Citrix's Knowledge Center at `http://support.citrix.com/article/CTX134979`.

How to do it...

To plan Citrix XenApp High Availability, follow the guidelines as shown:

1. Consider the following guidelines for the server hardware:

   - Redundant backplane on blade chassis/redundant chassis; redundant power supplies and fans
   - **Uninterruptible power supplies (UPS)**
   - Multiple (diversely routed) network interfaces and switches (link aggregation), multiple fibre connections/HBAs
   - Hardware RAID levels for disks; ECC memory
   - Hardware monitoring

2. Consider the following guidelines for the hypervisor:

   - Heartbeats through storage and network components
   - Failover plans
   - Restart priorities
   - XenMotion/vMotion/Live Migration

3. Consider the following guidelines for the XenApp Controllers:

   - Implement at least two or more dedicated Controller Hosts (with Zone Data Collector functionality) in the XenApp Farm per zone to provide *N*+1 redundancy
   - Load balance at least two or more Controller Hosts (with XML broker functionality) in the XenApp Farm to provide *N*+1 redundancy and divide the user load
   - Use a more intelligent load balancing configuration than the supported basic round-robin load balancing provided by the Citrix Web Interface

 NetScaler provides intelligent load balancing based upon built-in XML monitoring and algorithms.

4. Consider the following guidelines for the License Servers:

   ❑ With a grace period of 30 days, a single virtual Citrix License Server is sufficient

   ❑ A pair of Microsoft Remote Desktop Services License Servers should be deployed to avoid a single point of failure as a valid RDS CAL is required to set up a XenApp user session

5. Consider the following guidelines for the Data Store (SQL Server):

   ❑ A XenApp server will fall back to the **Local Host Cache** (**LHC**) when database connectivity is lost

   ❑ No management consoles can be used or configuration changes can be made when the database connection is lost

   ❑ Ensure at least a daily backup is made to quickly restore a lost database

6. Consider the following guidelines for Active Directory and DNS:

   ❑ Implement at least two Active Directory servers with DNS services to provide $N+1$ redundancy and support user authentication

7. Consider the following guidelines for the published desktop:

   ❑ Use imaging technologies to provide all XenApp servers in the farm with the same identical OS and basic application installation and configuration

   ❑ Include the (standard) installed applications in the base image

   ❑ Use application virtualization technologies for non-standard applications

8. Consider the following guidelines for the user settings:

   ❑ Use user profiling technologies to implement a Hybrid profile solution, where a small (mandatory) profile is combined with a profile management tool to save profile changes made by each user separately for those configured user settings

9. Consider the following guidelines for Citrix Web Interface/StoreFront:

❑ Implement at least two Web Interface servers to provide *N*+1 redundancy

❑ Use an external load balancer to divide the user load between the Web Interface servers

❑ Group at least two StoreFront servers in a server group to provide *N*+1 redundancy and have the configuration synchronized between the servers

10. Consider the following guidelines for NetScaler/Access Gateway:

❑ Configure at least two NetScaler/Access Gateway appliances in High Availability mode to provide *N*+1 redundancy

❑ Use NetScaler load balancing if available (as part of the license) to load balance all XenApp infrastructure components

Migrating from Citrix® Web Interface to StoreFront Best Practices

This recipe will provide a recap of the advanced best practices for migration from Web Interface to StoreFront session (SYN415) that was given by *Sam Jacobs*, at Citrix Synergy 2013.

 You can watch the complete session at Citrix TV at `http://www.citrix.com/tv/#videos/8457` or download the slides from `http://www.ipm.com/technical-insight/techdev-corner/the-goods-from-synergy-2013-session-migrating-wi-customizations-to-storefront/`.

How to do it...

To migrate from Web Interface to StoreFront, follow these best practices guidelines:

1. Implement StoreFront next to the running Web Interface components. Both can be run separately, and connect to the same XenApp backend allowing smooth testing and migration paths.

2. Check if the 32-bit or 64-bit version of Web Interface/StoreFront is running:

❑ Open IIS Manager (**Start | Administrative Tools**)

❑ Expand the IIS server in the left pane and select **Application Pools**

      □   Select **CitrixWebInterface5.4.2AppPool** in the **Application Pools** pane

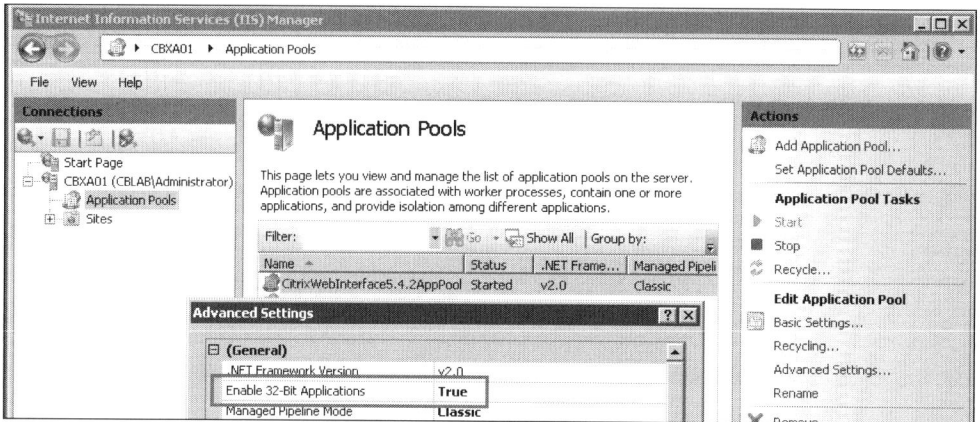

      □   Select **Advanced Settings** from the **Action** pane and check whether **Enable 32-Bit Applications** is set to **True** (as shown in the previous screenshot)

 Citrix StoreFront uses three Application pools, Citrix Delivery Services Authentication, Citrix Delivery Services Resources, and Citrix Receiver for Web. You can check for any of these application pools whether 32-bit is enabled or not.

3. Disable **Certificate Revocation List** (**CRL**) that checks Microsoft's **Internet Information Services** (**IIS**).

      □   Apply the provided workaround described at Citrix's Knowledge Center at `http://support.citrix.com/article/CTX117273` for either the 32-bit or 64-bit .NET Framework.

 The provided workaround for Citrix Web Interface also applies to StoreFront.

4. Increase website responsiveness by installing the Application Initialization Module for IIS 7.5

 The IIS extension can be downloaded at Microsoft's IIS site at `http://www.iis.net/downloads/microsoft/application-initialization`.

5. To apply customizations to the Web Interface, check the *Customizing the Citrix Web Interface look* recipe from *Chapter 3, Citrix® Web Interface*.

6. To apply customizations to StoreFront, check the Customizing Receiver for Web in StoreFront 2.0 Citrix blog at `http://blogs.citrix.com/2013/06/26/customizing-receiver-for-web-in-storefront-2-0/`.

There's more...

You can read more on Citrix's recommendations for StoreFront at Citrix's Knowledge Center at `http://support.citrix.com/article/CTX136547`.

12

Citrix® Community

In this chapter, we will cover the following topics:

- ▶ The Citrix® Community website
- ▶ Carl Webster – XenApp® 6.5 Farm documentation scripts
- ▶ Michel Stevelmans – Farm Nanny
- ▶ Dane Young – Citrix® Chained Reboot script
- ▶ Jason Poyner – XA6.5 Farm Health Check script
- ▶ Andrew Morgan – ThinKiosk
- ▶ Helge Klein – Delprof2, a User Profile Deletion Tool
- ▶ Smart-X – ControlUp Basic Edition

Introduction

The final chapter of this book focuses on some great tools and scripts built by a very active Citrix community. These tools and scripts will aid administrators, designers, and architects in their daily jobs to support and design Citrix XenApp infrastructures.

These recipes will not come close to addressing all the great tools out there, but I will try to include some added value tools that will make your job as a Citrix specialist and consultant easier. Please take advantage of the tools and tips offered in this chapter and explore the great knowledge that the Citrix community has to offer.

 There are many great tools to aid a Citrix XenApp specialist, so keep in mind that the mentioned tools in this chapter are a personal selection of tools that have proven themselves already in the consulting jobs I've had so far.

By no means is the list complete, and I do encourage you to find more tools and become an active community member and share your own knowledge, scripts, and toolset.

The Citrix® Community website

This recipe focuses on the Citrix Community website that shares information from Citrix and the Citrix experts with the community on Citrix technologies.

 You can find the Citrix Community website at `https://www.citrix.com/community.html`.

How to do it...

To join the Citrix community, perform the following steps:

1. Open an Internet browser and go to `https://www.citrix.com/community.html`.

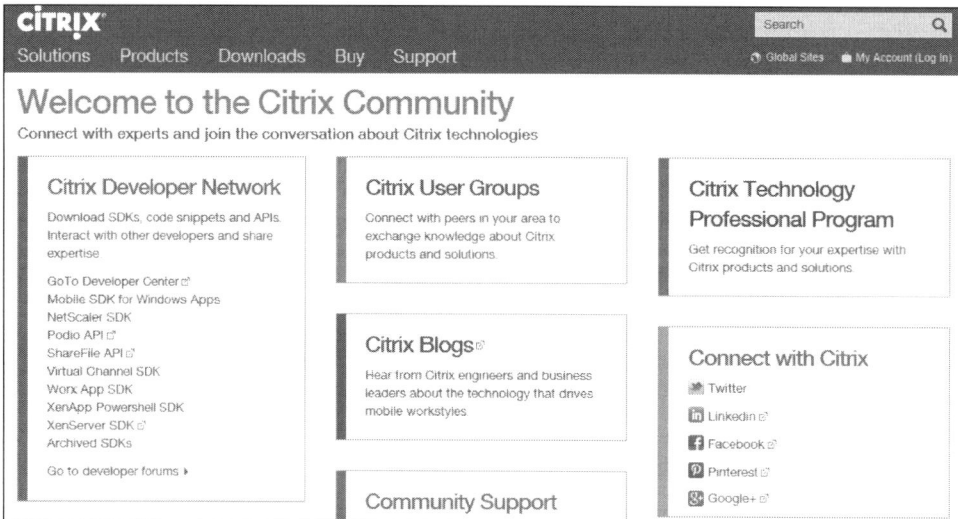

2. You can find the links to SDKs, such as **XenApp Powershell SDK**, in the **Citrix Developer Network** section of the site or directly jump to the developer forums.

3. Click on **Citrix User Groups** to check out the availability of a local Citrix User Group to meet with fellow Citrix experts and exchange knowledge with the (local) Citrix community.

4. Click on **Citrix Innovation Lab** to check out the new ideas and the early stage beta technology that Citrix wants to share with the community.

5. Click on **Open@Citrix** to learn about the open source initiatives that Citrix actively supports.

6. You can find links to different support forums and sites in the **Community Support** section.

7. Links to the different social media accounts for Citrix can be found in the **Connect with Citrix** section.

Carl Webster – XenApp® 6.5 Farm documentation scripts

This recipe will show you how to use the great PowerShell scripts *Carl Webster* has developed. These scripts will automatically document a XenApp Farm in Microsoft Word by using PowerShell scripting.

Use this permanent link to go to all the PowerShell Documentation Scripts by *Carl Webster*: http://carlwebster.com/where-to-get-copies-of-the-documentation-scripts/.

Getting ready

To run PowerShell, you should have the following prerequisites installed on the computer or server running the PowerShell script:

▶ XenApp Version 6.5 PowerShell SDK (provided by Citrix)

▶ Citrix Group Policy PowerShell module (provided by *Carl Webster*)

▶ XA65ConfigLog.udl (instructions provided by *Carl Webster*)

▶ Microsoft Word 2007 with Microsoft Office Add-in for save as PDF support, or Microsoft Word 2010 (provided by Microsoft)

▶ SoftwareExclusions.txt (a sample file provided by *Carl Webster*)

Installation instructions and download links for each resource is provided by *Carl Webster* in the ReadMe file provided with each script. Please follow the instructions carefully before running the script.

How to do it...

To document the XenApp Farm, perform the following steps:

1. Go to `http://carlwebster.com/where-to-get-copies-of-the-documentation-scripts/` to download the latest version of XenApp 6.5 Farm Documentation Scripts.

 For this recipe, Version 4 of the script was used.

2. Follow the instructions in the `ReadMe` file to install the prerequisites.
3. Unblock the `Citrix.GroupPolicy.Commands.psm1` file placed in the `Modules` directory.
4. Right-click on the file and select **Properties**.
5. Read the security message and click on **Unblock**.

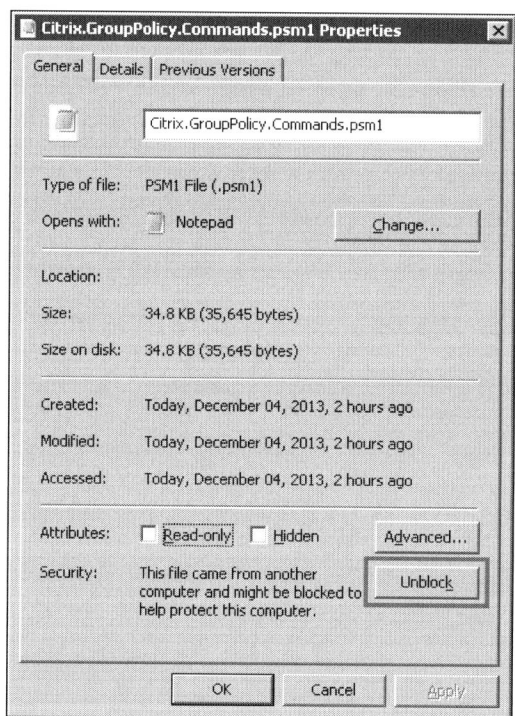

6. Open a PowerShell prompt by navigating to **Start | All Programs | Citrix | XenApp 6.5 Server SDK | Windows PowerShell with Citrix XenApp 6.5 Server SDK**.

![Administrator: Windows PowerShell with Citrix XenApp 6.5 Server SDK screenshot]

```
Windows PowerShell
Copyright (C) 2009 Microsoft Corporation. All rights reserved.

Loading Citrix.Common.Commands snapin...
Loading Citrix.XenApp.Commands snapin...
Loading Citrix.Common.GroupPolicy snapin...

To list all the Citrix commands: Get-CtxCommand
To list the Citrix commands related to a specific topic: Get-CtxCommand *topic*
To display all the help for a command: Get-Help command -Full
To see about XenApp topics: Get-Help about_XenApp*
To see about Citrix topics: Get-Help about_Citrix*

PS C:\Users\administrator.CBLAB> _
```

7. To ensure that all the required modules are loaded, you can manually import the `Citrix.GroupPolicy.Commands.psm1` file with the following command:

   Import-Module Citrix*

 You can check if the module is loaded correctly by running `Get-Module`.

8. Go to the script directory with the following command:

   cd \<path-to-script>

9. Run the script with the following command:

   .\XA65_Inventory_V4.ps1 -CompanyName "<companyName>" -UserName "<Author>" -verbose

![Administrator: Windows PowerShell with Citrix XenApp 6.5 Server SDK screenshot]

```
PS C:\Users\administrator.CBLAB> Import-Module Citrix*
PS C:\Users\administrator.CBLAB> Get-Module

ModuleType Name                          ExportedCommands

Script     Citrix.GroupPolicy.Com...   {Remove-CtxGroupPolicyFilter, Import-CtxGroupPolicy, Set-CtxGroupPolicy,...

PS C:\Users\administrator.CBLAB> cd C:\Scripts\Webster
PS C:\Scripts\Webster> .\XA65_Inventory_V4.ps1 -CompanyName "CBLAB" -UserName "Esther Barthel" -verbose
VERBOSE: 12/04/2013 15:49:45: Remoting is not being used
VERBOSE: 12/04/2013 15:49:46: Getting Farm data
VERBOSE: 12/04/2013 15:49:46: Verify farm version
VERBOSE: 12/04/2013 15:49:46: Setting up Word
VERBOSE: 12/04/2013 15:49:46: Create Word comObject.  If you are not running Word 2007, ignore the next message.
VERBOSE: The object written to the pipeline is an instance of the type "Microsoft.Office.Interop.Word.ApplicationClass"
 from the component's primary interop assembly. If this type exposes different members than the IDispatch members,
scripts written to work with this object might not work if the primary interop assembly is not installed.
VERBOSE: 12/04/2013 15:49:47: Running Microsoft Word 2010
VERBOSE: 12/04/2013 15:49:47: Validate company name
VERBOSE: 12/04/2013 15:49:47: Check Default Cover Page for language specific version
VERBOSE: 12/04/2013 15:49:47: Validate cover page
VERBOSE: 12/04/2013 15:49:47:
VERBOSE: 12/04/2013 15:49:47:
VERBOSE: 12/04/2013 15:49:47: Company Name : CBLAB
VERBOSE: 12/04/2013 15:49:47: Cover Page   : Sideline
VERBOSE: 12/04/2013 15:49:47: User Name    : Esther Barthel
VERBOSE: 12/04/2013 15:49:47: Save As PDF  : False
VERBOSE: 12/04/2013 15:49:47: HW Inventory : False
VERBOSE: 12/04/2013 15:49:47: SW Inventory : False
VERBOSE: 12/04/2013 15:49:47: Farm Name    : CBXAFarm
VERBOSE: 12/04/2013 15:49:47: Title        : Inventory Report for the CBXAFarm Farm
VERBOSE: 12/04/2013 15:49:47: Filename1    : C:\Scripts\Webster\CBXAFarm.docx
VERBOSE: 12/04/2013 15:49:47: OS Detected  : Microsoft Windows Server 2008 R2 Standard
VERBOSE: 12/04/2013 15:49:47: PSUICulture  : en-US
VERBOSE: 12/04/2013 15:49:47: PSCulture    : en-US
VERBOSE: 12/04/2013 15:49:47: Word version : Word 2010
VERBOSE: 12/04/2013 15:49:47: Word language: msoLanguageIDEnglishUS
VERBOSE: 12/04/2013 15:49:47: PoSH version : 2.0
VERBOSE: 12/04/2013 15:49:47:
VERBOSE: 12/04/2013 15:49:47: Script start : 12/04/2013 15:49:44
```

10. When the script is run, a Word file is created with the XenApp Farm's name in the folder from where the script was run, containing all the Farm configuration information.

 The script can run for a long time in a large XenApp Farm, so ensure you run the script with the `-verbose` switch to get progress reports while the script is running.

How it works...

With the help of the Citrix and PowerShell community, *Carl Webster* has created a powerful script to document all the settings in a XenApp Farm by using Windows PowerShell commands. With every new release of the script, new items are added and also even more Citrix products and components are provided with a PowerShell Documentation script of their own.

 Always ensure that you are running the latest scripts, by checking the latest version at `http://carlwebster.com/where-to-get-copies-of-the-documentation-scripts/`.

As Carl Webster does a tremendous job explaining the scripts, I encourage you to attend one of Carl's presentations on the documentation scripts (as I already have on two occasions) if you are able to. You will not only experience his enthusiasm first hand but also hear Carl's own quest of learning to script with PowerShell and how he is getting better with every new version.

There's more...

You can find all Carl Webster's PowerShell Documentation Scripts at `http://carlwebster.com/where-to-get-copies-of-the-documentation-scripts/`.

Michel Stevelmans – Farm Nanny

This recipe will show you how to use Farm Nanny, a free multifunctional application provided by *Michel Stevelmans* to help monitor, troubleshoot, and administer a XenApp Farm.

 You can read all about Farm Nanny and download it at Michel Stevelmans' website: `http://www.michelstevelmans.com/farm-nanny/`.

How to do it...

To use Farm Nanny, perform the following steps:

1. Go to `http://www.michelstevelmans.com/farm-nanny/` and download the latest Farm Nanny version present at the bottom of the page.

 For this recipe, Version 2.12 of Farm Nanny was used.

2. Unzip `Farm-Nanny.zip` to a folder on the XenApp server.

 For this recipe, Farm Nanny was run on a XenApp Controller Host.

3. Double-click on `Farm Nanny.exe` to run the program.

4. Expand `Farm Nanny` and select `Resource Monitor`.

5. Double-click on a server to get the detailed information about the XenApp server.

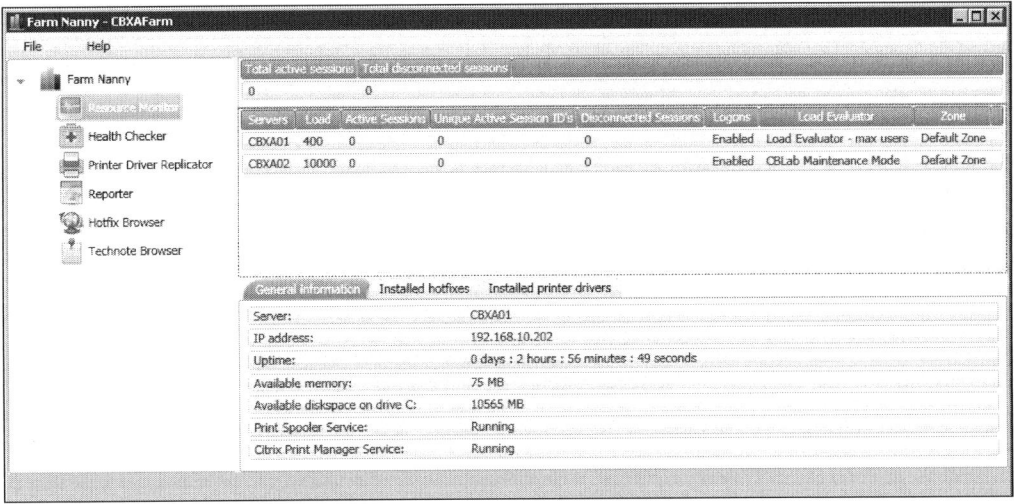

6. Select **Health Checker** from the left-hand side pane to run different commands to check the health of the Farm.

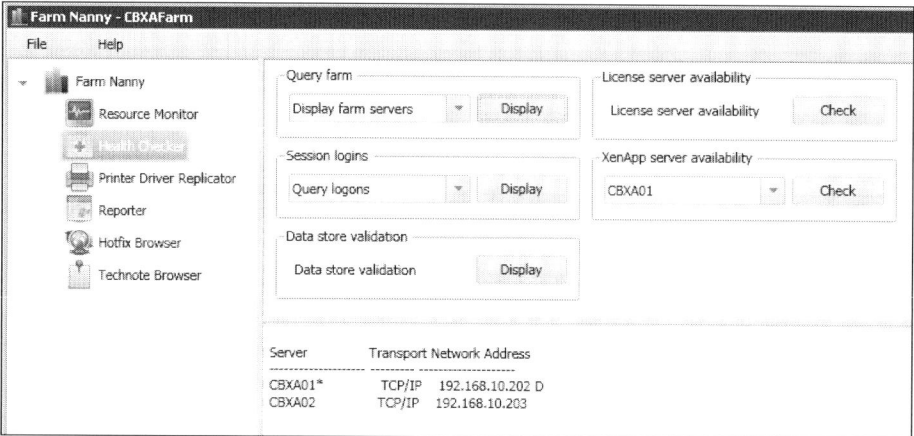

7. Select **Printer Driver Replicator** from the left-hand side pane.

8. Select an installed printer driver from the list on the **Source Server** tab and click on **Add** to add the driver to the auto replication list.

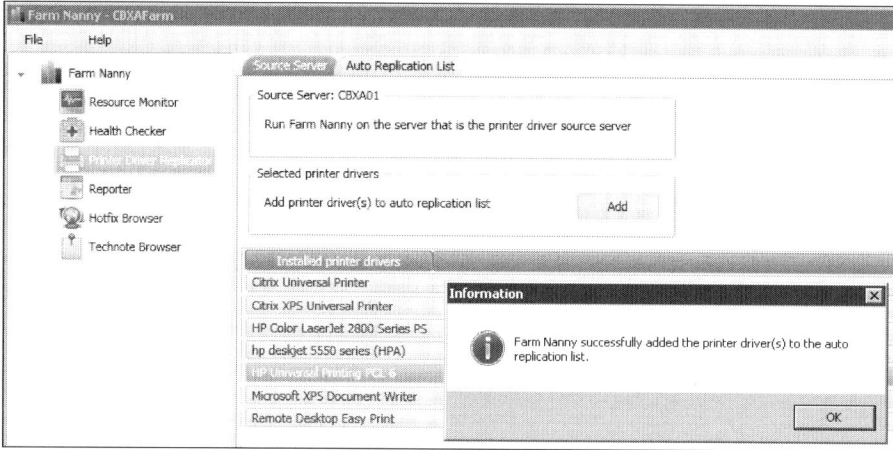

9. Check the printer drivers that are automatically replicated by selecting the **Auto Replication List** tab.

10. Select a printer driver and click on **Remove** to stop the driver from being automatically replicated in the XenApp Farm.

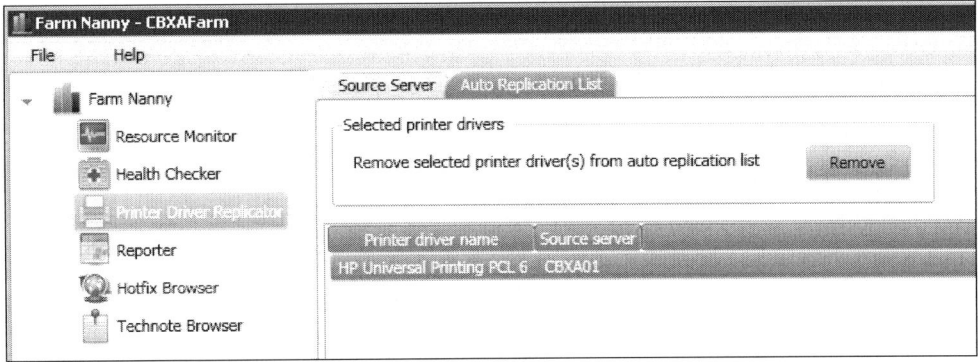

11. Select **Reporter** from the left-hand side pane and click on **Create Report** to create a report on the XenApp Farm.

12. Specify the folder in which the file has to be saved and click on **OK**.

13. The collected information from the **Resource Monitor** section in Farm Nanny is stored in a `Farm Nanny Report.xlsx` file.

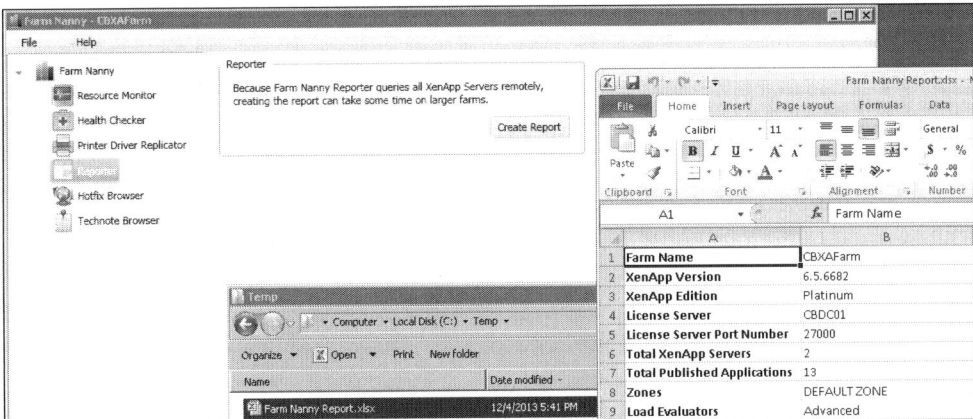

14. Select **Hotfix Browser** to get a list of all the available hotfixes for XenApp 6.5.

15. Double-click on a hotfix to open the web page in the lower-half of the right pane.

 You can view a list of the installed hotfixes per server in the **Installed hotfixes** pane of the XenApp server present in the **Resource Monitor** section.

16. An overview of the latest technotes can be found by selecting **Technote Browser** in the left pane. The technote can be viewed in the lower right pane by double-clicking on the technote.

How it works...

Michel Stevelmans provides a great freeware tool to monitor and troubleshoot live data from the XenApp Farm without having to install any additional software on a XenApp server. It even supports Farm health checks with a graphical interface for typical command-line tools such as query and dscheck. These tools allow you to check the connectivity to the Citrix License Server and XenApp servers.

When Farm Nanny is started, it runs an initial check and will show an error if all the requirements are not met as shown in the following screenshot:

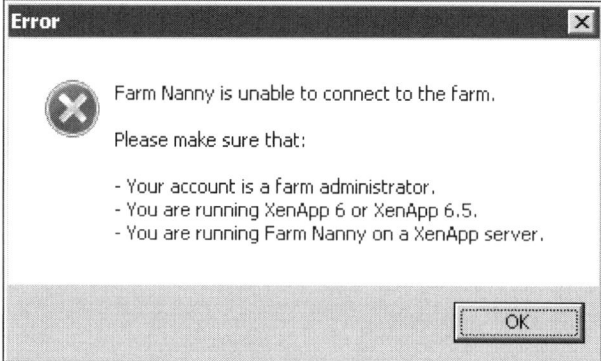

Farm Nanny is a very nice monitoring tool for XenApp Farms when budgets are small or administrators are less experienced. Farm Nanny offers a tool that allows administrators to quickly evaluate the health of a Citrix XenApp Farm.

There's more...

You can find information on *Michel Stevelmans*' Farm Nanny at http://www.michelstevelmans.com/farm-nanny/.

Dane Young – Citrix® Chained Reboot script

This recipe will show you how to use the Citrix Chained Reboot Script for XenApp 6.5, created and provided by *Dane Young*. This PowerShell script allows you to implement a reboot schedule, where the users are not kicked off the XenApp server for a reboot. Instead the server is removed from the XenApp Farm load balancing and will wait for all user sessions to be logged off before the reboot is performed.

You can read all about the Citrix Chained Reboot Scripts and download it from the following post by *Dane Young* in the ITVCE website:

`http://blog.itvce.com/?p=79`

How to do it...

To set up a scheduled task for the Chained Reboot Script, perform the following steps:

1. Go to `http://blog.itvce.com/?p=79`.

2. Select the **I Accept the Terms and Conditions** checkbox to download the XenApp 6.5 Citrix Chained Reboot script and the installation and configuration guide.

 For this recipe, the `XenApp6.5_Citrix_Chained_Reboot_Rev7` Powershell script was used.

3. Unzip the PowerShell script to a local folder on the server (preferably a XenApp Controller Host that is not hosting user sessions).

4. Configure the variables in the script as shown in the following screenshot:

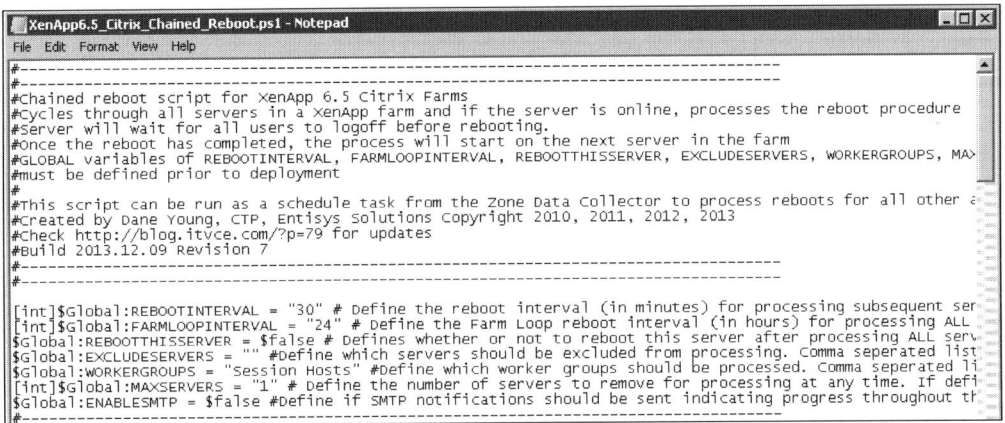

5. Open Task Scheduler on the server by navigating to **Start | Administrative Tools | taskschd.msc**.

6. Click on **Create a Basic Task** in the **Action** pane.

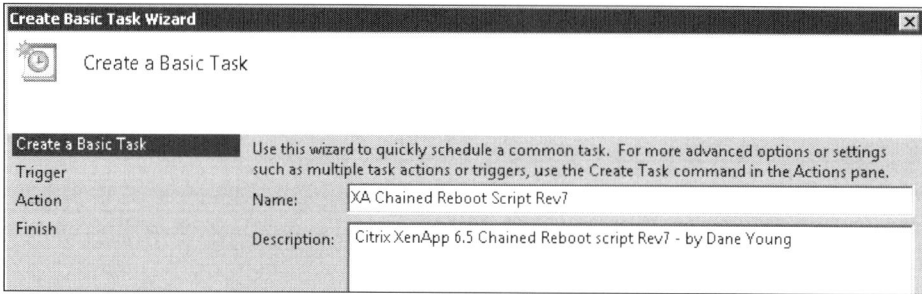

7. Enter **Name** and **Description** and click on **Next**.
8. Select **Daily** as the task trigger setting and click on **Next**.

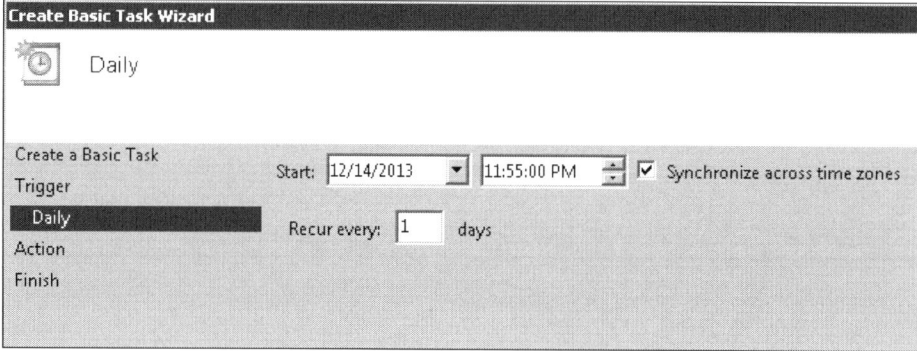

9. Configure the start date and time, select **Synchronize across time zones**, and click on **Next**.
10. On the **Action** screen, select **Start a program**, and click on **Next**.

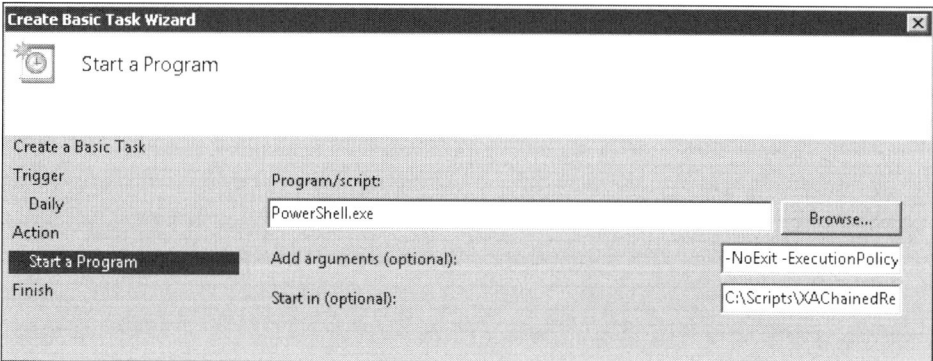

11. Enter the following information and click on **Next**:

    ❑ **Program/Script**: `C:\Windows\System32\WindowsPowerShell\v1.0\powershell.exe`

    ❑ **Arguments**: `-NoExit -ExecutionPolicy Bypass -File "<PathToScript>\XenApp6.5_Citrix_Chained_Reboot.ps1"`

    ❑ **Start in**: `<PathToScript>`

12. Check the scheduled task configuration on the **Summary** screen and click on **Finish**.

13. Click on **Task Scheduler Library** from the left-hand side pane of Task Scheduler and select the newly created task in the middle pane.

14. Click on **Properties** from the **Action** pane.

15. Select the **General** tab and change the default security options to:

    ❑ Select the **Run whether user is logged on or not** option

    ❑ Uncheck the **Do not store password** checkbox

    ❑ Uncheck the **Run with highest privileges** checkbox

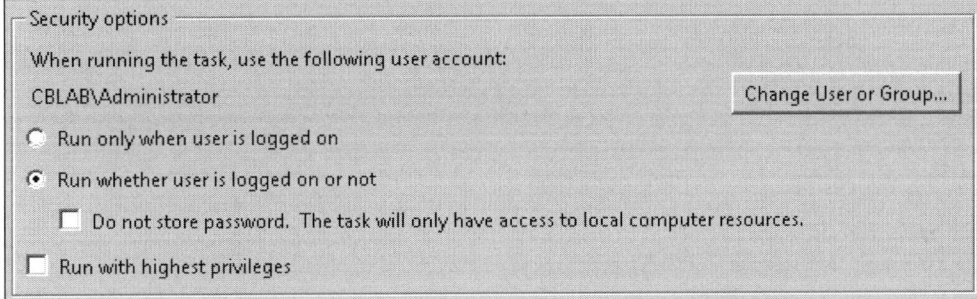

16. Select the **Settings** tab and change the default additional settings to:

    ❑ Select the **Run task as soon as possible after a scheduled start** option

    ❑ Set **If the task fails, restart every** to **1 hour**

    ❑ Unselect the **Stop the task if it runs longer than** option

> ❑ Select the **If the running task does not end when requested** option

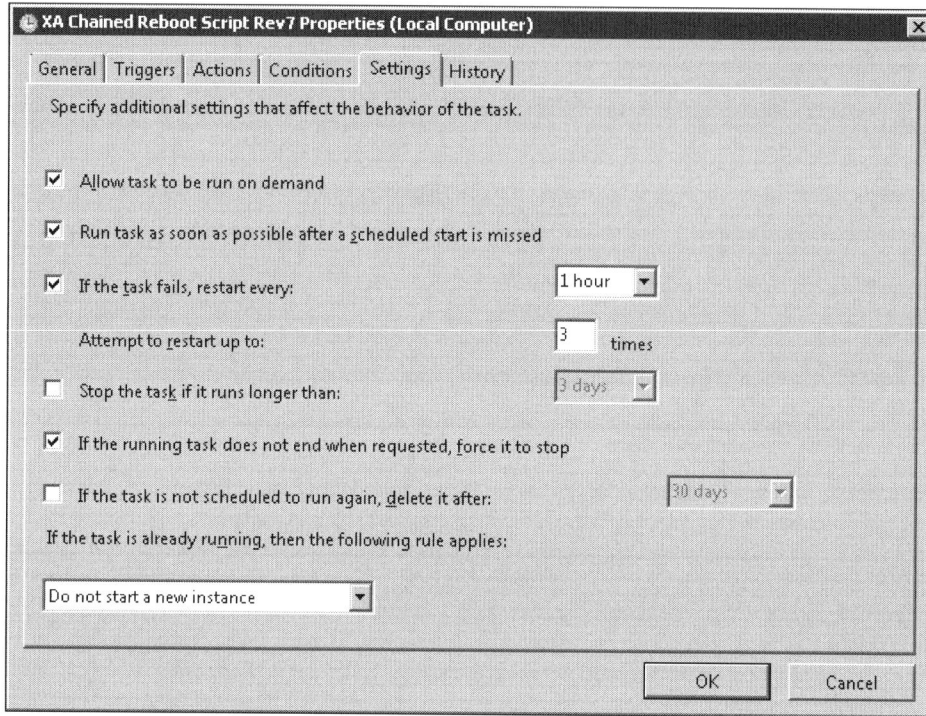

17. Click on **OK**, enter the user account information for running the task, and click on **OK**.

How it works...

The XenApp Chained Reboot Script runs in an infinite loop with its own checks, unless the scheduled task is terminated. The script uses the event log (events are logged at **Windows Logs | Application**) by default, to log progress and errors, unless the SMTP configuration is enabled.

 Regularly check the application event log for the logged events by the Citrix Chained Reboot script.

A simple run of the script can result in the events shown in the following screenshot:

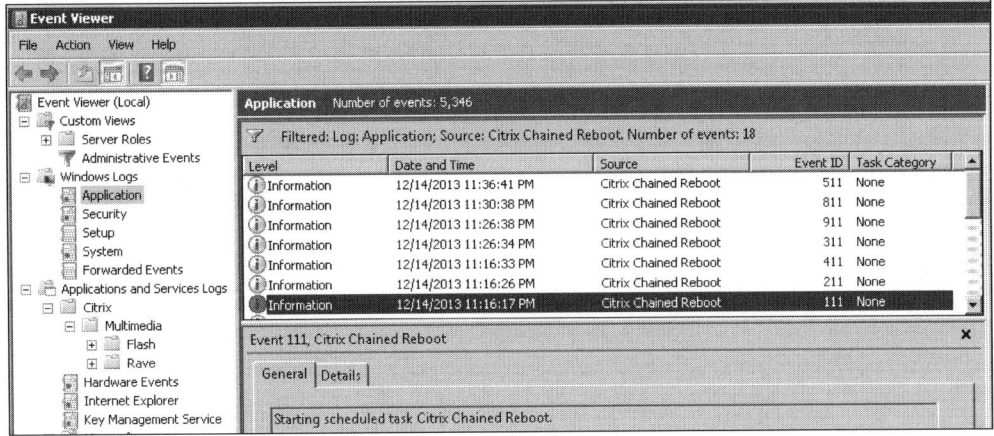

This script logs the following information:

```
Source              ID      Description
-------------------------------------------------------------------

Citrix Chained Reboot      511     It has been 0 hours since last loop
                                   for 'Session Hosts'. Waiting for
                                   another 1 hours.

Citrix Chained Reboot      811     CBXA02 rebooted properly, load
                                   rebalanced. Proceeding with
                                   subsequent servers.

Citrix Chained Reboot      911     Initiating reboot process on CBXA02.

Citrix Chained Reboot      311     Server CBXA02 has no active sessions.

Citrix Chained Reboot      411     Disabled logons until next reboot on
                                   CBXA02.

Citrix Chained Reboot      211     Processing server 'CBXA02' from
worker group 'Session Hosts'.

Citrix Chained Reboot      111     Starting scheduled task Citrix
Chained Reboot.
```

Jason Poyner – XA6.5 Farm Health Check script

This recipe will show you how to use the XenApp 6.5 Farm Health Check script provided by *Jason Poyner*. With his script, you can run scheduled health checks for a XenApp Farm and have the results sent via e-mail as an HTML report.

 You can read all about the XenApp Farm Health Check v2 script and download it from Jason Pyner's blog at http://techblog.deptive. co.nz/2013/03/xenapp-farm-health-check-v2.html.

How to do it...

To run the script, perform the following steps:

1. Go to http://techblog.deptive.co.nz/2013/03/xenapp-farm-health-check-v2.html and download the latest version of the script.

2. Save the script to a folder on the XenApp server.

3. Edit the script by changing the variables to match your XenApp environment.

 Ensure valid e-mail and mail server settings are applied.

4. Save the changes to the script.

5. Open a PowerShell prompt by navigating to **Start | All Programs | Accessories | Windows PowerShell**.

6. Go to the folder containing the script with the following command:

   ```
   cd \<path-to-script>
   ```

7. Run the script with the following command:

   ```
   .\XenAppServerHealthCheck_v2.1.ps1
   ```

 An e-mail report is sent out as well.

To run the script as a scheduled task, perform the following steps:

1. Open the **Task Scheduler** window by navigating to **Start | Administrative Tools | taskschd.msc**.

2. Click on **Create a Basic Task** from the **Action** pane.

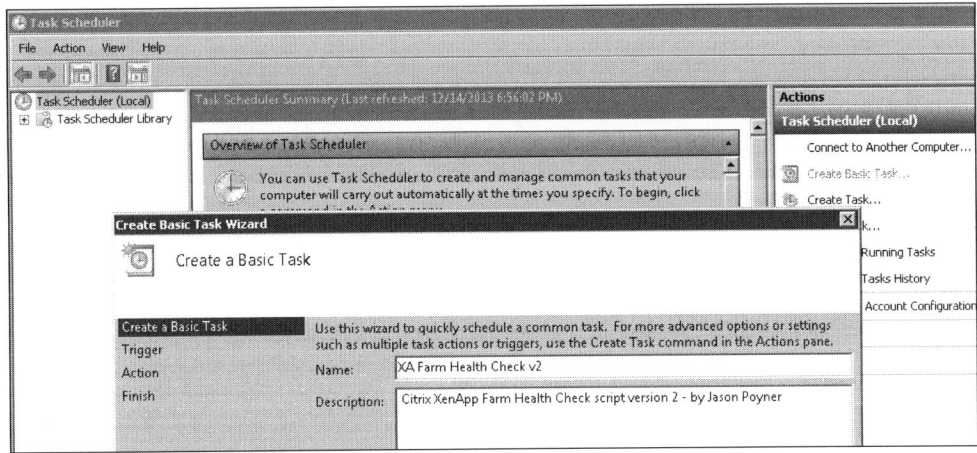

3. Enter **Name** and **Description** and click on **Next**.

4. Select when you want the task to start and click on **Next**.

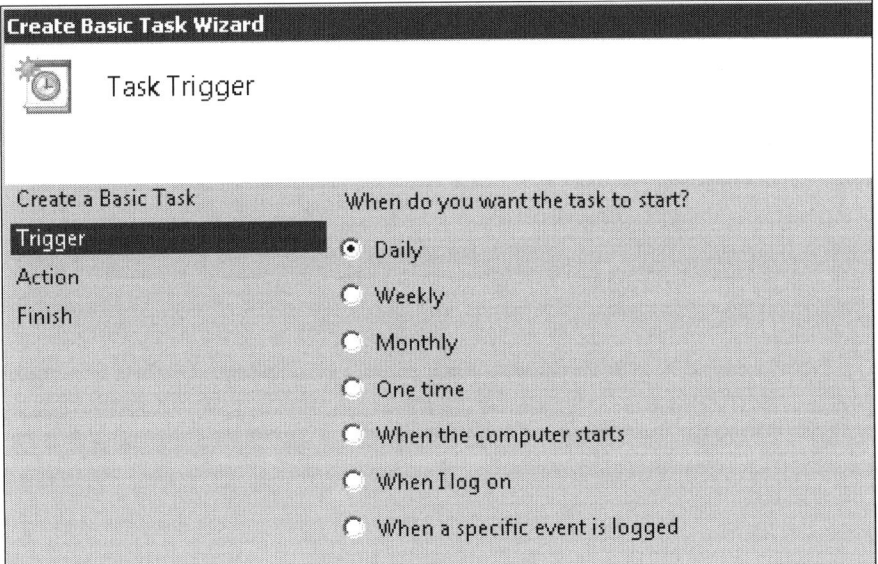

5. Configure the start date and time and when the task needs to recur and click on **Next**.

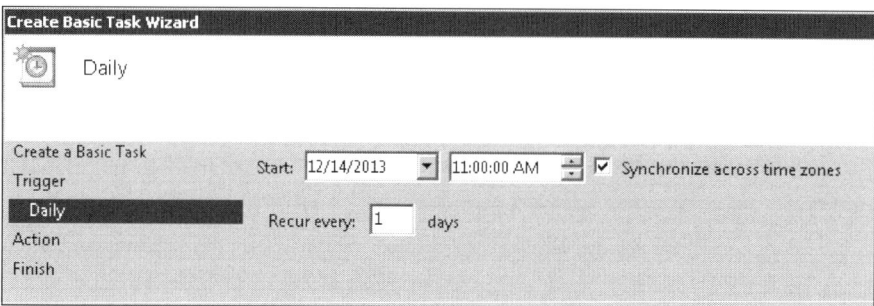

6. Select **Start a program** and click on **Next**.

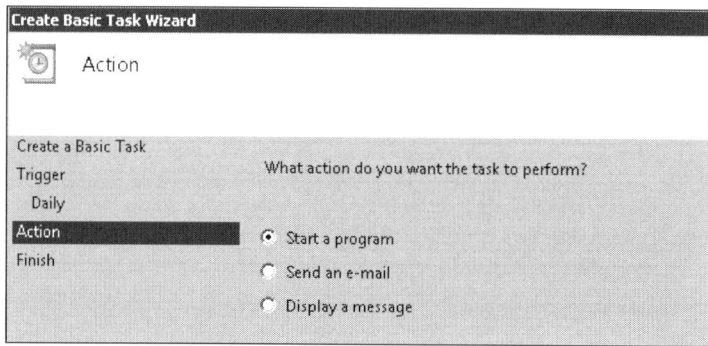

7. Enter the following information:

   □ **Program/Script**: PowerShell.exe

   □ **Arguments**: -ExecutionPolicy Bypass -File "<PathToScript>\
   XenAppServerHealthCheck_v2.1.ps1"

   □ **Start in**: <ScriptFolder>

8. Click on **Next**.

9. Check the summary and click on **Finish**.

10. You can check the settings and status of the scheduled task by selecting **Task Scheduler Library** from the left-hand side pane.

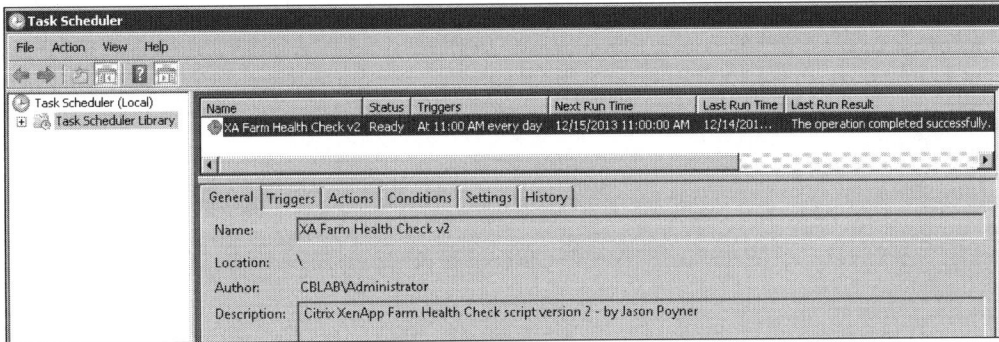

The script sends the HTML report to the configured e-mail recipient as shown in the following screenshot:

ServerName	FolderPath	WorkerGroups	ActiveSessions	ServerLoad	Ping	Logons	LoadEvaluator	ICAPort	CGPPort	IMA	CitrixPrint	WMI	XML	Spooler	Uptime	WriteCacheSize	vDisk
CBXA01	Servers		0	400	Success	Enabled	Default	Success	Success	Success	Success	Success	Success	Success	0	N/A	N/A
CBXA02	Servers	Maintenance Session Hosts	0	10000	Success	Enabled	CBLab Maintenance Mode	Success	Success	Success	Success	Success	N/A	Success	0	N/A	N/A

XenApp Farm Report

Active Sessions: 1   Disconnected Sessions: 0

Default Load Evaluator = Load Evaluator - max users

Default VDISK Image =

There's more...

You can find information on Jason Poyner's script at `http://techblog.deptive.co.nz/2013/03/xenapp-farm-health-check-v2.html`.

Andrew Morgan – ThinKiosk

This recipe will show you how to use ThinKiosk. This is a Windows-based, software-only PC to Thin Client converter. With ThinKiosk, old PCs can be locked down for users and can be re-used as Thin Client devices for connecting to **Server Based Computing (SBC)** and **Virtual Desktop Infrastructure (VDI)** platforms.

> You can read all about ThinKiosk, its editions (Community and Enterprise), and how to obtain the required licenses at: `http://thinscaletechnology.com/thinkiosk/`.

Getting ready

To use ThinKiosk, you will need the installation software and a license:

1. Go to `http://thinscaletechnology.com/thinkiosk/`.

2. Click on **Download ThinKiosk** and fill out the form to receive a download link for ThinKiosk.

3. Navigate to **Licensing | Request a license** and fill out the form to request a community license for ThinKiosk.

4. Download the installation files and ThinKiosk Administrators Guide.

How to do it...

To install the client software, perform the following steps:

1. Unpack the `ThinKiosk Client zip` file to a local folder and run `setup.exe`.

2. Click on **Next** from the welcome screen.

3. Select **I Agree** and click on **Next**.

4. Select **Local Profile** and click on **Next**.

5. Click on **Next** in the ThinKiosk Broker Server screen.

6. Click on **Next** in the FTP Server Information screen.

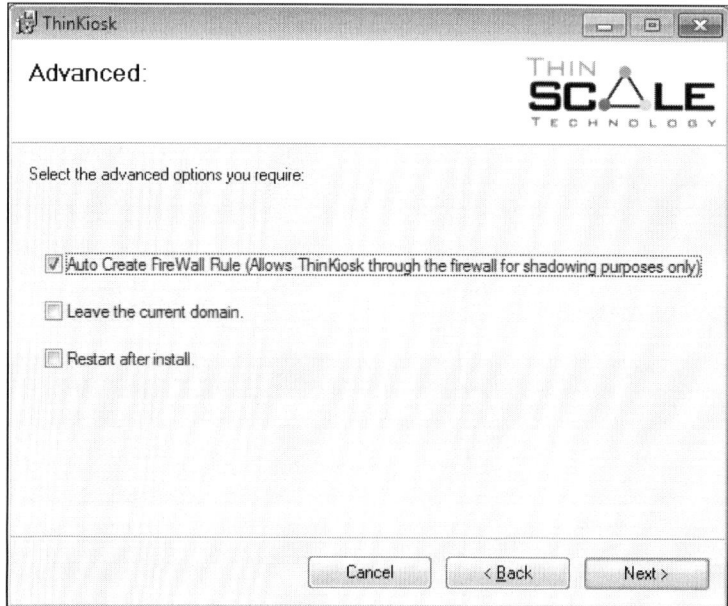

7. Select **Auto Create FireWall rule** and click on **Next**.

8. Specify the installation folder and click on **Next**.

9. Click on **Next** to start the installation.

10. Click on **Close**.

To configure ThinKiosk, perform the following steps:

1. Start the Machine Configuration tool by navigating to **Start | All Programs | ThinKiosk | Local Machine Configuration**.

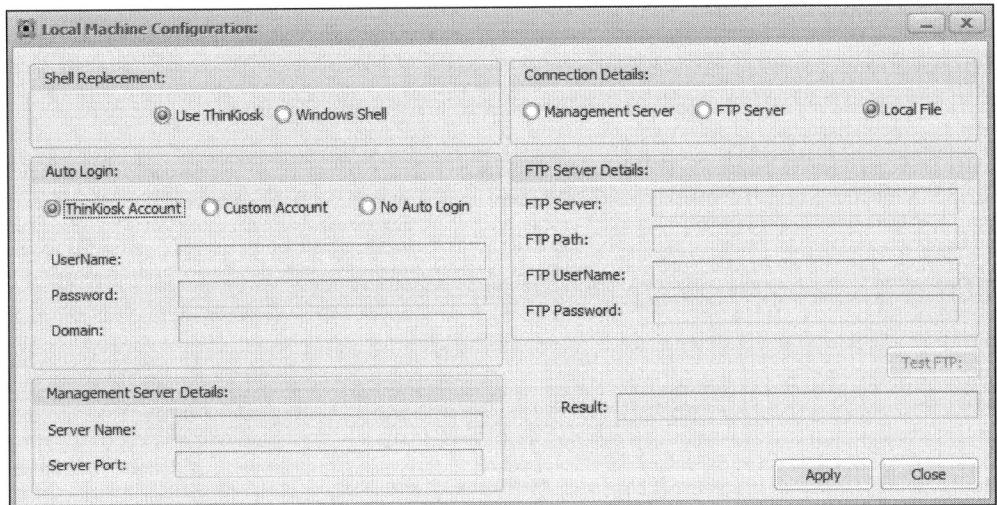

2. Configure the required settings for the device and click on **Close**.

3. Start ThinKiosk by navigating to **Start | All Programs | ThinKiosk | ThinKiosk**.

4. Click on the green lock icon at the bottom-right section of ThinKiosk to unlock the application.

5. Enter the unlock password (check the Administrators Guide for the default password).

6. Navigate to **Admin Menu | Profile Editor** to start the Profile Editor.

7. Click on **Licensing** from the left-hand side pane.

8. Enter the license code and select **Test License**.

9. Click on **Appearance** from the left-hand side pane and configure the desired settings:

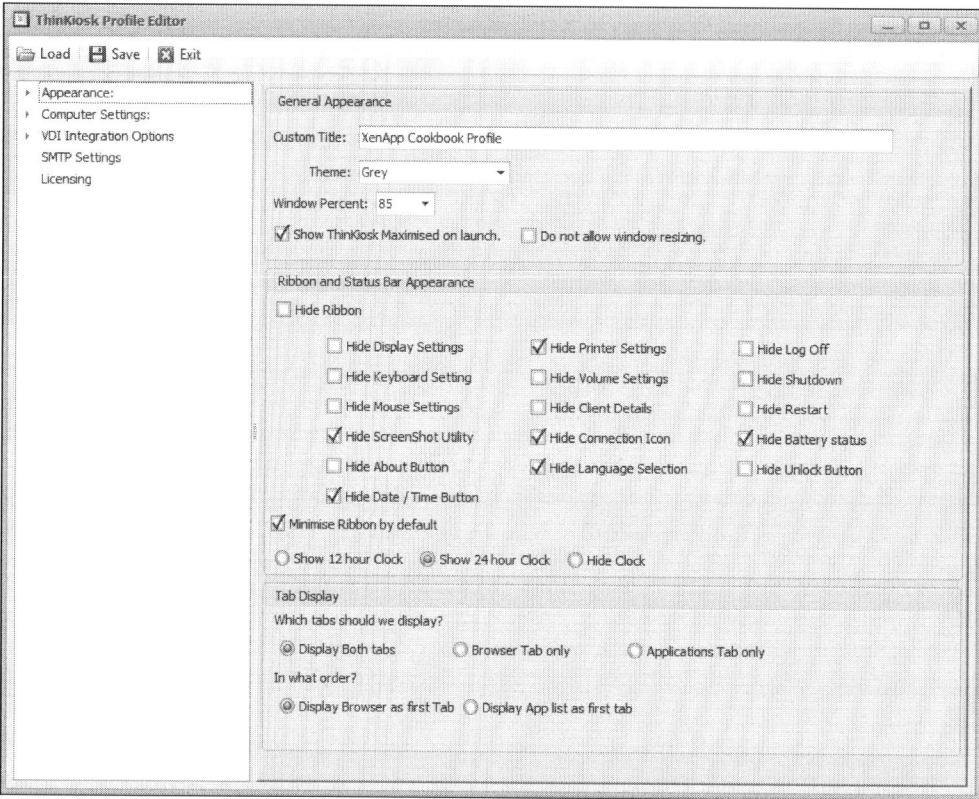

10. Click on the **Browser Tab** in the left-hand side pane to configure the websites users can select.

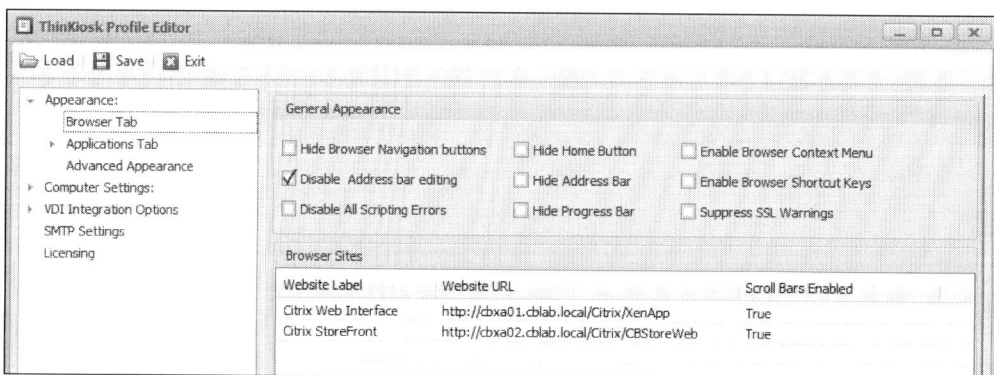

11. Click on **Auto-Login Options** in the left-hand side pane to configure **Shell Replacement** and **Auto Login** settings.

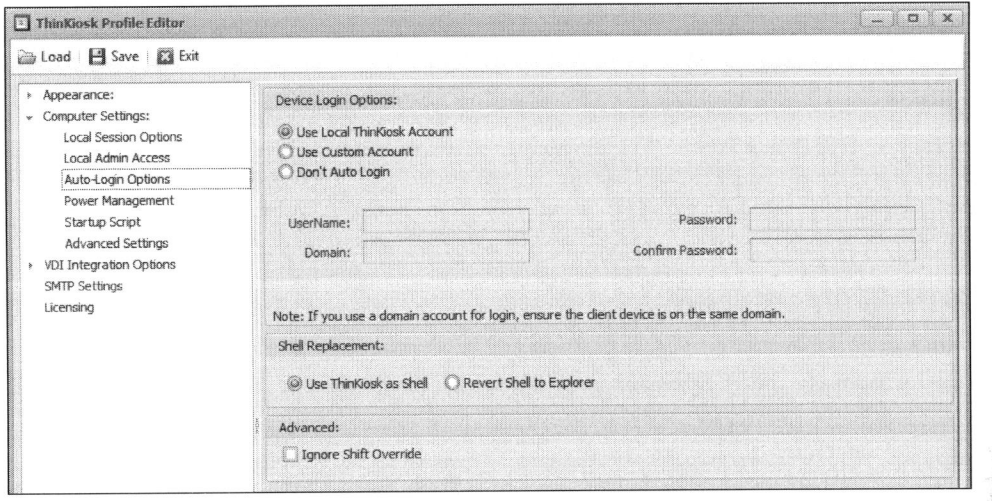

12. Click on **Power Management** to configure **Power Saving Options**.

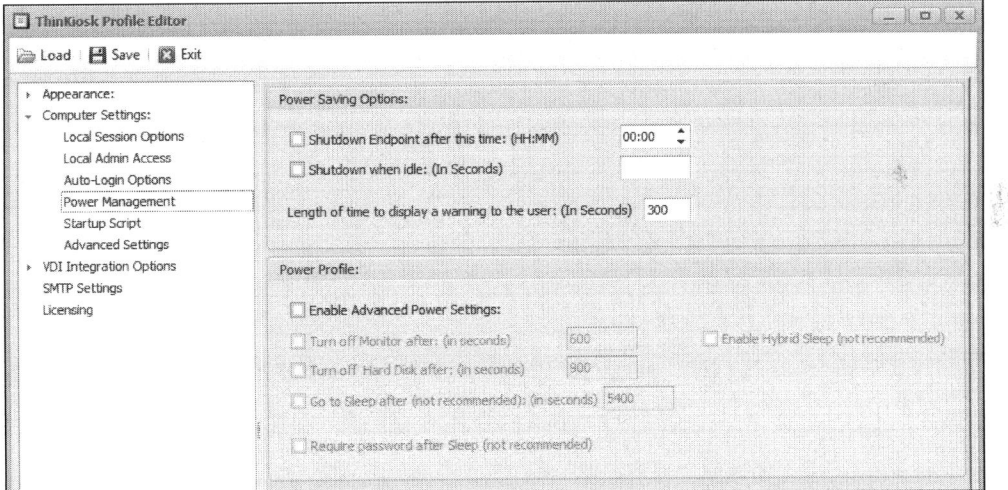

13. When all the settings are configured, click on **Save** and overwrite the `LocalProfile.xml` file to apply the settings to the device.

14. Click on the **Settings** tab and click on **Restart** to ensure that the device is restarted and the new configuration is applied.

How it works...

ThinKiosk is available in two editions: a Community Edition and an Enterprise Edition.

As ThinKiosk originated as a community-driven product, the community spirit is honored with the Community Edition that offers all the original functionality for free. You can request a community license by filling out the request form on the website.

After installing the ThinKiosk client software, you are provided with three new applications in the `ThinKiosk` folder in the **Start** menu. These are Local Machine Configuration, Profile Editor, and Thinkiosk.

Local Machine Configuration

This application allows you to configure the **Shell replacement**, **Auto Login**, and **Profile Delivery** options, as shown in the following screenshot:

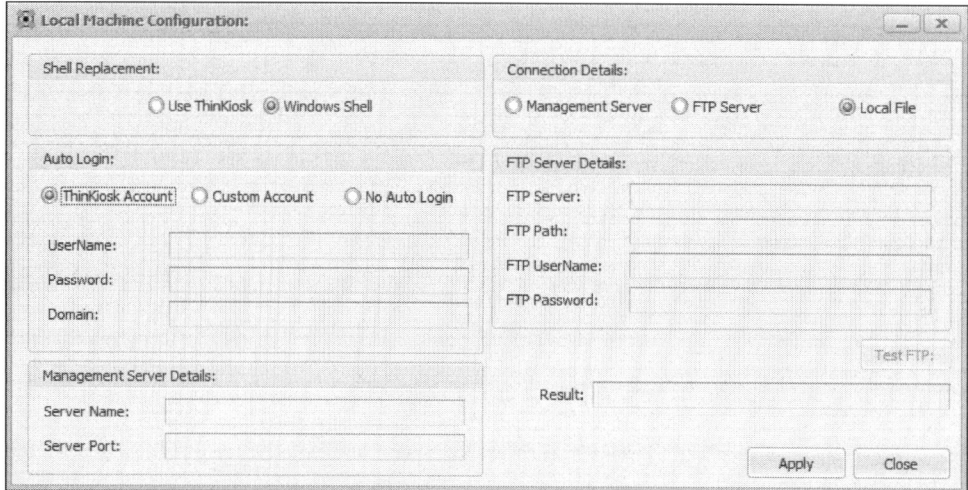

It is recommended to only use the Local Machine Configuration when you are logged on with an account that has administrative rights.

If the auto login and shell settings are set for ThinKiosk in the Local Profile, you should use the Profile Editor from the **Admin** menu of ThinKiosk to change these configuration settings. The Local Machine Configuration application cannot be started with an account that does not have administrative rights (for example, the ThinKiosk auto login account).

Profile Editor

This application allows you to create the required settings for the ThinKiosk profile XML file. The XML file can be deployed by FTP or Broker Service (Enterprise Edition) to the device.

If you are using the local file delivery method, it's recommended to start the Profile Editor from the ThinKiosk **Admin** menu to ensure that the right credentials are applied when the profile settings are saved to the Local Profile XML file.

> Keep in mind that you will need to restart ThinKiosk to apply the profile changes.

ThinKiosk

Depending on the profile configuration, ThinKiosk creates a locked-down environment on a PC and turns it into a Thin Client with limited application and website access for users.

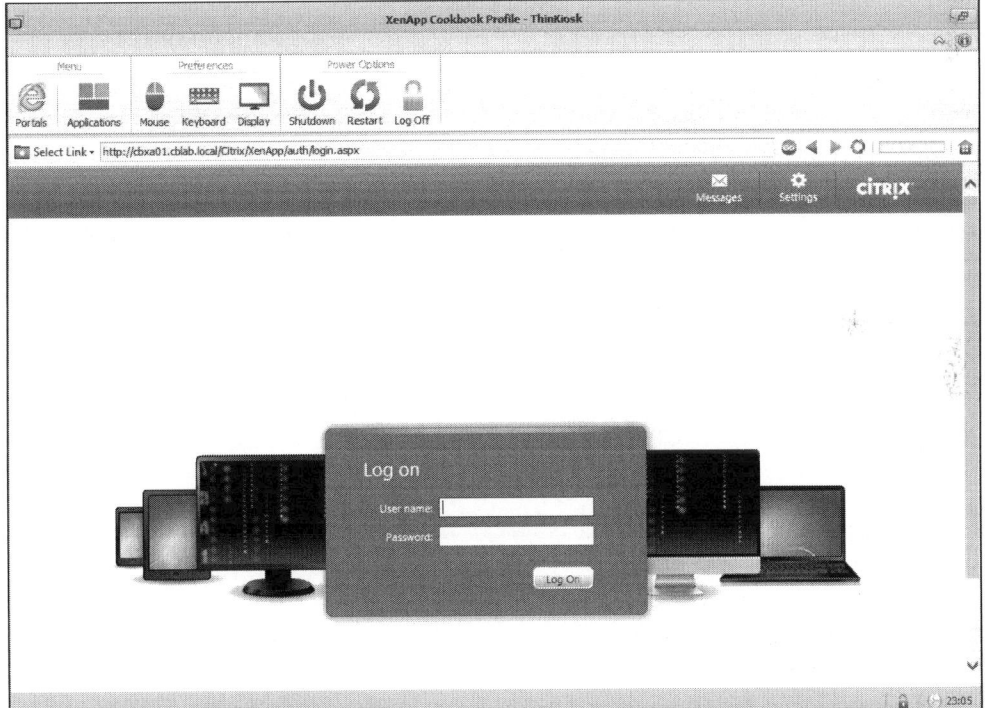

ThinKiosk Enterprise Edition

The Enterprise Edition of ThinKiosk comes with extra additions such as the Broker Service, Management Console, and a lot of extra settings to lock down the client devices and combine centralized device management with a true Thin Client experience.

With the Enterprise edition, you can also assign client devices to different device collections and assign a different profile to each collection.

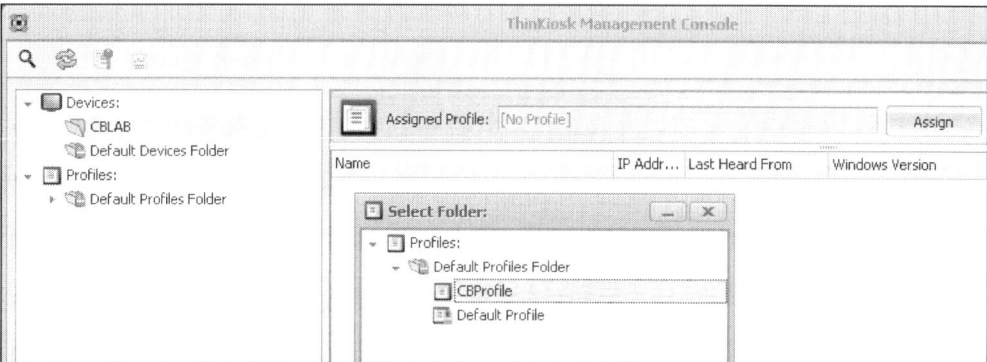

The Profile Editor is included in the ThinKiosk Management Console, which allows for easy profile changes without having to log on to a client device.

Helge Klein – Delprof2, a User Profile Deletion Tool

This recipe will show you how to use Delprof2, a User Profile Deletion Tool. Delprof2 was created by *Helge Klein* as the unofficial successor to Microsoft's Delprof, which does not work on Operating Systems higher than Windows Server 2003.

 You can read all about Delprof2 at `http://helgeklein.com/free-tools/delprof2-user-profile-deletion-tool/`.

How to do it...

To use Delprof2, perform the following steps:

1. Go to `http://helgeklein.com/download/` and download the latest version of Delprof2, which can be run on both 32- and 64-bit operating systems.

 For this recipe, Version 1.6.0 of Delprof2 was used.

2. Unzip `delprof2.zip` to a local folder on the XenApp server.

3. Run the following command to test the deletion of the specified profile:

   `delprof2 /id:cbtester05 /l`

   The result of the above command can be seen in the following screenshot:

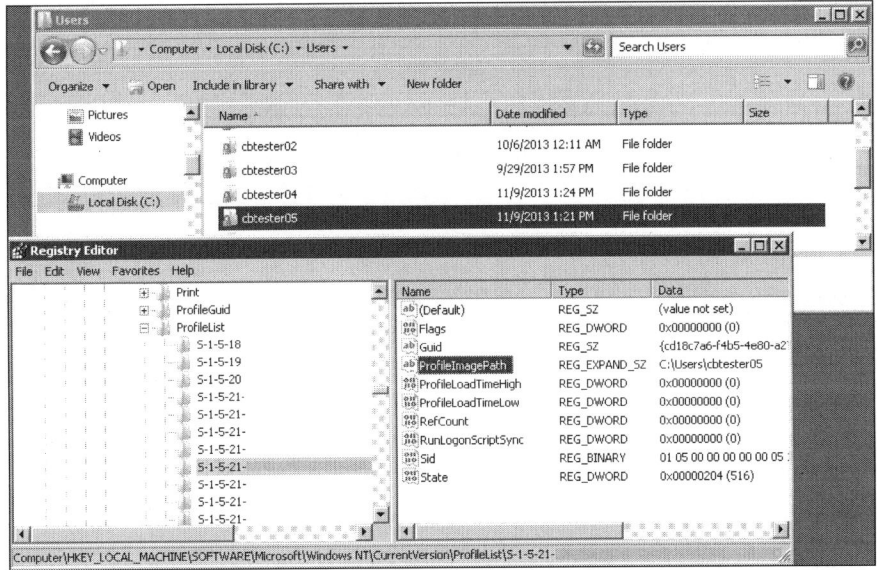

4. Check if the user profile settings are still present in the file.

5. Run the following command to delete the specified profile:

```
delprof2 /id:cbtester05 /u
```

The result of the above command can be seen in the following screenshot:

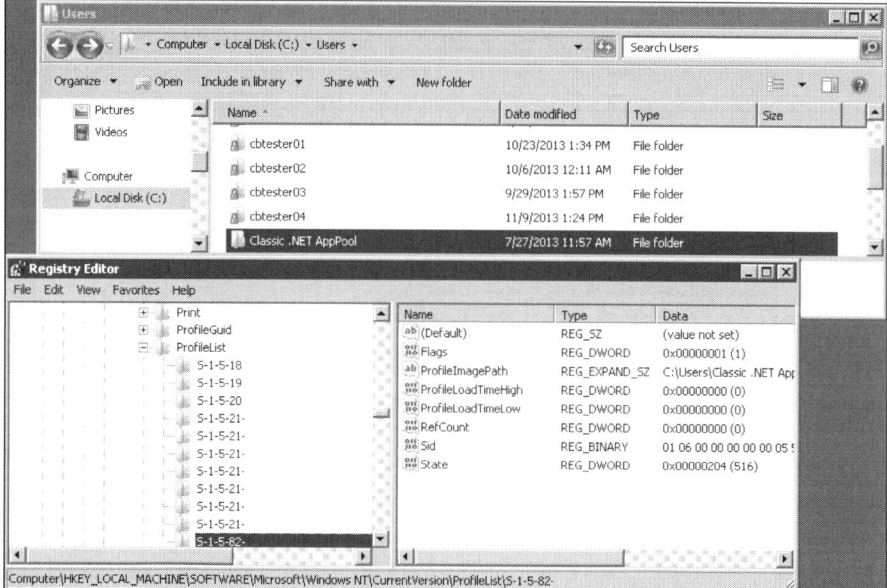

6. Check if the user profile folders and registry keys are deleted.

7. Run the following command to delete the profiles that are not used in 7 days, excluding the known Citrix profiles such as `Ctx_StreamingSvc` and administrative accounts:

```
delprof2.exe /ed:ctx_* /ed:admin* /u /d:7
```

The result of the above command can be seen in the following screenshot:

```
Administrator: Command Prompt

C:\Temp\Delprof2 1.6.0>delprof2 /ed:ctx_* /ed:admin* /u /d:7

DelProf2 by Helge Klein (http://helgeklein.com)

Listing inactive profiles on 'CBXA01' that have not been used for 7 days.
Excluding directories matching: ctx_*, admin*

Ignoring profile '\\CBXA01\C$\Users\Default' (reason: special profile)
Ignoring profile '\\CBXA01\C$\Users\Public' (reason: special profile)
Ignoring profile '\\CBXA01\C$\Users\Administrator' (reason: directory exclusion)
Ignoring profile '\\CBXA01\C$\Users\administrator.CBLAB' (reason: directory exclusion)
Ignoring profile '\\CBXA01\C$\Users\Ctx_StreamingSvc' (reason: directory exclusion)
Ignoring profile '\\CBXA01\C$\Users\cbtester01' (reason: not old enough to be deleted)
Ignoring profile '\\CBXA01\C$\Users\cbtester02' (reason: in use)
Ignoring profile '\\CBXA01\C$\Users\cbtester03' (reason: not old enough to be deleted)
Ignoring profile '\\CBXA01\C$\Users\cbtester04' (reason: not old enough to be deleted)
Ignoring profile '\\CBXA01\C$\Users\Classic .NET AppPool' (reason: not old enough to be deleted)

No user profiles match the deletion criteria.

C:\Temp\Delprof2 1.6.0>_
```

No profiles were deleted as the age constraint was not met for the user profiles.

> Unfortunately, in the test environment the `NTUSER.DAT` file's modified date is changed when the Windows 2008 R2 Server boots. A fix is available for this problem. You can read more on this known issue at Microsoft's Knowledge Base at `http://support.microsoft.com/kb/983544/en-us`.

How it works...

Microsoft's `Delprof.exe` file was part of the Windows Server 2003 Resource Kit and was used to clean up user profiles that were no longer in use on a terminal server or Citrix XenApp server. Unfortunately, Delprof does not work on Operating Systems higher than Windows Server 2003.

Fortunately, *Helge Klein* fixed this problem with Delprof2, which works on operating systems higher that Windows XP.

Delprof2 deletes inactive user profiles and is especially useful for Remote Desktop Session Hosts and XenApp servers, where local or hybrid user profiles are used that are not automatically cleaned up by the built-in User Profile Cleanup Service. Delprof2 will ignore the special profiles used by the system, such as the local administrator and default user accounts.

To clean up user profiles on a Windows Server 2008 R2, run the following command:

```
delprof2 [/l] [/u] [/q] [/p] [/r] [/c:[\\]<computername>] [/d:<days> [/
ntuserini]] [/ed:<pattern>] [/id:<pattern>] [/i]
```

This command uses the following parameters:

- ▶ `/l`: This represents the what-if mode; this mode only lists the actions without performing the user profile deletion.

- ▶ `/u`: This represents the unattended mode; this mode does not ask for a confirmation while deleting a profile.

- ▶ `/q`: This represents the quiet mode; this mode does not generate output nor does it ask for confirmation.

- ▶ `/p`: This prompts for confirmation before deleting each profile.

- ▶ `/r`: This only deletes the local caches of roaming profiles and not the local profiles.

- ▶ `/c`: This specifies the remote computer from which the user profiles need to be deleted.

- ▶ `/d`: This specifies the number of days a profile cannot be used; younger profiles are not deleted.

- ▶ `/ntuserini`: This is used in combination with `/d` and specifies that `NTUSER.INI` must be used instead of `NTUSER.DAT` for age calculation.

- ▶ `/ed`: This specifies which profile directories must be excluded. Wildcard characters `*` and `?` can be used in the pattern. It can be used more than once and can be combined with `/id`.

- ▶ `/id`: This specifies which profile directories must be included. Wildcard characters `*` and `?` can be used in the pattern. It can be used more than once and can be combined with `/ed`.

- ▶ `/i`: This ignores errors; Delprof2 will continue to delete the profiles that apply.

You can run `delprof2.exe` manually as a standalone command or include it in the startup script of a remote desktop session host to be run after a server reboot.

Smart-X – ControlUp Basic Edition

This recipe will show you how to use ControlUp, an advanced computer management and monitoring platform for simultaneously managing a large number of Windows servers, workstations, and user sessions. The ControlUp Basic edition can be used free of charge for up to 50 concurrent sessions and by one ControlUp user.

 You can read all about ControlUp at `http://www.smart-x.com/products/controlup/`.

How to do it...

To monitor a XenApp Farm with ControlUp, perform the following steps:

1. Go to `http://www.smart-x.com/products/controlup/` and download the latest version of ControlUp.

 For this recipe, Version 2.0.1.337 of ControlUp was used.

2. Unzip `ControlUp.zip` to a local folder on the server and run the `ControlUpConsole.exe` executable file.

3. Click on **Continue**.

4. Sign up for a ControlUp user account or log on with an existing account, select **Login Automatically**, and click on **Login**.

5. Accept the license agreement and click on **Continue**.

6. Enter an organization name and click on **Continue**.

7. Click on **Add Computers**.

8. Select the machines you want to monitor, and click on **Add** and then on **OK**.

9. Agents are automatically installed on the selected machines.

10. An overview of the performance of the added machines is given in the following screenshot:

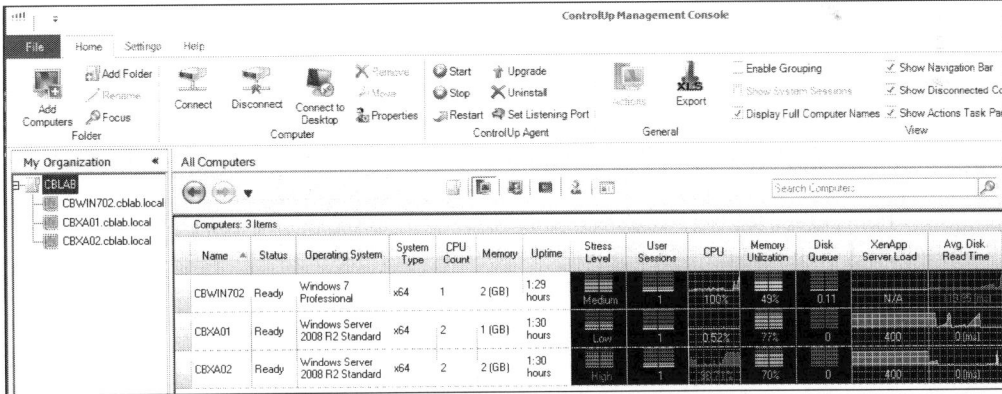

11. Right-click on a computer to view the available administrative tools and controllers. Computer management can be performed with the available tools.

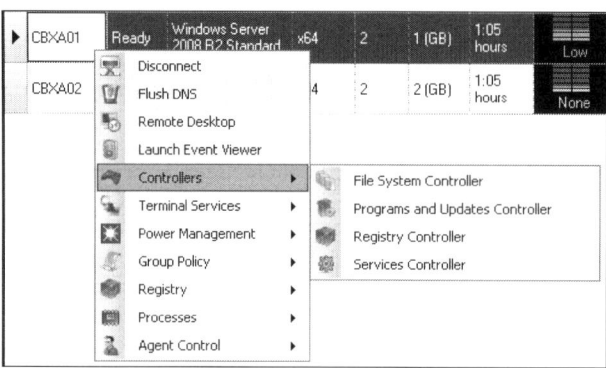

[The available tools are also visible in the **Action Pane** while selecting a computer.]

12. Double-click on the XenApp server with high stress level to view details about the hosted sessions, as shown in the following screenshot:

13. Double-click on the user session with high stress level to view details about the running processes within the session.

14. Right-click on the process with an elevated stress level and navigate to **Terminal Services | Send Message** to send a message to the logged on user, informing about the high server resource consumption.

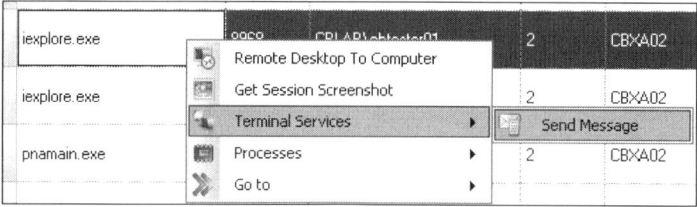

15. Select **Controllers** from the bottom-left pane and navigate to **Computers | Registry** on the left-hand side pane.

16. Add all the computers you want to compare by right-clicking the white space in the **Computers** pane and selecting **Add**.

17. Select a computer from the **Computers** pane and go to the registry key you want to compare in the **Registry Keys** pane.

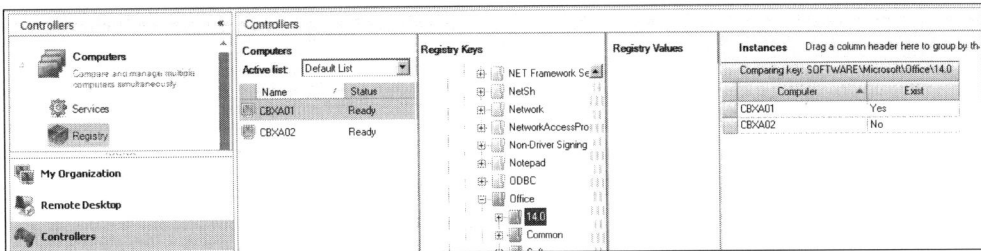

18. The right-hand side pane will show whether the registry key exists on all the listed computers.

How it works...

ControlUp combines different tools to manage a Citrix XenApp Farm. It offers real-time monitoring of the servers, sessions, and processes by providing a Task Manager like performance grid for the major metrics such as CPU, memory, disk queue, and XenApp Server Load.

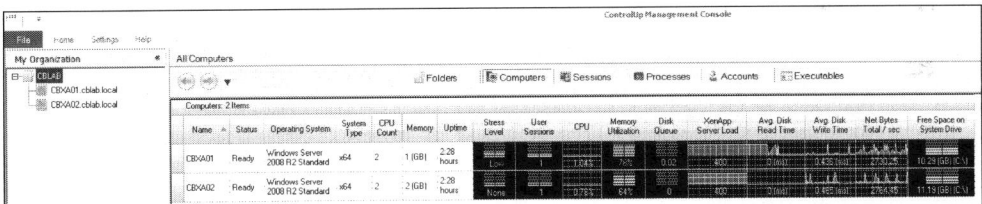

When a server, a session, or a process is selected in the middle pane, the **Action** pane will show the available tools that can be used to administer the selected item. This way, ControlUp offers a single console for all the XenApp Farm management tasks.

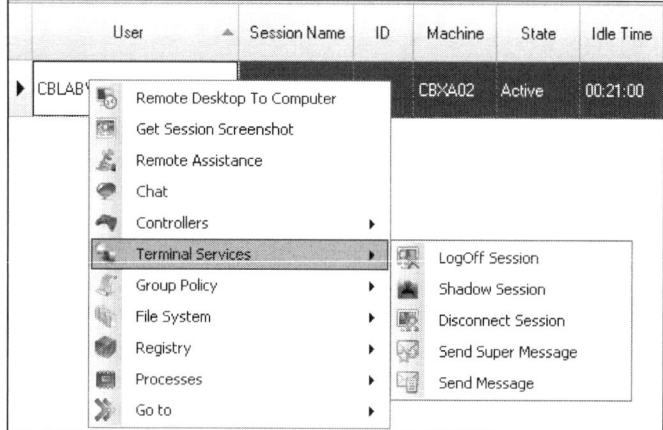

The **Controllers** section offers quick comparison options to search for differences between the XenApp server's **Services**, **Registry**, **File System**, and **Programs and Updates**. Tracking differences between servers has never been easier.

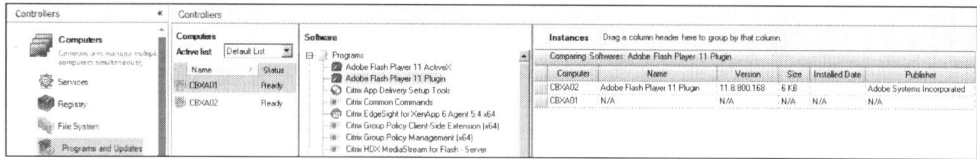

With the Basic Edition of ControlUp, you can manage up to 50 concurrent sessions with a single account free of charge. This also allows for centralized management of small XenApp Farms.

There's more...

You can read more on ControlUp at Citrix's Blog at `http://blogs.citrix.com/2012/09/06/controlup-real-time-management-tool-for-xenapp-xendesktop/`.

You can read more on ControlUp at Smart-X's website at `http://www.smart-x.com/products/controlup/`.

Index

K

keywords
used, for managing application behavior 125-127

L

language pack, CWI
building 90, 91
customizing 91, 92
LBDIAG command
used, for diagnosing XenApp® Farm load balancing rules 296, 297
legacy support, CSF
configuring 121, 122
License count
resetting 57-61
license files, CLS
installing 42-44
Licensing Diagnosis snap-in
using 27-29
lmdiag 64, 65
lmstat 63
lmutil 63
Load Evaluator
assigning, to CXA server 243-245
creating 166, 167
Local Host Cache (LHC) 204, 298, 327, 354
Local Machine Configuration 382
logon page, NetScaler Gateway
theme, changing 146
Low Graphics Display 75
LSQuery
URL, for downloading 55
used, for collecting data on CLS 55-57

M

management console, CLS
user accounts, adding 45, 46
Mapped IP (MIP) 137, 147
Microsoft Clustering
used, for clustering CLS 50-53
Microsoft Fix316926
URL 277

Microsoft Group Policies
used, for configuring RDS settings 18, 19
Microsoft Network Load Balancing (Microsoft NLB)
about 94
used, for load balancing CWI 95, 96
msiexec command 41

N

NetScaler AppFirewall 134
NetScaler Branch Repeater 134
NetScaler Gateway (NG)
about 115, 134
configuration, comparing 151-153
configuration, restoring 151-153
configuration, saving 151-153
configuring, for Citrix® Web Interface 140-143
configuring, for CSF 143-146
Enterprise Edition, licensing 135-138
logon page theme, changing 146
password, recovering 149-151
performance statistics, checking 148, 149
VLAN, using 147
NetScaler Gateway authentication point
used, for configuring web interface 138-140
NetScaler IP Address (NSIP) 136, 137
netstat 63
Network Interface Card (NIC) 135

O

Organizational Unit (OU) 18, 170, 173, 328, 331, 337

P

pass-through authentication
troubleshooting, with CWI 266-269
port numbers, CLS
changing 49, 50
PowerShell
used, for changing Citrix® XenApp® 6.5 product edition 308, 309
used, for checking XenApp® server load 315
used, for creating Citrix® policies 305-308

Thank you for buying
Citrix® XenApp® 6.5 Expert Cookbook

About Packt Publishing

Packt, pronounced 'packed', published its first book "*Mastering phpMyAdmin for Effective MySQL Management*" in April 2004 and subsequently continued to specialize in publishing highly focused books on specific technologies and solutions.

Our books and publications share the experiences of your fellow IT professionals in adapting and customizing today's systems, applications, and frameworks. Our solution-based books give you the knowledge and power to customize the software and technologies you're using to get the job done. Packt books are more specific and less general than the IT books you have seen in the past. Our unique business model allows us to bring you more focused information, giving you more of what you need to know, and less of what you don't.

Packt is a modern, yet unique publishing company, which focuses on producing quality, cutting-edge books for communities of developers, administrators, and newbies alike. For more information, please visit our website: www.PacktPub.com.

About Packt Enterprise

In 2010, Packt launched two new brands, Packt Enterprise and Packt Open Source, in order to continue its focus on specialization. This book is part of the Packt Enterprise brand, home to books published on enterprise software – software created by major vendors, including (but not limited to) IBM, Microsoft and Oracle, often for use in other corporations. Its titles will offer information relevant to a range of users of this software, including administrators, developers, architects, and end users.

Writing for Packt

We welcome all inquiries from people who are interested in authoring. Book proposals should be sent to author@packtpub.com. If your book idea is still at an early stage and you would like to discuss it first before writing a formal book proposal, contact us; one of our commissioning editors will get in touch with you.

We're not just looking for published authors; if you have strong technical skills but no writing experience, our experienced editors can help you develop a writing career, or simply get some additional reward for your expertise.

**Getting Started with
Citrix® CloudPortal™**

Get acquainted with Citrix Systems® CPSM and CPBM in order to
administer cloud services smoothly and comprehensively

Puthiyavan Udayakumar

Getting Started with Citrix® CloudPortal™

ISBN: 978-1-78217-682-4   Paperback: 128 pages

Get acquainted with Citrix Systems® CPSM and CPBM
in order to administer cloud services smoothly and
comprehensively

1. Overview of CPSM and CPBM architectures, and
   planning CPSM and CPBM

2. Become efficient in product management,
   workflow management, and billing and pricing
   management

3. Provision services efficiently to cloud consumers
   and clients

**Getting Started with
Citrix XenApp 6.5**

Design and implement Citrix farms based on XenApp 6.5

Guillermo Musumeci

Getting Started with Citrix XenApp 6.5

ISBN: 978-1-84968-666-2   Paperback: 478 pages

Design and implement Citrix farms based on XenApp 6.5

1. Use Citrix management tools to publish
   applications and resources on client devices with
   this book and eBook

2. Deploy and optimize XenApp 6.5 on Citrix
   XenServer, VMware ESX, and Microsoft Hyper-V
   virtual machines and physical servers

3. Understand new features included in XenApp
   6.5 including a brand new chapter on advanced
   XenApp deployment covering topics such as
   unattended install of XenApp 6.5, using dynamic
   data center provisioning, and more

Please check **www.PacktPub.com** for information on our titles

Getting Started with Citrix VDI-in-a-Box

ISBN: 978-1-78217-104-1   Paperback: 86 pages

Design and deploy virtual desktops using Citrix VDI-in-a-Box

1. Design a Citrix VDI-in-a-Box solution

2. Get the budget for Citrix VDI-in-a-Box by building a case

3. Implement a Citrix VDI-in-a-Box proof of concept and Citrix VDI-in-a-Box solution

Implementing Citrix XenServer Quickstarter

ISBN: 978-1-84968-982-3   Paperback: 134 ages

A practical guide to getting started with the Citrix XenServer Virtualization technology with easy-to-follow instructions

1. A simple and quick start guide for any system admin who wants to step into the latest and hottest virtualization technology

2. Learn how to convert physical machines to virtual ones using XenConvert

3. Get to grips with the advanced features of Citrix XenServer

Please check **www.PacktPub.com** for information on our titles

12596049R00232

Printed in Great Britain
by Amazon.co.uk, Ltd.,
Marston Gate.